THE GAME OF
disarmament

Also by Alva Myrdal (available in English)

Women's Two Roles (with V. Klein)

Nation and Family

America's Role in International Social Welfare
(with Dean Rusk, A. Altmeyer)

Are We Too Many? (with P. Vincent)

Women in the Community

Contact with America (with Gunnar Myrdal, available in Swedish)

THE GAME OF
disarmament

How the United States and Russia Run the Arms Race

ALVA MYRDAL

**Manchester
University Press**

341.733

Published in Great Britain by
Manchester University Press
Oxford Road, Manchester M13 9PL

ISBN 0 7190 0693 7

British Library Cataloguing in Publication Data

Myrdal, Alva
    The game of disarmament.
    1. Disarmament – History 2. U.S. – Defenses –
    History 3. Russia – Defenses – History
    I. Title
    327'.174'0904   JX1974

    ISBN 0-7190-0693-7

*Since this copyright page cannot accommodate
all acknowledgments, they are to be found on
the following page.*

Grateful acknowledgment is made to the following for permission to reprint previously published material:

The Center for the Study of Democratic Institutions/The Fund for the Republic, Inc.: Selected excerpts from *Pacem in Terris III*, vol. 2 *The Military Dimensions of Foreign Policy*, pp. 23, 24, 25, 27, and 29 (Santa Barbara, California); also, a portion of "Second Edition: Limiting War—A Younger Henry Kissinger Interviewed by Mike Wallace," from *The Center Magazine*, vol. 4, no. 1 (January–February 1971), p. 56. Reprinted by permission.

Rena Feld, Literary Agent: Excerpt from "Battlefields of the 1980's," by André Beaufre, as it appeared in *Unless Peace Comes*, edited by Nigel Calder (Penguin Books).

W. H. Freeman and Company: Brief excerpts from "National Security and the Nuclear-Test Ban," by Jerome B. Wiesner and Herbert F. York, reprinted from *Scientific American*, October 1964. Copyright © 1974 by Scientific American, Inc. All rights reserved.

New Scientist: Excerpts from "Changing Nuclear Myths," by Frank Barnaby, reprinted from *New Scientist*, A Weekly Review of Science and Technology, vol. 69, no. 983 (January 15, 1976).

The New York Times: Selected text excerpts from *The New York Times*, issues of May 27, 1975, May 24, 1974, and January 25, 1975. Copyright © 1974/75 by The New York Times Company. Also, a brief quote from "U.S. Arms Aide Warns A-War Could Destroy Earth's Ozone," by John W. Finney, reprinted from the September 6, 1974, *New York Times*. Copyright © 1974 by The New York Times Company.

Princeton University Press: Excerpts from "Law and the Conduct of the Vietnam War," by Lawrence C. Petrowski, from *The Vietnam War and International Law*, edited by Richard A. Falk, vol. 2, pp. 503, 506. Sponsored by the American Society of International Law. Copyright © 1969 by Princeton University Press.

Sierra Club Books: Excerpts from "Indochina Prototype of Ecocide," by Arthur Westing, from *Air, Water, Earth, Fire: The Impact of the Military on the World Environmental Order*, edited by Ruth B. Russell. Published in 1974.

Time, The Weekly Newsmagazine: Excerpts from "Global Growth in Guns," reprinted from *Time*, March 11, 1974, p. 87. Copyright © 1974 by Time, Inc.

UNESCO: Excerpt from "Science and Disarmament," by Philip Noel-Baker, reprinted from *Impact of Science on Society*, vol. 15, no. 4, 1965. Copyright © 1965 by UNESCO.

The Washington Post: Excerpt from "Brandt Supports U.S. Arms Cut," by Michael Getter, reprinted from the October 7, 1975, *International Herald Tribune*. Copyright © 1975 by The Washington Post Co. Also, an excerpt from "The Imponderables of Détente," by Peter Osnos. Reprinted from the September 2, 1975, *International Herald Tribune*. Copyright © 1975 by The Washington Post Co.

CONTENTS

Preface   xi

A Personal Note   xxi

PART ONE: THE FORCES BEHIND THE ARMS RACE   1

CHAPTER I *The Reign of Unreason*   3
  Section 1. A Global Folly   4
  Section 2. Greater Security?   7
  Section 3. The Costs of the Arms Race   8
  Section 4. An Arms Race Within the Arms Race   10
  Section 5. The Depletion of Resources for Development   12
  Section 6. The Wider Costs of the Weapons Culture   14
  Section 7. Any Road to Sanity?   21

CHAPTER II *The Superpowers' Game*   23
  Section 1. The Broad Picture   23
  Section 2. Gaming with Each Other   25
  Section 3. Gaming over a Passive Europe   30
  Section 4. "Limited War" over Europe?
              The Soviet Point of View   36
  Section 5. "Limited War" over Europe?
              The American Point of View   38
  Section 6. "Limited War" over Europe?
              The European Point of View   41
  Section 7. Scissions in the Alliances   50
  Section 8. The Superpowers' Gaming over the World:
              Some Special Cases   53
  Section 9. The Superpowers' Gaming over the World:
              The Rest of the World, Underdeveloped   61

CHAPTER III *A History of Lost Opportunities*   66
   Section 1. Disarmament Efforts Before World War II   66
   Section 2. United Nations and Disarmament   69
   Section 3. No Peace Plan for the Atom   72
   Section 4. Propaganda Game with General Disarmament Plans   78
   Section 5. The Test-Ban Issue—Before 1962   84
   Section 6. The Crisis, 1962–1963   88
   Section 7. An Ocean Treaty Truncated   96
   Section 8. SALT—Institutionalization of the Nuclear
        Arms Race   103
   Section 9. Where Are We Heading?   108

PART TWO: AN ACTIVATED AGENDA FOR DISARMAMENT   111

CHAPTER IV *Reversing the Arms Race*   113
   Section 1. Towards a Strategy for New Attempts   113
   Section 2. A Gross Miscalculation   115
   Section 3. How Can the Irrational Policies Prevail?   122
   Section 4. Some Brakes Suggested   124
   Section 5. Trends Threaten Change for the Worse   127
   Section 6. An Urgent Agenda   133

CHAPTER V *Stemming the Conventional Arms Rush*   137
   Section 1. Conventional Armaments in the Nuclear Age   137
   Section 2. Production of and Trade in Conventional Arms   141
   Section 3. Reversing the Conventional Arms Race   144
   Section 4. The Need for Conversion Plans   150
   Section 5. The Military Brain Drain   155
   Section 6. A World Folly   156

CHAPTER VI *Barring the Spread of Nuclear Weapons*   159
   Section 1. The Genie Came Out   159
   Section 2. The Lesser Nuclear-Weapons Powers   164
   Section 3. Futile Attempts to Ban Proliferation   166
   Section 4. A Grossly Discriminatory Treaty   169
   Section 5. How It Went Wrong   171
   Section 6 Any Limit to Proliferation?   177
   Section 7. The Prices to Pay   182
   Section 8. Make IAEA Safeguards Meaningful   185
   Section 9. Nuclear-Weapons-Free Zones—Voluntary,
        Not Imposed   194
   Section 10. In the Several Regions   196

Contents

CHAPTER VII *Closing the Loopholes for Nuclear-Weapons Testing* — 208

Section 1. *The False Alibis: Thresholds and Verification* — 208

Section 2. *"Peaceful" Nuclear Explosions—a Tenuous Link* — 212

Section 3. *The Most Dangerous Loopholes* — 217

Section 4. *An International Approach* — 218

Section 5. *A Test Ban Without Loopholes* — 221

CHAPTER VIII *Outlawing the Use of Cruel Weapons and Methods of Warfare* — 226

Section 1. *The Emergence of International Laws of War* — 227

Section 2. *Modern Warfare Violates International Law: The Case Against Use of Chemical Weapons* — 234

Section 3. *Modern Warfare Violates International Law: The Case Against Use of Dum-Dum Bullets* — 239

Section 4. *Modern Warfare Violates International Law: The Case Against Use of Napalm* — 242

Section 5. *Modern Warfare Violates International Law: The Case Against Terror Bombing* — 247

Section 6. *The Inegalitarian Character of Unethical Warfare* — 255

Section 7. *Updating the Humanitarian Laws* — 257

Section 8. *An Agenda for Each Nation* — 265

CHAPTER IX *Eliminating Biological and Chemical Means of Warfare* — 268

Section 1. *No Possession of Weapons When Use Is Outlawed* — 268

Section 2. *The Meandering Course of Negotiations* — 270

Section 3. *The Inglorious Fate of the B-Weapons Convention* — 272

Section 4. *Renouncing CB-Weapons—Treaty or No Treaty* — 275

Section 5. *Any Hope to Eliminate C-Weapons?* — 278

Section 6. *A New Shock—Binary Weapons* — 286

Section 7. *A Stepladder Approach to Prompt Action* — 290

CHAPTER X *Verifying Disarmament and Internationalizing Knowledge* — 293

Section 1. *The Obnoxious Role of the Control Issue* — 293

Section 2. *The Need for Controls* — 294

Section 3. *Control Requirements According to Scope and Character of Agreements* — 297

Section 4. *Ex Post and Ex Ante* — 299

Section 5. *Dismantling Secrecy* — 302

Section 6. International Verification of Disarmament   304
Section 7. Internationalization of Knowledge   313

CHAPTER XI *In Conclusion*   317
  Section 1. Looking Back   317
  Section 2. A World Disarmament Conference   322
  Section 3. Bypassing the Superpowers?   326
  Section 4. Not Against the Superpowers   331

Notes   335

Index   381

About the Author   399

Preface

This book is an attempt to study the policy questions of disarmament from an international point of view. It has grown out of a gradually increasing feeling of near despair after twelve years of participating in multilateral disarmament negotiations. There the superpowers have indulged in subterfuges and half-truths, with their closest and usually most dependent allies following suit or keeping silent. On balance, there has been no real advance towards limitation of armaments. The competitive race between the two superpowers has steadily escalated, and the militarization of the economy and national life of almost all countries has intensified.

Only with the passing of years did I come to realize how hollow was the rhetoric about "the will to disarm." As the book is founded upon crucial personal involvement, I have briefly told the story of my experience of the disarmament negotiations in "A Personal Note." I did not start out with a critical attitude or a missionary zeal, but with a rationalistic bent, hoping that by using diplomatic professionalism and advice from experts in many fields it would be possible to advance the progress of disarmament.

During the long years of negotiations and the following two years of working on this book, I have, of course, followed the international literature on issues related to disarmament. Nowhere have I found that book which could satisfy my quest for a presentation from a global viewpoint of the problems of the arms race and its ramifications.

Early in the Cold War, the reasoning about armaments and disarmament became encapsulated in a bipolar model, from then on
utilized in both official pronouncements and expert writings. On the
one side there is the United States, on the other side the Union of
Soviet Socialist Republics. These two countries are truly in a category by themselves as superpowers, as they alone have the might
to annihilate each other and all other countries. All others are
"lesser powers." But they are the great majority of mankind, and
they have a right to be heard; their interests would embrace those
of the superpowers if only they were thinking and acting rationally.
The bipolar model is revealed—both in diplomatic negotiations and
academic writings—by such phrases as "the other side," "the adversary position," if not "the enemy." In this model, the recent
détente has not meant any change, although it has led to a more
polite use of language, which by itself is all to the good.

The political and technical literature on arms and disarmament
in the Soviet Union is regrettably meager and unanalytical; however,
the debate in the United States is quite comprehensive and intensive.
Much of the information quoted in this book originates perforce,
directly or indirectly, in American sources. An important point
is that even those American writers who take a critical view of their
government's policy in regard to the armament race are usually im-
prisoned in the bipolar model. They are all addressing Washington.
They can find arguments against the official policy on various points
and propose radical changes, but they habitually adhere to the
model and plead in terms of American "security" in relation to the
Soviet Union as an adversary.

Although the issue of armaments and disarmament must in the
world of reality be intricately complex, with a multitude of interested parties, the field of vision has become strangely limited to
problems of military strategies between the two superpowers. Even
the emergence of China as a potential superpower and the somber,
crisis-ridden state of the world economy have not, as yet, succeeded
in lifting the debate on the senseless arms race to the level of a
supreme political issue, although it should clamor for urgent attention by all citizens of this world.

A platform for all nations, not least the lesser powers, to speak
out against the threat of superpower hegemony is provided by the
United Nations, through both the General Assembly and its Political
Committee. And since 1962 a forum for multilateral negotiations
has been institutionalized through the Geneva Disarmament Com-

mittee* comprising not only a number of lesser powers, who are members of the two military alliances, but for the first time representatives of states nonaligned to the two superpowers' blocs. A weakness of this potentially important body has been that France, although invited to join, has kept aloof and that China for almost twenty-five years was kept out of the United Nations and is not even now ready to cooperate so as to allow the creation of a more truly representative organ for disarmament issues.

Among the negotiators, those from the nonaligned nations have, more or less coherently, been able to apply a global outlook. The proposals they have made could not, in a sober analysis, be said to go against anybody's interests, not even those of the superpowers and their allies. Much military and scientific groundwork has been invested in their proposals, worked out mainly by Mexico, Sweden, and Yugoslavia, and by India in the beginning. Some of the allies to the two military blocs have often participated in elaborating or supporting constructive suggestions, especially Canada and the Netherlands, Japan and Rumania. But all these attempts have been thwarted because of the resistance of the two superpowers. More and more a regular pattern has become visible: that, although seemingly they struggle against each other, they are in a kind of conspiracy, dividing between them the responsibility for saying nyet and no. They apparently want to continue their arms race, to make mutual concessions, minor as they are, within bilateral negotiations, undisturbed by the majority of nations.

Statements by lesser, independent powers penetrate but faintly to the general public outside of the council chamber. The contributions they make, often with concrete constructive proposals, may be publicized in the mass media of their home countries, but very rarely are they reported in the world press and certainly not in the mass media of the superpowers. This is especially noticeable in the United States, which uses the media channels to play its own record of what takes place in the multinational debates so as to reinforce the image of a bipolar contest. This is regrettable, as the lively American academic and political debate on arms and disarmament issues is as a result kept strangely insulated and unnecessarily and irrationally nationalistic.

*This Committee, which is colloquially and in this book often referred to as "the Geneva Disarmament Committee," was first established as the Eighteen-Nation Disarmament Committee (ENDC), but in 1970 was widened to include eight more members and changed its name to the Committee of the Conference of Disarmament (CCD). It now has thirty-one members.

The books are as yet unwritten which would bring forth the views of the many who, domiciled in various parts of the world, share nonaligned views of disarmament policies. Setting out to fill what I consider to be an unfortunate intellectual and political information void about disarmament issues and negotiations, I want to say at the outset how I place myself in regard to the power constellation of the world: my ambition has always been to hold a position that is international and nonpartisan, siding with neither one nor the other of the two blocs, nor looking after narrow Swedish national interests.

My striving has been to widen the view to global proportions. And I firmly believe that trying to serve not your own country above others but mankind as a whole will in the long run serve the true interest of all nations. This is my main value premise by which I seek to present the reasons for disarmament, for holding military capacities to a sensible low by mutual agreement, formalized or not. In today's situation, with the superpowers dominating the scene, my sympathies definitely lie with all those nations, lesser powers in the world power game, who are weaker militarily and usually economically as well.

Nonaligned nations, by definition not under the strictures of the power blocs, can be the masters of their own voices and votes. I have considered it a great asset that during the long years of participation in the disarmament negotiations I have represented a nonaligned country, Sweden. With that background, it has been easier to make a nonpartisan evaluation of what has happened to the arms race and what has not been achieved in disarmament. It has even seemed to me a duty to try to outline an international strategy for disarmament. In addition to my nonpartisan, international point of view, I wish to characterize the direction of this treatise on disarmament as UN-centered.

This approach corresponds to what is the very essence of Swedish foreign policy. Neutral Sweden has deliberately chosen close participation in the efforts to reach international agreement in all fields; it has boldly expressed independent judgments about world events. In regard to the key question of military alliances, this policy was clearly stated in the 1945 official declaration when the present Labor Government recommended to Parliament our joining the United Nations; a policy which is, it should be added, largely shared by the opposition parties.

For the Swedish people, *both vital interests and idealistic motives* make it natural to hope that no political subdivision of the states in groups opposing one another will take place. We are willing to participate in a joint security organization and, in the event of a future conflict, to give up neutrality to the extent that the Charter of the organization demands. If, however, against expectation a tendency towards a subdivision of the great powers in two camps would appear within this organization, our policy must be not to let us be forced into such a group or bloc formation.[1]

Such a position of nonalignment, deliberately chosen and constantly defended, is, of course, easier to maintain when a nation is relatively independent economically and technologically. In this respect, Sweden is particularly favored. The policy of active neutrality, for which Sweden wants to be a champion, is reflected by Sweden's outspoken condemnation of the American war in Indochina, the invasion of Czechoslovakia by the Soviet bloc, the Greek military junta's repression of basic human rights, South Africa's inhumane apartheid policy, and the bloody military coup in Chile.

This declaration of what has been my particular trademark in regard to disarmament should, I feel, be stated from the beginning.

It should further be made clear that my purpose has not been to produce a fully documented study. The references and footnotes would then have multiplied by a factor of several hundred. My purpose has rather been to write a discourse, arguing as cogently as possible for a rational, international policy in regard to arms and disarmament.

I have developed these arguments over many years, and I make liberal use of quotations from earlier statements. The character of the book makes it essential that I also exploit what I have learned in disarmament negotiations as an insider about the positions taken by many governments. From the storehouse of official records I therefore have drawn frequent references, either by verbatim quotation or oblique reference. On matters not central to the main theme, I have used rather broad brushstrokes; for example, I have cited but few references to the historical shifting in the political background, as these developments are amply documented elsewhere.

To these explanations of my approach to the problems of the arms race and disarmament should be added a note on terminology. Throughout the book "disarmament" is used as the generic term, given a larger connotation than "elimination of armaments." It covers all degrees of reduction of armaments, and it includes the preemption of options for further arms development (non-armament) as well as measures for regulating the production or use of arms quantity or quality. In some contexts "arms limitation" may be used generally. As a more specific term, referring to international agreements or rules in regard to armaments, the expression "regulation of armaments" is more appropriate. This is also, with "disarmament," the expression employed in the Charter of the United Nations, for which terms authorized translations in the five official languages are available.

I wish it were not too late to start a boycott against the use of "arms control" as an over-all term. It is nothing but a euphemism, serving regrettably to lead thinking and action towards the acceptance as "arms control measures" of compromises with scant or nil disarmament effect. A further reason is that we need the term "control" in connection with verification problems which loom large in all disarmament debates. "Control" should apply only to verification, inspection, and the like. It should be extricated from the terminological jungle that has grown up since the introduction of the term "arms control," now spreading.

The semantic criticism against "arms control" is also political. "Arms control" as a synonym for "arms regulation" is an American innovation which has come into usage only in the last decade and a half. While "arms regulation" points in the direction of agreement to regulate, "arms control" connotes power to control. In different languages, this meaning of "control" comes more or less to the foreground; among the various translations given in dictionaries, words like *beherrschen* in German and *autorité* in French are prominent. In the *Oxford English Dictionary*, even "overmaster" is given as one of the meanings of "control." An overtone of some body having interest or power to control is quite audible in many of the United States pronouncements on "arms control." Politically, that choice of terms is very unfortunate as the Soviet Union on principle denounces the idea of control being exercised over armaments, only over disarmament. Crucial differences between the positions of the two superpowers refer to the issues of inspection and secrecy, that is, control and verification. Why cause political confusion by the choice of terms?

In this book I attempt to encompass the multifarious problems relating, on one hand, to the arms race, and on the other, to disarmament measures. The two main parts of the book, as well as the

separate chapters within them, cannot, however, be sharply delimited from each other, as there are many interconnections between
the topics. This makes it difficult to avoid some overlapping.

In principle, the first part deals with the complex problem from
some broad angles: as part of the general malaise of our era, particularly the unreason of competing for military might. It also retells
the disarmament history of political failures machinated by the superpowers.

The second part deals with the main issues that disarmament
negotiations and debates have centered around since World War II,
which are as yet unresolved. I endeavor to present constructive
proposals and I invite and welcome counterproposals. In a concluding chapter, a summary view is attempted of issues of the arms race
and disarmament, as they ought now to be pointedly addressed to
policy-makers and interest groups with varying degrees of power and
thus responsibility.

The guiding principle in my criticism is rationality. The building up of the giant military establishments has gone, and is going,
right against what would be rational from the point of view of the
interests of every nation. This applies as well to the superpowers'
policy of increasing armaments. It is beyond all reason. The book
was intended to be an appeal to reason, but it has also become an
appeal to morality. How can we let the nationalistic security needs
as defined and exaggerated by military and other vested interests
misguide our societies? How can we allow secretiveness and falsi-
fications of reality to motivate the continued arms race, with all the
dangers and burdens thereof? The common man should demand
honest accountability of the policy-makers. He has the right to question their ethics.

A supreme goal for all mankind is peace on earth, peace under
the rule of law, and peace for the progress of all peoples. This book,
however, does not deal with peace per se. Nor is its thesis that disarmament can by itself assure peace, as there are many other
avenues that must also be traveled to secure peace, above all
changes in the political climates within and between nations. But,
although disarmament has many interconnections with all problems
of peace, it is here treated as a subject in its own right. Disarmament, even if only incompletely achieved, would entail such obvious
advantages that it can be considered a valid objective constituting
a value premise on which to build a set of proposals for action. My
intention in writing this book is to sketch an international strategy for

reaching agreements that will lead to more disarmament and arms regulation measures, saving resources that are now wasted on weapons, reducing the use of violence in human affairs.

During the two years I have been working on this book, the horizon has darkened further. There has been no attempt on the part of the superpowers to fulfill their promises of negotiating seriously to reverse the nuclear arms race. Nonetheless, a final word is personal: despite all frustrating experiences, I feel that we cannot give up.

I address myself to the decision-makers—the governments and their advisers—but my ambition is to be heard also by independent experts and concerned citizens in all countries. In the last instance, it is only by intensified public debate that disarmament issues can be pressed forward. Something is fundamentally amiss when, even in democratic countries, disarmament can be such a dead issue.

Before acknowledging my many debts of gratitude, I should explain that I have not been able to aim at perfection in every detail. The work on the book would then have stretched over many more years. Worse, the facts change with every month. I close the manuscript over Christmas 1975. Before it reaches publication, many events may have intervened and many details changed which I can only take into account in exceptional cases. Also, many people, particularly those with access to classified information, may well be in possession of more recent and more accurate knowledge on many points. But I plead with my readers to be more interested in the ideas and trends which are there for all to see and for all to evaluate for their meaning to our future.

The surface treatment of some details, or outdated information let stand, has partly been forced upon me by circumstance. During my many years in the disarmament negotiations I enjoyed wonderful cooperation from Swedish experts in several fields. We worked as a team; often I began with an idea and an outline, often some wording and a draft, and my collaborators would then, from their specialized angles, criticize, prune, or elaborate. We had also to take into account that the final text would require the backing of the Swedish Government. These advisers, who have been many over the years, now often have continued their careers in another framework, especially the military advisers, one of whom now is Chief of the Swedish Defense staff.

But this time I have been on my own. I have struck out farther afield among the many problems of disarmament and the ramifications of the arms race. My views are expressed individually as my own and often in sharp form. I want nobody else to be held responsible, but I do want to express my gratitude for inspiring exchanges of ideas with several former colleagues, Ambassadors Axel Edelstam and Lennart Eckerberg from the Ministry of Foreign Affairs; Anders Thunborg, Secretary of State in the same ministry, formerly Secretary of State in the Ministry of Defense, has given me the benefit of a memorandum on conversion plans relating to military production (Chapter V). Ambassador Lennart Myrsten and Commander Torgil Wulff have been helpful in checking on a section on the Sea-Bed Treaty (Chapter III, Section 7). Dr. Hans Blix, Legal Adviser to the Ministry of Foreign Affairs, and Dr. Karin Hjertonsson have read and discussed with me the sections on inhumane warfare (Chapter VIII). I had over the years benefitted from expert advice from the Research Institute of National Defense, which continued after I left my Cabinet post, through many friendly conversations with Ulf Ericsson, Jan Prawitz, Lars-Erik Tammelin, and Johan Lundin, the latter having made valuable suggestions for Chapter IX on biological and chemical means of warfare. They all have my gratitude.

I have taken away the memory of many lively and informative exchanges of views with several colleagues from a long stay at the Center for the Study of Democratic Institutions in Santa Barbara, California, and from my repeated stays at the Massachusetts Institute of Technology as Visiting Professor.

As a firm base for factual and analytical information, I have throughout the book relied much upon the many pertinent publications of the Stockholm International Peace Research Institute (SIPRI), set up to commemorate the 150 years of peace for Sweden from 1814. I was chairman of the Government committee which formulated its constitution and plans of work. The follow-up of these was assured by Gunnar Myrdal, as chairman of SIPRI's international board, until we both left Sweden for two years in 1973, and thereafter by Governor Rolf Edberg and by the first two directors, Robert Neild and Frank Barnaby. SIPRI's internationally recruited staff has scrupulously kept its independence as a research organization. The fact that it is entirely financed on the Swedish national budget has assured independence from all foreign interests and from the Swedish establishment, as there are stringent legal rules about noninterference by any authorities in the work, including the selection of research projects by an institute like SIPRI.

Finally, I want to express my warm thanks to James Peck of

Pantheon Books, who has given much good editorial advice; to Gunnel von Döbeln at SIPRI, who has undertaken to check and complete the bibliographical references; and to Kersti Wänndahl, Barbara R. Green, and Vera Pressman, who have helped me with typing the manuscript.

I have had the invaluable intellectual support of Gunnar Myrdal, particularly during the later stage of the work on this book.

Alva Myrdal

Stockholm, New Year 1976

A Personal Note

The reader is entitled to a certain curiosity about how I have come to obtain the knowledge and form the views that lie behind this book. The positions I have taken are not derived from pre-conceived ideas. On the contrary, the road has been a long one. It has entailed some unexpected transformations of my work assignments and a sometimes painful process leading to mature insight.

I did not start out from the peace movements. As a matter of fact, my strong anti-Nazi partisanship in the 1930s and a deep allegiance to the Allies who fought Hitler in the war did not predispose me towards an ideology of radical pacifism or outright condemnation of arms. My opposition was directed more against the repression of human rights and the cruelties of war, particularly the bombing of civilians; I personally experienced some of it in London. The bombing of Hiroshima and Nagasaki with nuclear weapons shocked me as it did the rest of the world, but I shared the hope of many that the end of the war also meant the end of nuclear weapons.

In the immediate postwar period, I turned towards intensive work for the positive tasks of reconstruction, beginning in Europe. Then the great historic drama of decolonization gripped me. So I enlisted in the struggle for development of the underprivileged parts of the world. This linked up with my work from earlier years for social justice in my own country, for income redistribution and a better life for all weak groups, particularly children and youth. The ideal that always carried me was, and is, the one of pressing for equality.

This preoccupation with the belief that the historical mission of the postwar era was to build a better world left me as rather an idle bystander when atomic weapons first came onto the agenda of the United Nations. I missed the chance for consciousness-raising then and there, although I worked in close vicinity to the decision-making centers of the international community, holding posts in the United Nations and UNESCO from early 1949 to late 1955, as chief of the Departments of Social Affairs and of Social Sciences, respectively.

During all my adult years I have been an interested observer and critic of the contortions of foreign policy. I felt there were better futures to choose than the ones of a Russian-led world revolution or an American-led stride forward to a century of unrestrained capitalism. The high expectations of a more reasonable and peaceful postwar world were nourished by the fact that the two great nations who stood for an antithesis in political systems had become allies during the war. My disappointment was that much deeper when I saw the Cold War taking the place of that peaceful coexistence we hoped for. But even then my anxiety was first and foremost aroused by the threats to human freedoms, the oppression engendered by the Soviet Union in Eastern Europe and the hypnotizing horror of McCarthyism in the United States, which professed to lead "the free world" as its calling. I was not from the outset alert to the great risks of an incipient militarization of the world; I was not ready to cry out: Down with the weapons.

When in the latter half of the 1950s the debate about the sense or nonsense of equipping armies with nuclear weapons reached its peak, dividing even the Labor Party in Sweden, I had been far away from my country since 1947, and from 1955 continued to be abroad for more than five years as diplomatic envoy from Sweden to India and neighboring Asian countries. Thus it happened that I did not find occasion to leap to the barricades against including nuclear weapons in Sweden's armory, although many of my friends did, foremost among them my much admired chief, Foreign Minister Undén. Of course, I was generally in sympathy with any move that might restrain the use of violence and also, more specifically, inclined to suspect arguments proffered by the military in favor of more arms. But I did not publicly take a stand; my own knowledge of the problems involved was not much deeper than that of an ordinary, although avid, newspaper reader, and I would not want to base advice on so shallow a foundation.

Then, out of the blue, after my having returned from India in the spring of 1961, Mr. Undén gave me the assignment to prepare the briefs for a major statement on disarmament. It was going to be his farewell speech to the United Nations after having over a forty-year span been a stalwart worker for peace and justice in both the League of Nations and the United Nations. The task seemed so awesome that I asked him not to announce the assignment for a couple of weeks while I explored the possibilities to render service in a field of specialization so new to me. My apprentice work started by plunging me into the great flood of debate material and academic writings which was coming out at just about that time. To make the tale brief: once I had begun, I was never able to stop the search for the why's and how's of something so senseless as the arms race.

My advice to Mr. Undén was not unidirectional; I suggested four different topics for possible initiatives in the United Nations on behalf of the Swedish Government. One would probably have been the most timely, namely, internationalization of satellites, which were just at the dawn of their technological maturation. Another major one was a proposal for nuclear-weapons-free zones, which was preferred by Mr. Undén and which, after considerable inputs by himself and our Foreign Office colleagues, became the Undén plan.

While I had not from the outset joined the Swedish campaign against nuclear weapons, I soon became convinced of the uselessness of arming a country like Sweden with nuclear weapons, understanding more and more—as I was in the mid-1960s a member of the parliamentary Defense Planning Commission—that it would be counterproductive, a risk to draw nuclear fire onto us. This persuasion thus became a stronger and stronger basis for my adamant work against nuclear weapons in the international forums; from 1962, I became the representative of Sweden in the Geneva Disarmament Committee. My contributions could, of course, be wholehearted and more intellectually effective when I could point to the willingness of my own country to forgo weapons of mass destruction of its own free will. Vice versa, the response meeting such arguments in the international negotiations reinforced my own stand and that of my like-minded colleagues in the Swedish Parliament, to which I had been elected in 1962, and in the Swedish Cabinet, which I was invited to join at the end of 1966. In 1968, Sweden formally and unilaterally renounced nuclear weapons and soon thereafter all chemical and biological means of warfare.

What I have so far described is like the first act of my involvement with disarmament issues. The second act was played out during twelve long years of yeoman service to the cause of disarmament in the United Nations and various UN-related disarmament committees. Here another process gradually began to operate: my initial optimism began to look—to myself—more and more like naïveté. I could state in 1972: "We have accomplished no real disarmament, . . . we can see hardly any tangible results of our work, and . . . the underlying major cause must be that the superpowers have not seriously tried to achieve disarmament."[1] How that insight dawned and the cruel blows that have been dealt the cause of disarmament under the guise of flowing rhetoric is the subject of this book, in which the developments as they became externalized during the negotiations on one issue after another are related with as much objectivity as it has been possible for me to muster.

How my efforts and those of my colleagues from lesser powers, particularly from the nonaligned nations, were smothered will, however, have to be read largely between the lines. Our contributions were constructive ones, but they are hard for the general public to know and difficult of access even for serious students, academically concerned with international relations in general and disarmament discussions in particular. The mass media—except in our home countries—paid very scant attention, geared as they have become to consider only superpower dealings important. For scholars, interested and equipped to delve deeper into the material, the dynamics of negotiations and the superpowers' successful neutralizing or negligence of all the positive proposals are there to speak for themselves.

The inside story of how progress towards arms limitation was stymied is even more revealing, sometimes quite dramatic. I might briefly refer to three events. One is related to the negotiations on a comprehensive test ban (reported in Chapters III and VII). Soon after we had succeeded in Geneva in 1962, the first year of negotiations, in sweeping away the exceedingly cumbersome and costly technical superstructure—in reality just a house of cards—for verification of such a ban, a politically quite favorable climate broke in the aftermath of the Cuban crisis. The Soviet Union suddenly accepted the United States' demands for on-site inspections. The crucial difference was now only in the numbers: two to three or eight to ten inspections. Then the nonaligned delegates in order to be helpful worked out a quite ingenious scheme for bridging the gap,

in an operationally practical way, encouraged not only by the
rhetoric of the great powers and by the arguments of scientists but
also, as I recall, by prompting from Senator Hubert Humphrey.
What happened? Both Moscow and Washington started to exert
diplomatic pressure in our capitals, undercutting our work through
intimations to our own governments that we were jeopardizing important progress towards an agreement by the two superpowers.
Such pressure, which has never been exerted *in favor of disarmament*, led to the abandonment of plans for the total test ban of 1963.
What was achieved instead was a partial and ineffective test ban—
with added promises of completion unfulfilled after twelve years.

If in that case both sides resorted to arm-twisting, the other
examples show more one-sided responsibility. A memorable occasion was the effort in 1969 to obtain for the Geneva Protocol of
1925, banning the use of chemical and biological means of warfare,
the confirmation of the United Nations as constituting international
customary law, binding on all nations. When the so-called Swedish
resolution (Chapter VIII) to this effect was in the committee stage,
the United States mounted a fierce campaign against it—the political
reason of course being that chemical weapons were then being used
in the Vietnam war. The pressure was enormous. The test to me
personally came in the form of a luxurious luncheon, offered by the
United States delegation, where I was stood up against the wall as the
one to be blamed for United States inability to ratify this nearly fifty-
year-old piece of international legislation. "Are you sincere in saying
that nonratification is preferable to a ratification where we make
reservations so as to get the nonlethal chemical weapons exempted?"
Having at that time become sadder and wiser, my answer was a
firm yes. This time the proposal succeeded in the United Nations
with a remarkable support of the overwhelming majority of its
members.

The third example is one of adamant negativism on the part of
the Soviet Union. The concerted opinion of the smaller nations was
that the preliminary fact-finding for verification of compliance with
the ban on production of biological weapons should be assured an
objective, impartial handling. For that reason the task ought not to
be laid on the Security Council, with its veto powers for the five
permanent members (Chapter IX). I, and some others, fought
valiantly and with strong arguments all the way through the General
Assembly. But the Soviet Union just stonewalled. The Treaty on
Banning the Production of Biological Means of Warfare of 1972

came into force in March 1975, but without the Security Council even having accepted the responsibility as formally designed in a superpower draft resolution, submitted in accordance with Article VI of the Treaty. The Treaty prescribed that all biological means of warfare should be destroyed within a short span of time, but only the United States has in this case set a laudable example, with such a decision made already in 1969 and an apparently rapid implementation.

These are just a few episodes, unheralded by public attention, as other attempts at constructive contributions to disarmament made by representatives of lesser powers generally have been during the long period which I have called a *triste* second act in this personal narrative. They are characteristic for the Game of Disarmament.

The third act is, as yet, unwritten. It has not even begun. We are in a strange interlude of no-motion on all disarmament issues, the bilateral SALT negotiations implying only a kind of contractual institutionalization of the continued arms race, and the important Non-Proliferation Treaty becoming obsolete through its ineffectiveness. The stage has not as yet been set for a serious and concerted effort by all actors, as I would still hope, to win victory over the arms race, so senseless and cruel, and to bar a complete militarization of the whole world.

PART ONE

the forces behind the arms race

The Reign of Unreason

Our world is hovering at the edge of an abyss, driven there by man's unreason. One crisis is cresting on top of another.

There is danger pending of depletion of nonrenewable resources and of pollution of air, water, land, animals, and our own bodies.

The income gap between the developed and the underdeveloped countries is widening steadily. The recent food and oil crises have produced misery for large masses in the poorer countries. In the underdeveloped countries these problems are exacerbated by the population explosion. The increase of population to be fed in those countries is bound to continue for decades ahead.

Meanwhile, even the developed countries are caught in the process of stagflation—inflation of prices to a high level with simultaneous high unemployment, a process which is also causing international derangement of the world monetary system, threatening the attempts to lower trade barriers.

In a general way, these adverse trends are the result of a lack of foresight as well as unwillingness to cooperate within and between countries. The sinister developments in the advance towards the brink of disaster all interact, worsened by the calamitous threat this book has been written to analyze: the arms race and the militarization of the world.

1. A Global Folly

Clear-cut evidence of the irrational ordering of world priorities is provided by the rush for armaments, which is dependent on decisions taken and implemented by national governments. Upwards of $300 billion is spent each year in the armaments race. As a rounded estimate best serves the purpose of keeping the facts in the minds of the public, annual variations and statistical imperfections may be disregarded.[1]

This sum is in the same order of magnitude as the total production and income of those poor countries which comprise more than half of mankind. SIPRI presents another type of comparison:

> Thus, for example, world military expenditure is greater than either world expenditure on education or health; it is some fifteen times larger than official aid provided to the underdeveloped countries; and it is equivalent to the combined gross national product of all the countries in Africa, the Middle East, and South Asia.[2]

Such comparisons and estimates are quoted here to give an idea of dimensions and magnitudes. The concepts and the statistics on which estimates are built are flimsy, but they are reliable enough to illustrate a reality which the citizens of the world so far have been unable to grasp: nations seem to be bent on continuing along the road to more abundant, more sophisticated, more lethal, and more expensive armaments.

The distribution of military spending among nations broadly reflects power status and power aspirations. The two superpowers have regularly accounted for the major share of the global outlay for armaments. In addition to the two superpowers, four others are grouped as major military spenders. They are ranked by SIPRI according to the size of each military budget: China,[3] West Germany, Great Britain, and France. They far outdistance all other countries. Among other nations, NATO and WTO allies are shouldering a somewhat increasing burden.* Together these European-oriented alliances are responsible for about four-fifths of the total world military expenditure.

The tables of expenditures for various countries make interesting reading, revealing governmental priorities.[4] There is a remarkably low level for a fairly advanced country like Japan, around $26 per

---

* NATO and WTO will be used throughout the book for the North Atlantic Treaty Organization and the Warsaw Treaty Organization, respectively.

capita in constant prices in 1973, while Israel's is more than $1000. Israel has the highest rates of military expenditure, but is being closely followed by the other countries in the Middle East. The most dynamic, not to say dramatic, general trend is that countries reckoned as underdeveloped are nowadays loading their budgets with military expenditures. The Third World part of the global military resources rose from 3.2 percent in 1955 to 12.3 percent in 1974 without any corresponding increase in these countries' share of the world's financial resources. In these over-all figures, foreign credits, rebates, and military aid, even for training, are often not included; therefore, these figures should be relied upon only for a general but firm conclusion: military expenditures are throughout too high for public welfare and national development.

Where is the cold reasoning and weighing of priorities behind all this? This question has become pressing because the amounts of spending for military purposes have trebled since 1948. The trend from the beginning of the century into the 1930s—with the exception of World War I—had been for the United States to spend approximately 1 percent of its Gross National Product on the military.[5] Curves in constant prices for total world expenditure lie quite flat until the 1930s. After World War II, their steep increase is most marked between 1960 and 1970; since then they have flattened out again, although at a high level, now consuming some 6–7 percent of total world output.

Within these margins shifts have occurred, the dominant one at present being towards markedly faster increase of spending on the part of the Third World countries than in the advanced countries. By 1974 the number of countries spending over $1 billion at constant 1970 prices increased to twenty, a bare majority of eleven of these belonging to the two major alliances which together with China had totally dominated the scene until very recently. Of the newcomers no fewer than four were in the Middle East.[6]

This race for higher positions on the military expenditure ladder cannot be said to be related to greater war risks, although, of course, actual warfare in some countries has caused steep increases in costs. However, a kind of automatism with a ratchet effect is allowed to reign. As SIPRI states:

> On three occasions since the end of World War II, military expenditure surged upwards in connection with a war or major crisis, and in each case the subsequent fall in expenditure, if one occurred at all, was relatively modest.[7]

Even the end of the Vietnam war did not result in any marked decrease of the United States expenditure curve.[8] Weapons acquisition
continues; for the whole world it has become an end in itself.

In summary, all countries, whatever their level of development,
have at this juncture in history chosen to give their military needs
as they perceive them a high priority in comparison with alternative uses of the same resources for peaceful progress. Consequently,
the struggle for resources continually pits the arms race against
investments for social and economic development. The results are
more and worse slums, poorer health among the masses, and greater
educational deficiencies. This is a definite consequence, not only
for countries classed as underdeveloped:

> Comparisons of the military and social ranking of countries indicate
> that for most of the biggest military powers armed strength has been
> achieved at the sacrifice of the social welfare. With few exceptions,
> major powers stand lower, in the ranking of nations, in social indi-
> cators than in military.[9]

In the race for spending on armaments huge sums have been
sacrificed. The corresponding "gain" is measured in kill-effectiveness.
The two superpowers have been the principal actors in the race,
"gaining" incomparably more than others in military strength. They
have spent vast sums of money and usurped huge resources, particularly the rarest of all, human brain power, to develop nuclear and
other weapons. Their combined nuclear arsenal now possesses explosive capacity to the equivalent of several tons of TNT for each inhabitant of the earth—whether three or twenty tons, as variously estimated,
is of little significance. The fire-strength of their nuclear weapons
has increased several millionfold since Hiroshima. But the superpowers, the possessors of this overkill capacity, continue their race
in an upward spiral.

The number and quality of all other weapons, euphemistically
called conventional, have similarly increased. The familiar chain reaction of new weapons-counterweapons-counter-counterweapons is
taking its expensive toll in the form of outlays for both major and
smaller weapons to be used on land or for sea and air warfare. The
competition has also achieved vastly increased hit accuracy of
weapons through automation of systems for targeting and communications and other technological breakthroughs in electronic equipment, as well as lasers, sensors for spy satellites, etc.

The multiplying of kill-effectiveness through advances in military technology is an avowed aim of all major powers. But the acceleration of the armaments race is not confined to the relatively affluent nations. When the multilateral disarmament negotiations opened in 1962, only six nations of the so-called Third World of underdeveloped countries had supersonic military aircraft; at the latest count thirty-nine do.[10]

A first major conclusion as to the irrationality of the armaments race is that it results in a growing burden on the resources of all nations. A second conclusion is inevitable, although perhaps less visible prima facie, namely, that the military competition results in an ever increasing superiority—militarily and technologically—of the already overstrong superpowers, thus sharpening the discrimination against all lesser powers who have become, in fact, defenseless against them.

2. Greater Security?

Every government defends its participation in the arms race as necessary to guard its national security. But this is an illusion. What makes the arms race a global folly is that all countries are now buying greater and greater insecurity at higher and higher costs. The nonstop character of the arms race also poses ever steeper obstacles to disarmament negotiations. While the disarmers talk, the armories that were to be dismantled are being built higher and higher. Disarmament negotiations have, so far, been a sorrowful Sisyphus game and a long series of missed opportunities (Chapter III).

Although statesmen and their military advisers do not want to listen and learn, preferring to continue to use the woolly term "national security" in order to boost the defense budgets, the knowledge is now becoming commonplace among independent experts and writers that the stupendous increase in the quantity, quality, and cost of armaments has not resulted in any commensurable increase in aggregate national security for the world. A considerable body of evidence indicates that a mutual stepping up of armaments leads to a decrease in national security, that is, safety against attacks.

That the arms race is rapidly decreasing the security of all the lesser powers is obvious. Also, the dynamics of the arms race increases the incidental risks for third parties. If they line up with one of the superpowers in formal or nonformal alliances under the

illusion that this guarantees their security, they are then drawn
even more tightly into that superpower game which goes on above
their heads (Chapter II).

Not even the two superpowers can gain greater security through
the arms race. Their nuclear-weapons strength long ago exceeded
what might be needed even for a "terror balance," that is, for a
deterrent that forbids both, knowing what retaliation lies in store
at the already existing level of overkill, to use force against the other
(Chapter IV, Section 2). Temporary gains on one or the other side
cannot make it more tempting to use nuclear weapons for an attack.
In addition, competition, inherent in the arms race, tends to make
relative superiority unstable.

This element of instability in the arms race is a pending world
danger. The dangers of a collision are accentuated by technological
development itself, as warning times steadily decrease, thus making
it more and more probable that war might occur through technical
accidents and errors. This is illustrated by the fact that the time required for interhemispheric delivery of nuclear bombs by missiles
has shrunk to about ten minutes. The missile has also drastically
shortened the warning time and heightened the surprise element
possible between neighboring nations on a continental land mass.
The mechanical complexity and increasingly automated functioning
between signal received and attack released makes national security
more and more threatened by technical hazards.

3. The Costs of the Arms Race

The arms race has brought costs to levels that are ruinous to the
world economy. Even countries that are rich and technologically
advanced are hampered in economic growth. After World War II,
Germany, for a crucial period, and Japan until now were prohibited
from spending their resources on armaments. This undoubtedly is
part of the explanation why these countries had a growth rate that
motivated analysts to speak of a miracle. Other developed countries
in the postwar era would have shown a higher economic growth rate
if they, too, had abstained from participating in the arms race; underdeveloped countries would have had a greater chance for development.

As the defense expenditures in the national budgets mount,
it will become harder to obtain financing for the civilian purposes

of health, education, housing, and all other kinds of social needs. Public expenditures for such needs would, if well planned, increase productivity, as they are tantamount to investment in human capital which would raise the productivity of labor and prevent future remedial costs for individuals and society. In the long run, the arms race holds down civilian public expenditures, becoming thus an additional cause of stifling the rate of economic growth.

In underdeveloped countries, the allocation of scarce financial resources for the production or purchase of armaments will clearly have even more adverse effect than in the rich countries, having already hampered their economic development, grossly in some instances.

Military expenditure also plays a fateful role in the interrelations between richer and poorer nations. For example, there has been, globally speaking, a growing reluctance on the part of the richer, donor countries to give aid for development (Chapter II, Section 9). One of the causes of this is the financial difficulties in the developed countries, and those are partly related to high expenditures for armaments.

The discrepancy between what the rich countries devote to military purposes and to aiding the poor nations should shock our consciences, and would if the facts could be brought out and underscored in such a way that they would grip the ordinary citizen. The estimates, expressed in statistical terms, vary, but appropriations for the military are somewhere between fifteen and twenty-five times appropriations for development aid.[11] In justification, the rich countries can point to the financial and economic instabilities, or even to mismanagement, in the underdeveloped countries, which conditions are partly due to the high priority given to military expenditures in those countries.

A salient feature of aid is that much of these funds have gone into armaments, particularly aid from the United States to South Vietnam, South Korea, Taiwan, Pakistan, and many Latin American countries. All aid received by the poorer countries is in a general way increasing their ability to spend their resources on armaments and purchases of armaments abroad, and they are using these opportunities to their detriment:

> Whether a developing country pays for imported armaments in cash or through the export of primary products, its growth potential is adversely affected at a particularly vulnerable point, through the consequential preempting of scarce foreign exchange resources.[12]

The military element thus corrupts other economic relations between countries as well as the use of developmental aid. The recent scramble for arms procurement by the rich oil-producing countries does not change the over-all picture, but the dimensions of these purchases may serve as an eye-opener to demonstrate the craze of arms competition that has gripped the world.

4. *An Arms Race Within the Arms Race*

The calamitous arms race is here defined as an international one, between countries, but international policy is always a result of national policies. In all countries there are forces which irrationally drive the governments forward as participants in the international arms race.

Despite the heavy costs for armaments which impede growth and development of national economies, domestic discussion is rarely focused on over-all and long-term trends. In most countries, the misconceived view is that high military expenditures, particularly for weapons procurement, can be favorable for economic growth and safeguard a high employment level.

Once a country is engulfed in the arms race, continuing it often appears as a means of preserving employment and the level of industrial production. Considered from the point of view of an individual armament-producing region of a country or of a particular armament industry, this idea has a semblance of truth, although arms production has been shown to represent relatively low demands for labor. To be sure, any reallocation of resources always has initial difficulties and costs. These should, however, not be overestimated. They can be reduced if conversion plans are outlined and established well in advance (Chapter V, Section 4).

The arms race has become politically connected with the vested interests that President Eisenhower termed "the military-industrial complex." In military matters, no limit is set by market forces, by competitive demand, or by prices. Every new plant for military production, every new production contract, increases the weight of these vested interests. In democratic countries these interests, both labor and business, often become rooted in the parliaments and the provincial assemblies, whose representatives are expected to defend local interests. In authoritarian countries, these vested interests should be easier for a government to control, but apparently they are not. Potentially, the voice of the people, were they properly informed, should have a better chance to be decisive in the democratic nations.

But there are other forces in every nation irrationally driving the arms race forward. One is the investment in research and development work (R&D). This constitutes a considerable cost factor of the arms race in every country, but most of all in the advanced countries. Global investment in military research is devouring a very large share of the world's total research and development expenditures, approximately $25 billion out of a total of $60 billion annually, again to quote figures that, however frail, nevertheless give some idea of dimensions and priorities. This figure can be compared with $6 billion accounted for in the field of health research.[13]

What is driving this competition forward? What are the gains? The answer again is: increased effectiveness of arms to harm and kill. The race is led by the superpowers, who want to upgrade their nuclear-weapons systems and all other weapons across the board. This product improvement is the dynamic element in an open-ended, qualitative arms competition which is the most dangerous aspect of the arms race and which can be stilled only by banning new generations of weapons, operationally best achieved by banning weapons tests (Chapter IV, Section 6, and Chapter VII). The lead by the superpowers is followed not unwillingly by all governments who can master the techniques for upgrading any of their weapons systems.

Another, subtler, force is the ease with which individual scientists are apt to be tempted and therefore caught by the wide-open experimentation offered by military R&D. Often quite handsomely paid jobs in these fields make alternative work less enticing intellectually and less rewarding financially. Power and pride are obvious assets and the question "what for?" can, it seems, be comfortably forgotten. There is also the drive towards technology for technology's sake, often called the technological imperative, or the impulse to modernization, which has been described as a mental virus, typical for our time.[14]

Those scientists and technicians who work for research and development establishments, civilian as well as military, undoubtedly feel a drive for achievement per se, to proceed always to improved models and higher levels of sophistication, which means greater weapons efficiency for harming fellow men.

Industrial interests and imaginative scientists may have a natural inclination for new inventions, but there are within the military

R&D establishments also strong bureaucratic pressures to advance further. One reason for this is the interservice competition for shares of the military budgets, leading to an arms race within the arms race. This is difficult to control "because of the sheer complexity and variety of modern specialized weapon systems," which complexity supports the military establishment in its opinion that only it is competent to decide the size and character of the national security effort. The situation is then "exploited to support claims for higher military spending." If one service fears that its tasks are about to be reduced, the pressures become considerable. This reasoning is illustrated in a fictive case, posed by SIPRI:

> "With the termination of Minuteman III conversions, the Ballistic Systems Division [of the US Air Force] has no mission to perform while its organization competitors, the Office of Special Projects in the Navy and Strategic Air Command in the Air Force, still have the Trident submarine and the B-1 supersonic bomber, respectively, to develop." Similarly, on the USSR side, if land-based missile systems should be removed, "it will entail the dissolution of one entire branch of their armed forces, that is, the Strategic Rockets Division. It is reasonable to expect that this organization, with its powerful political backing, will resist successfully any efforts to negotiate it out of existence."[15]

A deep-seated spirit of competition reigns in this sector of our society as in so many others. The race is for *more* arms, for *more effective* arms—in short, for *new* arms—a fateful, self-generating process.

The spirit of competition also reigns in regard to the arguments for security, for strength, for being inferior to none, and for meeting threats from the enemy—making the decision-makers prisoners of prejudiced public opinion, nurtured by their own propaganda.

Without a straight and frank analysis from their leaders of real defense needs and appropriate arms requirements, citizens cannot function as a corrective force against the considerations of power, prestige, and oneupmanship which play a dominant role in arms decisions.

5.   *The Depletion of Resources for Development*

The costs of the arms race should not be measured in financial terms alone. The military consumption of material resources should also be specifically accounted for. What has been used for the production of aircraft, ships, and all kinds of hardware could have benefitted civilian needs instead. The armaments race has played a part in creating the present danger of depletion of the world's non-renewable resources. An analysis made in the United States in 1970 of the military take of some important raw materials showed a range of from 14 percent of total use of bauxite and copper to 7.5 percent of iron and manganese to 4.8 percent of petroleum.[16]

Seen from the point of view of social and economic development the use of research and development manpower resources for improvement of weapons must be deemed particularly disastrous (Chapter V, Section 5). Some 400,000 scientists and engineers, nearly half of the total engaged in research and development work, are employed in military pursuits in the advanced countries. The total manpower engaged directly or indirectly for military purposes is estimated at 50 million people, also a staggering figure.

Information about the misdirection of science and technology caused by the arms race can be found in UN reports.[17] In 1962, when serious multilateral disarmament negotiations were about to start, it was already estimated that more than 20,000 nuclear scientists and engineers could become available for other work through discontinuing the nuclear arms race.[18] Some of these scientists and engineers could be assigned to assist peaceful nuclear programs serving the interests of economic and technological progress in the less developed countries. Already in those early days some might have been assigned to help solve the obnoxious problems of nuclear-reactor safety and waste disposal.

Other research personnel could be employed in the education and training of manpower, in engineering, and in health work. One concrete example was presented in the United States Senate: to provide 100,000 elementary school teachers for a year (at a salary of $10,000 each) would cost $1 billion, which corresponds to the construction costs of just one nuclear-powered aircraft carrier—without equipment.[19] That would mean a much higher input for education in the underdeveloped world, where compensation to teachers is much lower, while arms are just as expensive as in developed nations, if they have to pay for them. The rivalry between disarmament and development must be brought to the foreground whenever development strategy is discussed in the UN, or whenever any donor nation designs its development aid program, or any aid-receiving country its plans for arms procurement.

The priorities given to the military, now absorbing huge and highly sophisticated research and technology resources, cause lack of development in the developed nations as well. In the United States, military expenditures in the past twenty years have been allowed to take what amounts to almost the total sum of personal income taxes paid during that period—while social needs have been neglected. There are back streets of dirt and ill-health, run-down houses, and neglected educational needs in the lands of the Great Military Spenders, too.

6. The Wider Costs of the Weapons Culture

Included in the true costs of arms belong the considerable non-economic human costs of the mass production and mass consumption of arms. The effects on people run much deeper than any financial and material reckoning can account for. First, there are the human costs, direct and indirect, of wars in which arms are actually used. Then there are the disruptive social, political, and psychological effects of the general spread and availability of weapons. These are hurting our bodies, souls, and societies everywhere. These essentially ethical problems of wars, weapons, and tools of violence have existed since time immemorial, but in the present era they have been steeply aggravated and will continue to be aggravated if a halt is not called.

A Judgment Book should carry at least six main entries on the ledger of guilt and unreason.[20]

a. The Human Costs of Actual Warfare.   Wars certainly have not been relegated to history. A count of armed conflicts since World War II would run into the hundreds if guerilla warfare, internal revolt, and violent coups d'état were included with international wars.[21] Tens of millions have been killed in action since 1945. Though not of the dimensions of World Wars I and II—wherein the victims, soldiers, and civilians, must be reckoned at some 100 million —the human costs of warfare continue.[22] Several major international wars have been in progress during the writing of this book, 1973–1975: the United States in Vietnam and Cambodia; Portugal in Angola, Guinea-Bissau and Mozambique; Israel with Egypt and Syria, border incidents with other Arab countries. Other border conflicts occurring in many places should not be overlooked, nor should internal revolts and guerilla warfare from Angola to Uruguay.

With the experience of the long war in Indochina fresh in our minds, we must, when estimating the human costs of wars, account not only for the numbers killed, lost, and wounded but also for prisoners of war and refugees. The material costs stretch from massive destruction of homes, hospitals, and schools to factories and fields, dams and dikes, land and forest. Additional losses are caused by the interrupted functioning of society, production, and consumption and the more permanent effects on health care and education. Behind this is the bitter sorrow of families separated or broken forever.

There are more subtle effects, even without actual war, when masses of men are held in occupation armies and military bases. These are social costs which make for long-term distortion of normalcy: the moral degradation of soldiers who become accustomed in their young and formative years to drugs, brothels, black markets—and, of course, to brutality. In the spate of self-incriminating comments after the end of the United States' active involvement in the Indochinese war, many somber facts were being reported about the 2.5 million American veterans who served in Southeast Asia:

> Of those who were married before they went to Vietnam, 38 percent were separated or getting divorced six months after their return.
> As many as 175,000 probably have used heroin since getting out of service.
> Over 400,000 servicemen who had participated in fighting were given other than honorable discharges.
> For the young Vietnam-era veteran, the ex-soldier of age twenty to twenty-four, unemployed rates have been running above 18 percent. If one looks at the black veterans' sub-group within this category (twenty to twenty-four years of age) the rates approximate 30 percent.
> Of the 124,000 draft evaders and deserters eligible for clemency, only some 20,000 ever applied.[23]

One hears of and cares about the hundreds of thousands of children fathered by American soldiers and left in Vietnam. Why is nothing said about the moral conditions of the men who abandoned them? Or about the guilt of soldiers, from generals to GIs, who turned hundreds of thousands of Indochinese women into prostitutes? Men engaged in the time-honored male pursuit of warfare

are evidently supposed to have the right to enjoy themselves—at the cost of women and children. Effects such as these are usually not counted as costs of war. But they should be.

b. The Brutalization of Warfare. Present-day theaters of war are used as proving grounds for new generations of weapons and the training of military forces in new techniques of destruction. Electronics equipment, lasers, and other new technological devices are tested to increase kill-effectiveness. New records are being sought and set for weapons that can cause greater suffering, more painful wounds, and more ghastly scars in the bodies of soldiers and civilians alike (Chapter VIII).

This proving opportunity is sometimes openly recognized as a benefit, as when the United States Air Force Chief of Staff George S. Brown was reported as saying that the service he heads "over-all is a stronger . . . more proficient and professional force than the Soviet air-arm" and that "combat-experienced leadership is a big factor."

> "One result is that we don't have anyone in any echelon of command in a responsible position who isn't combat experienced. That means a lot in terms of being used to the equipment, the tactics, and the people. They've all been exposed to gunfire. The Soviet Union has not been in combat since World War II. All things considered, our tactical forces are far more proficient than those of the Soviet Union." In contrast to what Brown sees as a Soviet fighter force oriented to defense, he says "our tactical forces are trained and equipped to work offensively in carrying the battle to an enemy."[24]

Wars are becoming "effectivized" as is everything else in our era. The development of weapons is going through a frightening escalation to higher levels of assured destruction. This trend to worse brutalization of wars may be deemed rational by the warmakers but must be condemned from a human point of view. Common ethical value judgments against unnecessary brutality have built up international law—some of it codified, some regarded as customary—to regulate warfare. However, it is clear that in our day of technological perfectionism respect by governments for rules of international law against inhumane warfare is drastically deteriorating.

Weapons and methods of mass destruction are now increasingly and willfully used against both man and his environment—such as area saturation bombing and other modern warfare methods which are indiscriminate in their effects on military and civilian targets. Weapons are developed, deployed, and used which cause excessive human suffering, such as napalm, flechettes, fragmentation bombs, and other new arms employed as antipersonnel weapons. They are developed despite—or is it because of?—the fact that they are unnecessarily cruel weapons, so defined because their effects in causing pain and agony are in excess of what the laws of war consider to be legitimate, namely what is required to put an enemy soldier out of action.

At the same time, the civilian populations are more and more the helpless victims of modern unrestricted warfare. The international Hague Conferences of 1899 and 1907 explicitly prohibited the bombing of cities. The hundreds of thousands of innocent victims of the bombings of Guernica, London, Hamburg, Coventry, Dresden, and Tokyo, not to mention Hiroshima and Nagasaki, illustrate how supremely disdainful governments have become of these humanitarian laws. "Megamurder" is the term General Burns of Canada has given to this new license which governments have taken over human lives, particularly since the onset of World War II, which marked a definitive turnabout in ethical norms concerning the protection of civilians.[25]

With each new war the proportion of civilians killed rises. On the basis of estimates in the *Encyclopaedia Britannica*, it may be surmised that of those killed in World War I more than 50 percent were civilians; if those dying from epidemics and famines are added, the proportion is even larger. In World War II, the civilian populations of Britain, Germany, and Japan were direct bombing targets. In Korea, only about 20 percent of the casualties were soldiers and 80 percent civilians.[26] The disproportion is even more frightening in Indochina, where the civilian populations of North and South Vietnam and Cambodia have been helpless victims of technologically masterminded methods of warfare.

This changed nature of war also shows itself in the many civilians being dislocated, uprooted, moved to refugee camps and strategic hamlets, or afflicted by forced urbanization—mostly women, children, and elderly people in ever greater numbers dragging themselves along to poverty ghettos. These costs are born by nations at war, whether they consider themselves winners or losers.

    c. The Encouragement of More War. The production and export of armaments, whether as sales or as grants, encourages nations to prepare for and engage in hostilities. This has proved particularly important in the new underdeveloped countries. Such increased weapons procurement may transform minor local conflicts into major confrontations. The recent wars in the Middle East have been crucially tied to arms deliveries from the two superpowers, which have thrown more and more fuel on a conflict that otherwise might have been kept at a smoldering low.

The inclination of governments to start or continue local wars is thus continually being bolstered and materially encouraged from the outside and, at the same time, the propensity to make war more devastating is increased. Therefore, the issues of arms trade and, more generally, of possibilities to limit both production and procurement of arms should be given a much more prominent place in deliberations concerning political solutions of ongoing conflicts in various regions of the world (Chapter V).

d. The Militarization of Nations. There are many invidious effects of living in a weapons culture. The acquisition of more and more arms with its built-in trend towards a continuing arms race contributes to a strengthening of the military in the domestic affairs of all countries. When dictators and oppressors take and keep power, they rely upon their military might, on weapons stored, and soldiers trained to use them. The installation of military regimes in Africa, Asia, and Latin America is among the prominent features of our time. This present-day power of generals and colonels is clearly related to procurement of arms, which is often a direct result of military aid. And, for policing such a nation, ordinary weapons such as tanks and machine guns count. Weapon development makes it ever easier for the few to dominate the many, thus constituting a crisis for democracy as well.

The militarization of political power is especially prevalent in new countries without firm traditions of the civilian government controlling the military. The military has often achieved a privileged position on account of favored access to education, whether or not it originated from groups enjoying high social status. Countries with an age-old tradition of civilian culture and democratic institutions are not immune to the danger of militarization. Most generally— and here I do not think I can exonerate any country—the hegemony of military priorities and the vested interests involved in the arms race are at present creating obstacles to disarmament. It is ominous that foreign affairs are more and more generally discussed in terms of military strategies, undermining peaceful international cooperation as a way of the future before it has even been given a chance.

This pervasive effect of militarism germinating everywhere should be given greater attention in connection with other issues on the agenda of the world community, those of colonialism, apartheid, human rights, refugees, military aid, and related problems of our marred civilization.

e. A Disturbing Psychological Impact. The shock of the nuclear terror weapons, the long drawn-out exposure to war horrors, and the glaring unreason of the ongoing arms race have had deep psychological consequences in the world. These are as undisputed as they are difficult to pinpoint and to measure.

> Against the background of the Second World War, the fear engendered by the nuclear arms race was one of the factors which stimulated the postwar disillusion of the youth in many countries, whatever the level of their military spending. Every child learned that he lived in a world in which violence had become commonplace, and which was now stocked with sufficient lethal power to wipe out all human life. He learned that weapons infinitely more destructive than the bombs which were dropped on Hiroshima and Nagasaki were in a state of constant readiness, and that a military or human or even a technical error could have devastating consequences. This awareness has undoubtedly helped to create a psychological background of uncertainty, of fear and anxiety, and sometimes of social rejection or disillusion. Some Western social psychologists tend to ascribe to the arms race and to the horrors of war a belief which prevails in some of the younger generation that the world is an irrational place in which the improvement of society, through economic growth, is a hopeless cause. There are, of course, other major contributing factors, such as the problems which the multiplying populations of the world will have to face if they are to find the resources with which to exist; or the rapid spoliation of our physical environment. Whatever the importance of these other major problems, there can be *no question but that the continuing arms race and the growth of violence in the world add to the disaffection of millions of people.*[27]

When nations invest so much in tools of violence, people may begin to feel hopeless about how to solve problems. Or, as an experienced statesman writes:

> No one has made the link between national and international developments; between the lawlessness in international conduct, the lawlessness in domestic politics, and the common habits of mind from which these lawlessnesses arise.[28]

The effect of the mass media in bringing war, with all its bloody realism, into the everyday experience of millions of people must be to gradually desensitize the general public to the occurrence of violence. War pictures show acts of violence sanctioned by having been ordered by governments. As such, they carry a mark of approval. A strong impact is particularly to be expected in the case of children and young people whose ethical concepts had not been stabilized before mass media, particularly television, began to vividly advertise acts of aggression against other human beings, undertaken by presumably civilized nations. The effects of the pictorial persuaders now undoubtedly reach down to subliminal levels.[29]

However, the blame should not be laid directly on the media but rather on the occurrence in real life of politically directed violence. It seems safe to assume that the wars in Biafra and in Bangladesh, in Indochina and in the Middle East, as depicted in the press and on the screens, have offered inducement to or at least justification of violence. Heroization of nonviolent and pacific attitudes seems less and less to respond to public expectation.

f.   The Risks for Banditry.   The effects of the brutality of war as presented in the mass media cannot be easily distinguished from the results of a more general preoccupation with crime-related violence programming. But the general impression is becoming widespread that officially condoned violence in wars is more and more creating an impression among the public that violence belongs to our way of life.

This is a more imminent danger where weapons are not handled and controlled by governments but are spread among the general public, as in some countries, particularly the United States. When instruments for aggression and violence are available relatively easily, the risks are great that they will be used by some individuals who are psychologically less balanced or morally more unscrupulous than others.

Where gun control is weak the risks are greater. The frequency of violence and murders, many committed with handguns, is several times higher in the United States than in otherwise comparable countries.[30] In Sweden, where gun control is effective, the irony is that violent crimes, although much rarer, are not infrequently committed with weapons stolen from military supplies. If tools for violence are readily available, the resort to violence becomes more probable, as its eruption in psychological terms is always a short-circuit type of reaction. Mohandas Gandhi once suggested "that the personality of a man changes when he acquires a weapon."[31]

The spreading use of incendiaries, explosives, Molotov cocktails, and suitcase bombs leads to increasing fears. A frightening prospect is that chemical weapons may, before they can be outlawed internationally, be used to serve movements of internal unrest. It is now prophesied that the days are not far away when even nuclear weapons may be taken in hand by terrorists, to be used for foreign policy by extortion (Chapter VI, Section 6).

These dangers of the future are as yet unmapped, despite some attention beginning to be given in national and international forums to the growing risks of terrorism. But there is not sufficient focus on the fundamental fact that the very spread of all kinds of arms and the official use of them is responsible, at least in part, for the proliferation of assassinations, highjackings, skyjackings, kidnappings, bank robberies, etc. This is another costly consequence of excess weapons production.

7. Any Road to Sanity?

Most generally speaking, the arms race and the conduct of foreign policy within which the arms race evolves must undermine the morality of the people.

In all our countries, most successfully in the highly developed democratic ones, the relations between individuals and groups have been controlled by ethical rules which are inherited and commonly accepted. These are changed gradually as society changes. They form the basis of the social order. Such a social order is not dependent upon criminal law, courts, and police. It would break down if people did not follow the rules voluntarily, habitually. In a well-integrated society there are other sanctions such as neighborhood controls, strengthened by all sorts of associations, professional and social. The ethical rules are also taught in the schools and churches. Of course, they are not perfectly obeyed. We all are aware that there are imperfections in the behavior of even the most social-minded and law-abiding citizens, and that some have to be dealt with as criminals.

But the fact that international relations are increasingly discussed as *Realpolitik*, outside ordinary moral precepts, and carried on in terms of power—which is taken to justify the use of violence and threats of violence, together with large-scale spying, bribing, and lying in high places—must have a debilitating outcome on the internal social order, founded as it is, and must be, on respect for ethical rules.

This view has always been the strong point of pacifism. In the present era, marked by the arms race and the militarization of our societies, the pacifist view should have greater and greater validity. It is not possible to preserve intact a social order founded upon ethical prescripts when foreign policy is openly conducted as amoral. Therefore it is necessary to turn international developments to a new course, divesting national policies of their aggressive, competitive components and building up instead habits of cooperation for attaining common goals of security and welfare. The arms race is intellectually unreasonable and morally unsound. Disarmament is the road to an ethical climate necessary to secure peaceful relations between nations.

Naturally there are other social trends creating friction between individuals and groups. There are testimonies enough about the aftermath of rapid urbanization, uprootedness, consumerism, and other changes which lead to alienation of individuals and carelessness about other human beings. But it is necessary to stress continuing militarization, through which people become tougher and are therefore more prone to disregard the rights of others and to forget that people beyond one's own frontiers have claims to human rights.

CHAPTER II

The Superpowers' Game

1. The Broad Picture

Since World War II, world history to a large extent has been determined by the tidal waves of relations between the two superpowers, the United States and the Soviet Union, and the repercussions of these for all other nations. Running from an uneasy wartime alliance through an almost immediately following sharply hostile cold war, the history of the superpowers' postwar antagonism has been interrupted occasionally by the seeking of accommodation in the act of balancing each other. The latest stage, called "détente," has, however, not stopped their fierce competition for world hegemony.

For a long time, as the cold war escalated, the hostility between the two superpowers and their allies was, on the Western side, motivated by a need for defense of the "free world" against the "communist conspiracy for world revolution." On the Eastern side, the motive was to stand up against "monopoly capitalism," "neo-colonialism," and "imperialism." The arms race was pursued by both sides under the assumption of an imminent risk of a military show-down between the two systems, or, at least, of a constant danger of encroachment from the other ideological camp.

Up to now the most important facet of the declared détente has been the playing down of the propaganda in ideological terms. In line with this there has been a mutual lowering of the belligerently hostile tone used by the spokesmen for the two superpowers. This is, by itself, certainly welcome.

23

A central element in the development of the relations between the superpowers has been the arms race going against the strivings for disarmament. The détente of recent years has led to a more polite choice of vocabulary as well as some, though limited, approaches to freer economic, scientific, and cultural relations and, generally, widened communications. The Helsinki Conference held in the summer of 1975 represented a kind of codification of the ideas of détente, but without any firm commitments regarding implementation. Détente, however, has not led to a reversal or even a cessation of the arms race. The main new element has rather been the institutionalization of the continuous character of the arms race. The two superpowers now stand more armed than ever with gigantic arsenals which continue to be increased.

The history of postwar disarmament endeavors can only be told as one of repeated lost opportunities (Chapter III), in which the crucial and determining factor has been sparring by the superpowers. From the beginning, both have excelled in high rhetoric about the goal of disarmament, often employing acrimonious polemics against each other's positions. But beneath the surface they have increasingly acted as if there were between them a conspiracy not to permit a halt, still less a reversal, of the arms race.

To this development belongs the tying up of other nations in alliances. Although the Soviet bloc had already been established and solidified, Europe was more firmly structured by the formation of NATO in 1949 and WTO in 1955. In other parts of the world, various regional or bilateral accords usually created less tightly regulated arrangements. Within these alliances, despite all pronouncements of mutuality and partnership, the power has remained firmly in the hands of the two superpowers.

Spurred on by the superpowers' arms race, most other countries have militarized unprecedentedly, not least the underdeveloped countries. The superpowers have actively contributed to this militarization by military aid and by the politicization of development aid.

They have not acted in concert to prevent or stop wars in various parts of the world, as the Charter of the United Nations prescribes that the great powers should do. In these wars, as in the Middle East, they have often taken sides, even when they have not got themselves involved in active warfare, as the United States did in Indochina. Still, they have until now been careful not to let their contributions to and involvement in these wars lead to an open military confrontation between themselves.

Talking disarmament while relentlessly building up their own armaments to dazzling levels; prodding and aiding allied countries to do the same, though on a necessarily more modest scale; making the world more dangerous; compelling even nonaligned countries to keep their defenses high—this is how peoples and governments of the lesser powers have experienced superpower politics after the war.

While these repercussions are played out all over the world, the two superpowers in their competitive antagonism are fixated on each other. Their posture is, I believe, well illustrated by the old Viking tale of the fighters who are required to carry on their knife-duel hitched together by a belt around their waists.

2.   Gaming with Each Other

The primary motivating force for the superpowers has been that each must be second to none. Such a goal can, of course, never be permanently fulfilled. That this is their absurd ambition can be concluded from their constant measuring and comparing of military might. Sometimes this ambition is revealed unblushingly:

> No power on earth is stronger than the United States of America today. None will be stronger than the United States of America in the future. This is the only national defense posture which can ever be acceptable to the United States.[1]

Whenever the will of the United States Congress falters regarding military expenditures, the Pentagon propaganda machine releases news about an approaching bomber gap or missile gap or megatonnage gap or some other alleged advance in the Soviet armory. The Soviet government is not dependent on a scrutinizing congress and the internal debate there is muted. But it can be safely assumed that those responsible for the Soviet budget are egged on by their military establishments which deliver correct or incorrect information about threatening changes in American capabilities. Thus are both powers pursuing an arms race within the arms race (Chapter I, Section 4).

The simple idea that the main motivation of the arms race between the superpowers is for each to match the other in destructive capacity is continuously revealed in official statements on both sides

(Chapter IV, Sections 2 and 5). Initially the Soviet Union started from a position of inferiority, but it has gradually advanced towards equality in the gross kill-effect of nuclear weapons deployed or in production. In regard to technology, the United States has always been and is for all foreseeable time far ahead. But in practical terms, especially from the beginning of the SALT negotiations in 1969, the two superpowers have acknowledged that what they possibly can agree upon is the establishment of essential parity—which each of them then attempts to surpass in order to reach superiority.

Fear of what the opposite side may be aiming for then acts on both as a force to drive the arms race onward. The military planners exploit this situation, the politicians do not oppose them, and the citizens therefore allow the two defense systems to spiral steadily upward in an action-reaction pattern. As long as the arms race is permitted to go on, more than momentary stability can never be secured.

The risk inherent in this open-ended competition is obviously increasing, as even the recent SALT agreements have not erected any barrier against qualitative improvement of existing nuclear-weapons systems nor against innovations being introduced by research and continued testing (Chapter IV, Section 5).

Apart from identifying the most dynamic elements in the arms race, we should also ask: how much is enough? Is there any rationale for continuing the quest to match the other side at ever higher levels—and for trying to surpass it? Such are the questions left unformulated by the superpowers themselves in bilateral negotiations and official statements to the public in their own countries.

Independent experts have often approached these problems and effectively pointed out how vast is the overkill capacity of both superpowers. The immediate aim of such observations has been to demonstrate the need to reach an agreement between them to scale down their nuclear ambitions. Seldom, however, is the question raised whether one of the superpowers could unilaterally and safely cease the competition and even decrease its nuclear arsenal without risking its deterrent effect (Chapter IV, Sections 2–4).

Expert discussion is most prolific and uninhibited in the United States. In the Soviet Union there is no corresponding free discussion. Russian participants in meetings such as Pugwash have been able to join in expressions of anxiety over the dangers of the continued arms race, provided they do not stand against Soviet policies which they have to believe are directed towards peace.

Independent analysts all agree upon one thing: the overkill capacity of each of the superpowers is far beyond "enough," even if the ambition should be to kill all of mankind. Often this argument is made in the form of estimating their ability to kill each human inhabitant so many times over. The theme can be played with many variations. Jules Moch, who for a long time was the leading French spokesman in favor of disarmament in the United Nations and on its various committees, made a striking calculation in his book *Destin de la Paix* (1969). Taking into consideration how many tons of explosives are needed to kill the average number of people on each area of a square kilometer, he figured out that stocks of nuclear weapons already then available were sufficient to annihilate the total world population 690 times over.[2]

The problem of overcapacities for fighting a war between the superpowers—realizing that far less is enough to deter such a war— has more recently been discussed in a number of expert papers commissioned for Pacem in Terris III, a 1973 Conference organized by the Center for the Study of Democratic Institutions in Santa Barbara. One of the experts, Herbert F. York, gives an answer in a nutshell:

> It is most important . . . to have clearly in mind what the current technical situation means: the survival of the combined populations of the superpowers depends on the goodwill and the good sense of the separate leaderships of the superpowers. If the Soviet leadership, for whatever reason, or as a result of whatever mistaken information, chose to destroy America as a nation, it is unquestionably capable of doing so in less than half an hour, and there is literally nothing we could now do to prevent it. The only thing we could do is to wreak on them an equally terrible revenge. And, of course, the situation is the same the other way around.[3]

The extent of expected damage is the question of most vital concern to the people living under what they believe is the protection of the terror balance. They must find that the physical, biological, and social consequences of ever *using* what the two sides have in their nuclear arsenals are completely out of line with any reasonable view of what could be the national objectives of the United States or the Soviet Union:

> In the event of an exchange of blows by strategic nuclear forces of the U.S. and the U.S.S.R., most of the urban populations of the two countries could be killed, and most of the industry and commerce could be destroyed by the direct and immediate effects of the nuclear explosions. The towns and rural areas of the two countries would at

the same time be subjected to varying amounts of radioactive fallout. The details of what would happen to the people living in such areas depend importantly on the weather conditions prevailing at the time and on the details of the attack pattern, but well over one-half of the town and country populations could be killed by the fallout. In addition, the living standards and the life expectancy of the survivors would be substantially reduced by secondary effects, including both the effect of less-than-lethal levels of fallout and the general break-down of civilized services.[4]

"Most of the urban population" and "over half of the total population" are current estimates of today. But few visualize the tragic reality that the price, in terms of destruction, is going up all the time, without the concomitant increase in security which the arms escalation was intended to buy. This was irrefutably stated in succinct language as early as 1964, in an article by York and another eminent colleague, Jerome B. Wiesner:

Ever since shortly after World War II the military power of the United States has been steadily increasing. Throughout this same period the national security of the U.S. has been rapidly and inexorably diminishing. In the early 1950s the U.S.S.R., on the basis of its own unilateral decision and determination to accept the inevitable retaliation, could have launched an attack against the U.S. with bombers carrying fission bombs. Some of these bombs would have penetrated our defenses and the American casualties would have numbered in the millions. In the later 1950s, again in its own sole decision and determination to accept the inevitable massive retaliation, the U.S.S.R. could have launched an attack against the U.S. using more and better bombers, this time carrying thermonuclear bombs. Some of these bombers would have penetrated our defenses and the American casualties could have numbered in the tens of millions.

Today the U.S.S.R., again on the basis of its own decision and determination to accept the inevitable retaliation, could launch an attack on the U.S. using intercontinental missiles and bombers carrying thermonuclear weapons. This time the number of American casualties could very well be on the order of 100 million. . . .

From the Soviet point of view the picture is similar but much worse. The military power of the U.S.S.R. has been steadily increasing since it became an atomic power in 1949. Soviet national security, however, has been steadily decreasing. Hypothetically the U.S. could unilaterally decide to destroy the U.S.S.R. and the U.S.S.R. would be absolutely powerless to prevent it. That country could only, at best,

seek to wreak revenge through whatever retaliatory capability it
might then have left.

*Both sides in the arms race are thus confronted by the dilemma
of steadily increasing military power and steadily decreasing national
security.* . . . The clearly predictable course of the arms race is a
steady open spiral downward into oblivion.[5]

The damage would, however, not be limited to the warfaring
nations:

In addition, the lives of many millions of people living in the immediate neighborhood of the superpowers would be imperiled by
so-called local fallout, and long-range or world-wide fallout would
endanger those living in even remote countries. It is very difficult to
make precise estimates, but it seems that a full nuclear exchange
between the U.S. and the U.S.S.R. would result in the order of
10,000,000 casualties from cancer and leukemia in countries situated
well away from the two main protagonists. In addition, genetic problems that are even more difficult to calculate would affect many, many
millions of others—not only in this generation, but for centuries
to come. Civilization would survive somewhere, but probably not
in the United States or the Soviet Union, and perhaps not elsewhere
in North America or Europe.[6]

The moral implications are rarely worrying strategists, military
or civilian:

During the Congressional debate and hearings on the SALT Agreements, only a few Senators and Congressmen raised questions about
the morality of threatening the mass killing of hostages. . . . The
question how our current nuclear strategy would conform with this
convention [against genocide] was never raised, so well have we
managed to conceal from ourselves the implications of "assured
destruction."[7]

To add to these already excessive military capabilities without
first answering the question of how much is enough to deter a war
between them is what the senseless game between the superpowers
is about. But it continues. As one of the present superactors, the
United States Secretary of State, Henry Kissinger, said in one of his
unguarded moments:

What in the name of God is strategic superiority? What is the significance of it politically, militarily, operationally at these levels of
numbers? What do you do with it?[8]

Disarmament efforts have for all practical purposes come to nothing until now (Chapter III). The problems are not insurmountable. It would be possible to formulate a new, realistic but courageous strategy for reversing the nuclear arms race and the race of conventional weapons (Chapters IV and V).

3.   Gaming over a Passive Europe

The prospects of the increasingly unthinkable danger to both the contesting superpowers in a head-on war explains their interest in planning for a "limited" war. Such wars do not imply the use of available strategic nuclear weapons against each other. Rather the homelands of the superpowers become "sanctuaries," while wars, if and when they would occur, are to be fought in the territories of lesser powers.

For historical reasons "limited war" primarily has been discussed in regard to Europe.* The long history of European wars, ending with World War I and World War II, has stamped the entire post-war discussion with the idea that a war threatening to involve the two superpowers might again originate in Europe. The core idea of the Potsdam Agreement in 1945 was to ensure "that never more should a war be started from German soil."

Yet today the consideration of who might ignite a war in Europe has been completely changed. The only possible origin of war would arise from a superpower conflict, which is rarely accounted for. The confusion must be shattered: a European war might mean a war fought over Europe and in the European locale but it would not be a war instigated by European states—except, for example, a localized war such as the Greek-Turkish conflict over Cyprus in the unruly Balkan corner. A "European war" would be categorically different from wars started independently in other parts of the world. In these, superpower interests might be involved, but not involved to the level of confrontation with each other. A few reminders of European history, though abridged to bare essentials, are needed here for an understanding of how the present situation has evolved.

---

* Europe is defined as the whole continent, except the Soviet Union. Eastern Europe refers to those countries allied to the Soviet Union, the membership of WTO being seven; and Western Europe refers to the countries allied to the United States, the membership in NATO being fifteen. In addition there are a few non-aligned countries, from those that remained neutral in the War, like Sweden and Switzerland, to some who joined the nonaligned ranks later, like Yugoslavia after 1948 and Austria after the 1955 State Treaty.

When World War II ended, the larger part of Europe, as well as the Soviet Union, was utterly devastated, suffering all sorts of social and economic disorganization. The Great Alliance from the War was breaking up; soon it would be followed by a gradually intensifying cold war between the United States and the U.S.S.R. Though the process ultimately took several years, the East European countries, including the then Soviet zone of East Germany, became satellites of the Soviet Union. There was never any attempt by the United States to suppress similarly the political independence of the West European countries. These were conceived of as democracies, including West Germany emerging at the end of the war from its humiliating defeat and material misery.

There were early moves by some West European countries to join in a defensive military alliance. When in 1948 the Western European Union was formed by Britain, France, and the Benelux countries in response to the Soviet coup in Czechoslovakia the same year, the protective role of the United States was recognized. The United States joined the alliance, the Berlin blockade having provided an additional warning of Soviet attitudes, and NATO was created formally in April 1949. It later included Greece, Turkey, and Portugal. Spain under the Franco dictatorship was never formally accepted as a NATO ally, but through United States bilateral arrangements involving military bases and other priorities it became included in the Western defense system. Finally, West Germany, having undergone transformation from occupation to partnership, was incorporated in NATO in 1955, following a long struggle within Germany and among NATO members over its rearming.[9]

In both Western Europe and the United States, NATO was from the outset conceived as a protective shield for Western Europe; the United States with its then monopoly of nuclear weapons was to provide a nuclear umbrella. When, in September 1949, the Soviet Union exploded its first atomic bomb, this created in many quarters of Western Europe (even if it was seldom expressed publicly) an apprehension that it was becoming engaged in a contest between the superpowers.

The military strategies that evolved became more and more clearly a reflection of the mutual contest between the superpowers, dominated by their shifts in strength. The American military policy was from the outset one of containment, which presumed the active threat of a Soviet military move against the West. As long as the United States had the monopoly of atomic bombs, the threat of counteraction implied security for Western Europe. When the Soviet Union acquired a nuclear arsenal, however, the security of Europe changed into the insecurity of the risk of being dragged into a nuclear confrontation between the superpowers.

Still, the reiterated promises to Western Europe of protection by the United States nuclear umbrella kept the worries from surfacing publicly. Some disquietude was often felt, as when John Foster Dulles in the early 1950s enunciated the doctrines of massive retaliation and roll-back. To the relief of the West Europeans, the latter doctrine was not applied to the uprisings in East Germany in 1953 and Hungary in 1956. No military countermeasures had been resorted to in Czechoslovakia in 1948 nor were they used later in 1968. The United States by then had apparently accepted the division of Europe as West European governments had done much earlier.

From the beginning the NATO alliance resulted in contributions from the United States other than the promise of an ultimate defense with its nuclear weapons. For many years the United States provided large-scale military aid and seemingly permanent garrisons of American troops to Western Europe. The Western European members of NATO were supposed to have increased their conventional defense; however, in spite of continuous prodding from the United States, to this day it is considered inferior in strength to what the Soviet Union could muster.[10] Some countries even occasionally reduced their forces.

The question of how far the defense of Europe should rely on conventional forces is, in reality, a crucial issue in the NATO strategic debate. While the European allies in NATO were unwilling to make a contribution in conventional forces that would match the Soviet bloc, and the American troops naturally could not be expanded to fill the void, the decision was to rely on nuclear weapons deployed in Europe. That the choice might have been a different one is borne out by the fact that the nonaligned countries of Sweden, Switzerland, and Yugoslavia have proven to be much more willing to build up strong defenses with conventional weapons and to rely on their own strength to be independent. They have continued this policy of strong national defense, forsaking not only alliances but nuclear weapons as well.

The real crossroad for the Western European defense strategy, signaled by the deployment of nuclear weapons in Europe, came when the United States, in the face of rising Soviet nuclear capabilities, no longer wanted to be committed to a near-automatic release of its massive nuclear retaliation. During the Eisenhower administration the possibility of fighting a more limited war with tactical nuclear weapons was envisioned.

Large numbers of tactical nuclear weapons, intended for use in a local battlefield, began to be shipped to Europe in 1954. Their deployment there was not negotiated, particularly with the major recipient, West Germany, not yet a NATO member. But they were nonetheless accepted, tacitly, as a substitution for stronger local forces, and, more openly, as a reassurance that the United States would not withdraw into isolationism (Chapter II, Section 6). What was less evident at the time was that these nuclear weapons on European soil inexorably linked the strategies for defending Western Europe with global American strategies for nuclear warfare, which did not necessarily serve Europe's best interests.

These tactical nuclear weapons deployed in Europe remain, like the strategic ones, under United States control. European feelings about this have perhaps been best expressed by Henry A. Kissinger in his earlier period as a professorial writer:

> The very quality of deliberation which makes this strategy militarily desirable for the United States creates a sense of impotence or pressures for autonomy among our Allies. The central command and control system, which is the key feature of the new doctrine, is American. The United States will determine—to the extent that the enemy cooperates—how and with what weapons the war is to be fought and on what terms it will be concluded.[11]

Although this statement refers to the "flexible-response" doctrine from the Kennedy years, the political, and military, situation has remained basically the same since the 1950s.

With Sputnik in 1957, the Russians demonstrated the possibility of Russian missiles with nuclear warheads reaching the United States and the credibility of the American nuclear umbrella was shaken. The shock of the Soviet testing of a ballistic missile that could cross the Atlantic led the United States in 1957 to negotiate, as a token of increased defense preparedness, installation of intermediate-range missiles (IRBM) in Britain, Italy, and Turkey. However, the IRBMs were never a real threat to the Soviet Union because of its strategic retaliatory force and thus were not effective protection for the Western countries either. They were removed in 1963 in a political bargain, part of the price paid for the withdrawal of Soviet missiles from Cuba. Afterwards, though promises of protection continued to be forthcoming from the United States, whenever new strategic doctrines such as that of "flexible response" or "realistic deterrence" were announced from Washington, Europeans experienced growing anxiety. The prospect of the superpowers fighting a limited war in Europe and the idea of their mutually establishing sanctuaries at home produced disaffection, but this was played down in public discussion and papered over in NATO compromises, as exemplified in 1967 agreement on a "flexible-response" strategy (Chapter II, Sections 6 and 7).

The initial premise about Soviet intentions, against which the capabilities had to be built up, became less and less a part of European thinking, though it spread rapidly in the United States. In these early years, because of my assignments in the United Nations and later UNESCO, I had wide contacts in practically all countries of the European continent, as well as in the United States, and can testify to this. In spite of European disapproval of the Soviet postwar annexation of the Baltic states and watchful protest against the Soviet suppression of political self-determination in the Eastern European countries, there was nevertheless a degree of understanding in the Western European countries that, after all the sufferings the Russians had sustained during the War, they could have valid reason to establish a belt of buffer states against Germany, whose onslaught on the European democracies was fresh in memory. In addition, the division of Germany was not felt by its neighbor countries to be entirely unfortunate. Still, overriding such considerations there was in Western Europe the widely shared conviction that the Soviet Union would not attempt to cross the line dividing the two Europes. Active planning by the Soviet Union for a military push westward was not perceived as realistic by most Europeans.

That picture took on a different cast in the minds of Americans. The Marshall Plan aid for reconstruction and development of Western Europe was, from 1947, of a scope and generosity greater than any aid later afforded the underdeveloped world, and it continued for many years. The basic American motivation was certainly human solidarity with the distressed European nations from which so many Americans reckoned their ancestry, while their own country had been spared, and this was gratefully acknowledged by Europeans. But, as the cold war between the superpowers gathered momentum, the United States motivation for providing aid increasingly reflected an anticommunist, anti-Soviet policy.

Western European governments for a time accepted this attitude as being necessary to secure passage of aid bills in the American Congress. Those Western European governments who in the immediate postwar years had included in their cabinets representatives of indigenous communist parties paid the price and excluded them. In addition several Western countries, including some nonaligned, paid the price of cooperating with the United States in a strategic licensing policy aimed at stopping exports to the Soviet sphere of a comprehensive group of commodities. In the United States this policy was widely publicized as being directly aimed at hurting economic development in the communist world. The West European governments' cooperation with the United States in this export embargo policy was kept mostly secret from European peoples.[12]

The West European nations had, in fact, been ready for a détente with the Soviet Union and its allies long before this could be advocated as policy in the United States. Stalin's death in 1953 signaled, from the West European point of view, an important political change. At about the same time Marshall Plan aid was being terminated and United States military aid also was decreased. Almost immediately the West European governments used this greater political independence to quietly liquidate the export embargo policy. What remained of the licensing procedures became more of a bureaucratic nuisance than a serious trade barrier. East-West trade in Europe increased, but the United States continued its discriminatory trade policy.

These historical glimpses, despite omissions, point up the differences of political developments on the European and the American scene. After the War, relations between the two Europes in trade, travel, and cultural contacts have been much closer than those between the United States and the Soviet Union, even such as could be projected as foreseeable results of détente. Europe must be understood to have been reliably cured from any propensity to war. Boundaries between its countries had been increasingly accepted as settled even when peace treaties had not been signed. Finally, there was the acceptance of the division of Germany and the demarcation between East Germany and Poland, the result of Willy Brandt's Ostpolitik at the beginning of the 1970s, which was solemnly countersigned at the European Security Conference in Helsinki on 1 August 1975.

4. "Limited War" over Europe?
The Soviet Point of View

As the available nuclear-weapons strength between the two superpowers grew more equal, at ever higher levels of destructive capabilities, it was inevitable that the idea of using these weapons against each other's homelands lost its appeal. The strategy of preserving the Soviet Union and the United States as sanctuaries is viewed differently by the superpowers than it is by Europe.

So far as one can gather, the official position of the Soviet government is a categorical disbelief in the possibility of a limited superpower war—that is, limited to a local battlefield such as Europe and limited there to the use of tactical nuclear weapons.[13] A. Ye. Yefremov, whose book *Europe and Nuclear Weapons* (1972) I have read in a complete Soviet-prepared Swedish translation, is quoted and summarized in *The Role of Nuclear Forces in Current Soviet Strategy*.[14] The use of tactical nuclear weapons in Europe is likely to lead to an escalation. Yefremov asserts that "military conflict on European territory," given the present network of military alliances, "would inexorably involve all other states of the world in the orbit of a thermonuclear collision," and that the "threat to use some of the American tactical atomic weapons to carry out local actions in Europe, figuring that the use of 'warning atomic shots' will not lead to escalation and a global thermonuclear war," is obviously "dictated by propaganda rather than military considerations."

Some authors are even more outspoken:

> By itself, the idea of introducing "rules of engagement" and artificial restrictions "by agreement" is illusory and untenable. It is difficult to visualize that a nuclear war, if it is unleashed, could be kept within the framework of "rules" and would not develop into an all-out war.[15]

Similar views have been expressed in speeches, articles, and books by high officials, such as Marshal Sokolovski's classic *Military Strategy*, and by the Soviet Minister of Defense, Marshal Grecko, and by the Marshal of Artillery, Peredelski, and others. In view of some hard facts this position appears reasonable. The most important of these is that Soviet proximity to European countries where United States nuclear weapons are stationed (some with definite capacity to hit targets in the Soviet Union) makes its territory more vulnerable than the territory of the United States. Also, the limited-war concept was part of the United States official strategic doctrine of flexible response, and is endorsed by its allies in Western Europe. As such it makes the Russians suspicious that the United States might pretend to engage in a limited war, and then use the occasion to escalate it.

Reflection on policy statements from Soviet sources raises the question of whether these statements may be merely propaganda threats, a warning to the United States that it will not be allowed to wage war in Europe without risking a nuclear onslaught at home. The Soviet Union must, equally with the United States, fear annihilation of its own country in case of a direct intercontinental confrontation. Thus underlying both strategies is a definite, joint interest in preserving their own territories. A former Secretary of Defense in the United States, David Packard, is quoted as having stated:

> The U.S.S.R. as well as the U.S. are going to use their nuclear potential against each other only when an unavoidable threat appears against their own existence.[16]

It is hazardous to take anything for granted in the gaming between the superpowers. The fundamental difficulty with the sanctuary theory is that the limitation of warfare must rely upon an understanding between the potential main enemies. Such a concordance is highly unlikely. Henry A. Kissinger, when still a professor, insisted that limited war is only possible if the contestants, through diplomatic understanding, agree to view it as a chance to emerge from the war without too heavy material and human damage and without too much injury to their prestige.[17] No attempt to reach such an agreement or understanding has ever been reported.

In this utterly unclarified situation, it may be surmised that the Soviet Union probably holds all conceivable scenarios open as alternatives, including that of a limited war in Europe. But in regard to such an eventuality, there seem to be two fundamental differences as to how the two sides view its course. One is that the prevailing view in the U.S.S.R. has always been that any war should preferably be limited to the use of conventional forces, a hitch being that a smaller or larger part of them may already be concentrated at other frontiers. Upgrading a war to the nuclear level would mean "unlimiting" it to the bitter end. A second difference is that we can deduce from all that is known about the deployment and composition of Soviet forces that their aim, different from the United States' (Chapter

II, Section 5), would be a massive attack or counterattack leading to a quick victory. The U.S.S.R. could then abstain from a nuclear assault on the United States, lessening the risk of assault on itself. Alternatively, the Soviet Union might use nuclear weapons for an early decisive victory on a European battlefield. The Soviet arsenal of nuclear weapons for war-theater use is concentrated on systems with higher yields, many in the megatonnage class, and with higher radioactive fallout than the corresponding United States weapons deployed in Western Europe for tactical warfare purposes. Soviet strategists do not make the same categorical distinction as the United States does between strategic and tactical nuclear weapons and they are evidently ready to use a part of their strategic arsenal on targets in Europe.

Several characteristics of the Soviet military posture point in the direction of a blitzkrieg: the continued resistance to any substantial decrease of its mighty conventional arms build-up; the reluctance, demonstrated by Soviet pronouncements, to draw a clear distinction between strategic and tactical nuclear weapons; and the unwillingness to admit that also for them there is an open choice to resort to limited war—on their terms.

5. *"Limited War" over Europe?*
The American Point of View

Contrary to Soviet skepticism about the possibility of conducting limited war in Europe with nuclear weapons, it has increasingly become declared policy in the United States to try to keep any war limited. The posture of "defense for Europe" thus relies more and more on tactical nuclear weapons. (Some 7,000 are now deployed by the United States in Western Europe [Section 3].) In current doctrines there is an ever clearer preference for, or belief in, limiting a war with strategic offensive weapons to selected targets (Chapter IV, Section 2).

An early reminder that Europe should not rely upon the strategic doctrine of massive retaliation was given by Professor Henry Kissinger in a 1958 interview by Mike Wallace:

KISSINGER: Our current military policy is based on the doctrine of massive retaliation—that we threaten an all-out attack on the Soviet Union in case the Soviet Union engages in aggression anywhere. This means that we base our policy on a threat that will involve the destruction of all mankind. This is too risky and I think too expensive.

WALLACE: You obviously think it is wrong—dangerous to our security. I wonder if you would expand on that. Just because of what you call the risk and just because of the expense, it is not worth-while?

KISSINGER: What it will mean is that in every crisis an American President will have to make the choice whether a given objective is worth the destruction of American cities. The American President will have to decide whether Beirut or whatever the issue may be is worth thirty million American lives. In practice I am afraid the American President will have to decide that it is not worth it and will therefore encourage the piecemeal taking over of the world by Soviet aggression.[18]

Referring more directly to Europe, Kissinger wrote in 1959:

The defense of Europe cannot be conducted solely from North America, because . . . however firm allied unity may be, a nation *cannot be counted on to commit suicide in defense of a foreign territory.*[19]

In 1965 Kissinger devoted a whole book with the telling title *The Troubled Partnership* to this subject.[20] In spite of considerable inconsistencies, he repeated his warning and continued to see Europe as becoming directly involved in war, although he recognized that war would in essence be a superpower contest. As Secretary of State, Kissinger has not changed his view on this particular point, although his pronouncements have been adjusted so as not to appear to retract the United States promise to hold a protective nuclear umbrella over Western Europe.

The United States clearly now has a double scenario, one for deterrence and one for war; both are focused on the Soviet Union as the enemy:

(a) deterrence for avoiding a superpower war chiefly through strategic nuclear weapons up to the level of MAD, Mutual Assured Destruction (Chapter IV, Section 2).

(b) if war occurs, it is to be fought as a limited war in Europe, possibly using tactical nuclear weapons as a counter-measure against a conventional attack, but not allowing that war to escalate to intercontinental warfare involving the territories of the superpowers themselves.

For good reasons this scheme is not often presented officially in clear terms. But former Secretary of Defense James R. Schlesinger repeatedly stated the present policy in an authoritative way, for example, in his 1976 budget report to the United States Congress:

We continue to deploy our own theater nuclear forces in both Europe and Asia. In the case of Europe, we have three basic reasons for our deployments. First, the maintenance of theater nuclear capabilities in NATO is essential to deterrence as long as the Warsaw Pact deploys theater nuclear forces of its own. They help to deter the use of nuclear weapons by the Pact and, along with our strategic nuclear and conventional forces, provide a general deterrent across the entire spectrum of possible aggression. Second, should deterrence fail, *our theater nuclear capabilities provide a source of limited and controlled options other than the early use of U.S. and allied strategic forces.* Third, in keeping with NATO's flexible response strategy, we do not rule out the use of nuclear weapons by the United States and its allies if that should prove necessary to contain and repel *a major conventional attack* by the Warsaw Pact.[21]

"Other than the early use of . . . strategic forces" is the crucial point. Even more revealing was a phrase used by Schlesinger in Senate hearings a year earlier when he argued for the strengthening of European conventional defense forces "so that they could sustain a longer war."[22] Different from likely Soviet strategy, the United States intention has been that the defensive forces in Europe should be built up, not for a quick victory, but for more enduring operations. Reinforcement from the United States would require time; the logistics have usually been planned for some sixty days before a war would reach its peak. No scenarios have been publicly revealed to what would happen then.

The vagueness about what might be the fate of Europe is reflected in the attitudes and opinions of American political leaders, editorial writers, and public opinion. It is fairly certain that neither the United States Congress nor American citizens in general would, even after a hypothetical Soviet attack against Western Europe, be in favor of letting such a war escalate to nuclear attack on the Soviet Union, which would initiate what has aptly been called mutual collective suicide. To judge by the results of some public-opinion polls there are signs that it might even be difficult to bring the nation along in active participation of a limited war.[23] That unwillingness to back allies even if attacked has undoubtedly increased after the debacle in the Indochina war. This brings into considerable doubt what is really meant by the loud exclamations after that defeat, that the United States stands firm behind its commitments. The entire doctrine of what is meant by limited war in Europe remains hazy, and ideas of what might trigger such a war are equally hazy if not actually erroneous.

6. "Limited War" over Europe? The European Point of View

Viewed from the angle of Europe—whether East or West— there are no possibilities for a major war to be launched by a European power on its own initiative. A major war could only originate from the protectors of the two blocs, the gaming super- powers.

If war comes to Europe, it will be because one or the other of the superpowers wish a contest to be played out there, which prob- ably would be ignited outside Europe, for example, in the Middle East. However, a military test of strength between the superpowers might then be transposed to Europe. Military planning is ready for such a contingency. Thus, the war machines may well begin to roll over Europe as a main battlefield. This kind of transferred incidental war in Europe would not be less gruesome than a deliberate one. No Europeans, East or West, would have their hearts set to win it, only to avoid or delimit it.

The possible origins of a war befalling Europe are not discussed very openly in Europe. Likewise, the nature and consequences of a limited war are not analyzed in Europe. This is natural for Eastern Europe, as such a war has never been announced as plausible strategic doctrine by the Soviet Union. There has not been much public discussion in Western Europe of such a war either, in spite of the United States having declared flexible response, with the em- ployment of nuclear weapons, to be NATO strategy. The European allies have duly lined up in support of this doctrine.

Helmut Schmidt was a prominent exception. For a time the leading spokesman on military questions of the Social Democratic Party, he is now the Chancellor of the Federal Republic of Germany. In his 1962 book, *Defense or Retaliation*, he quoted Kissinger on limited war and added:

> This one sober sentence sums up all the doubts of European states- men as to the efficacy of the strategy of nuclear retaliation.[24]

A decade later Schmidt stated:

> We have thus sketched out NATO's dilemma regarding deterrence:
> effective defense of Europe would only be possible for a short time or
> in a geographically limited area—and it would lead rapidly to the
> destruction of Europe.[25]

and he reiterated:

> a war which, though regarded as a "limited war" by the superpowers,
> would be no less than a war of annihilation for the countries of the
> battlefield.[26]

Let us separate the problem of a limited war in Europe with the
use of tactical nuclear weapons into two aspects. What would be
the consequences? What are the political conclusions?

Some experts, mostly German authors, have been quite outspoken about the possible effects. Retired German general H. H.
Trettner concludes a systematic review, that a "tactical nuclear
defense of [Western] Europe would lead to its destruction."[27] Carl
Friedrich v. Weizsäcker has edited the most intensive study to date,
a 700-page collection of detailed expert analyses devoted to appris-
ing the consequences to West Germany's civilian population of a
series of war scenarios with differing levels of input of nuclear
weapons. Even a brief and locally limited war could mean ten million deaths and cause total destruction of West Germany as an
industrial society.[28] Escalation to blind utilization of existing weapons capabilities could mean the extinction of all life in Germany.
V. Weizsäcker is reported as having testified elsewhere, in studies
for the NATO Nuclear Planning Group, that an input of just 10
percent of the nuclear weapons now stationed in Europe could
practically annihilate both East and West Germany.

Recently a different point of departure has been utilized in a
study by Herbert York, but with the same shocking revelations
about the consequences of tactical nuclear war in Europe.[29] York
finds that the approximately 7,000 tactical nuclear weapons in
Western Europe under the aegis of the United States and NATO
must be deemed provocative: though they are supposed to serve as
deterrents, war plans call for their actual use in case there is any
kind of attack, even conventional, on Western Europe (Chapter II,
Section 5). The corresponding Soviet nuclear weapons, designed
for tactical use, about half the number but of higher average yield,
are said by the Soviets not to be intended for an attack on the West
but Soviet officials add that, if for any reason, NATO should use
nuclear weapons they will be repaid in kind. York has elaborated in

considerable detail what would be the consequences of the use of Soviet weapons.

There is a difference in the targeting pattern of all these super-power weapons. Several less potent types are meant strictly for use in an ongoing battle and are kept in reserve for an input in Western Europe—that is, to stave off advances over important bridges, etc.

The larger NATO weapons are in the main targeted on Eastern Europe, with a few of longer range targeted or targetable on the Soviet Union. Obviously, if such weapons come to be used locally in Western Europe efforts must be made to limit collateral damage. It is reasonable to assume that those targeted Eastern European countries, which probably have few or no nuclear weapons stationed on their territory, would attempt to avoid massive civilian damage.

Conversely, Western Europe, having tactical nuclear weapons deployed in its midst, cannot avoid itself providing suitable targets for a retaliatory attack by the Soviet Union which, according to its different strategic doctrine, would strike first in a systematic attempt to preempt the larger weapons and to destroy command and communication centers which are generally in or near large cities.

York's study elaborates in considerable detail the consequences to Western Europe if the Soviet Union chose to launch just its 600 medium-range ballistic missiles with megaton warheads, specifically designed for bombardment of Europe. The projected result is very similar to von Weizsäcker's, which York presents in pictorial form. In one scenario York describes how 166 one-megaton ground-burst explosions with their wide area of lethal fallout could cover all of West Germany, killing all persons in the open. In another he describes the possible results of the use of an even smaller number of one-megaton bombs on Western European cities with more than 200,000 population. Fewer than 100 of these bombs against the European NATO countries would destroy these centers and kill at least a third of Western Europe's population.

What are the political and public reactions to these obvious dangers? The peoples of Europe—West, East, and neutral—have not been kept much aware of what is in store for them if the superpower rivalry leads to a military confrontation in Europe. There has been a carefully kept official silence as to the consequences. Only once, in 1955, when a NATO military field exercise, "Carte Blanche," resulted in 1.7 million Germans "killed" and 3.5 million "incapacitated," was a short-lived political furor caused.[30]

It is necessary to remember that Europeans had not asked for tactical nuclear weapons when they were first introduced in Western Europe in 1954 (Chapter II, Section 3). They were also reluctant to approve the United States' strategic doctrines. When finally in 1967 they accepted the flexible-response doctrine, the European NATO members exerted considerable pressure to have greater influence over the use of the nuclear weapons. The only concession they could obtain was the establishment of a Nuclear Planning Group in NATO for joint consultations in regard to, for instance, targeting of possible nuclear weapons operations. West German leaders in particular have wanted a considerably stronger role for the European allies in the control of nuclear weapons in Europe.

Since 1967 there has been little public discussion about any fundamental change in the policies of nuclear defense for Europe, little of the early clairvoyant anxiety of Helmut Schmidt. West European official postures have become frozen in a kind of silent approval of the status quo. In recent years, it has often appeared as if the NATO governments were backing continued deployment of tactical nuclear weapons in their countries even more than the United States. West Germany particularly seems to fear that withdrawal would signify a lessening of the United States commitment to act in the defense of Western Europe.

In 1975 I was conducting a seminar at the Massachusetts Institute of Technology on tactical nuclear weapons in Europe.[31] In order to isolate the determining factors in the justification of deployment of nuclear weapons, we posed the hypothetical question that, if there were now no such weapons, what would be the reasons for introducing them?

None of the participants, academics, diplomats, and some military personnel, could give tenable reasons, only numerous counterreasons for maintaining the status quo. The debate became nonconclusive as most of the participants cut off pursuit of the subject by asserting that any change in the present situation was totally impractical for political reasons—a nuclear-weapon-free Europe being altogether out of the question. This same concern for political sensitivities is probably the reason why writers like Enthoven,[32] after presenting a strongly convincing argument about the redundancy and danger of having tactical nuclear weapons deployed in Western Europe, conclude by recommending, not withdrawal, but reduction to 1,000; other authors suggest 500. Why?

The political sensitivities of the NATO countries, especially West Germany, must explain why Secretary Kissinger did not get very far when, as a bargaining chip in the Vienna negotiations on Mutual Reduction of Forces in Europe, he made an offer to reduce tactical nuclear weapons in Europe by some 1,000 of more than 7,000. He knew that many are obsolete and that all may be highly vulnerable in case of attack. The emptiness of this gesture which was approved by NATO in December 1975 ought to be obvious to all observers.[33] That the Soviet Union would accept such a bargain, particularly since those weapons which are longer range and there-fore targetable on the Soviet Union itself would not be the first withdrawn, is incredible.

It is refreshing to read the obvious truths so unpolitically pre-sented by Herbert York:

> In summary, today's Western Europeans have chosen to buy current political stability by placing the awful risks described above over their lives and their future. Perhaps their choice was inadvertent; perhaps they did not and even today still do not realize what they have done. In that case, it would seem that they ought to know, and that they ought to reconsider their choice in the light of such knowledge.[34]

Or, even more straightforwardly:

> To say it differently, NATO's plans for the defense of Europe are centered on an awesome bluff. . . . In short, the bluff could be called and Europe could be destroyed, not just partially as in 1914–18 and 1939–45, but totally.[35]

The discussion of the potential damage tactical nuclear weapons would inflict now centers around the pending changes in weapons characteristics, the substitution of lower-yield, shorter-range, more accurately targeted missiles for some of those now deployed. This would have the effect of increasing the total number. Plans to intro-duce a new generation of tactical nuclear weapons into the defense system of Western Europe are being met by criticism in many quar-ters, though criticism in NATO councils has not been audible outside them.

As a member of the Geneva Disarmament Committee, in 1973 I raised this whole question, asking for an unequivocal answer: were plans for a large-scale changeover to these so-called mini-nukes in the offing?

> developments seem to be under way, threatening to render the NPT even more discriminatory to the disadvantage of the non-nuclear-weapon States. I am referring to news items, that the major nuclear-weapon States are about to launch a new generation of *tactical*

nuclear-weapons systems, the so-called mini-nukes. Such a development would drastically aggravate the nuclear threat against non-
nuclear-weapon States everywhere. . . . Therefore, it is so disturbing
when we learn that ongoing research and development might lead
to a new generation of tactical nuclear weapons with yields in the
subkiloton range, overlapping the yields of the most powerful conventional charges, with extreme delivery precision, and with extra-
accurate intelligence support. These weapons systems are by their
proponents said to be not only usable on the battlefield but also
preferable as providing cheaper fire-power than conventional systems.[36]

This warning led to a series of curious denials, first by the United
States delegate to the Committee in the spring of 1974, and was followed up in an interview by the Director of ACDA, Dr. Fred Iklé.
That statement had obvious public relations intentions amounting to
a glaring example of doubletalk:

In elaborating on the policy statement, Dr. Fred C. Iklé, director of
the Arms Control Agency, said in an interview that its effect was to
"establish a barrier against taking advantage of available technology
to go into new types of nuclear weapons that make sense only if
viewed as substitutes for conventional arms."

"We are not now, nor have we been in recent years, at the brink
of some qualitative breakthrough in tactical nuclear weapons development," the statement said. It is known, however, that laboratories of the Atomic Energy Commission have on the drawing boards
concepts for a new generation of weapons with explosive yields of
less than 1,000 tons of TNT, such as small nuclear land mines or
bazooka-style rockets that could be fired by infantry squads. Their
developers contend that they could be used more effectively and
provide cheaper fire power than conventional weapons."

The statement notes that the United States has been "engaged
over many years in a gradual process of moderately upgrading our
tactical nuclear stockpile and indicates that the process will continue."[37]

Former Secretary of Defense James Schlesinger argued that any
ongoing changes are just part and parcel of a process of modernization, but at the same time he stated that

NATO should also consider whether, in the future, there are serious
possibilities of replacing the existing stockpiles with nuclear weapons
and delivery systems more appropriate to the European environment.[38]

The proponents of mini-nukes, chiefly the military planners in the United States, argue that they would reduce what is euphemistically called collateral damage. As Schlesinger expresses it, "denying the enemy his military objectives without excessive collateral damage."[39] This assertion is contradicted by experts who point out that a greater number of small weapons might well increase damage, and that even if they did decrease collateral damage to structures, people would be faced with a lingering death by radiation.[40]

In the academic debate on strategy, there is open advocacy of using mini-nukes for a rapid first use to fortify the sanctuary of the United States. Some Los Alamos experts openly make a plea for prime consideration of United States national interests by relying on an immediate input of low-yield nuclear weapons for the defense of NATO:

> The strategy proposed in this article . . . calls for immediately engaging an attacker with low-yield nuclear weapons for all but the most trivial incursions. Yet this concept would require no change in NATO's accepted strategy of forward defense, only in its interpretation.[41]

The ulterior motive is to steer war away from United States territory:

> Discriminating use of nuclear weapons from the outset would enable NATO to conduct a successful defense. . . . Dealing with threats of irrational attacks to destroy all or part of NATO is a problem for our European allies to face without counting on U.S. strategic nuclear weapons. It is their survival that such attacks threaten.[42]

As, due to European malaise, there has been little discussion and no public uproar about the plans for a superpower battle over European territory, I find it necessary to speak frankly about the limited-war concept being in reality little more than a plan for sanctuaries. Though there is open discussion of the risk of American *découplement* from Europe, that is not a grave risk at present; what is a risk is the existing *couplement* of superpower conflicts with the potential sacrifice of Europe.

Some other dangers also need attention, although more marginal in this dramatic context. If mini-nukes should become standard equipment, deployed interchangeably with conventional weapons, this would blur the distinction between nuclear and conventional weapons. But the "firebreak" between them must be absolute, as I strongly emphasized in the speech of 1973 quoted above (pages 45–46). If the present distinction between nuclear and conventional weapons becomes blurred it will be impossible to believe in limited war and to avoid uncontrollable escalation. Further, as communication links to the Supreme Commander in Washington, so far in sole control of the release of nuclear weapons, or with any specifically empowered NATO commanders would be difficult to keep clear, these smaller nuclear weapons would be more exposed to the danger of unauthorized use by overzeal, mistake, a failure of nerve, blackmail, or theft.

As the process of proliferation continues, moreover, there looms the specter of non-nuclear European allies acquiring mini-nukes for use by their troops. This would be a breach of the Non-Proliferation Treaty, to which they have acceded. Any spread in the West European defense system of nuclear weapons would in itself tempt other countries to nuclear-arms proliferation and cause a spurt to a new phase of the arms race.

Where is the thoroughgoing responsible analysis of all aspects of the deployment of tactical nuclear weapons in Europe? Where is the political debate about the effects of their use in a war and, generally, about their usefulness?

Discussion of the questions raised in expert circles about the wisdom of withdrawing all or certain types of them, the more vulnerable or more offensive, has not reached the peoples of Europe. There is definitely no interest in public discussion of a realistic analysis

> (a) of the implications of drawing nuclear fire onto the European countries, or
>
> (b) of the extent to which these countries and peoples would be devastated.

The ostrich attitude became apparent once again when the barter offer in the Vienna negotiations to withdraw a small part of the tactical nuclear weapons from Western Europe became known. In October 1975, Chairman Willy Brandt of the Social Democratic Party in West Germany declared himself in favor of the proposal. The news story was accompanied by some comments:

> But many U.S. allies in Europe, including West Germany, have previously expressed uneasiness over the proposal. They feel that any suggestion that U.S. atomic weapons are being withdrawn from Europe touches off fears that the United States is taking a step toward removing its guarantee of nuclear protection for its allies.[43]

As was already customary in earlier periods, the European partners in NATO have preferred to have little public attention directed towards the possible consequences of their NATO allegiance. Perhaps they feel that they could not handle a twofold argument—continuing to appeal to the Americans for military commitment while informing the people at home about the insecurity involved. The remarkable thing is that the public has acquiesced. Even in the nonaligned Western countries there has been astonishingly little discussion of these awkward issues or studies examining the consequences of various scenarios, for example, those involving the use of the thousands of tactical nuclear weapons deployed in the midst of Europe. These nonaligned neighbors to NATO countries have demonstrated a kind, but ultimately not very helpful, discretion in questions which concern the destiny of the continent as a whole.

There has as usual been more open discussion in the United States. There it has often been understood that the political consequences of presently relevant scenarios and damage estimates are ominous. As former ambassador to NATO Harlan Cleveland has pointed out:

> It is natural for Americans to press for effective, which is to say large-scale, use of nuclear weapons on the battlefield—enough to "stop the enemy in his tracks." But this conjures up for Europeans the picture of a Europe devastated while the United States and the Soviet Union remain intact.[44]

In the Brookings Institution study where Cleveland was quoted, the conclusion was put in sharper language:

> The idea that tactical nuclear weapons furnish a plausible "option" for *defending* Western Europe (as distinguished from their escalatory role) has had a lingering half-life. In fact, the use of hundreds of atomic weapons could cause so much collateral damage to the area being "defended" that the inhabitants might prefer surrender as a lesser evil. This would be less true of certain low-yield or "clean" weapons; but even if NATO so limited its weaponry, an enemy might not.
>
> The use of these weapons in Europe evokes a potential conflict of perceived interest between elements of the attentive publics in Europe and the United States.[45]

This matter was not brought up at the European Security Conference, where it ought to have headed an urgent agenda. Nowhere so far are views heard from the citizens of Europe, who will, after all, be the victims if there is a superpower war in Europe.

They should, if they were enlightened participants in a dialogue about the defense of Europe, join with the independent experts and state it clearly: *these tactical nuclear weapons are not needed in Europe, neither for deterrence nor for defense.*

In fact, and that should be the overriding concern, the United States does not need to have these weapons in Europe. If it maintains its strategy of using its nuclear strength to defend Western Europe, it need only detach some of its submarines, equipped with nuclear warheads on ballistic missiles, targeted and ready to fire in case of an attack against Western Europe (Chapter IV, Section 3). That should be sufficient to deter any such attack.

7.   Scissions in the Alliances

Even if their peoples have been kept uninformed, it must be assumed that the West European Governments and their expert advisers are fully aware of the wholesale destruction of their countries and the killing and maiming of a very large portion of their peoples that would occur in case of even a limited nuclear war in Europe.

No West European nation has tried to get out of NATO. Even France, which has withdrawn its forces from the NATO command, has remained within the alliance. From the point of view of an individual country, at least on the continent of Europe, a dissociation from NATO would not give more security. And neither is it foreseeable that the West European countries will collectively give up NATO, although the security originally pledged them has necessarily vanished with the developments.

The common belief in Western Europe that there is not much reason to fear a military attack from the Soviet Union has made the doubts about the United States commitment more bearable. On the other hand, in the political climate of the cold war it was natural to feel that a breaking up of NATO could be interpreted by the Soviet Union almost as an invitation to become aggressive.

Also, *fait accompli* is always important. Once an institution has come into existence it has a tendency to continue to exist. Even in Norway and Denmark, where there had been strong popular resistance against joining NATO in 1949, the opposition has died down in spite of nothing having happened to make NATO more attractive.

All this said, it is clear that there is a deep scission between West European and American security interests and that the differences have been increased by the more and more open preference in the United States for a limited war strategy which entails an early use of tactical nuclear weapons in Europe while refraining as long as possible from bringing the strategic ones into play. The mutual interest of the superpowers in keeping their homelands as sanctuaries and letting Europe bear the brunt of possible war has here been discussed in reference to nuclear war risks. Now there are SALT discussions about possible curtailing of new long-range weapons such as cruise missiles and Backfire bombers. The superpowers' idea is reported to be to cut short the weapons' ranges and not allow them to be used as strategic weapons across the Atlantic but to leave them free for use on closer battlefields, thus preserving their effectiveness for a war in Europe (Chapter IV, Section 5). This sanctuary idea naturally can never be a European interest nor be shared by any lesser power. If the war is a superpower war, so should the battle be.

Now and then there have occurred harrowing incidents which have focused the dissension dormant within NATO. One such occurred during the 1973 Yom Kippur war in the Middle East. The United States, without consulting or notifying its West European allies, on the night of October 24–25 ordered all its armed forces on alert, ready for war, including the nuclear forces in Europe. Europe shuddered, as did the whole world.

The alert came after the Security Council had on October 22 adopted a resolution calling for a cease-fire and had decided to dispatch UN peace-keeping forces. The West European governments judged that it would be, if not a violation, contrary to the spirit of the UN resolution not to observe strict neutrality in the Middle East war. Consequently they blockaded efforts to raise the military strength of Israel through deliveries from, or via, Western Europe. The only exception to this united front was Portugal, which allowed the use of United States bases on the Azores for refueling supply planes destined for Israel.

The NATO Treaty could not, in the understanding of the West Europeans, be interpreted as an obligation to participate if a member country got involved in a foreign war such as the Middle East one. In Indochina the United States had had to go it alone.

There were some acrimonious exchanges across the Atlantic, particularly French and German retorts to reproaches by Henry Kissinger. The conflict was deepened by a disagreement on oil policies in the wake of the Arab oil embargo late in 1973. The West European countries are to an incomparable degree dependent on oil imported from the Arab countries.[46] However, this dependency is seen as calling upon them to negotiate, or bargain, but not to fight their way to supplies.

When the United States Secretary of State Henry Kissinger and Secretary of Defense James Schlesinger, backed by President Ford, on several occasions indulged in veiled warnings that new embargoes on oil or exorbitant increases of export prices, "strangulating" the industrial countries, might lead to military intervention, the criticism in Western Europe became open and sharp. *The New York Times* reported from Germany:

> West Germans, even those at the highest levels, are worried about being drawn into an American military adventure in the Middle East and remarks like Mr. Kissinger's make their fears seem real. Asked about this in an interview in the weekly news magazine *Der Spiegel* today, Chancellor Helmut Schmidt answered:
> "That we could be drawn into conflicts against our will is something new in German political history." Dr. Armin Grünewald, a Government spokesman, said in a television interview yesterday: "I don't see the danger of "strangulation" at the moment. We are not interested in any kind of confrontation with the oil countries, but rather in cooperation. . . . We do not have the use of force in mind, and do not share such thoughts."[47]

"The Year of Europe," which had been proclaimed by Kissinger in April 1973 and which was occasionally used to explain the widening of NATO's mutual responsibilities and the broadening of the Atlantic alliance to take in Japan, was hindered from becoming consummated by these circumstances. At the NATO summit meeting in the spring of 1975 none of the interest conflicts, actual or potential, were settled or even much discussed. President Ford understood that his essential mission at that meeting, which he initiated, was to confirm that the United States stood firm in its treaty commitments. The making of such declarations in all directions was a strongly felt need in the United States after the disastrous end of the Indochina war. But further clarification of what that commitment entailed in terms of actual strategy was not proffered.

Indeed, the incidents of recent history have stirred European concern over the prospects of getting involved in the superpowers' gaming outside Europe. Henry Kissinger long ago had foreseen this Atlantic conflict of interest:

> When NATO was formed, the principal threat to world peace seemed to lie in a Soviet attack on Europe. In recent years, the view has grown that equally grave risks are likely to arise in trouble spots outside Europe. To most Europeans, these do not appear as immediate threats to their independence or security. . . . It is Europe that evades our entreaties to play a global role; that is to say, most Europeans do not consider their interests at stake in America's extra-European involvement.[48]

The fateful issue is the sort of war Europe must be prepared to face on its own continent. In that respect the Europeans obviously have little to say.

These observations also hold true for Eastern Europe. A breach in interest exists between the Soviet Union and its allies. These schisms surface even more rarely in that half of Europe, but unquiet rumblings are heard from time to time. In the issue of war and peace the destiny of all Europe is one. The same bitterness is smoldering within all its peoples.

8. The Superpowers' Gaming over the World: Some Special Cases

The bipolar confrontation between the superpowers has divided Europe, almost from the end of the war. But the superpowers have also been gaming with each other over the entire globe, bringing distant countries into alliances or otherwise exerting influence on their policies. Through their varying and changing accommodations with each other, they have sought to avoid a head-on clash. These problems must here be treated with broad generalizations.

a. The People's Republic of China—a Very Special Case. As the largest nation in the world, with some 900 million people, only China can be seen as challenging, politically or militarily, the future superpower positions of the United States and the Soviet Union. Its relations with the two have gone through dramatic shifts.

China emerged as a communist state in October 1949, after a long period of struggle with the corrupt Chiang Kai-shek regime, which for a considerable time was supported both financially and militarily by the United States. China was also harassed by continued invasions of Japanese troops. There is a general concurrence in many parts of the world that nothing can consolidate a nation as much as interference, particularly military aggression, from abroad.

In the beginning, relations of the People's Republic of China with the Soviet Union were close. China accepted much advice despite considerable differences in the two approaches to communism. After the estrangement from the Soviet Union around 1960, the Chinese government staked all on a national development policy of self-reliance. It demonstrated solidarity with the underdeveloped countries and gave some aid and technical assistance to a few underdeveloped countries, mainly in Africa. China in these years was blocked by the United States from joining the United Nations. In 1964 China exploded its first nuclear device. Having previously received Soviet aid to develop nuclear technologies, they then developed the program through their own efforts. In 1972 China was admitted to the United Nations, and permanent membership in the Security Council then followed constitutionally. The Chinese government has now become more active on the world scene, has opened diplomatic relations with the great majority of countries in the world, and has become a participant in several UN organs. It has nevertheless preserved a reticent position on many issues, not least on those pertaining to disarmament. From my own experience with Chinese officials, in China and in UN organs, I have come to understand that part of the explanation for this is an honest feeling on the part of the Chinese that after the long period of isolation they do not have at their command enough expert knowledge for participation in debates on such topics as communication satellites and cruel weapons, considering the political, legal, and technical intricacies which these matters have acquired in international forums.

A more substantial reason for reticence is China's determination to depend almost wholly on itself. It has expanded the exchange of commodities and technologies it long has had with a few countries like Sweden, but for the foreseeable future the market will probably not grow very much. Vastly exaggerated ideas of a huge market in China spread for a time in the United States when the twenty-five-year-old blockade of all American commercial and other relations with China ended. Such a market has for the time being proven illusory. China has firmly decided not to follow the example of other less developed countries who rely for their development on direct foreign investments or on large and long-term credits from abroad. Recently discovered extensive oil deposits in China and its surrounding ocean space make this policy of economic independence seem likely to succeed. China maintains its independence by importing technology and industrial equipment from developed countries without letting transnational corporations in.

China's posture in the United Nations and in its general political pronouncements is to condemn both superpowers' drive towards world hegemony. Today Chinese accusations are most vehemently directed against the Soviet Union. That China would decide to line up on the Western side, however, is difficult to believe, in spite of a deep distrust of the Soviet Union and the occasional conflicts along their long common border. In time, it is possible that China will settle some of its disputes with the Soviet Union. Yet, for the foreseeable future, China will continue to stand apart from the block-building which has resulted from the superpower bipolar contest.

In regard to disarmament, China has taken two positions. One is the traditional communist distinction between just and unjust wars, or, in Chinese political terms, between wars of liberation and imperialist wars. The other is a clarion call to complete nuclear disarmament. In a 1963 letter to all governments, a year before China exploded its first nuclear bomb, Premier Chou En-lai advocated "the complete, thorough, total, and resolute prohibition and destruction of nuclear weapons" and proposed a conference of the government heads of all countries of the world.[49] This was the quick Chinese reply to the Partial Test-Ban Treaty, which it called "a big fraud," not without reason (Chapter III, Section 6).

As a condition for its participation in the recently proposed World Disarmament Conference, the Chinese government demands that prior to convening the conference nuclear-weapons powers pledge not to attack non-nuclear powers with such weapons and not to be the first to use them (Chapter VI, Section 7; Chapter XI, Section 3). This agrees with demands generally made by far lesser powers.

b. Some Rich Countries, Western but Standing More or Less Apart. A few highly industrialized Western democracies have successfully extricated themselves more from the superpowers' bipolar grip. Australia and New Zealand, situated on the antipodes to Europe, were early brought into an alliance with the United States, ANZUS (Australia, New Zealand, United States Tripartite Security Pact). Unlike the West European allies, they both sent small contingents of troops to aid the United States in the Vietnam War. However, this aid was withdrawn when at the end of 1972 the Labor Parties took over the government in both countries.

The main reason this Treaty never became important and never involved the participants in problems similar to those of Europe was the absence of a nearby adversary. The Soviet Union was too far away to be a threat and China never entered into the same degree of war-prone hostility towards the United States. Both Australia and New Zealand have increasingly regarded their main foreign policy problem to be correct and friendly relations with Indonesia and other countries in the Southeast Asian region. They have come to realize that these relations, and those with China, should be established on an individual basis of mutual interests and not as part of a pact with the United States. The 1975 return to conservative governments in Australia and New Zealand will probably not signal much of a change in those basic policies.

In spite of immense American investments and a common border with the United States, Canada has kept a certain distance from the foreign policies of its mighty neighbor. Like Sweden, it early abstained unilaterally from becoming a nuclear power despite possessing the technical and economic preconditions, for it believes that decision to be in its best national interest. In the Geneva Disarmament Committee Canada has often taken an independent position, more than, for example, Britain.

Japan, now the second industrial power in the world, was bound after the War by the famous Article 9 of the United States–drafted Constitution "that the Japanese people forever renounce war as a sovereign right of the nation and the threat or use of force as a means of settling international disputes." The Japanese government and parliament, though not without opposition, has interpreted this article to allow the creation of Self-Defense Forces, but those have so far been kept at very low levels.

In recent years, particularly when James R. Schlesinger was Secretary of Defense, the United States urged Japan to increase its military forces and to be prepared to play a more active role in East Asian military matters. This idea has apparently not met much positive response in Japan. Against such a change there stand the deep antimilitaristic feelings that developed in Japan in the wake of World War II. Also there is awareness of suspicions in all of South Asia of a rebirth of Japanese militarism. In addition there are general budget difficulties caused by the present depression and the need to remedy social welfare inadequacies which were much neglected during the phenomenal growth years of the 1960s and early 1970s.

The 1960 Treaty of Mutual Cooperation and Security grants the United States use of many areas for its land, air, and naval forces "to ensure the security of Japan" and "the maintenance of international peace and security in the Far East." Japan has subsidized these bases, which in both the Korean and the Indochinese Wars have been used for United States military purposes. The bases are not popular in Japan. They occupy valuable real estate in a crowded country and remind the Japanese people of the occupation. Also Japan does not feel its national interests as so closely aligned with American military policy in the region.

Though in a recent joint announcement President Ford reaffirmed the United States' commitment to defend Japan, the nuclear umbrella is becoming increasingly open to doubt, as it is unlikely that the United States would accept the destruction of its own homeland to save Japan. For Japan itself, a nuclear war would be a most horrible prospect, both because of traumatic memories and because its population and industry are confined to such a small area.

That Japan would go nuclear does not seem likely. The living mementos of having been the first and so far the only victim of an atomic assault has made Japan particularly allergic to nuclear weapons. Allowing the United States the right to deploy nuclear weapons and letting United States warships equipped with such weapons use its port facilities is widely felt as deeply disturbing. Japanese aversion has succeeded in getting the United States to withdraw its huge stockpiles of chemical weapons from Okinawa.

Although the situation of Japan is more complicated than that of the other three countries included in this group, it seems probable that Japan will gradually seek to loosen its military obligation to the United States. A main background factor is that, like Australia and New Zealand, it is not located on a direct confrontation line between the two superpowers as is Western Europe. The Soviet Union has on the whole been rather inactive in regard to influencing Japanese policy. A dominant interest of Japan is to stabilize its relations with China. Nor is China pressing Japan today to follow any anti–United States line of policy. The United States détente with China has, finally, helped to increase Japan's freedom to choose a more independent line of policy. For all these reasons, there is in Japan a reluctance to get into such a close anticommunist alliance with the United States as has NATO.

In the disarmament negotiations, Japan has played an increasingly active role, endeavoring particularly to strengthen the arguments for various measures by solid technical groundwork (Chapter IX, Section 5).

These four countries, militarily considered to be lesser powers, comprise all the industrial nations outside the United States, the Soviet Union, and Europe. All are political democracies which can be assumed to resist being drawn too closely into the strategic planning or possible military adventures of either of the two superpowers.

    c. Latin America, Still a United States Precinct. Another large region, Latin America, has on the whole escaped being intensely involved in the superpowers' gaming. The Soviet Union has largely respected United States hegemony over Latin America, established by the Monroe Doctrine at the beginning of the nineteenth century, and anchored now in the Organization of American States (OAS). This organ for hemispheric cooperation may be showing signs of weakening the preponderance of the United States; Canada has conspicuously declined to participate. Anyhow, it is not a military alliance. The Soviet Union has not evidenced much interest in Latin America, not even in the guerilla movements which from time to time have operated against the various Latin American governments, nor has it encouraged or effectively backed branches of communist parties in the region.

An exception to Soviet recognition of Latin America as the interest sphere of the United States was its rash attempt in 1962 to install nuclear-weapons missiles in Cuba. For some dramatic weeks the world feared an imminent nuclear war between the two superpowers. Khrushchev backed down, the missiles were withdrawn, but a heavy burden of financial aid and commercial commitments was accepted by the Soviets to safeguard Cuba's survival in the face of the economic boycott upheld by the United States.

The United States hegemony over Latin America was generally undisturbed, even when occasionally it took the shape of gunboat diplomacy, for example, in relation to Guatemala and the Dominican Republic. As late as 1965, the United States sent marines into the Dominican Republic and then followed with an invasion of tens of thousands of soldiers to prevent a changeover to a socialist regime. The most shattering experience for the Latin American countries has been United States interference in the political destiny of Chile,

facilitating the ousting of the Allende government and the installation of a reactionary and brutal military regime, through various
manipulations including covert operations of the CIA.

Meanwhile, the United States has contributed arms and military training to most Latin American countries and used development aid to favor governments amenable to United States political
and economic interests. The United States has accepted the trend
in Latin America, as in so many countries of the underdeveloped
world, towards military dictatorships. Accustomed as it has become
after the War to ally itself to reactionary governments all over the
world, the United States government has apparently not felt any deep
regrets. Huge capital investments and control of natural resources
by American corporations has, however, engendered considerable
Latin American criticism of the powerful neighbor to the north.
However, almost the only unity demonstrated by the Latin American
governments has been their demands for a new deal in commercial
and financial matters.

In addition, one direct conflict with the United States is brewing
over Panama's request for a new settlement of the conditions for
United States control of the Panama Canal. This has developed into
an ever hotter dispute, Panama accelerating its demands and na-
tionalist forces in the United States Congress refusing them. Still,
even this conflict has not led the Soviet Union to show much inclination to interfere. The important initiatives taken by some of the
Latin American countries on the horizon of disarmament negotiations will be discussed later, particularly the roles of Argentina,
Brazil, and Mexico. In this process, no one has played a more important role than Mexico's long-time ambassador to the United
Nations and lately its foreign minister, García Robles.

d.   Wars in Asia—Confrontation Risks.   Although Canada,
Japan, New Zealand, Australia, and Latin America have remained
relatively undisturbed by the nuclear powers' competition, there are a
number of special cases where the gaming has been much more con-
sequential. The Israel-Arab conflict in West Asia is a conspicuous
case of limited war, as it has developed outside Europe. This conflict
has evolved as a blatant war by proxy. The sharp-tongued German
weekly *Der Spiegel* observed at the beginning of the 1973 war, "but
it is only Jews and Arabs that are killed."[50] The superpowers have
each armed their own side in a conflict which has continued for
decades, making it impossible for the Security Council to prevent the

wars, which have followed one upon another, always ending in uncertain armistice. An agreement by the two superpowers to stop the competitive supplying of weapons after the Suez war of 1956—when both stood against the adventurism of Israel's allies Britain and France—would have gone far to pacify the region. The opposite has occurred; even after the last war in 1973 the arms lost were rapidly replaced, resulting in a net increase. Today, both sides are getting ready for the next round.[51]

Though the arms have been provided mainly by the two superpowers, they have been sold by Britain, France, and West Germany as well. A relatively new act in the gaming has been United States willingness to provide aid to Egypt and to several oil-rich Arab states, which are in turn often supplying their co-religionists directly involved in military conflicts.[52]

In East Asia there has been a similar, although more lopsided kind of gaming. The story of the United States' gradual involvement in what was originally an independence war against French colonialism in Vietnam need not be retold. After a massive military invasion and the spread of war and destruction to the whole of Indochina it ended in total failure for the United States. The Soviet Union and China supplied weapons and food to the other side but abstained from military involvement, thus avoiding direct confrontation.

In the Korean War, on the other hand, a confrontation between the United States and China was brought on at the end. In that war, singularly cruel as it was for the civilian population, the United Nations itself became tragically involved. The United States command was covered by the UN flag. This unique character and the prolonged UN involvement in supervising the cease-fire should make the Korean war the prime subject for a profound study of the origins of wars and the public misconceptions and official misrepresentations largely responsible for them as well as the art of concluding wars by building up safe peace conditions instead of perpetrating divisiveness. Nothing of the sort has as yet been undertaken. A strong contingent of United States troops remains in the southern half of Korea and the situation between the two Koreas is still quite troubled. I firmly believe that the whole modern drama of Korea should be the prime subject for a deep-probing United Nations fact-finding study, entailing alternative futures to choose between.

Even with their different configurations, these three special cases—Middle East, Indochina, Korea—are all variations on the theme of the superpowers having kept the wars locally limited, refraining from escalating to the use of nuclear weapons. But the question of the superpowers' involvement is different from that in Europe. In the Middle East they have both abstained from direct participation; in Indochina and Korea, only one was directly involved. In Europe, however, both are presumed to become actively engaged in fighting each other—a war in Europe being so much more *their* war, so much less a war between countries in the region.

But the three cases of extra-European limited wars show a pattern. They demonstrate how little concerted effort there has been to prevent threatening conflicts and to end wars, as is prescribed by the Charter of the United Nations. Preserving peace would require cooperative efforts by the superpowers. However, what has been achieved are only some, though valuable, missions by UN peace-keeping forces to guard cease-fire lines and the sending of UN observers to trouble spots. The contributions made by the UN to avert threats to peace have been much weaker than was foreseen by the Charter. Some, although not always very clear, resolutions have been passed, the most important being the Security Council resolution 242 of 22 November 1967, in essence a request that boundary lines prevailing between the state of Israel and its Arab neighbors before that year's war be restored; followed up by the 338 one of 22 October 1973. No UN resolution establishing true peace has been adopted; neither have efforts been backed by using the instrument of sanction or the promise of sanction nor by the stopping of arms deliveries.[53]

9. The Superpowers' Gaming over the World: The Rest of the World, Underdeveloped

There are vast areas of the world where the international relations of countries are less fixed and where the superpowers are vying with each other to establish spheres of interest. That is the case for the large number of underdeveloped states, some small, some very populous in Africa and in Asia south of China. Unlike the Latin American countries, which, even if they have remained poor and economically dependent, earlier acquired status as politically independent states, these are (excepting Ethiopia and Thailand) new countries. They have emerged as states out of the stormflood of decolonization which swept the world after the War.

Except for the few countries that have oil these countries are all very poor, a poverty recently aggravated by the oil and food crises. The food crisis particularly is bound to worsen because of the population explosion. Whatever the national constitutions, these nations are generally ruled, both locally and at the center, by the well-off elite. In blunt contradiction to their declarations of greater equality, their development has mostly increased inequality, so that vast masses in rural and urban slums have remained destitute. There is almost everywhere a trend towards authoritarian government, to which the majority of educated, alert citizens show increased opposition, but these represent only a tiny minority in their nations. These governments are mostly military in origin and composition; this new, traumatic development fits in with the subject of this treatise: the trend away from disarmament and peace to militarization of the world. These extremely condensed generalizations also apply to the Latin American countries, though most of them enjoy a somewhat higher economic level.

In the African states the boundaries of these new countries resulted from colonial struggles and settlements and were drawn without much consideration for social, ethnic, linguistic, or economic conditions. The colonial powers established communications and other connections to their own metropolitan centers, but disregarded those to neighboring countries which often belonged to another colonial power. As it has everywhere been extremely difficult to build up and consolidate these new nations and for them to believe the boundaries with adjacent nations are natural and final, the seeds have been sown for conflict both within and between the new countries.

Not unexpectedly, the two superpowers saw this situation as inviting them to fish in troubled waters. Many countries leaned towards the United States, as did the Philippines, which had been a United States colony, and others for whom the United States was the natural inheritor of British colonial domination. Both superpowers are busily competing to spin a network of alliances, or dependencies, all over the Asian and African continents. They are not here bound by established and agreed spheres of influence as they are in Latin America.

While the United States since the beginning of the 1950s has tried to adhere to a pattern of multistate alliances, the Soviet Union has from the beginning relied on bilateral alliances, simple understandings, or friendship pacts. Lately, this has tended to become a pattern for the United States as well.

As the Vietnam conflict increasingly became more of a United States responsibility, the SEATO alliance (South East Asia Treaty Organization), comprising Australia, New Zealand, Pakistan, the Philippines, and Thailand and the United States, Great Britain, and France, was developed. The Baghdad pact in West Asia, later CENTO (Central Treaty Organization, comprising Iran, Pakistan, Turkey, and Britain with the United States as an associate member), became another such alliance which was definitely conceived as a bulwark against the Soviet Union. Britain and France have been more or less sleeping partners to these treaties, which have never been taken to imply serious obligation by the Asian participants, but the United States, acquiring the right to establish military bases, for some time referred to SEATO as juridical justification for its participation in the Vietnam War.

After the defeat of the United States in Indochina, the SEATO alliance was finally abrogated (September 1975) on the insistence of its Asian members. A number of Asian, noncommunist countries have now joined in an organization of their own—Indonesia, Malaysia, the Philippines, Singapore, Thailand—called ASEAN (Association of South East Asian Nations), professing neutrality and beginning to open relations with China and the former Indochinese states, Laos, Cambodia, and Vietnam. The United States is, however, continuously trying to keep ASEAN states within its sphere of influence.

In Africa, Britain and France have a policy of continued close contact with their former colonies, though not for strategic purposes. Many of the African countries have been linked to Western Europe through economic arrangements with the European Common Market organization. Still, the United States, the Soviet Union, and China have tried to exert their influence. In Africa, however, there is often a resistance to close bonds, although the North African states hold to links with their Arab co-religionists. On the whole, this continent in its attempts at regional and internal cooperation has been hampered by its own divisivenesses and complex destinies. It must be noted, however, that when Portugal gave up its African colonies the two superpowers became more involved than ever before, particularly in Angola. The present situation necessitates a question mark as to the future, with the anxiety focused on South Africa's ominous role.

Whether within or outside formal alliances the means of the superpowers exerting influence on underdeveloped countries have been of several types. A major vehicle has been the provision of arms: by sales, often at reduced prices; as direct military aid, including technical assistance; by licenses for arms production; by training of officers and other military specialists (Chapter V).

A second approach has been the establishment of military bases, either as wholly foreign bases or joint bases with the host country. Such bases are numerous, if all are included, such as those providing communications facilities. They are now the subject of strident debate, particularly in relation to the Indian Ocean (Chapter VI, Section 10).

The superpowers' military assistance is given to reliable governments. To the Soviet Union and its East European allies this has meant governments bent upon a socialist course, a condition which has, however, not been restrictively enforced if the client government has kept up a sufficiently anti-American posture. United States military aid has gone to supposedly staunch anticommunist regimes; in practice this has meant mostly very reactionary ones. In the twilight zone of the competition between the two superpowers, some underdeveloped countries have at times succeeded in getting aid and weapons from both of them; as did Indonesia under Sukarno, and, more recently, Egypt and Iraq.

The policy of unilateral economic development aid by the two superpowers, and, in the case of the Soviet Union, from its European allies as well, has been shaped by the desire to establish a network of reliable dependent countries. This becomes clearly visible in the distribution of aid to different recipient countries. Other countries giving aid—Britain, France, and West Germany—have also been motivated by national interests, but these were commercial and sometimes cultural.

Development aid from abroad has stagnated, and, globally, even decreased in real terms from about 1960, when the General Assembly declared that the 1960s should become the Development Decade, and this has continued through the second Development Decade of the 1970s. The falling off has been most pronounced in United States aid, and, if account is taken of the juggling of statistics, hardly more than a third of the figures presented as aid from the United States can be reckoned as development aid in any real sense.[54]

In recent years, as the economic situation of most underdeveloped countries has deteriorated seriously because of the food and oil crises and depression in the developed countries, the underdeveloped countries have increasingly joined together in ever louder demands for a new economic world order. The majority which the poor countries hold in the General Assembly and other organizations within the UN family has enabled them to force the acceptance of resolutions in line with their demands. In some developed countries there has been general and genuine sympathy for the demands, occasionally leading to votes for these resolutions. In some other rich countries, criticism and resentment have surfaced, particularly in the United States.

A new world order would necessarily mean that developed countries would use less of the world's resources and redirect downward consumption of many industrial and agricultural products. No developed country has as yet shown any will to move in this direction, even among those who have voted for the UN resolutions or expressed sympathy for the righteousness of the demands of the poor countries. I am embarrassed to confess that I cannot exclude my own country, Sweden, from this reproach of insufficient sincerity. The developed countries point to difficulties in regard to foreign exchange balance and to inflation and unemployment at home. Their foreign economic policies have turned away from common interests with the underdeveloped countries towards their interest in relations with other developed countries and with those exporting oil.[55]

CHAPTER III

A History of Lost Opportunities

1. Disarmament Efforts Before World War II

The questions of how to preserve peace and promote disarmament were burning issues after World War I. It was called the Great War or the World War and consensus reigned that it should not, and would not, be repeated. The world should be made to "return to normalcy."

There were two aspects of the disarmament issue. The first, motivated by sheer revulsion against war itself, led to attempts to proscribe the *use of cruel weapons*. The horrifying experience of the use of gas and the hundreds of thousands of victims killed, maimed, or blinded emphasized the need. Such work tied in with the traditions from the turn-of-the-century Hague Conferences which had established rules of international law for the conduct of warfare. In this first area, the work was crowned with considerable success in the form of the Geneva Protocol of 1925, which prohibited the use not only of gas warfare but of chemical and biological weapons in general (Chapters VIII and IX).

The second approach was aimed at *reduction of armaments* by mutually agreed limitations on possession and production. The reaction against the arms race that had preceded the War and, according to popular view, had been a cause of the War was one of the main constituent factors when the Versailles Peace Treaty was made and the League of Nations created in 1920. The Covenant of the League demanded that armaments be reduced to "the lowest point consistent with national safety." There was a strong political commitment to the League's work on the issues of disarmament, especially after 1926 when a Preparatory Disarmament Commission was established wherein both the United States and the Soviet Union (at the time nonmembers) participated, as did Germany (a new League member).

There were times when negotiations were on the verge of major breakthroughs, as often has been emphasized by Philip Noel-Baker, a prominent participant.[1] These potentialities were not realized, however. Governments were too preoccupied with what they considered to be their own security interests. They could not free themselves from questions of prestige, and they underestimated the greater security that could have been gained by mutual agreement. Then when Hitler came to power the disarmament negotiations had to be abandoned as being unrealistic. The world was drifting towards a new world war.

We ought nevertheless to learn a lesson from the sincerity and the boldness with which the disarmament tasks were tackled in that period. The situation was, of course, more manageable at the time of the League of Nations since the organization consisted largely of advanced European countries with similar problems. Technologies were then far less diversified. Wars traditionally had been fought on the surface of the earth and on the seas and only recently had the submarine environment and the air been opened up to military pursuit. Rules for the conduct of wars, from Grotius to the Hague Conferences,[2] had traditionally been based on comparatively manageable environments.

After World War I efforts were made to restrict armaments by matching, item for item, the number of troops, guns, tanks, warships, etc. in order to agree on a low ceiling or to eliminate arms altogether. There were early successes in a limited way and for a limited time such as the Washington Naval Treaty of 1922, which restricted the tonnage and gunpower of the navies of the major powers. Although it soon became obvious that the intent of the Treaty was forfeited by the *qualitative* improvement of cruisers and destroyers, the tradition of setting *quantitative* norms, or ratios, persisted and persists to this day.

Nonetheless, the progress of the League of Nations in settling disarmament issues was, all matters considered, remarkable. The leading statesmen of the era set high stakes on far-reaching proposals. Strong support came also from powerful civic-interest bodies like the trade unions and the cooperative movement. Their views were presented at the Preparatory Commission. For more than five years this body labored ambitiously on plans to be negotiated at the World Conference for the Reduction and Limitation of Armaments, which finally met in February 1932. As a matter of fact, it was at the first appearance of Soviet delegates at a meeting of the Preparatory Commission that Russia's Foreign Minister Litvinov introduced a plan for "general and complete disarmament," a term revived after World War II—a high aspiration which fifty years later seems to lie farther and farther away.

Strikingly ambitious proposals about specific arms reductions were made, beginning in the Preparatory Commission. Lord Cecil of Britain submitted a proposal on naval disarmament, suggesting that all countries should forgo three types of fighting vessels (which the Versailles Treaty explicitly had forbidden Germany to possess): surface vessels over 10,000 tons' displacement, all submarines, and aircraft carriers. The underlying principle was that weapons with primarily offensive functions should be outlawed. In relation to the interesting new weapons category of airplanes, this criterion meant that all military air forces be forbidden, including naval ones. In today's reality the principle would apply to almost all major weapons systems with high mobility, as being principally offensive in character, whether intended for preemptive defense of home territories or more farflung undertakings.

The most comprehensive plan, with proposals for drastic curtailment of armaments by land, sea, and air, was American, presented to the full Conference in June 1932. It is often called the Hoover Plan, as the United States President took great interest in these disarmament endeavors. At that juncture, according to Philip Noel-Baker, the Conference "came within an ace of success."[3] After a long struggle within the British Cabinet, the British presented counterproposals which, although Stanley Baldwin was fighting for the Hoover ideas, came out considerably less restrictive. Still, these were put in the form of a Draft Disarmament Convention and would seem surprisingly radical if measured with present-day yardsticks. It then was already March 1933, and Hitler had won in Germany. The work of the League's Disarmament Conference petered out. It held a last session in mid-1934, but then it suspended its work without setting a date for reconvening.

The failure of the League was political: propitious opportunities had not been grasped in time. However, the many substantive points for arms limitation that had been raised and partially agreed upon in the course of the work of the League of Nations are a testament from one generation of disarmers to the next, to us.

2. United Nations and Disarmament

The statesmen who had lived through the cataclysm of World War II, reflecting the feelings of the peoples in all countries, declared their determination that wars should be prevented by collective efforts. The United Nations was created in order "to save succeeding generations from the scourge of war." Peace was its primary purpose. The responsibility for enforcing peace was laid upon the Security Council, while the General Assembly was to have the right to consider questions of peace and security and to make recommendations to the members and to the Security Council on all matters within the scope of the Charter.

In the spirit of optimism and mutual confidence that reigned when the Charter was drafted, the question of disarmament was not brought forward as a major task or one of immediate urgency. The Charter did not prescribe that the Member nations should reduce their armaments or even that they should not increase them. Restraints were only placed on the defeated nations, but this was done through settlements by the victors outside of the United Nations.[4]

In order that the Security Council should be able to assure peace and security, the power of sanctions and of employing force for the solution of conflicts was to be in its hand. The structure of the Security Council thus became of utmost political importance. Recognizing the role some nations had played in winning the war and, even more important, their overwhelming control of the world's military strength, the drafters of the Charter gave permanent seats to the United States, the Soviet Union, and Britain, as well as China and France. This status carried with it veto powers. Decisions by the Security Council were to be by an affirmative vote of seven of the eleven members "including the concurring votes of the permanent members."[5] This provision implied that only when they agreed could binding decisions as to enforcement action through sanctions or military action described in Articles 41 and 42 be taken.

This was an entirely realistic rule, as majority decisions not including one of the major powers, or, later, one of the two superpowers, would be meaningless, even dangerous. To any lesser power

the possibility of such a majority decision in the United Nations could
mean automatic involvement in a war against a major power or a
military bloc. When Sweden joined the United Nations in 1945 acceptance of the veto was an explicit condition for combining membership
with its settled policy of nonalignment in times of peace and neutrality in war.

Almost immediately after the end of World War II the cold
war broke out between the two superpowers, within a few years
leading to the establishment of the system of military alliances
(Chapter II, Sections 3 and 8). As a result of deep-seated disagreement
between the two superpowers the Security Council became largely
ineffective. Although peace as the absence of war has been preserved
between the two blocs and, indeed, among all developed countries,
wars have been raging between, and within, many of the new states
in the Third World of underdeveloped countries. Quite regularly
the parties to these wars have been backed by one or more of the
veto powers, especially the Soviet Union and the United States, the
latter having been in Indochina a direct participant in a most devastating war. Both have, in certain cases, given such strong support to
opposing sides in a conflict as to virtually transform it into a war by
proxy."

In Chapters VI and VII of the UN Charter the Security Council's main functions had been laid down to be "pacific settlements of
disputes" and taking "action with respect to threats to the peace,
breaches of the peace, and acts of aggression." These functions of
the Security Council have become largely immobilized by the veto
and, more fundamentally, by the deep-rooted disagreements between
the superpowers. But rather hidden in Chapter V, otherwise dealing
with the rules for the constitution of and the decision-making in the
Council, there is an Article 26, prescribing:

> In order to promote the establishment and maintenance of inter-
> national peace and security with the least diversion for armaments of
> the world's human and economic resources, the Security Council shall
> be responsible for formulating, with the assistance of the Military
> Staff Committee referred to in Article 47, plans to be submitted to
> the Members of the United Nations for the establishment of a sys-
> tem for the regulation of armaments.

This task of regulating armaments has never in a systematic way
been performed or even approached by the Council. No work plans
have been seriously undertaken, and the military staff committee has

never been engaged to assist the Council in such work. The paragraph itself stands as a hollow promise.

In no other field has the disagreement between the superpowers so totally obliterated the purposes of the Charter. The next article excepts only procedural matters from the rule of the veto. As things have developed, I think that, among other matters, the preparatory work for plans relating to the regulation of armaments safely could have been left outside this veto rule.[6]

With the Security Council thus politically paralyzed, the main initiatives and discussions on disarmament matters have been moved to the General Assembly and its subsidiary bodies. This was not foreseen as a main duty for the Assembly, only that it "may consider the general principles of cooperation . . . including the principles governing disarmament and the regulation of armaments" (Article 11). Any recommendations accepted there by majority vote do not bind the member nations. But the General Assembly offers a forum where world opinion can make itself felt, policy proposals can be submitted, and compromise resolutions worked out. As to its work methods in regard to disarmament the General Assembly has a choice of a wide variety of possibilities, particularly through its competence, which in a nonexclusive way is shared with the Security Council, to set up commissions and other subsidiary bodies, thus creating negotiation machinery either ad hoc or on a more permanent basis.

In the field of disarmament the establishment of such organs usually occurs in some specific form, often agreed upon in advance by the superpowers as being the most appropriate to the particular case. The structures utilized have shifted considerably, particularly during the first fifteen years of United Nations work. Therefore any attempt to narrate the history of disarmament efforts tends to become confusing if exact references to the various commissions, conferences, or committees are constantly given. In what follows only the main sponsors of proposals and the year in which they have been discussed are recounted.

The main lines of the structural changes in the UN machinery for dealing with disarmament can, however, be discerned. In the beginning, membership in the subsidiary organs was rather restricted and heavily weighted in favor of the United States and its allies. The tasks tended to be of broad scope, starting with suggestions for rather immediate implementation in some fields and then attempting to set out a more general program for the regulation and balanced reduction of armaments by stages. This marked the high tide of expectations, and centered around an Atomic Energy Commission and a Commission for Conventional Armaments. From about 1952 the principle of parity between representatives of the two blocs, urged by the Soviet Union, was applied. At the same time ad hoc conferences gave an impetus to partial approaches. To facilitate references a brief summary is appended.[7]

Only in 1962 was the framework for negotiation made truly multilateral as nonaligned member states were allowed to participate. A disarmament committee, reporting to and instructed by the General Assembly though still under the formal guidance of the superpowers as co-chairmen, started to meet regularly in Geneva, under the name of the Eighteen-Nation Disarmament Committee (ENDC). Later it was expanded as the Conference of the Committee on Disarmament (CCD) with a permanent character. Despite its meager results nobody wants to see it capsize. Undoubtedly it has value as a forum for the exchange of ideas; it is often nonspecifically referred to as the Geneva Committee on Disarmament, a term used for its predecessor ENDC, which will be followed in this book.

At the start of the Geneva Committee, interest revived in a broader scope for disarmament; both superpowers presented comprehensive schemes for general and complete disarmament. However, hopes and expectations were soon confined to more specific collateral measures of disarmament, the most important of which were a ban on further testing of nuclear weapons and a ban against proliferation of such weapons to non-nuclear-weapons countries (Chapters VII and VI).

3.   No Peace Plan for the Atom

After 6 and 9 August 1945, when the United States demonstrated the awesome explosive power of the atom at Hiroshima and Nagasaki, governments realized that fundamental conceptions of war, peace, and security had been changed radically. From then on it was clear that disarmament efforts were highly urgent. It was clear to responsible thinkers that efforts should be directed towards the elimination of nuclear weapons, not just limitation and regulation of what was coming to be called conventional weapons.

The exploding of these atomic bombs was a blow dealt the new world organization only a few weeks after the signing of its Charter,

26 June 1945, and a few months before its first General Assembly met in session in London on 24 January 1946. Its very first resolution, numbered 1 (I), by unanimous decision established an Atomic Energy Commission with the urgent task of making specific proposals "for the elimination from national armaments of atomic weapons and of all other major weapons adaptable to mass destruction."[8] In pursuing its work the Commission concentrated entirely on nuclear weapons.

Acceptance of this sweeping resolution by all the fifty-one members should have opened possibilities for international agreement on this issue of momentous importance. It should have been the right moment to act, as it was still possible to envisage complete non-nuclear armament. At that time only three nuclear devices, of varying construction, had been produced and consumed: one, in the proving grounds of Alamagordo; two having brought death and destruction to Hiroshima and Nagasaki. The opportunity to stop production, which had not yet begun in earnest,[9] was never to recur.

The immediate blame must be laid on the Soviet Union for being such an insistent naysayer when the United States, at the first meeting of the UN Atomic Energy Commission on 14 June 1946, presented a plan for the prohibition of the manufacture of atomic bombs and for placing all phases of the development and use of atomic energy under an International Authority.[10] But this seemingly magnanimous plan, known to history as the Baruch Plan, contained explicit and implicit reservations which as they were revealed raised suspicions and caused resistance on the part of the Russians.

Indeed, the Baruch Plan was formulated at a time when U.S. foreign policy was moving towards a more nationalistic Realpolitik.

With the death of Franklin Roosevelt on 25 April 1945 there passed from the scene an American president who, in spite of basic nationalism and considerable apprehension caused by Stalin's takeover of Eastern Europe, had continued to support the wartime alliance with the Soviet Union and to believe in the workability of the United Nations. Even after his death his farsighted views continued to be expressed, as in this memorandum of 21 September 1945 by Henry Stimson, the Secretary of War, who had been advised by scientists James Conant and Vannevar Bush:

> Those relations may be perhaps irretrievably embittered by the way in which we approach the solution of the bomb with Russia. For if we fail to approach them now and merely continue to negotiate with them, having this weapon rather ostentatiously on our hip, their

suspicions and their distrust of our purposes and motives will increase.[11]

Before the cold war solidified, a preliminary version of a plan
for international cooperation in the atomic field had been worked
out. Robert Oppenheimer was among the participants. A later
version, which became known as the Acheson-Lilienthal Report, had
much of the original awareness of the need to accommodate the
Soviet Union. When it was presented publicly over the radio on
23 April 1946 it stated prophetically that:

> the extremely favored position with regard to atomic devices, which
> the United States enjoys at present, is *only temporary. It will not
> last.* We must use that advantage now to promote international
> security and to carry out our policy of building a lasting peace
> through international agreement.[12]

But the visionary view gradually dimmed, and each succeeding
draft of a proposed plan grew less generous and equitable. As Harry
Truman got more into his presidential stride, the outlook narrowed
considerably.[13] Taking the advice of his Secretary of State, James
Byrnes, Truman decreed that the plan should be made more workable and, against Dean Acheson's protests, the old financier Bernard
M. Baruch was chosen. He set about translating the Acheson-
Lilienthal Report into terms more workable from the American
point of view.

A major change was the addition of "condign punishment"[14]
for violators of a UN treaty that would ban atomic weapons and
control production and use of fissionable material by inspections.[15]
At the bottom of the controversy that opened up in the Commission
was the Soviet Union's deep distrust of any actions by the United
Nations, which it regarded, then with considerable justification, as
being dominated by the United States.

Thus, when Baruch presented his plan to the Commission as
"plain, peaceful, generous, (and) just," the Russians regarded it as
considerably less so. The Baruch plan contained several wise and
statesmanlike proposals, but it assigned obligations to the United
States that were extremely vague, while the obligations of the Soviet
Union were to be quite strict and harsh. Baruch's insistence on
condign punishments and the implied abolition of the veto rights for
such extremely important decisions were political elements that
wrecked the plan. Moreover, until a UN treaty could be agreed upon
and come into force the United States was to retain its monopoly on

atomic secrets and it did not promise to end production of new atomic weapons. Under these conditions, the United States was the only nation in a position to impose condign punishment. There was no doubt that the Soviet Union was the only potential violator upon whom punishments might be visited.

> The Soviet Union was undoubtedly doing all in its power to develop nuclear weapons at the moment. . . . If so, the "swift and sure punishment" provision could be interpreted in Moscow only as an attempt to turn the United Nations into an alliance to support a United States threat of war against the USSR unless it ceased its efforts, for only the United States could conceivably administer "swift and sure punishment" to the Soviet Union. This meant certain defeat of the treaty by Soviet veto.[16]

This warning lent some credence to the possibility of the United States with UN support waging preventive war against the Soviet Union before it would have had time to catch up with its nuclear-armed adversary.[17]

In all probability, the Soviet Union had already chosen the alternative course to procure the atomic bomb for itself, although Andrei Gromyko, Soviet delegate to the UN Security Council, immediately countered the Baruch plan with a proposal to destroy all nuclear weapons in existence and cease all production and use of atomic weapons categorically. The United States instead immediately demonstrated its unwillingness to sacrifice its advantage by conducting its first postwar atomic test over Bikini, on 1 July 1946—seventeen days after Baruch had presented his plan to the Commission and before its relevant technical subcommittee had met.

The political positions of both sides allow us to learn a lot from what happened in the Commission at the dawn of the atomic era about how to negotiate and how not to negotiate disarmament agreements. Besides the politically loaded issue of punishment, the controversy circled around two moot points.

The first concerned the exchange of information. Despite much doubletalk from both sides it was clear that the United States would refuse to share the know-how about the military application of nuclear-fission technologies—that is, the very secret of explosions; nor did it promise to release secrets to the envisaged International Authority. In return, Gromyko stressed the need for a total sharing of all knowledge under the planned Authority. This question of secrecy is a major issue that still befouls disarmament negotiations (Chapter VI, Sections 1–2, and Chapter X).

The second crucial point was the United States insistence on inspections, which a war-weary Russia and a paranoiacally suspicious Stalin were not willing to accept. This would remain an issue bedeviling later disarmament controversies in many fields. Much later Khrushchev, reiterating the criticism that the Baruch plan aimed "to set up an international control organ," said, "We, of course, could not agree to this."[18] In fact, Acheson had argued against using inspection as a means of opening up the Soviet Union:

> We should not . . . use the effort for international control of atomic energy to attempt to open up Russian society.[19]

A serious omission in the negotiations was that the world community did not sit down to reason things out, from the outset, using sincere analyses and a will to construct instead of obstruct. The Baruch plan and the Soviet counterproposals could have served as points of departure in the attempt to settle questions like those of international control of proliferation. Instead, several years were wasted by meandering discourses in the Commission and in the General Assembly when the Commission's reports were discussed. In September 1949 the United States announced that the Soviet Union had exploded an atomic bomb.

On 19 January 1950 the representative of the Soviet Union proposed the exclusion of "the Kuomintang group" from the negotiations and soon after walked out of both the negotiations and the Security Council on this question of Chinese representation. The UN Atomic Energy Commission was formally dissolved in January 1952, after nearly three years of inactivity.[20] But it was not until later, when the United States (1952) and the Soviet Union (1953) had exploded hydrogen bombs, that the idea of an international custody of the nuclear horror cabinet disappeared from American proposals. In 1954, again on the basis of a U.S. proposal, the International Atomic Energy Agency (IAEA) was set up by the UN General Assembly with the humbler assignment of controlling and promoting the use of atomic energy for peaceful purposes (Chapter VI, Sections 5 and 7).[21]

The opportunity to bring nuclear weapons under international control had been lost from the beginning. Knowing now the course of history in the decades to follow, we must deem this a tragedy, the enormity of which cannot be exaggerated. Serious negotiations had never been attempted. Even before the Commission's work had begun the nuclear arms race had already started and would continue unabated. The pattern of the superpowers' game of disarmament had been set: both sides would present proposals for disarmament agreement, of often wholesale dimensions, but would be careful to see to it that these would contain conditions which the opposite side could not accept. This is the way disarmament was, and is, continually torpedoed.

Using hindsight, it seems astonishing that the other UN members let this happen. The controversy in the UN Atomic Energy Commission was conducted mainly by the two major powers. Britain acted as a faithful supporter of the United States. France showed a somewhat greater independence, but did not try to change the controversy into purposeful negotiations that would have bound it. Both these countries initially had been in advance of the United States in the fundamental research that resulted in the construction of atomic bombs, and they continued to be interested in becoming nuclear powers. Therefore they did not take on the role of spokesmen for the rest of the world, which had no national interests to defend but only a common interest in prohibiting the new horror weapons.

The large majority of the world was remarkably silent. True, it all happened in the turmoil after the War, while Europe was trying to recover from devastation and disorganization and other continents were beginning to face the emerging groundswell of fighting for independence and decolonization. Membership in the United Nations was still limited. In any case, only the United States, Britain, France, and the Soviet Union commanded the expertise to make them truly cognizant of the problems under discussion. Canada should, however, be reckoned among the insiders with expert knowledge and with fewer distracting problems at home. But in the Commission, Canada remained inactive on the burning political issues.

Only in 1948, after the controversy between the superpowers had hardened beyond repair, did Canada with India try to get the Commission's work to continue. Poland and Yugoslavia spoke up on the side of the Soviet Union. Substantive, though negative, interest was shown by three other countries represented in the Commission, Brazil, El Salvador, and South Africa, "countries possessing ores containing atomic energy source materials"; they "referred to the possible difficulties arising from any effort to transfer ownership to an international agency."[22]

Looking back it seems incredible how nations all over the

world, though each was preoccupied with its own national problems and interests, could, in these first years of the world organization, accept with relative equanimity that body's inability to stop nuclear weapons. It is this dismal failure the world now has to live with.

4. *Propaganda Game with General Disarmament Plans*

Although the dramatic debate in the UN Atomic Energy Commission finally ended in total failure, it went on in the General Assembly and was stretched out to cover the whole field of "General and Complete Disarmament."

Reviewing the early speeches made and draft resolutions tabled, of such far-reaching dimensions, it is tempting to say that they were of a more declaratory or declamatory nature than serious proposals meant for implementation. They were apparently not backed by the necessary military staff work. The lack of specificity may be excused to a certain extent, as it could be presumed to be rectified at the later stage of negotiations. Spokes were also set in the wheels by the constant insistence of the Soviet Union that all weapons of mass destruction including atomic weapons be treated on the same comprehensive agenda. The United States and its allies asserted that negotiations in regard to conventional armaments be dealt with in the Security Council, while the atomic questions be dealt with solely within the Atomic Energy Commission.

Attempts to settle these over-all issues had been made by the General Assembly in December 1946, resulting in a unanimously accepted Resolution, 41 (I), which outlined an ambitious plan for the Security Council to tackle the disarmament task. It recommended

> that the Security Council give prompt consideration to formulating the practical measures, according to their priority, which are essential to provide for the general regulation and reduction of armaments and armed forces and to assure that such regulation and reduction of armaments and armed forces will be generally observed by all participants and not unilaterally by only some of the participants. The plans formulated by the Security Council shall be submitted by the Secretary General to the Members of the United Nations for consideration at a special session of the General Assembly. The treaties or conventions approved by the General Assembly shall be submitted to the signatory States for ratification in accordance with Article 26 of the Charter.[23]

The same resolution, whose basic premise, although it has so far led to nothing, should not be forgotten, also recognized

> that essential to the general regulation and reduction of armaments and armed forces is the provision of practical and effective safeguards by way of inspection and other means to protect complying States against the hazards of violations and evasions.[24]

Although this resolution centered on conventional arms, such safeguards were also to be worked out for control of atomic energy. Other matters which fell within the competence of the Atomic Energy Commission would continue to be dealt with by that body, with the Security Council to expedite consideration of its reports.

What was asked for in this resolution of early origin and high aspirations was the disarmament plan which the Security Council was already bound by charter to establish (Section 2, above). It has never tried to formulate this plan. It has never had secretariat resources comparable to those available to the study of economic and social questions. The Security Council did establish a Commission for Conventional Armaments early in 1947, with the same composition as the Council itself. In turn the Commission set up a working committee of the whole. When the reports were submitted, the debates took many turns, although they proved inconclusive. Some of the suggestions that were made relating to the control issue may be worth nothing here. In 1948 the Soviet Union introduced a draft resolution with specific proposals for the commencement of disarmament by the five permanent Members of the Security Council which underscored the need for effective control:

> . . . that, as a first step in the reduction of armaments and armed forces, the permanent members of the Security Council reduce by one-third, during one year, all land, naval, and air forces; that atomic weapons be prohibited as weapons of aggression but not of defense; and that an international control body be established within the framework of the Security Council for the supervision of and control over the implementation of the measures for the reduction of armaments and armed forces, as well as those for the prohibition of atomic weapons.[25]

When this draft resolution was rejected by the Western powers, the control issue was kept alive in the substitute French-Belgian text which was adopted:

> [The General Assembly] *trusts* that the Commission for Conventional Armaments, in carrying out its plan of work, will devote its first

attention to formulating proposals for the receipt, checking, and publication, by an international organ of control within the framework of the Security Council, of full information to be supplied by Member States with regard to their effectives and their conventional armaments.[26]

The requested records were not produced (Chapter V, Section 3). The Commission on Conventional Armaments duly submitted reports, but its proposals were sharply divided between the Western majority and a minority, consisting usually of the Soviet Union and the Ukraine. This minority upheld the demand that the regulation of armaments including atomic weapons be treated as a single indivisible question. The Commission's work soon ebbed; the Soviet Union ceased its participation after its demonstration against the "Kuomintang group" in 1950; the Security Council dissolved the Commission in 1952. The General Assembly then established a new Disarmament Commission by merging the two Commissions.

An attempt to breathe renewed life into the disarmament issue was made by Britain, France, and the United States with this proposal to establish another Disarmament Commission. The new Commission was directed to draft a treaty for the regulation, limitation, and balanced reduction of all armed forces and all armaments. The task was lofty, but the guidelines for the work were niggling. The first and indispensable condition was said to be disclosure and verification on a continuing basis, to reveal all armed forces and all armaments including atomic. International inspection to verify the adequacy and accuracy of the information was a must. The Soviet Union disagreed, and voted against the majority resolution which set up the Disarmament Commission.[27]

So restrained, the Commission could not be effective. There began a lame duck period, extending through the Korean War until 1953. Western proposals concentrating on inspection have always been an effective way to counteract grandiose disarmament schemes presented by the Soviet Union in the General Assembly— propaganda gaming from both sides. In the West, where there is always more scope for self-analysis, one of the American strategic theorists revealed this tactic:

> The United States, Britain, and France felt it wise to dramatize the Soviet Union's responsibility for the arms race by offering a disarmament plan and letting Moscow knock it down. . . . Some skeptics wondered if the provisions for inspection first and unspecified reductions later were not designed to assure Soviet rejection.[28]

What was lost, this time and again later, were the opportunities to enter into meaningful negotiations.

A more weighty effort engendering a more spectacular failure occurred in 1955, when the world and the United Nations seemed to be able to move in less stormy waters. The Grand Old Man of disarmament, Philip Noel-Baker, titles a chapter in his book *The Arms Race*, "The Moment of Hope: May 10, 1955." The political climate was unusually favorable. The Korean War had ended in 1953, and the French in 1954 were ready to quit Vietnam after their defeat in the colonial war. There was no imminent threat of a confrontation between the superpowers. Soviet attitudes had mellowed after the U.S.S.R. acquired the hyrogen bomb in August 1953, thus ending its nuclear inferiority. New leaders had taken over; Khrushchev evidently was preparing for some relaxation, as indicated by the welcome *Staatsvertrag* with Austria and his reconciliation visit to Tito in Belgrade (both these events only materialized in 1955). And Eisenhower came with a peaceful bent of mind.

The initiative for a new attempt to agree on disarmament was now taken in hand by France and Britain. In a well-studied memorandum of June 1954, submitted to the Five-Power Subcommittee of the Disarmament Commission, which held no fewer than one hundred fifty-seven meetings between May and September that year, they offered a comprehensive program "as a possible basis for compromise."[29] Stages were suggested—after divulgence of and ceilings for military expenditures came prohibition of use and manufacture of nuclear weapons (close to an old Soviet requirement)—and, proceeding step by step, the coupling of controls with progressive limitations on atom-bomb stockpiles, military manpower, and conventional arms to be down from the levels obtaining on 31 December 1953.[30]

The epic then became dramatic. First, the Soviet Union delivered the big surprise by declaring that it would accept in principle the British-French memorandum as a basis for negotiations, giving up its fundamental requirement that nuclear weapons be eliminated first. This was in September 1954 at the General Assembly, and it might be interpreted as a last-minute effort to stop West Germany from joining NATO and becoming remilitarized. The next step was taken by the United States falling in line, by offering in March 1955 several important concessions in harmony with the French-British plan of the previous year. After some exchanges of memoranda and more meetings in the Subcommittee, the Soviet Union on 10 May

1955 presented a detailed plan, the most comprehensive so far.[31] It was quite close to the Western position, postponing prohibition of the possession of nuclear weapons to the second step on the disarmament ladder. It contained a gesture of compromise, the acceptance of the installation of control posts in the territories of all states concerned, and it was closer to the Western recommendations for ceilings on armed forces.[32]

For the first time there now seemed to exist a genuine basis on which to negotiate. A give-and-take of further modifications was expected to begin in earnest. There were several indications that the interest in disarmament was sincere, and sincere for the first time on both sides of the East-West rift. Anyway the bridge, if built, might well have allowed further progress.

But political events intervened. The Russian hope of stopping West Germany's affiliation with NATO had been extinguished. This development led to the corresponding Warsaw Treaty Organization, WTO. Yet the Russians were evidently still ready to go ahead with the negotiations.

The Subcommittee had adjourned over the summer. The Geneva Summit Conference took place in July 1955. Detailed memoranda on disarmament plans came from all participants, the only new idea being Eisenhower's Open Skies proposal—that is, reciprocal rights to aerial photography. The Soviet Union replied that ground inspection seemed preferable. This could be interpreted as a positive response to Eisenhower's proposal, despite the fact that the Open Skies plan was presented to the conference without prior consultation with the Russians or even the Western allies.[33] A few years later the Open Skies concept was surprisingly undermined by its unilateral use in the so-called U-2 incident, until overtaken by satellite capabilities.

But even this auspicious episode in Geneva ended in collapse; not a nyet but a no, applied when the Subcommittee reconvened in August 1955 by the United States representative, Harold Stassen. This was put in the rhetorical form of the United States placing "a reservation on all of its pre-Geneva substantive positions."[34] The attitude of the United States had definitely hardened.

There are signs that during this period Khrushchev was in search of détente. What had happened to the political constellations of the United States? Reference to McCarthy's red-baiting campaign can hardly suffice to explain, but one thing seems certain: there was at this time never any real backing by American public opinion for the

ambitious General Disarmament plan. Eisenhower and his emissary
Harold Stassen met with strong opposition at home, in the Congress,
the Pentagon, the State Department, and the United States Atomic
Energy Commission. There was a general unwillingness to extend
the necessary trust to the Soviet Union. The governments of Britain
and France also probably found the United States' generosity on
nuclear disarmament unsettling to their plans to develop atomic
weapons. West Germany was disturbed by anything like a threat of
United States disengagement in Europe; there were rumblings within
NATO as the allies suspected the United States of getting ready to
reach agreements with the Soviet Union over their heads.

Still, it is perhaps more difficult to understand the moves in this
earlier period which led to the moment of hope of May 1955. It is
much easier to understand that 1956 was too late for disarmament,
as Britain and France were involved in the Suez War and the Soviet
Union violently repressed the Hungarian uprising.

The lame disarmament negotiations fell back into discussions
of partial approaches, none leading to any agreement. The United
States was not ready to offer more than some minor measures in
regard to nuclear weapons, for example, a cut-off of production of
weapons-grade fissionable material, and its Open Skies proposal.
The Soviet Union kept open the possibility of agreement by the two
nations to aerial inspection of at least the Arctic regions, but it
occupied itself primarily with propaganda for an agreement on
"non-use" of nuclear weapons. The attempt to "Regulation, Limitation and Balanced Reduction of All Armed Forces and All Armaments," as the UN agenda was entitled, continued until Moscow
punctured the make-believe with the launching of Sputnik in October 1957—the first orbiting of an earth satellite. The United States
was then jolted into proving that it could catch up with the Soviet
Union, and both were soon far into a new era of aiming missiles
at targets within the other's homeland.

During the first fifteen years of UN existence disarmament
negotiations had not solved any of the arms-race problems; nor had
they succeeded in an advance towards General and Complete Disarmament.

The technological breakthrough of 1957, when Moscow crossed
the space frontier and ushered in the possibilities of intercontinental
strategic warfare, marks a change second in importance only to 1945.
We are still waiting for both major enigmas to be resolved: the
acquisition of nuclear weapons by more nations, and the continual

competitive challenge of the two superpowers. The disarmament negotiations carried on in the meantime can be judged as not much more than a pastime, a game.

5.   The Test-Ban Issue—Before 1962

The holocaust of World War II did not end in peace. Its tragic climax at Hiroshima and Nagasaki, and the news of how these atom bombs killed and horrendously maimed hundreds of thousands of human beings, made the whole world panic. One might have expected that the United Nations would have been shocked into sanity. It evidently was not so. Then, people rightly should have become more startled and fearful as the nuclear arms race went into swing. It is a psychological riddle how people everywhere conditioned themselves to live with fear without mobilizing vigorous opposition. Most people still live so.

Complacency ruled during the United Nations' first decade (Chapter III, Sections 3 and 4). When after 1954 an uproar broke out in world public opinion, it centered on the testing of nuclear bombs, not on the existence as such of these horror weapons, nor on the race for more and better such weapons.

In 1954 an accident served to alert the world. When the United States tested a multimegaton thermonuclear bomb, called Bravo, at the Bikini Atoll, its radioactive fallout barely missed killing hundreds of Marshall Islanders and did score a murderous hit on some Japanese fishermen. Its harmful effects, like that previous Bikini blast of the 1 July 1946, are still marring the lives of the surviving population. This event moved many to think anew.

Scientists led the protest. Albert Schweitzer called on the scientists of the world: if they all raised their voices, he said, each one feeling impelled to tell the terrible truth, humanity would understand that the issue was grave. Bertrand Russell and Albert Einstein authored a Manifesto of 1955, which, born in the aftermath of this new awareness of the dangers of nuclear weapons, became the Charter for the Pugwash movement. Prominent scientists joined in urging governments to realize that nuclear weapons threaten the continued existence of mankind and that they must therefore find peaceful means for the settlement of all matters of dispute between them.

But it was the continual testing of nuclear weapons that became a matter of concern. In the United Nations the initiative to ban such testing was spearheaded by the Prime Minister of India, Jawaharlal Nehru, who in April 1954—barely a month after the ill-fated Bikini test—asked for a standstill agreement in respect to the tests, even if the discontinuance of nuclear-weapons production was not immediately possible.

A sustained effort during this period was kept up by the countries then taking on the label "nonaligned," first applied to the group having assembled in the Afro-Asian Conference in Colombo in 1954 and Bandung in 1955. These Afro-Asian nations, which were joined by Yugoslavia, raised the demand in the United Nations that nuclear testing be dealt with as an urgent (although partial) measure, separate from General and Complete Disarmament. But their draft resolutions failed to be adopted for several years. The Western powers, then commandeering the world organization, led a vigorous resistance, not least when countries like Austria, Japan, and Sweden joined the chorus demanding a ban or at least a moratorium on testing. The Soviet Union had in its May 1955 disarmament plan (Chapter III, Section 4) taken a leaf from the nonaligned book and included demands for the discontinuance of nuclear testing. This Soviet support functioned, however, like a kiss of death, serving to turn away American interest for several years.

> . . . that the interests of the nonaligned states in an immediate test ban came to coincide with the tactical position on disarmament priorities of the Soviet Union placed the nonaligned states, politically and diplomatically, on the defensive to the extent that test-ban initiatives appeared suspect from the American point of view as manifestations of a pro-Soviet bias or even merely of naïveté.[35]

A second unfortunate development was that the issue of disarmament and prohibition of production of nuclear weapons was de-emphasized, while the effect of nuclear tests increasing radioactivity in the atmosphere became the main issue. Almost all tests at the time were atmospheric and the radioactive fallout from them was on everybody's mind. In response, a Scientific Committee on the Effects of Atomic Radiation was set up by the General Assembly in 1955, after a resolution had been passed by acclamation, its preamble referring to "the importance of, and the widespread attention being give to, problems relating to the effects of ionizing radiation upon man and his environment." Nothing, however, was mentioned about nuclear bombs or tests, the danger of the wider issue of which India had underscored when proposing that this very item be placed on the agenda.[36]

Concern over radioactive fallout from the tests did help to broadly mobilize public opinion against nuclear bombs. From then on and well into the 1960s a veritable public uproar swept over large parts of the world. Agitation for ending tests because of possible harm through radiation was mixed with the revulsion against the bomb. In January 1958 Linus Pauling submitted to the UN Secretary General a petition signed by 1,000 scientists from forty-three countries urging an immediate international agreement to ban nuclear tests. In Japan the protest movement for obvious reasons had a particular appeal to the people. In large parts of Europe, both East and West, there was awakened a strong popular movement for banning the bomb. Protests like the Aldermaston Easter march in 1960 expressed the feelings of alert sections of the British people. Opposition against armies procuring nuclear weapons contributed in some countries to national strictures against their development, thus effecting a first phase—unilateral—of nonproliferation, although it was not successfully to change the decision by the governments in Britain and France to go ahead and become nuclear powers (Chapter VI, Section 2).

The protest movement was a definite success in Sweden. Military planners from the early 1950s advocated acquisition of nuclear weapons as part of the strong defense system which they deemed necessary to Sweden's decision to stand outside military alliances. Initially, civilian and military applications of nuclear energy did not require different approaches in research and development, and for a long time the issue did not arouse much attention. But in 1955 a convulsive debate gripped Sweden. The Cabinet found itself deeply divided; several of its members were leaders on the nay-saying side, such as the Foreign Minister Undén and the Finance Minister Wigforss. Strong mass support was organized by an indefatigable campaign of the Social-Democratic women's union, under the leadership of its then chairman, Inga Thorsson.

The first victory came in 1959 when funding for research of nuclear-weapons construction was cut off. Opposition to nuclear weapons had by then grown into a strong popular movement, as indicated by the public opinion polls. This movement embarked on a tactically successful approach: there should be a moratorium of several years before any final decision was made. In the meantime, no purchases from abroad nor any steps towards development of nuclear weapons were to be allowed. The Social-Democratic Government was not to be free to make any change in this approach until further studies and a future party conference so decided.*

While the heat was off public debate, intensive discussions took place within the deliberative parliamentary organs. The 1965 Parliamentary Defense Commission, of which I was a member, released its report in February 1968. The government thereafter submitted a bill to Parliament in which Swedish renunciation of nuclear arms was upheld both as a doctrine and as a policy.[37] The decision was taken without a voice raised against it (Chapter VI, Section 5).

Slowly, the nuclear-weapons powers seemed to be responding to the protests against the testing of nuclear weapons. In 1958 the Soviet Union, the United States, and Britain agreed to gather together a group of experts, called the Geneva Experts Conference on Nuclear Tests (Chapter III, note 7, p. 344). Scientists from East and West worked out a very detailed scheme for a world-watch system to monitor possible violations, if a test-ban agreement were achieved. Extensive negotiations followed between government representatives of the three powers concerned; staff regulations for personnel and many other details were discussed at great length. The experts also unhesitatingly recommended a powerful international control commission, to have the authority to send an inspection group to the site of any unidentified and suspected event. To the issue of a control commission, and its power, composition, and administration the Conference devoted some one hundred meetings between 1958 and 1962 (Section 6 below and Chapter VII).[38]

The beginning of a more substantial response to mounting popular pressure was a voluntary moratorium on nuclear-weapons testing observed from 1958 to 1961 by the Soviet Union, the United States, and Britain. The Soviet Union shocked the world on 30 August 1961 with its announcement that testing would be resumed, crowning the new series with a fifty-megaton blast soon thereafter in Novaya Zemlya. The United States resumed testing, first underground from 15 September 1961, and then atmospheric testing, officially declared on 2 March 1962.[39]

After the first complacent decade there had come one of consid-

---

* I was not part of this early debate, as I was, until 1 April 1961, Swedish Ambassador to India. After that date, in my new post within the Foreign Office and later through membership in the Senate and the Cabinet, I was a close cooperator with Mr. Undén (see "A Personal Note," p. xxiii).

erable activity, centered on the issue of banning nuclear tests. This
upsurge of concern was carried forward both by the general public
and, in the United Nations, by the nonaligned and other non-nuclear-
weapons powers, led by India. The number of these had increased
with the wave of decolonization in Asia and Africa. The 1959 French
announcement of testing in the Sahara drew protests against this new
manifestation of colonialism.

Joint consultations among delegations from specific regions and
other nonaligned nations caused a perceptible change in the balance
of moral opinion between the superpowers and the majority, which
consisted of lesser powers. The first trial of strength was to be on
the issue of banning nuclear-weapons tests.

6. The Crisis, 1962–1963

A promising juncture occurred in 1962 when a chain of events
seemed to place agreement on a test ban within reach. One was the
inclusion of nonaligned members in the newly formed Geneva Committee for disarmament negotiations. The other was a period of
relative détente between Kennedy and Khrushchev, which, though
severely strained by the Cuban missile crisis, thereafter remained
at a promisingly high level until Kennedy's death in 1963. The
political auguries thus seemed fairly favorable. Nevertheless, endeavors to stop nuclear testing, which after the break in the moratorium went on unabated, were unsuccessful.

The Geneva Disarmament Committee, then called ENDC,
opened a new phase in disarmament negotiations. Eight nonaligned
countries (Brazil, Burma, Ethiopia, India, Mexico, Nigeria, Sweden,
and Egypt) were included, and this group of newcomers actively
seized the initiative in the first week. In the nonaligned countries
there was a strong public resistance to nuclear bombs. In Asia it
was never forgotten, and was sometimes expressed publicly, that
the bombs had been used against a nonwhite country, the implication being that they might not have been so casually heaved upon
a European nation.

While the gaming of the superpowers on the broad issue of
prohibiting manufacture of atomic weapons went on as part of their
parallel proposals about General and Complete Disarmament
(Chapter III, Section 4), there was among the nonaligned countries
taking seats at the negotiating table a strong will to try to stop the

testing immediately. These argued that agreement on a test ban could curb the further development of nuclear weapons and their proliferation. These important goals could be obtained only if the test ban were comprehensive and included underground tests, which had then increasingly been used. The danger of augmenting radio-activity by atmospheric testing, which had been the principal issue, could not be left to stand alone.

The first action by the nonaligned countries, after the Committee convened in March 1962, was to press the Soviet Union, the United States, and Britain to change their attitudes on the test-ban issue, which had been deadlocked since the breaking of the moratorium. These nuclear powers were made accountable to the ENDC through a subcommittee whose specific mandate was to produce a draft of a convention prohibiting nuclear tests.[40]

The major move by the eight nonaligned delegations was the presentation (made within the first month) of a memorandum offering a new scheme for a radically simplified and effective system for the control on a technical, nonpolitical basis of a comprehensive ban on nuclear tests.

> On 16 April 1962, in a plenary session of the ENDC, a joint memo-randum was submitted by the eight nonaligned members of the ENDC: Brazil, Burma, Ethiopia, India, Mexico, Nigeria, Sweden, and the United Arab Republic. The joint memorandum stated that there were possibilities of establishing, by agreement, a system for continuous observation and effective control on a purely scientific and nonpolitical basis. Such a system might be based and built upon already existing national networks of observation posts and institu-tions or, if more appropriate, on certain of the existing posts desig-nated by agreement, together with new posts, if necessary, also to be established by agreement.
>
> The memorandum also referred to the possibility of setting up an international commission, consisting of a limited number of highly qualified scientists, possibly from nonaligned countries. The com-mission should be entrusted with: (a) processing all data received from the agreed system of observation posts; and (b) reporting on any nuclear explosion or "suspicious event" on the basis of thorough and objective examination of all the available data. All parties to the treaty should accept the obligation to furnish the proposed commis-sion with the facts necessary to establish the nature of any suspicious and significant event. Pursuant to this obligation, the parties to the treaty "could invite" the commission to visit their territories and/or the site of the event the nature of which was in doubt.[41]

This new approach to the control and verification of a ban, using inspection by invitation and verification by challenge (Chapter X), provided a good handle to tear to pieces the ridiculously over-elaborated structure of verification agreed on by the 1958 bipolar conference of experts. While some experts had proposed even grander schemes, the joint proposal then advocated was for an international network of control, including 160 to 170 land-based control posts, new and international, and about 10 ships. The spacing between the control posts would be about 1,700 kilometers in continental aseismic areas, thereby placing a great number in Soviet territory. About thirty specialists and auxiliary servicing personnel would be required at each post. In addition to the basic network, air sampling would be accomplished by aircraft, and special flights would be organized to collect samples of radioactive debris if suspected clouds appeared. A central international control commission would be authorized to send inspection groups to sites of suspected events. Though the costs were never formally summarized, they must have run into billions of dollars. The staff requirements alone ran into several thousand[42] scientists and technicians, who would be sitting isolated far away, watching day after day and night after night for some suspicious sign—a horrible thought for any academic!

After a brief study, I was able to demonstrate to the Committee that a substantial measure of international collaboration for control already existed among national observation posts:

> The Swedish delegation had discovered from public sources that there were 7,800 land stations making meteorological observations and 12 anchored weather ships. In addition some 3,000 ships had agreed to make observations while crossing the oceans. At that time the United States also had at least two satellites in orbit making meteorological observations. Under arrangements for the transmission of data then in effect, data gathered at one of the stations would be available throughout the world in about one hour.
>
> So far as seismology was concerned, the Swedish delegation had discovered that there were approximately 800 stations in operation and that about half of them had participated actively in the International Geophysical Year in 1957. Mrs. Myrdal mentioned the collaboration of many of the stations with the United States Coast and Geodetic Survey and stated that 65 nations throughout the world had reported the French underground nuclear test of May 1 to the Coast and Geodetic Survey within six weeks of its occurrence. . . . The combination of countries, representing East and West as well as North and South, was indeed impressive.[43]

Or, as I said in a more explicit address, those who pretend that no truly international cooperation exists are retreating from reality as much as are those who assert that international cooperation might mean espionage.[44]

> There was to my mind a most imperative reason for preferring to utilize existing observation stations rather than create a new international network. Only in this way could the scientists be saved from becoming subservient to a system which had as its exclusive task policing a nuclear test ban.[45]

The eight-nation proposal for verifying the comprehensive ban on nuclear testing was simple, submitted in all due modesty, and wholly in constructive terms. It relied not on obligatory inspections to prove violations but on the only possible sanction: abrogation of the Treaty by other nations, if suspicions about a member could not be dispelled. Behind our belief that the new scheme was workable and would deter violations of a test-ban treaty there lurked suspicions that the nuclear-weapons powers had not really aimed at a cessation of testing. Our scientific advisers found several signs of their subterfuge. The 1958 conference of experts had, for example, concluded that the methods available at the time "made it possible, within limits, to detect and identify nuclear explosions, including low-yield explosions (one to five kilotons)."[46] In the ensuing negotiations, however, all technical work seemed to be bent on increasing the difficulties rather than surmounting them. (For an evaluation of the present situation, see Chapter VII).

As our experts were able to follow the technical discussions, we knew that the delegations from nuclear-weapons powers were wary of revealing the truth. Thus, it was well known that limits for detection and identification by seismic means were being constantly lowered. Further, the United States' position that teleseismic signals were not enough but that on-site inspection was needed in addition had quite early been undermined by their own experts in a twofold way. First, other methods of monitoring test sites and activities through satellites were being developed early in the 1960s, making clandestine testing unlikely. The capabilities of these national means of verification are still not openly discussed by the superpower delegates. Second, the fallibility of on-site inspection had been proven, indicating the difficulty of actually obtaining radioactive debris as proof that a test had been made. This was recorded in the scientific literature, although the representatives of the nuclear-weapons powers in Geneva were not eager to remind anybody of it. This fallibility had been clearly demonstrated by the United States GNOME test shot in 1961. This information was not publicized as it "would greatly complicate the problem of on-site inspection of unidentified events."[47] In 1963 we learned, from hearings in the United States Congress, about the conditions for on-site inspections—that, for example, digging of just one hole to find radioactive debris as uncontestable evidence of a test explosion would be completed as much as fifty-five days after the suspected event.[48]

Although American response to the radical proposals presented in the memorandum by nonaligned nations was emphatically negative, and the Soviet response lukewarm, success was not too long in following. The memorandum did achieve a considerable weeding out of the technical overgrowth covering the test-ban issue. The requirement for a colossal network of control posts first was reduced and then eliminated. The idea of using regular and open seismological observations from nationally manned stations and the idea of a scientific commission for evaluating their findings was gradually accepted. The Western position was reexamined in Washington and amended to the effect that it would respond "as closely as technical knowledge will permit to the eight-nation proposal of April 16."[49] President Kennedy himself (1 August 1962) affirmed the assessment of the neutral memorandum: "new technical assessments . . . give promise that we can work toward an internationally supervised system of detection and verification for underground testing which will be simpler and more economical than that contemplated in previous U.S. proposals."[50]

During 1962 the Geneva Committee continued to work diligently on detailed proposals, outlining rules and provisions for a comprehensive nuclear test ban, as well as the structure and modalities of a control scheme. At the end of the year, the Cuban missile crisis brought the nuclear disarmament issue to the fore. After Kennedy had ordered the United States nuclear forces on red alert and Khrushchev, in the face of this ultimatum, had ordered the Soviet missile shipments to turn back, there followed a lively correspondence between the two leaders which soon was concentrated on what was obviously the most popular resolution, namely a ban on nuclear testing.

The discussion on the moot issue of controls focused on underground explosions. At this point, the two superpowers were negotiating the conditions for a comprehensive test ban. In the winter of 1962–1963 the margin between their positions was narrowed to the choosing of the number of annual on-site inspections a party accused of violation of the treaty would be obliged to accept. The original minimum number acceptable to the United States was eight to ten; this was later reduced to seven; the Soviet Union suddenly and surprisingly agreed to two or three, but final agreement was not reached. Instead, a new round in the series of lost opportunities was begun. The United States did not grasp that the Soviet Union had made what they considered to be a major concession; had this happened, the question of the actual number of inspections could have been relegated to the sphere of trivia.[51]

The smaller nations did not perceive the depth of seriousness signified by this refusal of the United States to accept a compromise. Nor were we aware that, as a consequence, the Soviet Union would withdraw its offer to permit obligatory inspections as part of the verification system. The Geneva Committee continued during the spring of 1963 to labor in good faith on a total test-ban proposal, attempting to devise a scheme for compromise between the superpowers' positions. Although we never subscribed to the doctrine that inspections in loco were necessary or even purposeful, we stood ready to mediate on the number of such inspections in order to facilitate what appeared to be an attainable compromise. We were encouraged from several quarters. Senator Hubert Humphrey suggested to me that we strike a middle chord, which would mean some five annual inspections.[52] The Swedish delegation then contributed the idea of setting not an annual quota for inspection but a quota to span several years. The nonaligned countries agreed and soon, in their private meetings, were homing in on a proposal for twenty to twenty-five inspections over a five-year period. Then the blow fell that there was to be no comprehensive test ban at all (see "A Personal Note," above). This approach towards inspection was at the time not disclosed in ENDC, but I unofficially presented it to a nongovernmental organization meeting in Copenhagen that spring of 1963.[53]

I must confess that we did not wake up to the somber reality even when the superpowers suddenly, in the summer of 1963, switched the test-ban negotiations from multilateral talks in Geneva to bilateral talks in Moscow. There, within weeks, a *partial* ban was produced. I only gradually experienced this fateful turn of events as a rude awakening. So hopeful were we that we euphorically hailed this agreement as of utmost importance. We took it for granted, as we were told, that it was the first step towards the discontinuance of all testing of nuclear weapons.

The preamble of the Moscow Partial Test-Ban Treaty explicitly spelled out the commitment of the parties to "seeking to achieve the discontinuance of all test explosions of nuclear weapons for all time, determined to continue negotiations to this end." This we took as solemn, honest promise which we believed would be fulfilled.

Our credulity, or plain naïveté, was such that we smaller nations did not see through to the emptiness of the promise, evidently not meant to be binding, or perceive the lack of true willingness to proceed with nuclear disarmament. Evidently we did not listen closely enough. The absence of this intention was stated in President Kennedy's own words when he gave Senate leaders and, through them, military interests "unqualified and unequivocal assurances"[54] that the underground testing would be "vigorously and diligently carried forward." [He promised explicitly] that the United States would maintain its readiness to test in the prohibited environments, and that it would "resume atmospheric testing 'forthwith' if the Soviet Union violated the Treaty," and that the Treaty in no way limited the "authority of the Commander-in-Chief to use nuclear weapons for the defense of the United States or its allies."[55]

Instead we paid attention to and believed what President Kennedy said in his television address to the American people on 26 July 1963. He did not draw attention to the continuation of testing, except obliquely, saying that the treaty "permits continued underground testing and prohibits only those tests that we ourselves can police." But in the main Kennedy held out a bright prospect:

> Nevertheless, this limited treaty will radically reduce the nuclear testing which would otherwise be conducted on both sides. . . . It reflects . . . our common recognition of the dangers in further testing. . . . This treaty can limit the nuclear arms race in ways which, on balance, will strengthen our nation's security far more than the continuation of unrestricted testing. . . . While it may be theoretically possible to demonstrate the risks inherent in any treaty . . . the far greater risks to our security are the risks of unrestricted testing, the risk of a nuclear arms race, the risk of new nuclear powers, nuclear pollution, and nuclear war.[56]

The Soviet Union had abandoned its long-standing "maximalist" position in favor of a total test ban. Perhaps its willingness to give up continued testing of military interest had all along been hollow. The Soviet Union might also have performed all the high-altitude tests needed to produce its missile defense system (ABM) (Chapter III, Section 8). Thus, the sacrifice involved in a ban on atmospheric testing was not difficult for either side. The truth has since become irrefutably clear: the Moscow Treaty probably was never intended as a measure to curtail the development of weapons. In any case, it has not had a restrictive effect on nuclear-weapons development, not even on the number and yield of tests by those nations who already possess such weapons.

If the Partial Test-Ban Treaty can hardly be considered among disarmament measures, it should be given some credit as a public-health measure, since it has reduced radioactivity in the atmosphere, even if the degree of such pollution has never been as dangerously high as sometimes reported. In retrospect, it is probable that popular concern about radioactive fallout oversold the health aspect of a ban on nuclear-weapons testing. The public was too easily satisfied with the ostrich-like solution of driving the tests underground— which had no effect on the major objective, to hamper and curtail nuclear-weapons development.

The failure to achieve a total ban on testing of nuclear weapons was ominous for all disarmament efforts. Agreement would have erected a double barrier of formidable strength: it could have ended the qualitative development of nuclear weapons, ended the competitive race between the nuclear-weapons powers, and provided an effective bar against acquisition of such weapons by other countries.

It is worth stressing that, at this early stage, nations on the threshold of developing atom bombs declared themselves in favor of self-sacrifice; several appeared as signatories to the memorandum of April 1962 (Chapter VI, Section 5).

A comprehensive ban on nuclear testing has been voted continuously in the United Nations General Assembly by great majorities of non-nuclear-weapons countries. Since 1962, the resolutions have contained as a final paragraph that "condemns all nuclear weapon testing." A specific cut-off date has been stipulated several times; the first one was "not later than 1 January 1963." But to no avail. The solemn pledge of the Partial Test-Ban Treaty, "seeking to achieve the discontinuance of all test explosions of nuclear weapons for all time," has been broken. (For further developments see Chapter VII.) In a CCD meeting on 7 August 1973, I declared on behalf of the Swedish Government "a day of mourning."[57]

7. An Ocean Treaty Truncated

The wide oceans have always been considered free for all, even when they were far from fully known. In reality this was freedom for the strongest among the seafaring, whether merchant or military. Since the beginning of the seventeenth century the principle of the freedom of the seas has been a part of international law, Grotius's formulations being commonly accepted.[58] Also respected was a general rule about the rights to territorial waters (immediately adjacent to the shores of a state), to a distance that varied during the last two hundred years between 3, 4, 6, 9, or, at most, 12 nautical miles, the latter limit claimed by Russia.

For several hundred years the world seemed content with the relative orderliness thus established, although free competition favored the stronger seafaring nations. There was no real challenge to this tradition despite the technological developments that made seagoing vessels larger, faster, and safer, and the contacts they brought about between different nations more and more complete. Technological changes sometimes evolved into military competition, the naval arms race from the turn of the century being a case in point. A dramatic spurt occurred as Britain and Germany, in a strict pattern of action-reaction, built dreadnoughts and superdreadnoughts against each other, one of the precipitating factors leading to World War I.

At about the same time, there occurred another technological change which considerably undermined the relatively equitable free sharing of the ocean space by merchant marines and military vessels. The advent of the submarine and other devices for reaching greater and greater ocean depths gave to the ocean environment a dimension of depth. The militarization of the oceans, particularly after World War I, on the surface, on the sea-bed, and in the space between has become a significantly worrisome feature of our time.

Simultaneously, civilian development of the oceans for peaceful exploitation has led to conflict. No longer a question merely of fishing rights, discoveries of mineral riches on the ocean floor have led nations to claim rights to the sea-bed.

The reach for extension of national-waters rights started with oil exploration in the United States. In 1945 President Truman issued a proclamation extending national jurisdiction over oil-bearing offshore strata. The proclamation was originally an attempt to forestall conflicts between states in the Union, but a pattern became set for international application when oil was discovered in the continental shelves which stretch along the coasts of many nations, sometimes far beyond the conventional territorial limit. These oil discoveries caused a rush to explore and exploit the riches of the sea-bed; in due course the need for international agreements was recognized.

In 1958, an attempt to establish new codes was made at a conference in Geneva. The result was four Conventions.[59] One, the Convention on the High Seas, upheld the clear distinction between the territorial sea under the sovereignty of a coastal state and the high seas, where freedom was to prevail—freedom to navigate, freedom to fish, freedom to lay cables and pipelines, and freedom to overfly. Another, the Convention of the Continental Shelf, introduced an imprecisely defined, new concept of a part of the sea-bed constituting a continental shelf. Coastal states were given some exclusive rights to such continental shelves, but only "for the purpose of exploration and exploitation of its natural resources." An incredibly elastic formula was used for the delimitation of the continental shelf. Definition was not measured in distance from land or depth from the surface, but was left open-ended by using the term "exploitable." That means that the acceptable territorial area will become greater as technologies advance giving access to greater depths. This again implies greater power to the technologically advanced nations, as they have the knowledge and equipment to reach and exploit greater depths which have often been developed by the technological advances of the military.

When the Geneva code was formulated, military implications were not considered. The focus was on the risk for discriminating in favor of coastal against land-locked states, and advanced countries against less advanced ones. An attempt to assure international peaceful use of the wealth hidden in the oceans was then made by an item introduced in 1967 in the General Assembly. It was also formulated as to exclude military interests:

> Examination of the Question of the *Reservation Exclusively for Peaceful Purposes* of the Sea-Bed and the Ocean Floor, and the Sub-Soil Thereof, Underlying the High Sea Beyond the Limits of Present National Jurisdiction, and the Use of their Resources in the Interests of Mankind [italics added].

The initiative for this had been launched by the representative of Malta, Dr. Arvid Pardo. Formally, it was a great success and resulted in a unanimous decision by the General Assembly to set up an Ad Hoc Committee to Study the Peaceful Uses of the Sea-Bed and the Ocean Floor beyond the Limits of National Jurisdiction.[60] In 1968 the Committee was expanded and now is continuing as a regular UN Sea-Bed Committee. It has organized the important new Laws of the Sea Conference, which held sessions in Caracas in 1974, Geneva in 1975, and New York in 1976. Lately the work has predominantly dealt with national extensions beyond the present continental shelf through introduction of the concept of economic zone rights foreseen to extend to two hundred miles.

An early, important fruit of this work has been acceptance by the Sea-Bed Committee and by the General Assembly of a declaration of principle establishing that the sea-bed under international waters is the common heritage of mankind, and should be reserved for peaceful purposes. No state should be allowed to claim sovereign rights over any part of it, and an international body should be established for exploration and exploitation.[61]

As the disarmament aspect concerning reservation of the sea-bed for peaceful purposes was largely lost sight of in the United Nations and is not in the purview of the Sea-Bed Committee and the UN Laws of the Sea Conference, I raised an early warning and tried to achieve a moratorium against militarization of the sea-bed:

> The military problems that may be connected with the ocean bed also appear to be in urgent need of discussion before some irreversible course of action is taken by any Power. . . .
>
> It may be hoped that especially the States having great financial and technological resources would heed an appeal that, pending the United Nations deliberations, they would refrain from taking any measures with a view to appropriating any parts of the ocean floor or resources on it, and in it, and refrain from activities on the ocean floor for military purposes. Such declarations on their part would amount to an important "gentlemen's agreement."[62]

The aspect of "nonpeaceful," i.e. military, activities was referred to the Geneva Disarmament Committee and, once there, the superpowers truncated it. First negotiations were confined to the issue of the ocean floor. Because this was important enough, nobody opposed it as a first step. Next only fixed installations on the sea-bed were to be negotiated. A new treaty finally resulted only in a rather meaningless "non-armament" measure, restricted to non-nuclearization of the ocean floor.

In the continual gaming between the superpowers the Soviet Union as usual took the maximalist approach which appealed to the majority of lesser powers and was especially supported by the nonaligned among them. The United States was recalcitrant from the beginning, but, under the pressure of international opinion, inched towards minimal disarmament. The conclusion followed a now well-known scenario: the Soviet Union, in a clearly premeditated move that was made to appear as a gracious gesture of compromise with the United States, agreed to the scuttling of its own proposal, thus freeing itself of an obvious overcommitment. So started what was to become known as the Sea-Bed Treaty.

Let us review the story a little more closely. When the Geneva Disarmament Committee met on 16 July 1968, the Soviet Union submitted a memorandum which declared

> that the progress of research and the prospects of development of the sea-bed and the ocean floor made it possible to give timely expression to a regime to ensure "the exclusively peaceful use of the sea-bed beyond territorial waters," in particular to prohibit the establishment of fixed military installations in that area; and it proposed that the ENDC start negotiations on this question.[63]

This stress on *fixed* military installations was an obvious stratagem in the well-known game of distracting attention from the major problem of the arms race of the seas which concerns, of course, mobile rather than fixed weapon capabilities. The United States carried this a considerable step further. On the same date the President of the United States called for negotiations on an agreement "which would prohibit the use of the new environment for the emplacement of weapons of mass destruction."[64]

And so it was to be. On 18 March 1969, the Soviet Union had submitted a draft treaty providing for complete demilitarization of the sea-bed beyond a coastal zone of twelve miles. At about the same time the United States wanted to assure "that the sea-bed, man's latest frontier, remains free from the nuclear arms race," seemingly oblivious of the fact that the major share of that arms race takes place above the sea-bed. On 7 October 1969, the Soviet draft was withdrawn and a compromise was reached on the basis of the United States' suggestion only to denuclearize. After years of strenuous efforts to widen its import by representatives of lesser powers, a Sea-Bed Treaty was approved by the General Assembly in December 1970[65] and entered into force 18 May 1972. Its scope, as indicated by its full name, "Treaty on the Prohibition of the Emplacement of Nuclear Weapons and other Weapons of Mass Destruction on the Sea-Bed and the Ocean Floor and in the Subsoil

Thereof" is very limited indeed. What the Sea-Bed Treaty is supposed to prevent has never been of military interest. Most nations
have no nuclear weapons to hide, and of those five who have such
weapons only three have signed the Treaty, and the last thing they
would do with them would be to emplant them in the ocean floor.
As a SIPRI publication explains:

> The military significance of the Sea-Bed Treaty must be regarded as
> very low. In its present form, the treaty essentially only bans fixed
> nuclear missile installations from the sea-bed. While such weapons
> systems were once under consideration, for instance in the United
> States, any plans were soon abandoned for good military, technical,
> and economic reasons *before* the sea-bed became a disarmament
> issue. From a military point of view the deployment of nuclear
> missiles on board mobile carriers, e.g., ballistic missile submarines,
> is much preferable in order to use to the full the ocean's advantages
> for protection—essential to any credible second-strike force.[66]

SIPRI also draws on information from hearings before an American Senate Subcommittee headed by Senator Claiborne Pell, who
has devoted much study and legislative labor to ocean matters:

> The point may be illustrated by a quote from a 1969 statement by a
> former Assistant Secretary of the United States Navy: [in a reply to
> Senator Pell] Dr. Morse: One has to remember that the great ad-
> vantage of deploying a weapons system at sea is mobility, and that
> if one bands only fixed nuclear weapons systems at sea he may well
> be banning something that doesn't have any value anyway. Consider
> the Polaris, if the Polaris fleet were anchored at fixed points it cer-
> tainly would not represent the threat that it does today.[67]

Here the brief story on the nonarmament Sea-Bed Treaty may
end. I have examined it more closely elsewhere.[68]

It is seldom explicitly admitted that the Sea-Bed Treaty does not
inhibit military activities of real interest, that it does not limit installations on the ocean floor for military purposes other than the
embedding of weapons of mass destruction. It does not prohibit the
installation of facilities which service crawling or free-swimming
military systems, even those with nuclear weapons, nor the temporary
stationing of nuclear missile submarines on the ocean floor. Thus, the
treaty does not stop the nuclear arms race under international waters.
Still less does it place any obstacle in the way of that arms race of
wider import based on mobile carriers: submarines with ballistic missiles; vast and sophisticated antisubmarine warfare systems; manned

and unmanned underwater stations; moored platforms for bunkering, refueling, repairing, signaling, etc. It does not limit the deployment of hordes of detection devices on the sea-bed. There is no international prohibition against the ocean space being used as the main or sole abode for deployment of strategic nuclear weapons systems, just as there are no limiting rules about fleets cruising the surface of the seas. A nonstop arms race is going on in the underwater environment with stupendous new developments under way, particularly for tracking enemy submarines, for positioning one's own, and for targeting of both military and civilian objects and installations (Chapter IV, Section 5).[69]

None of these military activities on or in the oceans is the subject of multinational negotiations. There is rarely mention of them in the Geneva Disarmament Committee or the General Assembly. Under strong pressure from nonaligned members an Article V was introduced into the Sea-Bed Treaty which states:

> the Parties to this Treaty undertake to continue negotiations in good faith concerning further measures in the field of disarmament for the prevention of the arms race on the sea-bed, the ocean floor, and the subsoil thereof.

Hope is faint that it will be more than a lip-service article, that it will lead to any vigorous action at the obligatory review conference of May 1977.[70] One step forward could be the international registration of trade and transfers of surveillance devices. This would allow the tracing of client countries and, coupled with the registration of trade in conventional arms which has been suggested, would be a preparation for future prohibitions (Chapter V, Section 3).

Two interconnected aspects ought to worry the world community: encroachment and verification. The development and deployment of communication and detection devices means that the oceans are becoming more and more thoroughly bugged. Some of the devices such as hydrophones and sonars for acoustic surveillance are mobile, but some are fixed. There may be hundreds or thousands of fixed sonar systems in the oceans, bottom-mounted, upward-listening, interconnected with each other and transmitting information to airborne or satellite-borne receivers. The outlook for the future is described in relation to a particularly ambitious new scheme by SIPRI: "this system is intended as part of the United States effort to achieve total surveillance of the oceans. . . ."[71]

There is no reason to believe that oceanic activities are carried on by only one of the two superpowers, although the information available is lopsided. What is threatened is encroachment or usurpation of parts of the ocean floor by some nations. These areas may be small in size—for example, just the mooring line for a buoy—but from the point of view of principle any fixed installations are antagonistic to, or, I dare say, a violation of, the international decision to keep the ocean floor as the heritage of mankind, available for peaceful purposes only.

These encroachments should also be viewed in relation to what might happen if economic exploitation of the ocean floor, say for oil or mineral extraction, were leased or licensed to national interests. What if they would demand the right to establish a security area as is already done for similar installations on the continental shelves? What kind of military apparatus might such an area contain? Perhaps nuclear weapons might be concealed? In 1971 I warned:

> There is an inherent contradiction and incompatibility in legislating internationally to use the sea-bed and ocean floor for exclusively peaceful purposes and at the same time allowing nations to pursue clandestine military activities of any kind in that area. This idea is here expressed with a pointer to the future: *military and national interests must cede the primacy to civilian and international ones.*[72]

Two politically important questions are left dormant. First, how can international verification in keeping with Article III of the Sea-Bed Treaty be implemented? This article stipulates the "right to verify by observation the activities of other States Parties to the Treaty." Right of inspection of any installations is thus laid down in law.

Second, there is the question of the twelve-mile limit which is exempt from external inspection and from the prohibition against fixed installations of nuclear weapons. Beyond the twelve-mile zone the prohibition rules against the emplanting in the sea-bed of nuclear and other mass destruction weapons and also specifically prohibits "facilities for launching, storing, and testing such weapons." Permission to protect enclaves outside the twelve-mile limit, however minute in size or peaceful in purpose they may be, are not allowed by the Sea-Bed Treaty. There is an inherent incompatibility between the Sea-Bed Treaty, with its provision of this twelve-mile limit for nonverified military activities and the same twelve-mile limit expected to be agreed upon in future as the generally accepted span of territorial water rights, as against present planning for economic exploitation that might prove to be paramilitary encompassing such zones as the continental shelves or the economic zones discussed above, stretching probably to two hundred miles. There the right to international verification must be vindicated.

As the need for verification is a necessary basis for international security, the foregoing should be a reminder of how much of an unfinished agenda the disarmers face in regard to the demilitarization of the oceans. The Sea-Bed Treaty in truth is a frustrated, partial attempt, another lost opportunity.

8. SALT—Institutionalization of the Nuclear Arms Race

The latest of the lost opportunities I want to record in this review of disarmament history are the bilateral negotiations under détente. These superpower negotiations are known as SALT (Strategic Arms Limitation Talks). Strategic weapons in modern parlance are weapons with which the superpowers can serve direct hits on each other's homelands. The SALT negotiations have concentrated on these strategic-weapons systems, especially the offensive types, but questions are not asked about possession, reduction, or elimination; rather there is only a haggling over marginal differences in their continued increase.

The SALT negotiations represent a belated attempt, at least ten years overdue, to broach the problems engendered by the development of intercontinental ballistic missiles. These negotiations ought to have come as a political follow-up to the technological breakthrough of the late 1950s. At that time the United States began intensive development of land-based, long-range and medium-range missiles with nuclear warheads and submarine-based missiles, and the Soviet Union gave surprise notice of its own considerable advance along the same course by launching the first intercontinental ballistic missile in August 1957 and, in October, Sputnik.

These arms-limitation negotiations, originally to begin after the Johnson-Kosygin summer meeting in 1967, revealed the superpowers' desire to turn the negotiations onto a bilateral track. Some signs had already pointed in this direction. When the superpowers had removed the negotiations for the test ban from Geneva to Moscow they took the responsibility for alone framing an international although partial treaty and they asked no other country but Britain to be present. When the superpowers began the SALT discussions, they did not invite even Britain or any other of their respective military allies.

This bilateral staging of the SALT negotiations corresponds to the actual power situation in the world. Still, as the destinies of others are so much dependent on their decisions, we are in our full right to express our opinions and raise our voices. This is being done in international forums, in the General Assembly and the Geneva Disarmament Committee. The SALT negotiations are also critically scrutinized by experts and independent research bodies. This is done in SIPRI publications on a continuing basis, which I have used to a large extent to fill in the technical background for the following comments.[73]

The first SALT agreements were ready to be signed in May 1972 at a summit ceremony in Moscow, when then President Richard Nixon visited the Soviet General Secretary of the Communist Party, Leonid Brezhnev. The climate of détente was reflected positively in some simultaneous agreements, which introduced the principle of cooperation to a number of scientific and technical issues in the fields of medicine and public health as well as in the exploration and use of space, protection of the environment, prevention of incidents on and over the sea, etc. The agreements referring specifically to arms limitation were basically two, a "Treaty Between the United States of America and the Union of Soviet Socialist Republics on the Limitation of Antiballistic Missile Systems," and an "Interim Agreement between the United States of America and the Union of Soviet Socialist Republics on Certain Measures With Respect to the Limitation of Strategic Offensive Arms," the latter accompanied by a protocol specifying details.

The one definitive agreement, the ABM-treaty, concerned the antiballistic missile defense systems. Its conclusion is related to the fact that there is no effective defense possible against offensive nuclear weapons, not even for the nuclear-weapons powers. In the first round of talks in 1972, afterwards called SALT I, it was agreed that each side should limit ABM installations to two sites: one ABM system was for defense of each nation's capital and one was to defend a launching area for intercontinental ballistic missiles (ICBM); one site to protect people and one to protect retaliatory nuclear forces. Each of these two complexes was permitted 100 individual launchers and 100 interceptor missiles. This was not restriction but quantitative expansion. At the time of signing the United States had no ABM system. It was beginning to build two sites. The Soviet Union had one ABM system functioning, located near Moscow, deploying sixty-four launchers. At a new Nixon–Brezhnev summit meeting in June 1974 agreement was reached to reduce the ABM installations to one site for each side, the Soviet Union choosing to retain the Moscow site and the United States an ICBM site.

The systems were to be land-based, and the testing and further developing of sea-, air-, or space-based or mobile ABM systems was prohibited as were auxiliary lines of research and development. These limitations on the further development of defensive missile systems are not disarmament but nonarmament measures and they represent the only elements of the SALT agreements which meaningfully attempt to inhibit the competitive arms race.[74]

The second SALT I decision resulted in a five-year Interim Agreement covering 1972–1977 on measures to limit the increase of offensive strategic arms. These were launchers capable of firing missiles to reach the other superpowers, land-based intercontinental ballistic missile (ICBM) launchers, and ballistic missile launchers on submarines (SLBM). No additional fixed land-based ICBM launchers, submarine launchers, or ballistic missile submarines were to be constructed beyond those in production at the time of signing. Exact numbers of these items in each category belonging to each side were not given but were subject to understanding. The quantitative ceilings discussed were so high that there was no sacrifice of either operational or construction capabilities.

On the contrary, considerable increases of nuclear arms were allowed. Future developments permitting *qualitative* improvements of both missiles and warheads were left open. There was also a quantitative loophole in this SALT I agreement. The *number of warheads* fitted to the missiles was not limited. The right to equip various types of missiles with Multiple Reentry Vehicles, either MIRV (independently targetable on several targets) or MRV (detonating over the same target area), pushed multiplication of the number of nuclear warheads a single missile can deliver. This has made the numerical limitations on the missiles themselves almost irrelevant. Similarly, the agreement allows replacements and modernization of existing weaponry. The mass media have abounded with news about the competition of MRVs and MIRVs, missile-launching systems like the submarine Trident, and new generations of improved bombers such as the American B-1 and its Soviet counterparts.[75]

Hopes for real progress rose when negotiations continued into SALT II for a permanent agreement by 1977. Although there have been numerous meetings in Geneva between delegations from the two powers and several summit meetings, no formal agreements have been readied for ratification. There is no need to describe in detail the meanderings. The net result so far is a reaffirmation that for the five-year Interim Agreement of SALT I, 1972, a permanent ten-year agreement on offensive strategic arms will be substituted. The world was informed after the meeting of President Gerald Ford and General Secretary Leonid Brezhnev in Vladivostok, November 1974:

> They reaffirmed the great significance that both the United States and the U.S.S.R. attach to the limitation of strategic offensive arms. They are convinced that a long-term agreement on this question would be a significant contribution to improving relations between the U.S. and the U.S.S.R. to reducing the danger of war and to enhancing world peace. Having noted the value of previous agreements on this question, including the interim agreement of May 26, 1972, they reaffirm the intention to conclude a new agreement on the limitation of strategic offensive arms, to last through 1985.

To this was added a promise that

> the new agreement will include a provision for further negotiations beginning no later than 1980–1981 on the question of further limitations and possible reductions of strategic arms in the period after 1985.[76]

As yet, this agreement has not been reached. The understanding to agree on numbers provides that each side would be allowed a ceiling of 2,400 strategic nuclear delivery vehicles, including intercontinental ballistic missiles, submarine-based ballistic missiles, and strategic bombers. Included in this number are 1,320 missiles equipped with multiple warheads. This last stipulation would permit the quantity of nuclear warheads in 1985 to be at least double that of 1974. SIPRI has calculated that by 1985 the United States could have between 18,600 and 19,980 strategic nuclear warheads and the Soviet Union 9,420 to 11,300, the difference being dependent on MIRVs or MRVs.[77]

By no stretch of the imagination can this be called arms limitation. Instead it is a mutually agreed continuation of the arms race, regulated and institutionalized. The competition for quality of nuclear weapons remains totally unregulated, leaving open the avenue

for gaming without end. After SALT I, my judgment was expressed
to the Geneva Disarmament Committee:

> Logically, the next step to follow the limitation of the defensive super
> system of ABM ought to be a freeze on the *qualitative* development
> of *offensive* weapons. A cessation of nuclear-weapons tests then be-
> comes an imminent urgency.[78]

SIPRI states:

> A major weakness of both the SALT I agreement and the proposed
> SALT II agreement from the disarmament point of view is the total
> lack of any prohibition on qualitative improvements in nuclear
> weapons. The nuclear arms race has, in any case, already moved
> from a race for quantity to a race for quality.[79]

All categories of tactical nuclear weapons remain totally outside
regulation. These number in the tens of thousands around the world.
All delivery vehicles, aircraft, missiles, etc. which can be used for
both nuclear and conventional warheads are regulation free; such
double-purpose weapons can be both produced and exported. If
the two superpowers now feel their homelands more secure thanks
to the SALT agreements, they are entering upon a sense of security
nobody else can share (Chapter II, Sections 6 and 8).

There is one gleam of satisfaction resulting from the SALT
negotiations: both sides have been more willing than before to have
the actual numbers of their weapons made public. This elimination
of secretiveness is confirmed by their willingness to forgo obtrusive
control requirements, both now obviously relying on national means
of verification, which in technological terms means satellites.

But the superpowers have become confined in a cage of their
own making. The very fact that their nuclear arms race has been institutionalized in SALT agreements must mean that their freedom of
action for any disarming is reduced. They will be even more
shackled than before by domestic interests, military, industrial, and
political, which construe continued arms build-up to match the enemy
as an assured right. It will be difficult for critics and opponents to
go against what has been firmly institutionalized by bilateral contracts. It will be even harder to repeat the victory which was scored
on the ABM issue. The power of the arms-control community to
oppose the arms race has been undermined. (For further developments as to both SALT negotiations and nuclear strategies see
Chapter IV, Sections 2 and 5.)

The international prospects seem forbidding. Some members of the United Nations, led by the nonaligned nations, have repeatedly issued warnings since 1968. Requests for a moratorium on further development of missiles for the duration of the SALT negotiations, although supported by a substantial majority, have gone unheeded, as I have complained publicly.[80] (See Chapter IV, Section 4.)

As far as the count is final, SALT so far merits only the net verdict of being one more of the lost opportunities to limit the senseless arms race.

9. Where Are We Heading?

The United Nations was created thirty years ago. Its proud promise "to free coming generations from the scourge of war" is getting frailer and frailer, as violence mounts and wars rampage. And its bold goal of a disarmed world seems to recede farther and farther into a misty future. The efforts to negotiate General and Complete Disarmament have failed. Results of all negotiations have fallen far short of the goal of disarmament. Dealing with issues minor in comparison with the threatening ones, they have been insufficient in coverage, weak and ineffective in implementation, and generally discriminatory against the lesser powers. I have characterized them as lost opportunities, the history of which is one of uncoordinated single applications which have been further impeded by stubbornness.

But the list of opportunities so far rendered is not complete. Several more will have to be noted in subsequent chapters where the major issues are analyzed at somewhat greater length. A comprehensive list of agreements, including some not dwelled upon here, like the Antarctic Treaty of 1959 and the Outer Space Treaty of 1962, are recorded in reference works such as SIPRIs.[81] Several bilateral agreements, not in essence part and parcel of a disarmament agenda but called U.S.–U.S.S.R. "arms control" measures, should also be duly recorded.[82]

What has gone wrong? What is lacking is not machinery, but the will to use it for progress in the direction of disarmament. Thus, at the bilateral level the machinery set up and stabilized for bipolar SALT negotiations could be used for much more vigorous moves. There is also some machinery available for European agreements. Not much has been or will be said in this book about the European Security Conference held in 1975, as it yielded political but not disarmament results.[83] Not much more can be told about the negotiations going on in Vienna since 30 October 1973 on Mutual Reductions of Forces and Armaments and Associated Measures in Central Europe (usually referred to as MBFR, but the term balance was later dropped).[84] It will be worthwhile to watch these negotiations as they continue, for questions of nuclear weapons in Europe will be broached in the Vienna talks, if not in SALT (Chapter II, Section 6).

It will be interesting particularly to see if the smaller European states within the two alliances can make their voices heard; there is in principle nothing to hinder them from conferring with each other in order to exploit and expand the margin of maneuverability. The European non-nuclear-weapons states have themselves considerably muted their voices in the negotiations by the long haggling over who would have the right to participate and the resultant division of the participants in tiers of differing status. At the center are the states with troops in Central Europe, Canada, Britain, the United States, and the Soviet Union together with seven of the Central European countries. Another tier comprises flank countries: Bulgaria, Denmark, Greece, Hungary, Italy, Norway, Rumania, and Turkey. The wide composition should, however, give scope for European countries to talk to each other above and beyond the boundaries set by their blocs.

That the UN machinery for disarmament negotiations needs overhauling has been recognized by a resolution voted in the General Assembly: an Ad Hoc Committee on the Review of the Role of the United Nations in the Field of Disarmament has been set up.[85] The infrastructure of the United Nations concerned with disarmament is evidently to be examined (Chapter XI, Section 3).

There has been no will to use this machinery to full avail. There does not even exist an agenda for continued disarmament negotiations. When the superpower drafts of 1962 for General and Complete Disarmament had to be seen as defunct, a rescuing operation was attempted by some UN members to establish at least an agreed program for continued negotiations. The occasion was grasped when the UN Secretary-General launched the idea of the 1970s as a Disarmament Decade. He had emphasized:

> A concerted and concentrated effort during this Disarmament Decade to limit and reduce nuclear and other weapons of mass destruction, to reduce conventional weapons and to deal with all the related problems of disarmament and security, could produce concrete, measurable progress towards general and complete disarmament by the end of the decade of the seventies.[86]

The idea of a timetable had to be dropped because of super-power opposition, but a resolution was passed approving the idea in general terms.[87] The next year Mexico, Sweden, and Yugoslavia presented a draft of a systematic program for future disarmament efforts, as the Geneva Disarmament Committee's contribution to the twenty-fifth anniversary of the United Nations. However, it was not formally submitted, but instead annexed to the Committee's report and later to the corresponding resolution of the General Assembly.[88]

Experience has been gathered over the years and there is not much illusion left to the lesser powers. This was the blunt answer I gave when a UNESCO periodical asked me, "Who is at fault? Are the two nuclear superpowers really serious about nuclear disarmament?"

> Let me immediately reveal how the experiences of a decade of disarmament efforts have gradually led me and many others participating in these efforts to some terrifying conclusions: that we have accomplished no real disarmament, that we can see hardly any tangible results of our work, and that the underlying major cause must be that the superpowers have not seriously tried to achieve disarmament.

And the editor summarizes:

> She discerns little genuine disarmament progress over the years, despite certain limited treaties, primarily because the two superpowers have not really worked for this, but rather to achieve a balance between themselves.[89]

There the matter rests.

Those who have power have no will to disarm. At least they constantly demonstrate this by negative response to each and all of the proposals that would entail genuine arms limitation.

The history of disarmament should have been a series of positive, purposeful, effective steps towards the goal which is acclaimed by everybody. We are still waiting for a first decisive, or even a serious, step to be taken.

PART TWO

an activated agenda for disarmament

Reversing the Arms Race

1. Towards a Strategy for New Attempts

Against the background of the long history of defeat, it sometimes looks as if the task to reach effective agreements on important disarmament measures were impossible, that mankind is doomed to continue an ever intensified arms race and a relentless militarization of the world. If this is to be our fate, it would be equally impossible to trust that the political balance between the superpowers will secure peace. This balance is being undermined by technological advances which keep open the possibilities of surprising breakthroughs in new weapons systems (Chapter III, Section 8), decreasing warning time and weakening the barriers against all kinds of mistakes and misinterpretations (Chapter I, Section 2). Security is further eroded by the probable future spread of nuclear weaponry to more countries (Chapter VI). The danger of a major cataclysm is real. Bertrand Russell, towards the end of his life, reckoned the possibility of human survival on earth till the next century to be only 50 percent.[1]

I decline to accept a defeatist view. To be realistic it is necessary to recognize the facts. The arms race is irrational, and we are not permitted to let unreason stand unchallenged. Hope of reversing the trend must be built by untiring efforts to educate peoples and governments to recognize their true interests. This means effectively attacking the forces within the countries that are propelling the arms race within the arms race (Chapter I, Section 4). There are mistaken but widely spread ideas about the importance of production

113

and modernization of armaments for industrialization and employment. There is ambition in the military sector to dispose of bigger defense budgets and competition between the armed services for a share in new investments. The technological imperative to improve the performance characteristics of all military devices is kept alive by scientists and the technical cadres. Additionally, the very idea of balancing and the thoughtless acceptance of the thesis that every advance in military strength by "the other side" is reason for matching it is irrational (Chapter IV, Section 3).

Many of the above factors are expressions of the competitive spirit prevailing in our societies. All converge in what Dwight D. Eisenhower in his last presidential message to the American nation called the military-industrial complex, to which must now be added "academic." These forces are represented in legislative assemblies. They are particularly strong and visible in the United States, but they operate in all countries, including the Soviet Union.

We must oppose the arms race on the grounds of morality. Each new generation of arms becomes more inhumane. Every new war tends to become more cruel. For centuries rules about how warfare is to be conducted have been accepted as international law, but these rules are now disregarded in the most flagrant way. They must be expanded, modernized, and respected. They must guide our efforts to restrain the use and production of and trade in cruel weapons (Chapters V and VIII).

This book is an attempt to educate politicians, experts, opinion-makers, and ordinary people to use common sense and follow moral values. It is part of Western cultural heritage that basically we believe that our moral values are in accord with reason. If we are not going to succumb to cynical defeatism, we must hold on to the precepts of rationality and morality.

In attempting here to formulate a rational and ethical strategy for disarmament, I conclude from experience that we have regrettably to give up the holistic approach of General and Complete Disarmament by means of an orderly series of steps for implementation and a preset timetable. That approach has a long history in both the League of Nations and the United Nations (Chapter III, Sections 1 and 4). It has always ended in failure.

The sober conclusion of those who stand for the ideal of disarmament is that in the present world situation what we must aim at is a strategy for limitation and reduction of specific arms and other preparations for war as part of a comprehensive program.

Attempts hitherto made to agree on specified arms-limitation measures, however, have been far too piecemeal. No treaties to abstain from production and use of weapons have been concluded, only marginal steps have been taken, and even these are not effective (Chapter III, Sections 6–9). On the prime issues, such as the nuclear arms race between the superpowers, the negotiations up to now have been futile.

A strategy that is both realistic and courageous must be found to limit and reduce arms and eliminate some of them immediately. A new comprehensive grasp of the disarmament problems is necessary. While abandoning the attempt to get a general agreement in one stroke, we must seek a solution that combines specific measures into an integrated whole. These may take the form of international legislation, of multi- or bilateral agreements, or of unilateral moves forward on the road to the acknowledged goal.

2.   A Gross Miscalculation

The despondency over mankind's present drift towards disaster is exacerbated by senseless overkill capacity, more arms having already been produced and deployed than could ever be used. This is particularly true of nuclear weapons, especially strategic ones in the arsenals of the superpowers; tactical weapons, intended for battlefield use, deserve special attention from a political point of view with a focus on specific regions (Chapter II, Sections 4–6).

For this evil the superpowers are almost entirely responsible. Each has accumulated and is continuing to accumulate stockpiles of atomic weapons which have long since been much more than enough to destroy the other power and the whole world many times over. By the end of the ten-year term of SALT, each will be capable of destroying the other, not fifty times over as at present, but a hundred times over.[2] Why?

Realistically, the problem is how much weaponry is needed for a strategy of deterrence. This is the only relevant question. Continuing to match each other's destructive capacity is irrelevant. Only as a second, separate exercise (if deterrence should fail) should what is needed for war-fighting be considered, and then only in terms of various specific scenarios, which would clearly expose the end result of such a war.

Of course, deterrence, the price that an adversary must be expected to pay in order to risk a military offensive, is a concept used

in all strategic reasoning. However, with nuclear weapons, no customary mathematical exercises relating to conventional matériel
hold. The number of troops, tanks, aircraft, and barges that may be
sacrificed and the reserves of similar defense forces to withstand a
counterattack are irrelevant. With nuclear weapons on both sides, the
question is raised of the would-be attacker's willingness to lay his
own territory and people open to an instant nuclear assault.

The price is so high that a military adventure should be unthinkable. In reality the situation between the two superpowers is
this: neither the United States nor the Soviet Union can possibly
deliberately want to use nuclear bombs against each other, knowing
that they would immediately draw the holocaust onto themselves.
This is the assumed purpose of the terror balance. When we and they
know that a fraction of their nuclear fire-strength is enough to deter
the other side from ever courting such a fate, the intrinsic irrationality of the superpowers' holding and augmenting their giant nuclear
armories is immediately evident.

Militarily, the size of nuclear forces needed for deterrence are
spoken of as second-strike capabilities. In simpler words, what
counts is how much is needed for retaliation. The superpowers must
calculate how much they would have left after having suffered a
nuclear attack, and how much they estimate they would need for retaliating with unacceptable damage on the adversary.

It should be quite clear that the size of the second-strike capability cannot be measured in the number of warheads and delivery
vehicles they have now, but must refer to the chances of having
enough operable which could be fired from an invulnerable position.
Thus the salient military concern must be to harden the silos for land-
based missiles, or to make them mobile, or, as the most effective
means so far available to preserve invulnerability, to give preference
to submarine-based ballistic missiles. Without entering here into a
discussion of how much might be left for a second strike, it is enough
to know that both superpowers are confident of having such securely
retained capabilities far beyond what is enough for retaliating with
an insupportable blow. As the threat of such a blow is most effective
when directed against centers with civilian populations, the second-
strike force is usually described as a countercity force. And the force
available for that deterrent is surely much more than sufficient on
both sides. But the relevant answer as to how much capacity retained
is enough for deterrence cannot be, and need not be, given in quantitative terms. The calculation becomes psychological-political more

than military. Is it or is it not enough deterrence for each of the superpowers already to run the risk of being hit by a one-megaton nuclear bomb? Or do they see any war aims for an offensive that could justify several of their own big cities being sacrificed when the retaliatory blow comes? Even their entire nation devastated?

A succinct answer, indicating that the low figure of one bomb is probably enough for a credible deterrent, was given in a statement by McGeorge Bundy, former Special Assistant to the President for National Security Affairs, made shortly after leaving his post:

> In the real world of real political leaders—whether here or in the Soviet Union—a decision that would bring even one hydrogen bomb on one city of one's own country would be recognized in advance as a catastrophic blunder; ten bombs on ten cities would be a disaster beyond history; and a hundred bombs on a hundred cities are unthinkable.

The above statement was quoted by Herbert York, who has held many prominent posts, among them the job of Director of Defense Research and Engineering in the Department of Defense under Presidents Eisenhower and Kennedy. He added:

> My personal view is that Bundy is right; that from one to ten are enough whenever the course of the events is being rationally determined.[3]

The reservation about a decision made on rational grounds is important. Of course, there can be no calculus for lunatic decisions.

In Chapter II, Section 2, I presented quotations from top United States experts on the facts of existing overkill capacities of both superpowers. I stressed the increasing insecurity brought about by continued expansion of nuclear armories and the wanton devastation posed by possible use. Besides highlighting the irrationality of military thinking, the quotations indicated sufficient nuclear strength for deterrence, including a margin for indeterminate military and political considerations. Some fifteen years ago, when the debate raged over the so-called missile gap, General Maxwell Taylor is reported to have advised President Kennedy that a deterrent of 100 to 200 ballistic missiles on each side would be a sufficient umbrella for security.[4]

It was at this juncture in history, when Sputnik shocked the United States into realizing that ballistic missiles from one superpower could reach the other, that attempts began to measure what the "terror balance" would need. A consensus developed among U.S.

experts for a somewhat higher estimate. The strategic goal was then formulated as Mutual Assured Destruction (MAD) of the enemy. The present Director of the United States Arms Control and Disarmament Agency (ACDA), Dr. Fred Iklé, illustrates what such a strategy of coldblooded mass killing involves, at the same time as he criticizes the rationality of decision-makers, and their lack of moral hesitation before a strategy of mutual genocide:

> the threatened "retaliation" must be the killing of a major fraction of the Soviet population, moreover, the same ability to kill our population must be guaranteed the Soviet government.[5]

The calculations for MAD then envisaged the capacity to deliver approximately 400 one-megaton warheads as an adequate deterrent. The basis of this estimate is explained by York:

> In order to quantify the question, it was assumed that "assured destruction" meant guaranteeing the deaths of twenty-five percent of the population and the destruction of a majority of its industrial capacity. From that, it was calculated that as many as 400 bombs on target might be needed.[6]

In the light of such estimates, how can it be explained that the numerical limits foreseen in the Vladivostok agreement would allow each of the superpowers to increase its arsenal up to 2,400 strategic missiles and bombers, multiplying the warheads into tens of thousands, all together representing more than a million Hiroshimas? (Chapter III, Section 8.)

What has happened is best studied in the United States. There the deterrence concept has been lost sight of and military planning, with the aid of the balance concept, has gone wildly astray. It is asserted that the higher figures are needed to safeguard the "balance of terror." *But this is a miscalculation.*

To clear up the morass partly of faulty thinking and partly of opportunistic misinterpretations, a critical analysis of concepts and terms is needed.

First, the very idea that the terror must be balanced leads to the erroneous conclusion that the arms level must be equal and increase at the same rate. In a situation where both sides already have far above "enough" of terror capacity, marginal increments become meaningless. *The military capabilities do not need to be "equal" or "balanced" when the limits for effective threats of terror devastation are long since overreached.*

Second, the only militarily important fact is how strong capabilities would remain for retaliation in a second strike, i.e., after having suffered a hypothetical first strike by the enemy. This implies that the crucial strength is determined by how many nuclear arms are invulnerable and how effective they will be, not how many nuclear warheads and delivery vehicles can be marked up in the inventory for each side.

Third, in the real world the only important fact, and that is what ought to guide the procurement of nuclear arms, is *how much would be enough*. This can be estimated only when all relevant political and psychological factors are taken into consideration for each country and for each epoch.

The miscalculations simply derive from the planners taking a giant jump between the two terms of the "terror balance," from the threat of terror needed for deterrence to the simple arithmetic of wanting always to have "equally much" to balance the other side.

In short, what is occurring in strategic planning is a conjurer's trick, a shift from estimates of deterrence for a second strike to estimates of war-fighting forces that would allow for a first strike. How this takes place was illustrated by Paul Doty, Director of a Program on Science and International Affairs at Harvard and former Chairman of the Federation of American Scientists, when he recently testified to a Senate committee. He first analyzed a reasonable deterrent, adding considerations for hedging against vulnerability, and then concluded that an ample number would be what the United States already had a decade ago. Approximately 1,600 warheads (not missiles) would suffice to retaliate and would allow for low-level nuclear exchange between the superpowers as well. Negotiations should be based on mutual reduction to that level.

When the military planners demand more they are clearly abandoning the concepts of deterrence for fantastic war-fighting scenarios. Or, in Doty's words:

> the need of further warheads is justified only by the claims of large scale war-fighting. . . . Scenarios can be created that would call for either hundreds, or thousands, or tens of thousands of warheads. . . .
>
> Clearly, this broad spectrum of putative need calls for imposing a cutoff. An acquaintance with the magnitude and duration of damage that would be inflicted at the lower end of this spectrum counsels severe restraint. Before we reach midway in this spectrum, the superpowers would cease to function as coherent societies even if urban areas were not intentionally attacked. We must, therefore, view the temptation to move into this realm of war-fighting as increasingly

contradictory to our national survival. My own view is that beyond a few hundred weapons the hard justification vanishes, the rationalization for the remainder is sustained only by unreal scenarios that mask national suicide. Yet it is this war-fighting concept that provides some military planners on both sides the basis of continuously raising their requirements.[7]

York carried this reasoning further with searching arguments:

If one, or ten, or maybe a few hundred bombs on target are all that are needed to deter, how did it happen that we came to possess more than 10,000? And why so much total explosive power? These numbers are *not* the result of a careful calculation of the need in some specific strategic or tactical situation. They are the result of a series of historical accidents which have been rationalized after the fact. In the late 1940s and early 1950s, before the invention of the H-bomb, it was determined that we needed on the order of 1,000 delivery vehicles (then land-based and sea-based bombers) in our strategic forces. . . . Then suddenly, when the H-bomb was perfected in 1954, the explosive power of the bombs multiplied 1,000-fold. When the effectiveness of each nuclear weapon was thus so enormously increased, one might have supposed it would have resulted in a reduction in the number of delivery vehicles needed, *but no such adjustment was made.* In fact, because the perfection of the H-bomb was one of the technological advances that made long-range missiles practical, the H-bomb actually resulted in a proliferation of types of delivery systems. . . . In the late 1960s, further technological advances made it possible to provide each individual missile with more than ten individually-targetable warheads. Again, one might have expected some adjustment in the number of delivery vehicles, but there was none. . . . In brief then, even if we accept for the time being the need for a policy of deterrence through mutual assured destruction, the forces now in being are enormously greater than are needed for that purpose.[8]

The thinking of the planners is obviously deviating constantly towards war-fighting rather than deterrence. But then war would proceed to the bitter end where both sides would have fought to the last bomb and possibly the last major population center, with the menace of radioactivity covering a large part of our globe. Which government would then call itself the victor would have lost all reasonable meaning.

The devastation that would be caused by a fraction of the bombs presently available in nuclear arsenals should be enough to make such a war unthinkable, if the thinking is at all rational. The lower level of terror envisaged in the deterrence concept is long since past. The idea of terror balance introduces a dangerous, perhaps even willful, error of logic, as it is used to justify matching at levels far beyond deterrence needs.

There is clearly no sense in keeping deterrence forces at such high, continuously rising levels, as permitted by the SALT agreements. Rationally, the two superpowers could at any time agree to lower the guard. The suggestions made by the authors quoted here would, if implemented, be a move to stop and reverse the arms race, a real advance towards disarmament. In addition, it would encourage political steps towards nonproliferation of nuclear weapons and conventional arms-limitation measures. That is exactly what has not happened in the SALT negotiations. Matching is a stupid game, for there would be no risk if one of the superpowers by a unilateral decision lowered its stockpile of nuclear weapons.

Any such unilateral move could certainly not risk an attack from the other superpower, particularly if it were duly advertised how much retaliatory capability would still be left. Instead, such a move reasonably would cause the other side to think things over. The recommendation is for a *series of reciprocated moves*, unilaterally initiated, not necessarily agreed in advance. These should be signaled as expecting a response and ought thus to lead to negotiations on how to stop the arms race and gradually to firm agreements for substantially lowering existing levels of nuclear weaponry.

Even the United States Congress has become worried over the unpromising prospects. In early 1975 a resolution (No. 20) was passed in the Senate, with comments on the outlines for a new SALT agreement presented at the Ford-Brezhnev meeting in Vladivostok. The Senate was eager to forestall a perpetuation of the arms race and therefore expressed

> firm belief that this agreement in principle must lead to further mutual arms limitations and reductions and that both the United States and the Soviet Union should make every effort to halt the continuing competition in strategic arms by exercising mutual restraint in the deployment of nuclear weapons systems beyond currently-deployed levels and types of weapons systems.[9]

The Senate advised the President to make every possible effort to continue negotiations so as to reach further agreements, including

> mutual commitment to continue negotiations on a timely and sustained basis to achieve further mutual limitations with regard to

military forces and armaments not presently limited as part of the 1972 United States-Soviet Union strategic arms control agreements and the Vladivostok agreement.[10]

This sounds well and good, but since the catastrophic end of the war in Indochina Americans have become disturbed lest the political and military prestige of the United States should decline. The climate around SALT has become chillier; critics of United States concessions as weaknesses might succeed in stalling the negotiations to restrain the nuclear-arms race to any appropriate degree.

These comments have all referred to the United States. The Soviet Union is not so easily scrutinized. I suspect that many of the same competitive forces are operating there, though in a different institutional setting. The Soviet military establishment is important and the technological imperative is alive among its scientists and engineers. However, as the Soviet Union started from a position of having to catch up, a unilateral initiative by the most advanced country, the United States, should help both to step out of the irrational race for more and more nuclear arms.

3.   How Can the Irrational Policies Prevail?

In the United States, where views are expressed without too much inhibition or fear of reprisal, it is astonishing to me that the facts about overkill capacity and the costly irrationality of keeping the nuclear guard at such unnecessarily high levels have not been given more public attention.

In the United States there are several thousand professors and intellectuals who have no excuse for not standing up with that expert elite whose writings are quoted here.[11] Most of them have, however, elected to stay out of the controversy, when they have not actually supported the official doctrine about the necessity to continue the nuclear-arms competition. To choose a random example, Professor Marshall Shulman, who as former director of the Russian Institute at Columbia University has had reason to keep himself informed about the facts and the problems, sermonizes along the familiar lines:

> The first thing to be said about the mixed relationship between the U.S. and U.S.S.R. is that it is one of competition, and is likely to be so for some time. . . . Both see that a paramount objective of the first stage of détente is to translate this shared interest [the recog-

nition that war would be a universal catastrophe] into practical terms. This means, in the first instance, trying to stabilise and codify the strategic military competition. . . . Clearly, any realistic notion of security involves maintaining a military equilibrium.[12]

This is advocacy for the United States position—as well as the Soviet one—in the SALT negotiations, which are leading away from, not toward, disarmament measures.

That such a position rests on erroneous reasoning is, I hope, clear from what I and many experts have tried to explain. If Shulman and other writers in the political science field repeat what defense authorities assert they may be excused. A Secretary of Defense succeeded in putting all the basic errors in a nutshell when he argued:

An equally essential requirement of deterrence is parity with the Soviet Union in strategic offensive forces.[13]

For deterrence there is *not* need of parity in offensive forces; there is not even a need of parity in reserve retaliatory forces; there is only need of *a sufficient threat of unacceptable damage*.

The general public in the United States can hardly be reached by the critical arguments presented in the last section. To the unsophisticated mind it is probably quite natural to draw a false analogy from elementary physics and believe that balance presupposes that both sides have equally much. In reality, the needed balance of terror is obtained when both have enough for deterrence. It is easy for propagandists to get the uncritical public to participate in the comparison game and to agree that the United States must always militarily match the Soviet Union. That their country should be second to none is taken as a self-evident norm in a nation that has always had an inclination to be the biggest in many ways with a strong craving for competition. The public can then be easily impressed by the most comprehensible of all comparisons—the simple number of missiles, now much lower than the number of nuclear warheads—as the quintessential image of national strength.

A journalist writing in the *International Herald Tribune* has no doubts:

In the jargon of disarmament specialists, the prevailing doctrine of mutual deterrence is that both superpowers must be equal in terms of nuclear strength and be seen to be equal in the eyes of the world. What Moscow and Washington are negotiating in SALT 2 . . . is that parity.[14]

In turn, the official position of the government banks on this unsophisticated doctrine of matching, of continually pressing to advance ahead of the adversary. This attitude is partly an adjustment to thinking of the multitude and the biases in the mass media. On the other hand, the experts and the bureaucrats must know better: balance in that sense is not a measurement of security. Moreover, the nuclear defense cannot be balanced in relation to the Soviet Union in all terms in which comparisons can be made, numbers of delivery vehicles, range of missiles, megatonnage of warheads, penetration capacity, precision targeting. To continue to seek matching or even essential parity in all these asymmetric respects must lead to an incessant technological race. To a large extent, that is what is happening.

An informed President, his Secretaries of State and Defense, and the Congress ought to spell out the irrationality of the traditional policy line and stand up for inaugurating a new one. This would need the courage of a Lincoln or a Roosevelt. But the leaders have become prisoners of their concessions to special interests and of their own propaganda.

People in the Soviet Union and its satellite countries are given much less information about the realities of the nuclear arms race. How their experts reason is not known. The discussions that go on between them and within the Politbureau are kept secret. Only the positions the government decides upon are disclosed, plus highfaluting statements about principles and goals: détente, disarmament, and peace. To have such tremendous power covered by so much secrecy increases the fears of the rest of the world about the future of the arms race.

4.   Some Brakes Suggested

There are certain aspects of SALT and other bipolar negotiations which are of positive value; this should be acknowledged by disarmers even though they want a maximum of the deliberations to take place under international responsibility.

SALT has provided the beginning of less secretiveness (Chapter III, Section 7). The potential of the superpowers' nuclear arsenals is no longer kept secret, though they are not open about their intentions: under what circumstances would they be prepared to use nuclear weapons?

SALT has only two partners who need to arrive at an under-standing. They know what the whole world knows: that other nu-clear-weapons countries, actual or potential, lag far behind. What really matters is that the two giants meet the challenge of starting an arms limitation process which would demonstrate to all others the fallacy of nuclear extension.

A value of SALT is, furthermore, its machinery for negotiations. SALT has proven a certain efficiency in arriving at agreements to forgo plans for a huge land-based defense system against missiles, ABM, and in dealing with the numbers of offensive weapons. The superpowers could go ahead to a safe standstill and then agree to reductions, based on the stated acceptance of the present postures as being of essential parity. But the real question is if they will use the SALT machinery for barring all competition for new improvements which would upset parity. We have seen few signs that they are willing to stabilize the present situation by stopping not only the quantitative but the more dangerous qualitative arms race. That is the big order: the *perpetuum mobile* of the arms race must be stilled.

Considering SALT's overwhelming preoccupation with quan-tities, we may accept for the sake of argument that the next move must also be quantitative. The first question is: what should be the follow-up to SALT I and Vladivostok? If we narrow the question even more and focus in the conventional way on offensive strategic nuclear-weapons systems, what should be the next step beyond set-ting the ceilings there discussed?

The official posture of both superpowers is for an increase before any freeze is established; there is yet no negotiation about reduc-tions. However, in the United States some unofficial suggestions have been made for reductions, sometimes even for capping the quali-tative competition. One idea, presented as a "bold and imaginative proposal for serious disarmament" by Senator Henry M. Jackson, is to reduce sharply the number of offensive strategic weapons author-ized by SALT. The proposed reduction would affect bombers, sub-marines, and land-based intercontinental missiles; the reduction would not be by fixed numbers but possibly by reducing the ceiling to 1,760 missiles or less, or by a third.[15]

One method to achieve reduction would be to set aside a certain number of missiles which would be allowed to become obsolescent. By 1985, at the end of the Vladivostok agreement, there would then have been a convenient, consecutive reduction in numbers. The aspect of obsolescence or qualitative restraint should be considered a possibility in other contexts. (Chapter IV, Section 6.)

In academic debate, there is a wealth of suggestions about methods to achieve a quantitative reduction of strategic forces. One such is to eliminate bombs of high megatonnage (York). Another idea to achieve partial nuclear disarmament is to eliminate strategic bombers and drastically reduce the number of nuclear submarines and intercontinental missiles, retaining only 10 percent of the United States and Soviet strategic nuclear forces (Rathjens). Several authors include qualitative restraint by emphasizing the value of nonmodernization and nonreplacement (Doty), or suggest coupling a freeze on numbers with a ban on construction of new launchers and on any change of the characteristics of those already deployed (Scoville), or strangling most new development programs (La Roque). At the 1975 Pugwash Symposium in Kyoto, an attempt was made to propose jointly an even more specific reduction program to maintain only a few almost invulnerable submarines. Immediate negotiations should begin: (a) to reduce and phase out all land-based ICBMs; (b) to reduce and eliminate strategic bombers; (c) to reduce submarine-launched ballistic missiles by 90 percent. Several papers were presented proposing that the United States should retain, say, five Poseidon submarines, which would provide it with 80 missiles carrying 800 MIRVed nuclear warheads. The Soviet Union would retain, say, seven missile-launching submarines which would provide it with 105 missiles carrying 1,050 MIRVed nuclear warheads.[16]

A quite radical and well-reasoned argument by one of the experts who has since become an influential official of the United States establishment, Dr. Fred Iklé, now Director of the United States Arms Control and Disarmament Agency, should be cited. He has expressed stark and honest doubts about "such vulnerable arrangements as aircraft in delicately ready conditions and missiles exposed on or near the surface."[17] Submarine-based nuclear-weapons systems, hidden as they are from offensive targeting from the other side, are more invulnerable. A low number of them could therefore substitute for the very great numbers of land-based missiles and airborne bombers.

Typical of the majority of proposals presented is that they focus mainly on the quantity of weapons, or often just on the delivery vehicles, rarely taking into account the number of warheads these can carry. In other words, the United States experts "talk to their capital" as it is wont to hear the arguments of the military interests. There is, of course, no harm in pleading restraint with the mighty, but this leaves out the international perspective. This is a regrettable lack, as very few action proposals are formulated in countries other than the United States.

In the United Nations appeals for restraint are repeatedly made in strongly worded resolutions, but little if anything of an agenda has been discussed. An endeavor to fill the gap was made by a number of nonaligned nations during the recently held Review Conference for the Non-Proliferation Treaty (Chapter VI, Section 4). While it has value as an impatient call for action by several nonaligned nations, the substantive idea to couple reduction of strategic nuclear weapons with the numbers of adherents to the Non-Proliferation Treaty seems artificial, even incongruent. If some goodwill had been forthcoming from the nuclear-weapons power, that particular feature of the proposal might have been amended in a positive way and brought to an affirmative vote.[18]

What should now be taken up at the international negotiating table is some scheme, bold but practical, for a genuine limitation of the nuclear arms race. I therefore suggest that with SALT obviously just treading water, one should break with the previous debate about ceilings for nuclear delivery vehicles and turn several pages back in the history book to the radical concept of a *minimum nuclear deterrent*. Discussed in the United Nations some ten years ago, this envisaged fixing the size and the mix, both the quantities and the characteristics of ultimate nuclear strength, incorporating the qualitative with the quantitative curb (Section 6 below will be devoted to such planning).

5.   Trends Threaten Change for the Worse

The greatest dangers in the nuclear arms race lie in trends towards changing the quality of weapons systems. The growth in the numbers of missiles and bombers becomes insignificant in comparison. The overriding criticism against SALT is that it is not even endeavoring to stop the nuclear arms race, because no limits are set on the technological changes which aim at increased qualitative performance capabilities. The awareness that the arms race is kept open-ended has moved the General Assembly to issue repeated warnings, expressing deep anxiety at the lack of progress:

Urges the Union of Soviet Socialist Republics and the United States
of America to broaden the scope and accelerate the pace of their
strategic arms limitation talks, and stresses once again the necessity
and urgency of reaching agreement on important qualitative limitations and substantial reductions of their strategic nuclear-weapon
systems as a positive step towards nuclear disarmament.[19]

The appeal was the same in 1975, though sharper in tone towards
the powers who lead this march towards new horrors. The General
Assembly particularly stressed "its concern . . . for the total absence
of qualitative limitations of such arms. . . ."[20] Both superpowers
remonstrated by voting against, with a few of their allies abstaining
from the vote.

Within the SALT framework the first step would be to agree on
a freeze, barring continuation on the as yet barely mentioned work
on improved generations of certain weapon systems. On the United
States side there is still a chance to stop full production and deployment of the B-1 bomber and the long-range cruise missiles, as there
is strong opposition to them in the arms control community and
also in the Congress. On the Soviet side, the strategic-range Backfire
bomber as well as the SS-19 and SSX long-range missiles should be
stopped, as they also belong to what the United States often
refers to as bargaining chips.

More shielded from mutual inquisitiveness but still formally
open are final decisions on important new generations of strategic
submarines with their plethora of perfected missile systems, the
United States Trident as well as the Soviet Delta submarines. The
competition is sharp and uneven. The Soviet Union is beginning to
equip its missiles with the multiple independently targetable reentry
vehicles (MIRV), while the United States is advancing the technology from MIRV to MARV, Maneuverable Reentry Vehicles,
that is, vehicles with multiple warheads maneuverable when already
in flight.

Worse is in the offing. The unsettling aspect of the qualitative
arms race becomes more pronounced with each new technology
publicized in the specialist journals. Funding is now being sought
for experimentation, but that is, of course, the narrow wedge with
which the doors to a new hellish development are pried open.
Vigilance must be kept up against a whole category of unmanned
vehicles. Remotely piloted drones, in particular the cruise missiles
with computerized programming and data link with their operators,
have a formidable capacity for selective targeting and retargeting

while in flight and a low trajectory that allows them to avoid detection by radar. Many of these and other sophisticated new systems, some laser-based and with sensors and precision-guided munitions (PGM), utilize ultra-advanced technologies. Not only do these loom large in laboratories and military budgets, but some have been tested in actual combat experience, both in Vietnam and the Middle East wars. That many of the precision-guidance systems can be fitted into non-nuclear-weapons systems makes them even more important.[21]

Practically all these novelties can be employed against the lesser powers. Yet in this respect no attempts are being made to curtail the right to use them. For instance, it is a drastic confirmation of the superpowers' sanctuary doctrine that, when in SALT an accommodation is discussed in regard to United States cruise missiles and Soviet Backfire bombers, only those of strategic range are considered. That means that the potential enemies mutually help to protect each other's homelands, leaving all other countries in the lower shooting range in the line of fire.

The development of new military ultratechnologies clearly signals that the superpowers are now gaming for superiority, not predominantly in regard to quantity, when parity is discussed in SALT. The competition is away from quantity to quality:

> For about the past ten years in the United States, and probably not much less in the USSR, the challenge has been to increase the number and accuracy of warheads per missile together with reliability, ability to penetrate, and so on. In other words the emphasis has been on technological advances and qualitative improvement.[22]

So far in this chapter, I have talked positively in accordance with most of the public debate about the promise of mutual deterrence being what the world has to rely upon for peace to be kept between the two superpowers. But now a new period is opening where the race between the superpowers seems to be leaping away from the maintenance of deterrence. We are obviously in a dangerous transition period. We must try to know whether the two are abandoning their goal of maintaining a second-strike capacity in favor of seeking a first-strike one. Behind these technical terms there are horrid realities. The second-strike strategy is bad enough, as its means of deterrence is to keep forces for retaliation against the civilian population of the other side, a country-city force. It exists, as we know, in more than sufficient strength.

But the ambition exists to move ahead to new strategic doctrines on the basis of the qualitative arms developments, to obtain first-strike capacities for a strike at the missiles or warheads themselves, to assure the destruction of all or nearly all the military potential of the other side. To let SIPRI explain it:

> Counterforce strategy does not replace deterrence; rather it supplements it with the additional capacity to strike, either preemptively or in response to an attack, at the opponent's military targets, including hardened missile silos. Such a strategy requires a large number of accurate powerful nuclear warheads targeted not against cities and industrial and transportation centres but against military installations. In addition, a counterforce strategy implies the capability of fighting a nuclear war if deterrence fails to prevent its outbreak.[23]

An open declaration that the strategic policies have been changed in favor of a first-strike capacity has not yet appeared. However, we must interpret the signs which are becoming visible, both in the debate on strategic doctrines and, more irretrievably, in the trend towards new warfare technologies.

As usual, the signs are most easily read from open accounts in the United States. (All I have previously mentioned about the tilt towards nuclear war-fighting capabilities (Chapter IV, Section 2) indicates such a leaning in the United States despite its being played down in favor of deterrence since about 1960.) In January 1974, the then Secretary of Defense, James R. Schlesinger, enunciated a new strategic doctrine which was euphemistically presented as one of selective targeting. But the succinct version in SIPRI's chronology spells it out:

> 10 January. The U.S. Secretary of Defense announces that a change has taken place in the nuclear targeting strategy of the U.S. to provide selective options against different sets of targets, including military targets.[24]

The debate is still going on in the United States. President Ford has explicitly supported the Schlesinger ambition. The Soviet Union certainly will not acquiesce in decisive nuclear superiority by the United States but it will try to keep pace.[25] The horrible risk for qualitative escalation of the nuclear arms race is something the world will have to stem or find itself facing the more certain risk of perishing.

The ominous conjunction of opportunities for new offensive strategic planning with new technological trends is particularly marked in regard to precision targeting. It will soon be possible to deliver missile-borne thermonuclear warheads over distances of 6,000 miles to within a few tens of meters of the target. SIPRI's conclusion is

> the amount of *effective* damage that the U.S. and the U.S.S.R. can inflict on each other will rise astronomically over the next decade even if the limits on the total number of strategic delivery vehicles and MIRVed missiles in the proposed SALT II agreement are established.[26]

The consolation offered by the military planners that precision targeting would limit collateral damage should not decrease the fears of the civilian population. The risk in any situation depends on whether the military targets are located at a safe distance from their places of work and habitat. Precision targeting does not mean, as is popularly believed, that the targets are hit with needlepoint accuracy; the area of damage caused by any bomb is of the same extent regardless of the accuracy in selecting its center.

> It has been argued that the improved accuracy of strategic nuclear weapons will permit the adoption of a policy of limited and flexible response by making possible attacks against military targets near urban centers without massive damage to civilian populations and property. But this is a false argument. Two reentry vehicles with identical 0.2 megaton warheads, but with accuracies of 0.25 nautical miles and 30 metres respectively will both devastate the same area, a circle with a radius of between two and three nautical miles. . . . Therefore, if the intended target of the reentry vehicle is more than two or three nautical miles away from a city neither weapon will cause grave damage, while if it is closer than this, both weapons will cause damage. The more accurate weapon is not more humane. . . . The radius of destruction of nuclear weapons is so much larger than the relative improvement in accuracy envisioned that the results of an attack near a city are the same irrespective of the sophistication of the weapon.[27]

A second technological trend which points in the same ominous direction occurs in the domain of submarine warfare where huge investments are now being made on both sides. The missiles carried by submarines have hitherto been considered highly effective as a deterrent force. Although relatively inaccurate in targeting, submarines have been able to threaten a certain retaliation with considerable damage to populated areas, a countercity role. New developments are imminent. By equipping submarines with the multiple and separately maneuverable MIRVs and by innovative improvements in their navigation systems, they would be allowed to determine position more precisely. With the capacity for swift surprise movements, the submarines, with thousands of nuclear warheads, might then have a first-strike role, a capacity to strike the home bases of other nuclear weapons.[28]

The competition for offensive nuclear forces is mirrored in practically all the other new developments. They all, particularly the cruise missiles, increase the capabilities for fighting wars considerably, while their role for deterrence disappears in the background. The Director of SIPRI, Frank Barnaby, summarizes the mounting risks for a recourse to war-fighting in an article "Changing Nuclear Myths."

> For war-fighting purposes . . . it is important that the yield-to-weight ratio of the warhead be maximized. The atomic bomb dropped on Hiroshima weighed about four tons and had an explosive yield equivalent to about 12,000 tons of TNT. The yield-to-weight ratio was, therefore, about 3,000. The ratio for a conventional bomb cannot, of course, exceed unity. A typical modern nuclear warhead is the American multiple independently-targetable reentry vehicle deployed on the Minuteman III ICBM. This has a yield of about 200,000 tons and weighs about one-tenth of a ton. The yield-to-weight ratio is, therefore, over a million. This is within a small factor of the theoretical maximum; further improvement would be virtually meaningless.[29]

Barnaby also points out how the near science-fiction improvements of weapons "are unnecessary and even harmful for a strategy of deterrence but are all highly desirable for effectively fighting a nuclear war."

In this situation, there are certain underlying causes which make effective arms limitation measures singularly hard to clinch, even were political leaders willing to do it. For this reason, plans for weapons procurement years from now have to be decided on the basis of strategies conceived and information available today. Meanwhile, production plans run their costly course automatically. When they are changed, it is often overreaction. In the action-reaction pattern of competition the superpowers use what is called the worst case method, letting technological imagination guide them rather than reason. The result is that the weaponizers always overtake the disarmers. By 1985, according to the plans so far recounted, they will have secured the weapon systems for 1995.

6.   An Urgent Agenda

Our future is being ever more heavily mortgaged by the acceleration of the qualitative arms race. The superpowers' master game, underpinned by their near-monopoly on ultratechnologies, is turning them towards new strategies of first-strike superiority. It is therefore imperative that a barrier be built as soon as possible against further competition: weapons improvement, new generations of weapons, new weapons. As little is to be expected from the bilateral negotiations between the superpowers, in SALT or elsewhere, it becomes urgent to return to multilateral negotiations and to do so with a new determination not to be dismissed with crumbs or hoodwinked with promises.

Both the short-range and the long-range problems must be tackled to institute an immediate, decisive end to production and to decide which if any nuclear weapons should remain. The first imperative is a *banning of all nuclear-weapons tests*; the second, a *minimum nuclear-weapons deterrent*.

The ban should start with Research and Development work, but these activities are admittedly particularly difficult to verify. The most important recommendation is to open up all accumulating information and to monitor research that is already under way. Both subjects are treated in connection with suggestions for an international disarmament verification agency (Chapter X).

Intervention must concentrate on internationally agreed banning of testing of new weapons systems. Banning the testing of nuclear warheads has been our avowed aim for more than two decades. It was recognized as an urgent obligation when the Partial Test-Ban Treaty was signed more than ten years ago. Now a comprehensive ban on testing of nuclear explosions must be seriously and conclusively negotiated (Chapter VII; see also Chapter III, Section 6). Such testing is easily controlled. Assertions to the contrary are only excuses, void of factual content. Concerted attention must also be given to the issue of banning the testing of missiles. The question of whether the international community will continue to tolerate the closing off of large areas of the oceans for weapons testing ought to be raised. To me and to many others, this appears to be a violation of the freedom of the seas.[30] Missile tests are also relatively easy to monitor with national means, particularly for nations which have the whole technical spy apparatus of cameras and sensors of all kinds on aircraft and satellites at their disposal (Chap-

ter X). International demand to restrict activities such as missile tests
—the most urgent being flight-testing of cruise missiles—has largely
been lacking. This is deplorable as many missile tests occur over
international ocean space, and sometimes over foreign territory.

Leaving the urgent but short-range questions of prohibiting
weapon tests of various kinds, let me turn to one of the most important and least discussed of questions: what nuclear weapons
should be permitted in the longer view? Once lost, the state of innocence can never be recreated. There is scant hope for total nuclear
disarmament. The clandestine production of even one bomb would
always be feared as a potential disaster. Neither is it believable that
there will ever be complete international control of all that pertains
to the nuclear process. Greater safety, however, should be feasible
through the existence of a few nuclear weapons for deterrence. To
examine how few, how constituted, and how kept in custody is our
most urgent task. Therefore, I strongly recommend that both
academic studies and negotiations return to trying to fix rules for a
minimum deterrent.

The Soviet Foreign Minister Andrei Gromyko, in the General
Assembly in 1962, and in more detail in September 1963, suggested
a goal of drastically reduced nuclear forces. This idea, often called
the nuclear umbrella or the Gromyko umbrella, was accepted by
the United States and Britain as one of the bases for discussion (a
term often used when a proposal is neither turned down nor approved as a commitment). At the time, it was the object of considerable detailed comments both at the United Nations and the
Geneva Disarmament Committee.

While Gromyko seemed to favor a gradual approach, negotiating
from present levels downward to a minimum level for nuclear forces,
I proffered a number of suggestions in order to make the proposal
more practical. The most important of these was to turn the exercise
upside down and start with decisions as to the final, minimal level.
The idea was that the actual size and composition of a minimum
deterrent force, to be kept by nuclear powers at the end of a general
and worldwide process of disarmament, should be the subject of
calculations by a working group of experts. I also explicitly asked
that the term "nuclear shield" instead of "nuclear umbrella" be used
to indicate that the suggested working group study not only the so-
called Gromyko proposal.

During this phase of multilateral negotiations the debate centered
on an approach in three stages, so I suggested:

focus first on what kind of nuclear shield should exist at the end of the disarmament process—that is, in stage III—leaving to a second round the questions of the methods and the pace by which that level is to be reached. . . . Politically speaking, such a procedure . . . would avoid having to deal with the questions of balance in the period nearest to the actual existing situation . . . From the technical point of view the advantage is no less important, since, without the issue having been prejudged, the working group can attempt to estimate directly what would constitute a suitable "mix" for each side in order to secure the desirable nuclear protection.[31]

In other words a decisive political agreement should be made as soon as the study group has reported, to fix precisely the size and mix of a minimum deterrent, leaving to detailed negotiations the establishment of a timetable for the process of reducing present levels.

The overriding phenomenon, of which we must never lose sight, is that a compromise has been achieved and that there is agreement in principle that a certain nuclear striking force may be retained by each of the two nuclear superpowers to the end of the disarmament process. All other issues—such as those of the size, character, composition, and deployment of those forces, as well as the timing of the reductions needed to reach the agreed level, amounting to an elimination of all other means of nuclear delivery—must be considered in the second place as "modalities" appropriate for settlement after technical scrutiny in a working group.[32]

The task seemed a very challenging one, even allowing for alternative futures:

I believe we must leave the working group free to discuss relative quantities in terms of any conceivable "mix." It might even use some modern technical devices for trying to determine an appropriate composition for the shield. In this operation several hypothetical "mixes" must be tried out. I believe the working group should also be afforded the possibility of presenting not only one but several alternative constructions in its report to us.[33]

No such working group has been established and the SALT negotiations are steering a very different course, stepping up the arms race, not reversing it. The proposal remains valid today. I hereby emphatically reintroduce it. It would seem practically feasible and politically promising if an international working group were established to study the parameters of such a nuclear shield. They would suggest a minimum deterrent whose size would be enough, while freezing new weapons developments, thus guaranteeing a stop to qualitative competition. This would mean true deterrence and assure us of what we seek most: security.

Mention should be made of another possibility which was introduced in the debates on General and Complete Disarmament in the early 1960s: that all permitted nuclear weapons be in the hands of the United Nations. I do not share this view. For the sake of the United Nations itself and for the sake of a peaceful world in the future, such contentious instruments of might cannot be allowed to be the prize of any, maybe whimsical, majority vote, or, worse, of aggressive power formations within the international community. The nuclear shield has a role, safer for us all, as an agreed minimum deterrent functioning which would let the superpowers, two, or, in the future, possibly three, including China, keep each other at bay. It is the fighting propensities that must be shackled. Of course, if proliferation is let loose (Chapter VI) and we get a world of many nuclear-weapons powers, no ideal solution, even if once established, can prevail.

CHAPTER V

Stemming
the Conventional Arms Rush

1. Conventional Armaments in the Nuclear Age

Almost the entire discussion of international arms limitation has focused on the race for nuclear arms and the need to stop the further proliferation of states having such weapons. This is true of proposals being submitted, resolutions being voted upon, and negotiations taking place within the United Nations or its several commissions and committees. It has dominated the agenda of the Geneva Disarmament Committee, and the bilateral SALT talks between the two superpowers. It is true also of the literature on disarmament problems. And this is understandable, as nuclear weapons pose the supreme threat to the security of mankind.

The issue of limiting conventional armaments has largely been permitted to remain outside the intensive international debate, and this is clearly indefensible. True, compared with nuclear weapons, conventional arms have a limited range of threat and their damaging effects are less frightening, but they are far more widespread. They have been used in innumerable wars, while nuclear weapons (since the two explosions over Japan) have, as yet, only been stockpiled. Conventional arms have increasingly been used in ways contrary to international law: they have become increasingly cruel and they have become more widely directed against civilians and the environment (Chapters VIII and IX).

Measured in terms of costs, conventional arms and the man-power immobilized by their production and servicing represents the world's major military financial burden. While the expenditure for all military hardware, arms, munitions, and other equipment has been estimated at 30 percent of the total world military outlay, producing nuclear weapons takes only a minor share, perhaps a third of the total.[1] The balance goes to personnel, construction, and research and development, mostly for conventional armaments.

The cost of conventional armaments is a drain on resources in developed countries and a still worse one in underdeveloped countries (Chapter I, Section 3). Conventional arms are also mainly responsible for the militarization of our societies. In the underdeveloped world, the increase of conventional armaments supports the trend towards military dictatorships. Such arms carry a heavy liability for moral, social, and broadly human costs beyond the financial burden of wars and war preparations (Chapter I, Sections 5 and 6).

The superpowers are the leading spenders in the field of conventional as well as nuclear weapons, excelling all other countries in total military costs, but most other countries follow suit. A prominent dynamic trend at present is that military spending in the underdeveloped nations is rising proportionately more than in the developed countries, which traditionally have been the great military spenders (Chapter I, Section 3).[2]

The advent of nuclear weapons and the ensuing arms race between the superpowers was such an enormous change that it might have been expected to affect the military planning of conventional arsenals in some fundamental way. But this has hardly taken place anywhere. Conventional armaments have continued to be developed along the beaten track as a parallel phenomenon. And this despite the fact that the nuclear weapons in the hands of the two superpowers have long since reached such destructive capacity that all lesser nations are defenseless against them. In Europe this holds true even for Britain and France, and in the whole world for all countries, even those readying themselves for the proliferation of nuclear weapons (Chapters VI and VII).

This defenselessness would continue even if the superpowers stopped the nuclear arms race and began to reverse it. They would nevertheless have a sure overkill capacity. So the lesser powers would remain defenseless under any condition against a superpower willing to use its full strength or threatening to do so.

For lesser powers to build up their conventional armory can make sense only in so far as they can count on not getting into a war with a superpower. Even when the United States got heavily involved in warfare in Korea and in Indochina, it did not resort to the use of nuclear weapons. These wars were fought only with conventional weapons, though highly sophisticated ones, used with utter disrespect for international law. In Indochina the United States did not use nuclear weapons, partly because it was motivated by insecurity concerning the reaction of Russia, and partly because of the deep horror such action would have created in the world, including the United States. Representatives of the Department of Defense have hinted that nuclear weaponry might be used in case a new conflict should break out in Korea. However, it is doubtful that such a threat would ever be carried out for the same reasons that more subdued threats made in regard to the Vietnam War were not.

Such a threat has been considered more likely in regard to Europe, if a superpower confrontation were played out there. As such, it is discussed openly in the scenarios on both sides and more specifically as part of the announced United States strategy for a limited war on a European battlefield (Chapter II, Sections 3 and 5).

This threat of widening options being revealed, the mass media must try to educate the public about the difference between first use and first strike. First strike means an all-out surprise attack by one superpower against the other, relying on such an overwhelming superiority that it would substantially eliminate an enemy's retaliatory second-strike forces (Chapter IV, Section 2). First use is to meet any, even a conventional, attack—for example, in Europe—with an input of nuclear weapons. Scenarios for first use of some nuclear arms do not in principle exclude any theaters of war; threats by the United States are addressed in all directions—Europe, Korea, and even the Soviet Union. A sample quotation referring to the Soviet Union may be taken from an interview with the United States Secretary of Defense:

> First use could conceivably—let me underscore conceivably—involve what we define as strategic forces and possibly, possibly—underscore possibly—involve a selective strike [against military targets] at the Soviet Union. We do not necessarily exclude that, but it is indeed a very, very low probability.[3]

Such threats, however hypothetical, of nuclear weapons being used in situations where the other side employs only conventional weapons opens new dimensions of fear. These fears are now besetting countries allied to the superpower blocs, but nonaligned nations must bear the nuclear danger in mind, their independent defense forces being based solely on conventional armaments.

Qualms about ultimate defenselessness become very pointed for the nonaligned countries, which cannot resort to any illusion of being protected by a superpower nuclear umbrella. The nonaligned European countries, close to prospective battlefields, have paid a great deal to build up their defenses with conventional armaments. They are gambling, if war breaks out in Europe and exposes their territory to being drawn into it, that nuclear weapons will not be used or threatened.

The overriding goal for the defense of nonaligned nations is for forces strong enough so that—under the favorable assumption of a non-nuclear war—the costs to a would-be aggressor would appear greater than the advantage he could gain by an attack. At bottom, this is built upon a manifest resolution that a country does not want to go down without fighting for its freedom.

A nation as indisputably bent on defense as Switzerland, recognizing that effective retaliation is an impossibility, states the truth in two terse sentences in its policy statement of 1973: "The heaviest threats cannot, even with the greatest input, be fully deterred." And: "More armaments do not today bring more security."[4]

The main concern of countries facing the possibility of nuclear war in their vicinity is to make maximum preparations for protecting themselves against the radioactive fallout. Arrangements to safeguard their populations have been considered most important. In Sweden civilian defense plans are a considerable part of defense preparations for shelters and evacuation, envisaging, first, protection of the civilian population against direct attacks with conventional arms, and, second, measures to protect them against drifting clouds of chemical and radioactive substances.

The risks of becoming involved in a nuclear war between the superpowers are, of course, less in other regions of the world. In the Middle East there is, however, some danger that one or several of the contending countries will equip themselves with nuclear weapons (Chapter VI, Section 6). This danger is also present on the Indian subcontinent and in other parts of the underdeveloped world, as the proliferation of states with nuclear-weapons capabilities proceeds. Generally, the superpowers in their competition for hegemony will have their fingers in the pie, occasionally making a local conflict almost a war by proxy. Under what circumstances they would enter a local war and introduce nuclear weapons remains a disquieting question.

2. Production of and Trade in Conventional Arms

The same internal forces propelling the nuclear arms race are operating in the field of conventional armaments within all countries. Everywhere, vested interests—financial, industrial, and local— are pushing armaments upward, as are competition between the several services and the technological imperative of seeking improvement of weapons (Chapter I, Section 4).

As conventional weapons have become more and more sophisticated, and more and more costly, they have also become more cruel. The production of them is drawing an increasing share of scientists and technologists into research and development work who then acquire vested interests in the continuation of their specialized work. A bureaucratic hierarchy spreads which can successfully withstand those who are striving for restrictions to arms production and programs, most often on budgetary grounds.

Obviously the developed countries have a huge superiority in conventional weapons, but the underdeveloped countries are now raising their armaments level even faster than the developed ones. There is a resultant trend towards equality between developed and underdeveloped countries in military equipment rather than in economic growth and standards of living. However, the underdeveloped countries have to rely largely on imports. The industrialized countries not only are independent when building up their arsenals but reap profits, in cash or political influence, when arms are sold or given away.

Only the two superpowers are entirely self-sufficient in arms production. All other countries are more or less dependent on imports of certain weapons, parts and equipment, or licenses needed for the domestic production of arms. SIPRI shows how this interlocking pattern works for the thirty-three countries listed as economically advanced:

> for transactions in complete major weapons systems there were twenty-nine importing countries and sixteen exporting countries; nineteen countries manufactured foreign-designed major weapons under license and eight countries granted these licences; three countries used major components of foreign design in their indigenous weapon programs and thirteen countries supplied these components. . . .[5]

This pattern is particularly fine-meshed for the NATO countries, but even an industrially and technologically advanced non-aligned country like Sweden, which prefers to produce its armaments itself, is dependent on imports for special weapons or component parts. Some of the larger underdeveloped countries, such as Brazil, Argentina, and India, have in recent times begun to produce quite advanced weapons, but remain largely dependent on licenses and components from developed countries. Some of them have even on a small scale entered the export markets.

> In 1960, virtually no Third World country possessed the capacity to produce major arms—with the notable exception of Argentina and Brazil. By 1974, eighteen Third World countries are listed in the SIPRI register of licensed production of major weapons. Of these, fourteen also appear in the register of countries which have acquired a domestic design and development capacity.[6]

This must imply a considerable dislocation of development efforts:

> The efforts required, in terms of funding, infrastructure, training of manpower, and establishment of related industries to produce the raw materials and components needed in the arms industries are incalculable and almost impossible to translate into monetary terms, especially for such countries as India with a constant profile of underdevelopment, foreign aid needs, and hunger catastrophes.[7]

Excluding what the superpowers produce for themselves, the value of the total weapons market is probably well in excess of $20 billion annually.[8] This only refers to conventional weapons, as nuclear weapons are sold by no one. The largest share of this market is taken up by the advanced countries in an intricate pattern of interdependence characterized by bartering on the basis of sophisticated specializations. But the less advanced countries, including those which increasingly acquire a capacity for domestic arms production, are also in the market for weapons as well as for components. Recently their share in the international trade in arms has risen quite spectacularly. SIPRI estimates the value of such transfers of major weapons systems to underdeveloped countries to have risen 60 percent between 1973 and 1975. Every succeeding estimate moves upward; the current value of the trade is probably $10–12 billion.[9]

Some of the weapons imports in underdeveloped countries now come from other countries in the Third World as production capacity increases there or, like Iran, they are reexport arms. But most of the arms trade goes unilaterally from the technologically more advanced to the less advanced countries. Until recently this could be translated as from the richer to the poorer countries, but now, with the monopolistic rise in oil prices, some underdeveloped countries have suddenly become very rich and these countries have become major importers of highly sophisticated and expensive weapons.[10] Besides the superpowers' continued deliveries to them, almost all the developed Western countries (in the wake of the 1973 Middle East war and the Arab oil boycott) have been racing to please the Arabs and simultaneously reap profits. There has been a resultant strong upsurge in trade according to the new pattern of arms-for-oil deals. When contracted orders are filled, Kuwait, for instance, with only around a million inhabitants, will have one of the world's most modern air defense systems, and all the Gulf sheikdoms are acquiring sophisticated counterinsurgency weaponry.[11]

While the motive behind importing weapons is, or pretends to be, the strengthening of national security, no such motivation can be attributed to the advanced countries for the exports. Their security is not increased by this trade and would not suffer if the export of arms were discontinued. The motivations of the exporting developed countries differ considerably. The superpowers have sold arms to underdeveloped countries, sometimes at reduced prices, or offered them as aid, mainly for strategic military reasons in the cold war. Aid in the form of military or technical training has usually accompanied the exports. Such political motivations have been weaker in other developed countries. Yet all countries can realize a profit from arms export, strengthened by the economics of longer production series. France particularly has for a long time promoted profits uninhibited by restraints, and it has now become the world's third largest arms exporter.

The picture is as much one of glee for the weaponeers as of gloom for the disarmers. There is a fierce competition building up for the export of arms. Unlike in earlier periods, the arms trade, particularly in major weapons, is no longer left mostly to the private arms traders and weapons manufacturers, the "merchants of death." Governments themselves have taken on a responsibility both for contracting production of armaments and for promoting sales abroad. They cannot avoid the contagion of the tremendous payments for bribes, agents' fees, and other corrupted practices infecting the arms traffic.

Several governments, indeed, are going beyond merely licensing arms exports and taking over much of the burden of salesmanship. Britain has compiled a 734-page catalogue of almost every military item that the nation's manufacturers offer, from Corvettes to combat socks. France maintains a permanent exposition near Versailles for the drop-in trade, and publishes its own three-volume catalogue. Sample prices: hand grenade, $1.80; AMX-30 tank, $400,000; Mirage III reconnaissance jet, $1,500,000. Only about 20 percent of United States arms exports are negotiated by private manufacturers who obtain export licenses from the State Department. The rest are sold by the Government, acting as a middleman.[12]

Sheer financial gain clearly outweighs any ethical arguments in favor of restraint. Even so, sales profits are not sufficient to offset military costs more than marginally, not even for France, which has proved ruthless in promoting arms sales wherever it can. Arms sales of $570 million in 1973 did not compensate for more than some 6 percent of the French military budget for the same year. The corresponding British figures were $333 million and 4 percent.[13] West Germany was for a long time restrictive in arms export but has increased its export levels sharply in recent years.[14]

3.   Reversing the Conventional Arms Race

Little thought has been given to measures that might block and perhaps reverse the race for building up the conventional armories. In the Geneva Disarmament Committee this issue does not even figure on the agenda. Measures to cope realistically with this problem must perforce be enmeshed in the complicated web of development, production, and sales of arms, where individual threads can hardly be kept separate. A first step is to lay bare the somber facts. Active measures for introducing restraint must then be sought, either by the indirect method of reducing military expenditures across the board or by the direct way of prohibiting certain lines of production and of trade in conventional weapons. Because of the interdependent nature of the problem, the steps I propose will necessarily follow a somewhat zig-zag course.

a.   *Disclosure of Military Expenditures.*   The first requirement for an international taking stock of where the world is heading is to lay all the facts on the table. An annual yearbook on armaments and arms trade was published by the League of Nations until 1938.

At that time the publication of national military budgets was recommended, a standardized accounting system was beginning to be developed, and a number of states did, in fact, submit their military budgets to the League Secretariat in roughly standardized form.[15]

There is no reason why these traditions could not be taken up again. The most practical way to obtain a registration of military expenditures would be to request through a majority of the General Assembly that the Secretary General appoint an expert group to spell out the procedures for gathering the required information from the Member countries for its central compilation by an agency of the United Nations. In Chapter X I make a proposal for an International Verification Agency that could undertake such a duty among its other fact-finding chores.

Emphatically, the military budgets should become part of international public knowledge. There are difficult problems in making figures for military expenditures comparable, particularly because some are often hidden in other parts of a national budget. But these do not pose insurmountable technical problems. A deeper difficulty comes from the imperfect methods of estimating the sacrifice of gains that might have been won through alternative use of resources.

The problem of abolishing the secrecy of military expenditures has a long history. It has usually been connected with the further issue of recommendations for freezing or reducing military budgets. As far back as 1899 at a Hague Conference the Russian Czar proposed ceilings for military expenditures with the aim of capping an arms race. During the time of the League of Nations the Preparatory Disarmament Commission again wrestled with the problem of standardizing military budgets as a step towards agreeing on their reduction.

In the United Nations, proposals for more open divulgence of military costs have for a long time been a kind of Swedish specialization. As early as 1958 Foreign Minister Östen Undén had recommended a technical study of the problem. I reemphasized this need in the Geneva Disarmament Committee in 1963 several times over.[16] Swedish proposals have lately been made both in the Geneva Disarmament Committee[17] and in the European Conference for Security and Cooperation, with the intent that budget-accounting should constitute one of the confidence-building measures.[18]

When in 1973 the United Nations General Assembly took up the problem again, it was because of a proposal by the Soviet Union that the permanent members of the Security Council should reduce their military budgets by 10 percent, and use 10 percent of the funds thus saved to provide assistance to underdeveloped nations (altogether sacrificing roughly 1 percent of their total military budgets). Although this proposal was, with certain additional recommendations, accepted by a majority of UN Members, it could not be expected to be implemented. Four of the five veto powers, who were supposed to reduce their military budgets, did not accede to the proposition. As a gesture of compromise, on a separate proposal by Mexico, the Secretary General was instructed to set up an expert group for further study of the problem, and it reported in 1974.[19] Work along these lines is being pursued, and seems to be moving from the statistical level to an in-depth analysis but not to recommendations for action. The further study should now also include

> valuation of resources in the military sector, considering different economic systems and different structures of production within the military sector, with the purpose of examining methods concerning the relationships between resources and military output.[20]

Making public the military expenditures and monitoring them by a UN agency is in line with the general request made in this book for reducing secrecy (Chapter X, Section 5, also Chapter VI, Section 1). As the vested interests pressing for higher military expenditures in one country are often banking on spreading exaggerated views on what an adversary country is undertaking, full disclosure could strengthen the forces for restraint. It would also draw attention to ill-advised outlays not in proportion to actual needs in many countries. In this way, it would to some extent serve disarmament purposes.

But, of course, the purpose of more openness about military expenditures has always been and should today be to make possible international agreements to reduce these very expenditures. The simplest form would be a straight reduction of a percentage of the military budget, but only the availability of standardized and fairly specialized national accounts for military expenditures, according to procurement categories, would open up the way for critical comparisons and disarmament advocacy. Points will then be won for abolition or reduction of spending for specified weapons or other war preparations, including R&D expenditures (Chapter V, Section 4).

   b. Disclosure of Production and Trade in Arms. There are many arguments against any restriction of aid and trade in arms which must be met head on. A prohibition against transfer of arms from outside states, presumed to be neutral, to any state taking part in warfare is already laid down in the Hague Convention of 1907. Like many other stipulations of international law, this one has often been broken, without drawing much criticism from either legal scholars or concerned citizens. Neither have such violations, common as they are, been discussed within the United Nations.

Here again there is scope for the Geneva Disarmament Committee to take an initiative and for the General Assembly to instruct the Secretary General to create a high-level group of legal scholars and military experts to analyze the international flow of arms. Many problems are now more complicated than in the time of the League; exceptions must be made for sharing of weapons within formal military alliances. Other problems are: if the prohibition to import and export arms should be clearly stipulated to cover all undeclared wars, which have become a modern fashion; if it should cover those situations where countries are more or less imperceptibly drifting towards wars; and if it should cover civil wars.

With the development in the Middle East uppermost in mind, it might be reasonable to question whether arms-exporting countries should not be urged to agree to balance their arms deliveries and do so at lower levels. If the Security Council were less immobilized by the superpowers, such restrictions would already have concerned it.

There is a need to scrutinize the rules various countries unilaterally have laid down for the transfer of weapons to war-prone countries. Most countries seem to have no hard and fast regulations but let government policies be decided from case to case. Another method, utilized in Sweden, is to legislate as a general principle the rule of no arms sales abroad, granting exceptions only on application in special cases, thus greatly facilitating strict restraint. Such a rule is easier to administer and have accepted, both at home and abroad, than the practice of allowing the transfer of weapons to flourish unregulated. An expert group should see whether a uniform international rule could be recommended for arms transference. Full disclosure of the arms trade and all military aid should be given, the aim to be a continual registration by a United Nations agency of all arms transfers in any category.[21]

Proposals in the United Nations for divulgence of the arms trade—by Malta in 1965, the United States in 1967 (for sales to the Middle East), and by Denmark in 1958—have failed to win approval. They have met with resistance, mostly from underdeveloped countries who strongly argue that accounting for trade in arms without accounting for production of arms is discriminatory. Some of them would resent revealing how much of their foreign exchange reserve pays for armaments. Countries which have little or no domestic production themselves often fear that any control over arms transfers would be directly discriminatory against them. The mere fact that developed countries produce most of their weapons at home and have a surplus to sell for profit or to give away is felt as discrimination by the underdeveloped countries. My opinion is that they would object less to having their weapons imports registered if that were combined with a comprehensive registration of all weapons production in all countries. I therefore propose that the expert group be instructed to widen its study to include both production and trade in arms.

    c.   Restraining Production and Trade in Arms.   Registration of military budgets in some standardized form and publication of statistics on production and transfer of weapons is only a first step towards agreement on controls. In addition to the need to reach agreed limitations of the whole arms budget, it would be possible to seek out certain items on which to forbid production and transfer. Obvious candidates for such limited disarmament measures are mass-destruction weapons, such as the biological and chemical ones, which are already under a ban against use and near to being banned on production (Chapter IX).

Highest priority for international prohibition must be given to the huge number of conventional weapons which are cruel and inhumane: high-velocity weapons, fragmentation bombs, napalm, etc. They are now in ample stocks in many military establishments and have been massively used in wars, although that is contrary to international law. Their eradication from national armories and the prohibition of their production should be thought of as part of the reestablishment of the rules of international law (Chapter VIII). The benign neglect with which military violations of these rules have been treated must cease. To forbid the transfer of cruel weapons from one country to another would be a suitable entering wedge for total prohibition of these devices.

Particularly important would be the forbidding of, or at the very least restraint of the production and transfer of, arms that are typically offensive in character, while leaving purely defensive capacities less restrained. During the time of the League of Nations this problem of outlawing weapons produced for aggressive, offensive purposes and restricting arms to purely defensive functions was tackled in the Disarmament Conference, although the end was failure (Chapter III, Section 1).[22]

Admittedly, the classification must have been easier to make in the days of less sophisticated weapons and less tolerance of total warfare. But the issue must be brought to life again in the disarmament negotiations. Once more I see the need for an expert group working under the aegis of the United Nations and drawing on experiences from many countries. It would, for instance, lead us much farther in understanding what weapons are truly needed for defense if the analysis took as a point of departure a neutral and independent country like Switzerland. The superpowers are so engaged in dreaming up nuclear deterrence and war-fighting capabilities that conventional defense has been overshadowed.

While these approaches are addressed to partial disarmament in regard to specific conventional weapons, a wider and more general approach is essential to bring to a halt the competition for ever more sophisticated weaponry. As with nuclear weaponry, the same request for stalling the qualitative arms race must be made and stressed. To some extent such a desirable development may be pursued through limitation of military budgets. The constant modernization of weapons is so tremendously expensive that sheer cost considerations should support this request in all countries.

The Swedish Parliamentary Commission which is preparing the next five-year defense plan is considering a new "Swedish profile." It stresses the procurement of a greater number of technically satisfactory but less advanced weapons systems in preference to a few expensive systems of very great sophistication.[23] This was presaged in the 1972 plan. From all national points of view it should be a rule that "a greater number of technologically less sophisticated weapon systems . . . should be procured rather than a lower number of highly advanced ones." This is also in line with Sweden's unilateral abstention from atomic weapons and from biological and chemical weapons.

Finally, new efforts must be made not only for worldwide but also for regional disarmament agreements. There is every reason why neighboring countries should voluntarily agree on mutual limitations of their armaments, and why the rest of the world should be in favor of such regional agreement. Such a movement, beginning with jointly restraining the possibility of nuclear-weapons proliferation, could lead to a joint interest in wider demilitarization (Chapter VI, Section 10).

4.   The Need for Conversion Plans

The build-up of the arms industry is not conducive to the economic growth of a country (Chapter I, Section 3). If parts of this industry were curtailed it would create only transitory economic difficulties as specifically demonstrated by the UN expert report on *Economic and Social Consequences of Disarmament*, 1962. A later Report by the UN group of experts on the economic and social consequences of disarmament, of which I was chairman, *Disarmament and Development*, 1972, states succinctly:

> We agree with the authors of earlier studies that there would be no insuperable technical difficulties in ensuring the redeployment of the released resources to peaceful uses.[24]

I emphatically agree with the summary conclusion:

> The transfer to peaceful uses of resources used in each country for military purposes will bring about greater satisfaction of civilian needs of the country. The resources thus released, sometimes referred to as the "disarmament dividend," can be redirected to raise standards of living and to promote faster growth, in particular through higher expenditures in fixed investment and in education and training of manpower.[25]

Though this is true for a nation as a whole, it can look different from the point of view of a single industry or a local district. These interests are an enigma for legislators and candidates for election, who often become prisoners of the military-industrial interests dominating their constituencies. The causal relation is so strong that it has been intimated that the arms race is now largely autistic, as new armament programs are propelled by such domestic factors, in the form of a "follow-up" as soon as one line of weapons production nears completion.[26] The arguments are especially powerful in periods of high unemployment or when they refer to the danger of increasing unemployment. Still, they are shortsighted, as all studies indicate that military budgets do not have a great capacity to generate jobs. One such study was, for instance, made by the United States Bureau of Labor Statistics, estimating the employment generated by a billion dollars of expenditure

> for "national defense," for five types of construction, and for state and local government purchases for education and health. State and local spending for health and education would generate a significantly higher number of jobs per unit of expenditure than defense spending, while expenditures on construction would generate fewer jobs.[27]

Rational planning to transfer resources from military to civilian purposes has most often been absent on the national level. When questions were directed to the Member governments in connection with the above-mentioned 1962 UN report, only the replies from Norway and Britain were relatively comprehensive and supported by detailed studies. Somewhat later, a United States committee, headed by the chairman of the Council of Economic Advisers, faced the problem squarely:

> Two facts should be noted at once. First, such adjustments are necessary even when the defense budget is rising. Indeed, the major reallocations of the defense budget that have occurred in the postwar period have meant both large contractions and large expansions of production in particular firms, industries, and regions. Second, the adjustments required by defense shifts are not different in kind— or perhaps in degree—from the adjustments that are required and that occur every year from causes unrelated to defense.[28]

In practical terms, that committee recommended machinery for expanded assistance to communities and corporations to plan for conversion and reallocation, and for employees to be replaced and retained. But it has remained only a plan of lofty recommendations.

A new attempt to tackle the problem was made in 1969 when a bill by Senator George McGovern to establish a National Economic Conversion Commission was introduced.[29] The Senate Labor Committee began hearings with testimony by Walter Reuther, the United Automobile Workers' President, and many others. But so little was achieved that in 1972 Senator McGovern had to plead the sense of conversion plans anew:

> We also need to take steps to meet the economic fears of beleaguered Congressmen and defense-oriented communities by means some of us suggested in the Congress several years ago: that is, *an economic conversion act* to assist our defense industries and local communities by converting excessive military capacity to the production of urgently needed civilian facilities.[30]

Quite apart from a country's national planning for its total economy, having conversion plans for defense industries should be a self-evident duty. Governments have, as the monopolistic consumer of all weapons but handguns, taken direct or indirect control of the production for defense; government contracts sometimes, as in the aerospace industry, cause giant swings in starting or stopping a production line. In essence, conversion plans for defense industries are not different from the planning of future activities that any big corporation finds indispensable on economic grounds.

Sweden has had the conversion problem fairly prominently in view. As nonaligned, it has found it necessary to keep quite a strong defense and to produce most of its own weapons, even advanced ones like supersonic aircraft, submarines, armored fighting vehicles, and guidance systems. It has intentionally tried to keep defense contracts from monopolizing a production facility. Ordinarily a corporation is supposed to have less than 10 or at most 20 percent of its total production so earmarked. The same purpose is served by spreading defense production geographically so that individual communities do not become too dependent upon it for employment of the labor force. Some grants have been given to industries for research and development to prepare for a wider spread of production patterns and for contingency plans for redeployment of a plant's resources.[31] Nonetheless, local interests often raise loud arguments to safeguard employment against any changes in military planning, making it more difficult for government and parliament to follow a desired course.

The need for conversion plans was taken up as an international issue by the group that produced the UN report *Disarmament and Development*. Four assumptions were made and briefly studied as to the resources that would be released by these specific disarmament measures: (a) a comprehensive test ban; (b) comprehensive prohibition of the possession and production of chemical weapons; (c) demilitarization of the sea-bed and the deep-sea environment, and (d) the elimination of all foreign bases and withdrawal of foreign troops.[32]

The most general study was one of a hypothetical 20 percent cut in military spending and its effect in regard to various resources. In Appendix II, a calculation was presented of the impact on the economy of the United States of having to find compensatory use of resources and employment of manpower. The conclusions were quite hopeful:

Most of the resources released by disarmament, total or partial, would be readily transferable to other uses—for example, manpower, food, clothing, transport, fuel, and products of the metal and engineering industries. Budgetary action to raise civil demand will be enough to induce redeployment of released resources either to investment or to consumption, public or private.[33]

In some cases a more specific search must be made for alternative uses of resources, but even so there is no room for pessimism:

Some other resources, for example, nuclear weapons, military aircraft, and missile plants, may not be readily transferable. Some alternative civil uses may be found: for example, satellites and other techniques developed by the military could be used more than they are now in the search for natural resources and in international meteorological work. But only a part of the specialized resources could probably be absorbed in ways of this kind. For the rest, other industries will have to be brought into the areas where the specialized military production has been concentrated and retraining programs will be needed for those whose skills become redundant.[34]

On the basis of our study we recommended that pressure should be exerted by the international community in order for governments to elaborate alternative contingency plans in advance so as to facilitate a halt to the arms race:

The industry is often reluctant to change, and sometimes the Government places new military orders to sustain employment, thus perpetuating the arms race. To prevent this happening, the Group suggests that Governments, when placing orders for specialized military production or creating specialized plants likely to give rise to these difficulties in the event of disarmament, should make advance plans to deal with the redeployment to peaceful work of the manpower and plant (in so far as the latter is reusable). . . . The Group believes that the possibility of making such plans should be explored now.[35]

The spotlight should not be only on what would happen within the countries undertaking reductions in arms production. The experts were specifically instructed to study relations between disarmament and development in underdeveloped countries. Although we stressed the need for public awareness that a decrease in expenditures for military purposes could everywhere release enormous resources for development and that disarmament measures in developed countries should make possible more aid to underdeveloped countries, we were eager to emphasize that the two goals must be kept separate:

We believe that these two objectives—disarmament and development—are of the greatest importance to the world community. But
fundamentally they stand separately from one another. The United
Nations has agreed to seek each one vigorously in its own right, regardless of the pace of progress in approaching the other. Specifically,
nations have agreed that *national and international efforts to promote development should be neither postponed nor allowed to lag
merely because progress in disarmament is slow.*[36]

We must focus critical attention on a reasonable relation between a country's developmental aid and the total military costs it
carries. Sweden may be used as an example of how much aid can
be obtained without tying it to savings on the military side. The
Swedish target for straight development aid, provisionally set for
1 percent of the gross national product, was reached in the fiscal
year 1975–1976. (The UN target of 0.7 percent GNP in aid dis-
bursements was surpassed in Sweden in 1974). The military share
of the national budget corresponds to about 4 percent of the GNP.
Development aid, as official assistance carried on the national
exchequer, thus equals not 1 percent but some 25 percent of the
military costs. For poor nations to wait until Sweden would save 10
percent of its military budget, then retain nine-tenths of that saving
for its own domestic use and finally give one-tenth to development,
as suggested by the Soviet Union, would seem futile. Those who
want to promote development in the poorer countries should compare
the total allocation of the major powers for military purposes to the
total allocation for development aid.

The 1972 report was adamant in not allowing a lessening of
development ambitions by waiting for military savings. As we were
keenly aware of the tremendous disparity between the huge sums
squandered on armaments and the meager, decreasing allotment for
development aid, we were happy to conclude from a more detailed
analysis of the American material that

> the number of industries suffering negative impacts would be smaller
> when the replacement for military expenditure is assistance to de-
> veloping countries than when the replacement is domestic personal
> consumption.[37]

The twin myths about the excessive needs of military security and
the economic risks involved in redirecting production of goods and
services to peaceful purposes must be exploded. Only increased
knowledge can explode them. So I end by urging annual reporting

of conversion plans by governments to the United Nations. I recommend the setting up of an international commission, under the Geneva Disarmament Committee (CCD) or the future International Verification Agency (Chapter X), to outline a master plan for conversion of a large share of military resources that could be used to better the lives of human beings.

5. The Military Brain Drain

The most spectacular gains could be obtained by redirecting a great share of that most precious of all resources: human brain power. Technology is the great dynamic force behind the arms race. What the 400,000 scientists and engineers absorbed by military research and development are doing is escalating the performance levels of newer, more kill-effective weapons. That ability must be reoriented to work for development and peace.

The UN report, *Disarmament and Development*, gave special consideration to research and development activities.

> The world's expenditure on research and development has grown tremendously since the Second World War, but a very large part of the effort has been military. It is estimated . . . that world expenditure on research and development now amounts to $60 billion, or about 2 percent of world gross product, of which $25 billion is for military purposes. An overwhelming part of these expenditures are made in the advanced countries.[38]

Though approximate, the estimates serve to give an idea of dimensions and proportions.

The tremendous misuse of our most precious natural resource, brain power, is deeply tragic and totally indefensible. If there were no other reason for disarmament, saving this resource for the dire needs of development in a world with much privation in the developed countries and immeasurably more for the masses in the underdeveloped ones would be enough. SIPRI in 1972 published a volume, *Military Research and Development*, which details some shocking findings.[39] Six nations had the largest military budgets, being responsible for 80 percent of the total; the share of the same six in R&D spending is 98 percent. Among them the United States and the Soviet Union tower high above all other nations, an eloquent measure of their present, and their prospective, advance in military technology, and their superiority in power.

It is worth underlining that the gap in technological advance is ever widening, a discriminating pattern which reappears again and again as basic in the world situation. The grand nations compete only with the grand, the lesser nations have to compete with each other. The SIPRI study talks of two different technological arms races. The competition between the United States and the Soviet Union goes on at the very frontier of weapons technology, and there is no relenting where the most dangerous weapons development occurs. The world at large does not seem to be aware that this strong forward thrust is going on, including those inhuman weapons which are under international negotiations to stop production or those of which the possession and use has been condemned (Chapters VII, VIII, and IX).

The long list in Annex III to the report of 1972 contains many concrete suggestions for lifesaving and civilization-saving new directions of research, which would have extraordinary potential growth effects. These can be supplemented from the *World Plan of Action for the Application of Science and Technology to Development*,[40] and by innumerable suggestions from the idea banks in academic studies and periodicals. There are fields of current urgency such as the development of: solar energy and geothermal energy, natural disasters warning systems, systems analysis, techniques and computer technology applicable to development problems such as health service planning operations, efforts devoted to cancer research, storage and preservation of agricultural products, effects on man of noise and vibration, hitherto probed mostly in the interest of military needs or space adventures.

6.   A World Folly

In Chapter I, I called the arms race a global folly. Certainly it is not steered by rational thinking or valid national interests. The worst sinners against simple common sense and morality are the two superpowers, but neither are most other countries rational and conscientious in their military planning. If their analyses of the situation were rational they would agree to a reversal of the nuclear arms race and prescribe a series of reciprocal unilateral moves downward for the conventional ones.

It may be understandable that ordinary people are ignorant about the facts and inclined to think in crude terms of balance. It is indefensible, however, that the two governments, who know the facts, do not draw rational conclusions about the interests of their nations. Instead, by their actions and policy statements, they lead their people to patently wrong views.

It is equally indefensible that so many scientists and experts, who must know better, keep silent or voice the official doctrine, and that the mass media give so little attention to those few who stay independent and speak the truth. This last accusation is addressed mainly to individuals and groups in the United States and its allied countries, because in the Soviet Union there is still little opportunity for free public discussion.

The two superpowers are also leading the world in the race in conventional arms and in the provision of such weapons to the underdeveloped world through sales and gifts. Most other countries are participating in this race. The expenditures for conventional armaments are several times higher than for nuclear armaments. The conventional weapons race is also qualitative: the procurement of steadily more sophisticated and expensive weaponry like supersonic military aircraft.[41]

The difficulties involved in stopping this world folly are immense, and up till now we have achieved almost nothing. All citizens, especially young people, must be awakened and made to understand that there is no need for us to be slaves of the endless senseless military usurpation of a giant share of all fiscal, material, and mental resources. True security would require far less military input. Far more research and development must be turned towards civilian purposes, thus curbing the competition for improved new armaments.

The myths must be exploded that economic collapse would follow eradications of military procurements and development work. There is nothing unique about the capacity of the military to create jobs, and more of these job opportunities would be anchored in home communities serving the people. There are enormous riches in the world to be set free for public welfare, especially for the people in the poorer parts of the world. Ever since the first UN report on this subject in 1962, the challenge to redirect resources from military to civilian uses has been before the Member nations.

Would they rather have listened to military leaders? I can find no better way of concluding this chapter than by a quote from President Eisenhower, who more than any other American statesman felt the risk in the drift of military policy in his country. His famous farewell message warned against the "unwarranted influence, whether sought or unsought, by the military-industrial complex" and against the "potential for the disastrous rise of misplaced power." Several times he expounded on the theme, widening it to the whole scope of armaments versus security. Once he said:

> No matter how much we spend for arms, there is no safety in arms alone. Our security is the total product of our economic, intellectual, moral, and military strengths.
>
> Let me elaborate on this great truth. It happens that defense is a field in which I have had varied experience over a lifetime, and if I have learned anything, it is that there is no way in which a country can satisfy the craving for absolute security—but it easily can bankrupt itself, morally and economically, in attempting to reach that illusory goal through arms alone. The Military Establishment, not productive of itself, necessarily must feed on the energy, productivity, and brainpower of the country, and if it takes too much, our total strength declines.[42]

CHAPTER VI

Barring the
Spread of Nuclear Weapons

Although stopping and reversing the nuclear arms race between the two superpowers is the most important disarmament measure, preventing further proliferation is even more urgent, as recent developments open truly horrifying prospects for a future worse than the present. Stopping the spread of nuclear weaponry to additional countries, however, is crucially dependent on the superpowers stopping their own proliferation.

1. The Genie Came Out

A curse fell on the whole future of mankind when the atomic bomb exploded. So incredibly powerful is this weapon that in the early debates it was often spoken of as the ultimate, the absolute, or the decisive weapon.[1] It contributed in a singularly frightening manner to the militarization of our whole civilization. Political leaders became so obsessed with military strategies that most of them ceased to be statesmen responsible for the long-term destiny of their nations and the world.

One, and the most pervasive, of the political effects was the cold war. I will not attempt to judge to what extent the atomic bomb—or rather its genesis as a United States monopoly—was responble for the collapse of what was left of political trust and cooperation between the United States and Russia, but the bomb, and the overriding concern with secrecy that was its hallmark, was certainly a main constitutive element in the cold war. Such secrecy killed any rational

159

approach which might have been used to negotiate for international control at the very outset of the atomic era (Chapter III, Section 3).

Never has a new weapon been so successfully managed to come as a surprise to the world. In comparison, all other tools of warfare developed gradually, and new developments were easily conjectured. Conversely, the nuclear explosion was brought to readiness in closely guarded secrecy.

Secrecy was the keynote from the days when the race began on the part of the Western allies to tame the atom before Hitler's Germany could do so. The scientific discovery of nuclear fission became known early in 1939, on the threshold of war. Had Hitler not plunged the world into war, the subsequent development of nuclear power might have followed the tradition of international scientific cooperation. Typical of the scientific way of working up to that time, information was readily exchanged. Relevant discoveries were made public. Independent but surprisingly simultaneous research was pursued in many countries. But with World War II competition not only for the peaceful application of fission but for mastering the art of making nuclear explosives for war purposes became one of the fiercest, most highly secret scientific adventures.[2]

However, the secret could not be kept for long; basic knowledge was widely shared among scientists in several countries—Germany, Denmark, France, Britain, Italy, Japan, and Russia. Scientists from different nations had participated in the early stages of experimentation for producing the bomb. Extreme secrecy, resulting from wartime fears about security, soon led to a consolidation of research which left the United States in sole possession of the horror weapon when it was exploded.

However, moral responsibility for creating the atom bomb must be shared by several governments. Britain, in Churchill's historic memo of August 1941, was the first to make the decision to try for an atomic bomb. The United States took the formal decision the day before Pearl Harbor was attacked on 7 December 1941. Several scientists who had worked in France were brought to England after France fell to the Nazis. They in turn, together with an important group of British colleagues, went to Canada, where they cooperated with an American team, which was heavily fortified by a scientific elite of escapees from totalitarian Germany and Italy, many of Nobel laureate caliber.

Accounts of how the United States ousted the French and played hide-and-seek with the British have been published with bitter comments by British and French authors.[3] After the War, those scientists, who had started out as colleagues in a joint allied endeavor, had to go their separate ways. Many returned to England and France, taking their knowledge with them.

Some commentators may have overestimated the contributions of non-U.S. scientists, but their early insights had considerable value as seed capital for ensuing developments, leading to nuclear reactors in Canada, England, and France and to proliferation of nuclear weapons. Britain was able to produce its first atomic bomb in 1952; France, in 1960.

This is told not to distribute the honor of inventing the hellish bomb but to demonstrate the curse of secrecy. Secrecy simply cannot be kept for long, especially not of knowledge that rests on a basic scientific discovery. If that knowledge is considered important, the drive forward inherent in all science and technology will soon break open the locks. The main objective of the United States' secrecy was first to move ahead of Nazi Germany, then to keep the secret from the Soviet Union. This only delayed the appearance of the first Soviet atomic bomb for about four years (1949). This corresponded to what the scientists had estimated, four to six years, while United States military authorities were confident that the Russians were some twenty years behind.

Hindsight reveals that the delay was no net gain at all. Many ill-conceived strategic ideas of containment and massive retaliation originated in the interval when the United States relied on its monopoly of nuclear weapons and directed its military planning accordingly. One of the major roots of the cold war was the double-sided gaming of the two emerging superpowers: the United States' fear that the Soviets would pry open the secret and master the knowledge and Soviet resentment that they were to be kept at bay by a former ally that considered itself to be omnipotent.

International cooperation could have saved the situation by burying all plans for future production of nuclear weapons and sharing the knowledge of nuclear energy for the benefit of all nations. The compelling concern with secrecy and the belief that knowledge about nuclear explosives could not be independently obtained for a long time by other countries caused internationalization to fail. Any hope to move from one nuclear power to none was quenched in 1946 with the failure of the Baruch plan (Chapter III, Section 3). Even after the Soviet Union had acquired nuclear-weapons power it should have been possible for the two powers to cooperate in halting further proliferation. It would have left the world with two nuclear powers —hardly ideal, but corresponding to the political power situation prevailing then and now. The world might have learned to live with what has been called two scorpions in a bottle as well as with one.[4] The period when such a political maneuver might have been possible passed, however, without any real attempt to stem the tide of proliferation. For fifteen long years, until the early 1960s, a lack of concern was manifested by the negligence of action at the UN.*

Secrecy played a major role in the proliferation until the nuclear-weapons powers became five. In both Britain and France decisions to continue research and take steps towards manufacture of nuclear arms were taken without public debate or public knowledge. In 1946 the Attlee cabinet placed all nuclear activities under government control and proceeded to erect a plutonium separation plant and a gas diffusion plant for enriching uranium. The concern with secrecy served to keep public discussion subdued. No mention of these ominous decisions was made in the White Papers of these years. Parliamentary debates on the strategy and meaningfulness of an independent British nuclear force occurred only in the period 1957–1964, "The Great Nuclear Debate."[5] The public uproar, culminating in the Aldermaston march to ban the bomb (Easter 1960) came ten to fifteen years after the fateful decision and five to eight years after the United Kingdom had detonated its first bomb in a test at the Australian island of Montebello (1952).

When in 1952 France decided to produce plutonium as part of a five-year plan, nothing at the outset was said about its military utilization, although it was—according to Bertrand Goldschmidt— "undoubtedly predominant in the minds of those responsible." In 1954 the government of Mendes-France was ready to take the decisive step: "very conscious about the gap at the international level between the nuclear powers and the others."[6] In 1960 the first French nuclear explosive test was a fact for all to hear.

The delay between the acquisition of nuclear power by Britain and by France was because France was handicapped by lack of technological knowledge and supplies of fissionable material. The United States had refused all cooperation for French development of nuclear energy, which was begun by a nationalization act of 18 October 1945 similar to England's. The French, since early in the war never officially part of the United States-British-Canadian coopera-

* This statement is valid although Eisenhower's Atoms-for-Peace plan of December 1953 and the establishment of IAEA in 1956 were implicitly antiproliferation.

tion, and not constrained by its concomitant policy of secrecy, have always revealed more both about their nuclear research and descriptions of their reactors. Indirectly, this has served to break up American secrecy.[7]

The harsh conclusion, unavoidable, is that secrecy is writ large all over the history of proliferation—to no avail. The policy of secrecy and the resentment caused by it only acted to spur others' nuclear ambitions. Prestige became more and more involved. Secrecy was combined with political fumbling and a curious let-go attitude to bring us to the point that, when proliferation started to be debated as an important international issue, a "nuclear club" already existed. The Non-Proliferation Treaty solemnly confirmed its unassailable position by declaring those nations that had tested nuclear weapons before 1 January 1967 to be nuclear-weapons powers. There were then five. I said in a speech in Geneva, when the proliferation debate was finally beginning: "Nobody could assert that they [five] are the ones whose possession of nuclear fire power poses the minimal danger, in other words: that all is quiet on the nuclear front as it is drawn today."[8]

There are many complexities in the public concern with rights and wrongs of acquiring nuclear weapons. In the United States, some scientists themselves had led the ethical self-examination even before the first atom bomb was delivered and even more fiercely before work on the hydrogen bomb started, symbolized in the sacrifice of Robert Oppenheimer to the McCarthy forces some years later. A parallel debate on the ethical problems first ensued in Europe later in the 1950s (Chapter III, Section 5).

There was a similar dead period before the international debate on proliferation was revived in 1960. It started with academic concern with doctrines, bitterly argued despite the high level of theoretical abstractions. Popular interest was stirred in the United States by the *Daedalus* volume, commissioned by the American Academy of Arts and Sciences in 1960. It continued through a number of books by Thomas Schelling, Herman Kahn, Henry Kissinger, and many others, sometimes called The Strategy Intellectuals. In England books by P. M. S. Blackett, Bertrand Russell, B. H. Liddell Hart, Philip Noel-Baker, and others had at the same time or somewhat earlier challenged the official sanctioning of nuclear weapons as military necessities. In France the debate for or against nuclear weapons has never been active, and least of all has it spread to the general population.

2. The Lesser Nuclear-Weapons Powers

While debate in international forums became concentrated on the problem of *further* proliferation of nuclear weapons, the legitimacy of nuclear-weapons possession has not seriously been questioned. The nuclear arms race between the two superpowers is in a category by itself. Their responsibility is recognized as crucial. But what about the lesser powers known to have nuclear weapons—Britain, France, China? Even if their role is not decisive for the nuclear arms race as a whole, their responsibility for promoting or hindering nuclear weapons acquisition by additional countries is considerable. They should not be spared criticism, as has become the custom in the United Nations and, generally, international public opinion.

None of the lesser nuclear-weapons powers have been invited to the SALT negotiations (Chapter III, Section 8; Chapter IV, Sections 2 and 4). Their nuclear arsenals are not large enough for them to aspire to the type of balancing in which the superpowers are gaming. That does not mean, however, that their equipping their armed forces with nuclear weapons can be considered to have only a nuisance value. If they, or others who might be expected to join what is euphemistically called the nuclear club, ever use such weapons, this would cause damage on a scale much bigger than the two American bombs over Japan in the infancy of the nuclear age.

Why Britain and France insisted on becoming and remaining nuclear-weapons powers is open to speculation. For both these nations have from the outset directly wanted to procure nuclear arms, not just to secure a share in commercial possibilities for developing peaceful nuclear energy. Having nuclear weapons seems to be reckoned as a prerequisite for being included among the great powers, as in earlier times having overseas colonies was. Both Britain and France are in a sense compensating for the loss of status as colonial empires. Of course, to the extent that this is true there may be fewer motivated to emulate them.

There is another political angle to the aspiration for power and prestige. Both these countries, although to a different degree, have wanted to keep independent of their American ally. This was early expressed by British leaders. Churchill said that what was at stake was Britain's future independence.[9] During the great debate pro and con nuclear weapons in the 1960s, Gaitskell, being pro, felt nuclear production was justifiable to avoid excessive dependence on the United States. He had doubts regarding America's willingness to engage in nuclear retaliation on Britain's behalf and wished to retain maximum influence in political discussions with the United States so that decisions would not be forced on Britain against its will.[10]

Today Britain has on its territory several sets of nuclear weapons, some under sole United States command, some under NATO, some tactical nuclear weapons of its own, and a small independent strategic force of four nuclear-propelled submarines with Polaris missiles for nuclear weapons. How independently can such national forces function, for either defense or deterrent purposes?

Britain's motivation for remaining a nuclear-weapons power has become increasingly pathetic because it has continuously and in almost all respects lost its great power position, while at the same time it lags behind other industrial nations in economic growth and stability. It seems incredible that the British people would not respond positively to a political leadership prepared to give up nuclear weapons on the same rational grounds that countries like Australia, Canada, and Sweden have abstained from acquiring them (Chapter VI, Section 5). The question of disarmament or proliferation is one for responsible leadership.[11]

French leaders used the British example as justification for acquisition of nuclear weapons.

> In the view of many Frenchmen, France's interests were as extensive as those of Great Britain. If Great Britain felt that her security obligations required that she possess a nuclear weapons arsenal, then France should recognize the same need and take steps to assure herself a nuclear force.[12]

This is exactly the pattern that makes for proliferation. In France the political-military case for independence has been much more adamantly advocated than in Britain. Doubts have been expressed much more openly and frequently about the willingness of the United States to use its nuclear umbrella in defense of an ally. This belief in the sanctuary doctrine (Chapter II, Sections 2–7) has led France into a quite vigorous and costly program; both research and production have been carried out in considerable independence. The French project the size of the *force de frappe* to continue to expand for years to come. It will, however, never reach more than a small percentage of a superpower's strength.

Exactly how this nuclear force would be used is never quite clarified. It is claimed to have a deterrent function and serve to protect French territory, but how it could function in an independent way in conjunction with a shooting war in Europe begs the question. Neither the French nor the British could hope to strike effectively against the capabilities of the Soviet Union, presumably the enemy. Retaliation would have to be expected, a costly retaliation—this is the national dilemma for any nuclear-weapons power in the lesser category.

China is a case by itself. Having come late into the field, partly with the aid of the Soviet Union, China has been building up its nuclear arsenal, both bombs and delivery vehicles, and is also ambitiously launching surveillance satellites.

Politically speaking, because the size of its population and its political and economic coherence, China is the only country that could aspire to become a third superpower. It denies that it wants to achieve superstatus[13] and carries on a propaganda campaign against both superpowers, today most vehemently against the Soviet Union. Its role in regard to proliferation is uncertain. But if Asian countries should start to acquire nuclear weapons, China—as a precursor and as a threat—might well be used as a justification. This responsibility lies heavily on China in light of its strong stand for the right to wars of self-defense and liberation and its frequent exclamations about its readiness to use nuclear bombs against any nuclear attacker.

3. Futile Attempts to Ban Proliferation

When the nonproliferation debate belatedly opened at the outset of the 1960s, it resulted in two different solutions that were proposed in the form of draft resolutions in the General Assembly. One was an Irish plan to foreclose all options for additional countries to join the nuclear club. Another was a Swedish proposal for voluntary self-organization of a nuclear-free club, or, in the terms of the "Undén plan," nuclear-free zones. The plan emphasized the idea of self-determination for a group of countries and underlined that renunciations would be tied to explicit conditions.

The two proposals reveal a deeper difference in political philosophy. The Irish proposal was based on the concept that nuclear weapons could be a national asset, but that they should be compulsorily abjured in the wider international interest, although only by newcomers. The Swedish concept was much more akin to the spirit that had animated the ban-the-bomb movement, which received political expression in the British Labour Party proposal of 1959 for a voluntary non-nuclear-weapons club.[14] Its pamphlet *Disarmament and Nuclear War: The Next Step* was a laudable attempt to get Britain to renounce becoming a nuclear-weapons power. To have done so would have meant the British recognized their responsibility for proliferation, but, alas, the proposal was never followed up in actual policy.[15] Neither did the British movement to ban the bomb, although the corresponding Swedish movement succeeded (Chapter III, Section 5).

The Swedish proposal was based upon the notion that nuclear weapons could not enhance national security, especially that of the lesser powers. By having nuclear arsenals, necessarily small and weak, they might risk drawing fire onto themselves. National self-interest was seen to be at one with international security. The same reasoning, however, should logically lead the nuclear powers to divest themselves of their giant powder kegs, or, at the least, not to race for more, and, as expressed in the Swedish resolution, "to discontinue all nuclear tests."

Both resolutions were accepted on 4 December 1961, the Irish one, 1665 (XVI), unanimously and the Swedish one, 1664 (XVI), with a majority of fifty-eight votes against ten, with twenty-three abstentions, the Eastern bloc voting for and the Western against. The many abstentions were mostly caused by Latin American and African uncertainty.

Still, years passed before action was attempted. By 1965 the United States and the Soviet Union had become superpowers in the sense that they were the only ones who could destroy the whole world at their will. They were firmly entrenched in their locked-horn position of striving incessantly to outdo each other by escalating their nuclear arsenals. Confident of their power, they attempted to hold unrestricted rights to possess, deploy, and develop nuclear arms quantitatively and qualitatively, while showing overbearing disregard for the three minor nuclear-weapons powers, and resolutely closing the options for all other nations to go nuclear.

When impatience grew for some disarmament measure on the part of the nonaligned countries, the superpowers countered with a very inequitable model. India was particularly active during these years, submitting to the General Assembly in 1964 a proposal for a special agenda item "Nonproliferation of nuclear weapons." India and Sweden then joined forces in demanding as "a more equitable and practical basis of agreement . . . a package or integrated approach consisting of a nonproliferation agreement and some other measures affecting directly the nuclear weapons capability of the nuclear powers."[16] All the nonaligned members of the Geneva Disarmament Committee joined in a memorandum stressing that "measures to prohibit the spread of nuclear weapons should . . . be coupled with or followed by tangible steps to halt the nuclear weapons and the means of their delivery."[17]

To retain the initiative, in the fall of 1965 both the United States and the Soviet Union submitted to the General Assembly draft treaties designed to prevent the spread of nuclear weapons. Both favored the Irish solution, which allowed discriminatory distinctions to be established between nations possessing nuclear weapons and those without. During all the time the Non-Proliferation Treaty was actively negotiated in the Geneva Committee, in the General Assembly, and finally in 1968 in a special spring session of the General Assembly, improvements were suggested and warnings were heard that a treaty according to superpower design might not attract those countries whose aspirations would be stymied and whose activities would be controlled. However, the basic construction was retained. Obligations were laid on the non-nuclear-weapons countries, and only on them, to accept international control over nuclear installations. In the end they were able to extract only a promise (Article VI) from the superpowers to negotiate in good faith the cessation of the nuclear arms race at an early date.

There was no balance, no mutuality of obligations and benefits. I said then that it was necessary to emphasize "the reluctance of non-nuclear powers to shoulder a particular and, as a matter of fact, a solitary obligation to make renunciatory decisions in regard to proliferation of nuclear weapons."[18] To place the major responsibility on their shoulders amounted to a clever design to get NPT to function as a seal on the superpowers' hegemonic world policy.

An immediate result of the deficiencies of the NPT was, when the UN General Assembly (June 1968) voted to recommend the conclusion of NPT, that a number of important countries abstained —Argentina, Brazil, France, India, and several African states. India's refusal to join the NPT had been flatly stated during the negotiations, the argument being that the Treaty was discriminatory. This outcome of the negotiations was a tragic reflection on history, as India's Nehru had been the first to propose a ban on all nuclear testing.

4. A Grossly Discriminatory Treaty

The lack of balance between obligations and benefits in the Non-Proliferation Treaty (NPT) is blatant on at least five crucial points. They are the following:

First, the pledge (Article VI) for the nuclear-weapons powers to cease the arms race is still unfulfilled and there are no vital signs that it will be honored in the foreseeable future.

Second, the obligation (Article III) of the non-nuclear-weapons states to "accept safeguards, as set forth in an agreement to be negotiated and concluded with the International Atomic Energy Agency . . . for the exclusive purpose of verification . . . with a view to preventing the diversion of nuclear energy from peaceful uses to nuclear weapons or other nuclear explosive devices," is one-sided. This obligation has been implemented by the majority of states that have ratified the NPT.[19] The promise, held out in the debates, that the United States and Britain would be willing to submit their non-military nuclear facilities for verification, has not been put into practice. At an early stage some experimental testing of IAEA safeguards did take place (and some later in the Soviet Union). But the American and British promises had been made in no uncertain terms, secured by solemn but unilateral statements by the two governments in the last tense months of the NPT negotiations.[20]

Third, there was an understanding that non-nuclear countries which became parties to the NPT would be favored in regard to the supply of nuclear technology and material (Article IV). Combined with Article I ("not in any way to assist, encourage, or induce any non-nuclear-weapons State to manufacture . . . nuclear weapons or other nuclear explosive devices") this understanding amounted to an obligation for supplier countries to give parties to the NPT preferential treatment in information and material aid in the nuclear field. But NPT parties have not been the exclusive beneficiaries of such aid and trade.

In its press comments after the Indian nuclear explosion SIPRI said on this point:

There has been no inducement to join the NPT: States can remain outside the Treaty, and outside the new safeguards systems set up by the IAEA, without risking difficulties in their peaceful nuclear endeavours or even in preparing for a nuclear explosion. Indeed, the insousiance of supplier countries may have facilitated the Indian nuclear explosion.

The growing activities by IAEA in the field of technical and material assistance to less developed countries has not been restricted by consideration of whether a recipient nation is a party to the NPT or not.[21]

The rules in Article I and II concerning transfers and safeguards are extremely unfair to non-nuclear weapons powers. They favor the nuclear-weapons powers, which is indefensible from the point of view of disarmament. Those who had joined the nuclear club in time are free to transfer to each other both nuclear weapons and kindred nuclear explosive devices as well as to "assist, encourage, and induce" each other to acquire and manufacture equipment for nuclear-weapons production. The non-nuclear-weapons countries are not free to do any of these things; they are also explicitly forbidden to "receive any assistance in the manufacture of nuclear explosive devices" (Articles I and II). The freedom of transfer within the nuclear club includes all source materials, fissionable material at any degree of enrichment, and equipment. The non-nuclear-weapons countries, on the other hand, are not to receive any of these categories of material or equipment except under the rules whereby all nuclear installations within their territory are to be controlled according to the IAEA safeguards system. International transfers of natural uranium and heavy water, both of which can be used in nuclear processes, are still, at the time of writing, freely allowed.

Fourth, Article V of the treaty promised that benefits from nuclear explosions, conducted for peaceful purposes, would be made available to treaty partners at a low cost. More important, Article V also says that states should be able to obtain such benefits "pursuant to a special international agreement or agreements, through an international body with adequate representation of non-nuclear weapons states. Negotiations on this subject shall commence as soon as possible after the Treaty enters into force." No international agreement has been reached and no such international body established, nor have negotiations on the subject taken place during the more than five years which have elapsed. Needless to say, no benefits have been made available.

Fifth, a promise of security guarantees to non-nuclear-weapons countries against attacks or threats of attacks from nuclear-weapons states was given during the negotiations in order to allay the worries about security on the part of the nuclear-free nations. For this purpose the three NPT "depositary states"—that is, the superpowers and Britain—moved a resolution in the Security Council (Resolution

255, 1968) wherein they promised immediate assistance to a non-nuclear-weapons nation, party to the NPT, if it became the "victim of an act or an object of a threat of aggression in which nuclear weapons are used."

This pretended security guarantee has proved to be a misbegotten one. First, most countries have not appreciated the gesture; the non-aligned members of the Security Council at the time had reservations about it. Also it restricted rather than added to the obligation to render such assistance under UN Charter rules. Further, with veto powers—as they were in 1968—the promise was tantamount to protection only in the event of an attack from China. With China now able to use the veto, a UN-sponsored action against any possible nuclear attack or blackmail would fail to receive the necessary unanimity. Recently, a group of experts held a preview conference on NPT and frankly stated that, as a protection for non-nuclear-weapons countries, the resolution is valueless (Chapter VI, Section 7).[22]

As scheduled in the NPT, a conference to review the performance of the Treaty during its first five years met in May 1975. The harsh judgments made above were then confirmed on all five scores. So far, the NPT falls short of all reasonable expectations as a disarmament measure.

5. How It Went Wrong

The Non-Proliferation Treaty was soon signed by over one hundred nations. At the time of the Review Conference eighty-seven had also ratified, all being non-nuclear-weapons states, except the depository governments of Britain, the United States, and the Soviet Union. What superficially looks like a victory is, however, hollow. The overwhelming majority of nations making this gesture did not have much of a chance to produce nuclear arms. Of the fifteen to twenty countries who were thought to have such capacity,[23] only four had ratified the Treaty before the Review Conference, Canada, Sweden, East Germany, and Australia.

The renunciation of these four was not dependent upon adherence to an international treaty. Canada and Sweden, being close to the top of the threshold or near-nuclear countries, had already made independent decisions, founded upon what they conceived as their national interest, not to allow nuclear arms in their arsenals.

Canada from the end of the War had forsaken the option of producing an atom bomb. The Canadian delegate categorily stated early in the Geneva Disarmament Committee that Canada never contemplated joining the nuclear club:

> There has never been any serious question of Canada becoming a member of the nuclear club—that is, one of those nations which by its own national decision can launch nuclear weapons. This ability could only be obtained by the national manufacture of nuclear weapons. It is not contemplated.[24]

The Swedish history of the successful opposition to military plans to acquire nuclear weapons has been told (Chapter III, Section 5). The debate was virtually won by 1960, and after the question had been duly dealt with in a Parliamentary Commission, the Government laid the proposal before Parliament early in 1968. As the Minister of Defense and myself were the Government spokesmen in the two Houses for a decision to be taken against any nuclear weapons in the Swedish arsenal, we had the great satisfaction of finding that all political parties were ready to acquiesce. The historical decision was taken by Parliament on 22 May 1968. It has seemed appropriate to underline here how firm Sweden's renunciation of nuclear weapons is, as our adamant criticism of how the NPT came to be shaped is sometimes misconstrued as a thinly veiled threat of crossing over to the nuclear club. The *no* to a Swedish nuclear bomb is categorical.[25]

The belief that nuclear weapons would be more of a burden than an asset was the basis for both Sweden's and Canada's renunciation of them. It was also an Australian argument later. East Germany clearly belongs to a military bloc within which nuclear weapons are certain to be kept as a Soviet monopoly.

The situation in regard to nonproliferation by other nations in the near-nuclear category is a motley one. Of the NATO countries, such important threshold countries as West Germany, Italy, Belguim, and the Netherlands ratified NPT only days before the 1975 Review Conference.[26] In May 1976, Japan ratified the NPT. Switzerland probably will not go nuclear.

But it is of sinister importance that Argentina, Brazil, Egypt, Israel, Spain, South Africa, and Pakistan have refused to adhere.[27] And India has put an audible exclamation point behind its refusal. With its underground test in May 1974 India demonstrated possession of a device which is per se an atomic bomb, whether or not it is so used or intended. The Indian nuclear explosion symbolizes the mistaken and niggardly approach of the superpowers to the negotiations. Several nations are keeping their nuclear arms options open, either by refusing to become parties to the NPT or by procrastinating, signing but not yet ratifying the Treaty.

The conclusion is unavoidable: the NPT was not tailored to convince the nations at which it was aimed. No concrete give-and-take negotiations that could have lead to firm commitments were undertaken, not at the conference table nor through diplomatic channels in the capitals. That the NPT has become such a political miss is not yet succinctly analyzed and generally acknowledged. It should, however, have been recognized from the outset that if there are tenable arguments for some lesser powers in favor of possessing nuclear weapons, such must be equally applicable to others.

Even now, the three nations in the minor nuclear-weapons league—Britain, France, and China—continue unabashed testing, production, and development of new and more nuclear arms and the vehicles for delivering them. All three are causing worry to the superpowers while at the same time providing precedent and allurement to others who might contemplate becoming the sixth or nth nuclear-weapons power.[28]

The whole plan to have the non-nuclear-weapons powers accept responsibility for preventing the destruction of mankind by renouncing nuclear arms is in disarray. More nations will follow India's example, perhaps aiming straightforwardly at the weaponizing of nuclear explosives.

The failure of the NPT became evident at the May 1975 Review Conference.[29] Much hope had been set on there achieving a redressing of the discrimination to provide a more effective barrier against the further spread of nuclear weapons. To this end, before the Conference convened, a number of expert subconferences were held; many publications were issued to muster the arguments in persuasive detail, to influence governments and conference participants as well as public opinion.*

However, at the Conference practically everybody seemed to have accepted continued proliferation of nuclear weapons as something

* Reference should be made particularly to the preview conference held in Divonne 9–11 September 1974, under the aegis of the Carnegie Endowment for International Peace and the (US) Arms Control Association. Its findings are published in *NPT: Paradoxes and Problems*, 1975. I participated in that conference as well as in several meetings in Washington, e.g., one with a great number of United States Senators, 4 March 1975. Also, I presented my ideas in "The High Price of Nuclear Arms Monopoly," *Foreign Policy*, Spring 1975, and in SIPRI's *The Right to Conduct Nuclear Explosions: Political Aspects and Policy Proposals*, Stockholm paper 6, 1975, with a nearly identical article in *Bulletin of the Atomic Scientists*, May 1975.

inevitable. The nuclear-weapons powers had nothing substantive to offer to stem the trend toward proliferation. Their cynicism was made obvious by a categorical nonacceptance of all proposals, symbolized by a giant United States test explosion in the middle of the Conference. Additionally, the non-nuclear-weapons countries had not built up a common frontier in advance. The role of the nonaligned countries at this Conference was an uncommonly muted one. The causes are complex, but a major reason was that the nuclear-weapons powers had schemed to make the Conference impotent by rushing and railroading it. They took upon themselves the laying down of the main rules for the Conference and the financing of it in their capacity as depositary powers. To secure the smooth running of the Conference according to their wishes Britain, the Soviet Union, and the United States met in London in advance. There they decided, on the basis of their important funding of the Conference, that it would close on 29 May. They also drafted a declaration of what should be the outcome of the conference—a document that leaked to participants. During the conference they spoke in a singularly preharmonized manner. They stonewalled any attempt to get them to pay their share of the price of nuclear disarmament. As the Conference was only to act by consensus on substantive issues, there could, of course, be no more consensus than what the least willing Parties, i.e., the superpowers, agreed to—that is, to the most innocuous statements.

The lesser powers were divided. Some were in military alliance with the two blocs, sleeping partners of the superpowers. Some, like the very important threshold countries, not being parties to the NPT agreement, were not official Members of the Conference. Several of them, however, came as observers—Japan, Switzerland, Argentina, Brazil, Egypt, Israel, and South Africa. As a matter of fact, only fifty-eight Treaty Members participated.* Even among the nonaligned, usually stalwarts at disarmament meetings, there were too many divisive interests for them to act in purposive unison on the central issue of stemming nonproliferation.

The NPT Review Conference did not rectify the discriminatory imbalance in the Treaty nor was any recommendation made in that direction, as exemplified by the Final Declaration. As consensus could not be obtained at the Conference, the joint Declaration con-

* No less than nine states joined the NPT just before or during the Conference; recently the total number of adherents has been brought to ninety-seven at the end of 1975.

sists of a "summary of deliberations," drafted and presented by the chairman, Inga Thorsson. As such, it reflected the prevailing situation by some meek statements (though there were strong reservations made orally), such as the one in the Preamble about it being essential to *maintain* "an acceptable balance of mutual obligations of all States party to the Treaty, nuclear-weapons and non-nuclear-weapons States," as if any such balance existed.

Instead of castigating the nuclear-weapons powers for non-fulfillment of their pledge, a legal obligation under the Treaty's Article VI to negotiate "in good faith on effective measures relating to the cessation of the nuclear arms race at an early date," the Final Declaration is next to congratulatory:

> While welcoming the various agreements on arms limitation and disarmament elaborated and concluded over the last few years as steps contributing to the implementation of Article VI of the Treaty, the Conference expresses its serious concern that the arms race, in particular the nuclear arms race, is continuing unabated.[30]

While concern was expressed about the nuclear arms race, it must be concluded that Article VI is now dead, or at least its power to exert pressure is paralyzed.

To judge the Conference as a whole, however, the world community would do well to listen to the strong criticisms, even warnings, voiced by such countries as Mexico, Nigeria, Peru, and Syria (among the nonaligned) as well as Rumania, Australia, and New Zealand. Yugoslavia perhaps went farthest in threatening to re-examine its attitude to the NPT as such and "drawing corresponding conclusions."[31]

In the absence of so many Treaty Members the opposition was diminished in power and took recourse to a stratagem which had strong value as a demonstration but in practice was less successful. This consisted of presenting draft resolutions containing three additional protocols, of which only one, Draft Protocol III, asking for a pledge of nonattack with nuclear weapons, was strictly germane to the issues at the Conference.[32]

Another stratagem was to wrest some fulfillment of Article VI by asking for a comprehensive test ban, Draft Protocol I, but it did so by linking a moratorium of ten years to the number of NPT members reaching one hundred and the establishment of a full-fledged comprehensive test ban only when all "the other nuclear-weapon States" were willing to become parties. I have, although reluctantly, criticized this approach as less compatible with the NPT tasks, particularly in relation to another of the draft protocols, Draft Protocol II, setting a similar pattern for reduction of strategic missiles (Chapter IV, Section 4). Unfortunately there was no opportunity to put the superpowers' willingness to pay the main prices suggested in this chapter to a real test: a pledge of no nuclear attack on non-nuclear-weapons countries, and the subjecting of themselves to the general rules of nontransfer of fissionable materials (Chapter VI, Section 8).

An explanation of the relative complacency of the lesser powers, especially the less developed, is that they had become fascinated by the prospect of access to nuclear technology. Some are not immune to the lure of mastering the fateful double-edged nuclear explosions (Chapter VII), but most of them are enthusiastic to apply nuclear technology for the peaceful purpose of providing new sources of energy. At the Conference there was extraordinarily little heard of the debate rumbling within the advanced nations, of the warnings from environmentalists and other groups in favor of limiting nuclear energy production so that natural sources of energy—solar, wind, geothermal, etc.—could be given a greater chance. The reliance on the value of nuclear energy was rather one-sidedly expressed in the Final Declaration, in which was more than a full page of desiderata in relation to Article IV of the Treaty, which stressed the need for broadening cooperation for such purposes and noted

> the important role which nuclear energy can, particularly in changing economic circumstances, play in power production and in contributing to the progressive elimination of the economic and technological gap between developing and developed States.[33]

Warnings were, however, heard and practical recommendations given in regard to increased safeguards against theft of nuclear material:

> The Conference, convinced that nuclear materials should be effectively protected at all times, urges that action be pursued to elaborate further, within the IAEA, concrete recommendations for the physical protection of nuclear material in use, storage, and transit, including principles relating to the responsibility of States, with a view to ensuring a uniform, minimum level of effective protection for such material.[34]

The IAEA is devoting much attention to this subject. Also an idea for future improvement was articulated at the Conference: regional or multinational centers were advocated for coping with the full nuclear fuel cycle (Chapter VI, Section 8). In summary, there were positive but minor improvements suggested for the implementation of the NPT, particularly for strengthening the access to and safety of nuclear energy production.

Nonetheless, the imperative task of the NPT is to stem the further spread of nuclear weapons and the nuclear arms race as a whole. The impression remaining after the 1975 Review Conference is that a great many nations are giving up hope of stopping further proliferation. From that point of view it might have been better to have the Conference end in open failure. The superpowers anyway seem inclined to tolerate lesser powers equipping themselves with nuclear weapons, trusting that they would serve only as a defense against neighbors, while relying on their own ultimate strength to withstand any threat against themselves.

6.   Any Limit to Proliferation?

A general disbelief grows as to the inability of the NPT to stem proliferation of nuclear arms as the rapid spread of reactors for producing nuclear energy leads to worldwide multiplication of stocks of fissionable material. Technological knowledge is also spreading, creating the prerequisites for independently manufactured atomic bombs in a great number of countries. Some nations would be capable of producing sophisticated weapons, backed by adequate delivery systems. Others would have to be content with lower degrees of sophistication. Most would be able to produce first generation bombs of the plutonium-based Nagasaki type able to kill some 100,000 people in one strike. Even if such bombs remained untested, they would still add a considerable threat of death and destruction.

Estimates abound as to how soon and how many bombs could result from diverting fissionable material from the widely available stockpiles of plutonium which accompany the expansion of nuclear energy programs. There may also be an ability to divert reactor-grade uranium to enrichment for weapon-grade. The wide margin of uncertainty in all such estimates is in part dependent on differences in the technical parameters of the type of nuclear fuel cycles that would be used—such as light-water reactors with or without plutonium recycling, heavy-water natural uranium reactors, gas-cooled reactors using either natural or enriched uranium, or possibly fast breeder reactors.[35]

However, much uncertainty about future developments is related to the fact that several countries are going ahead with ambitious plans for expanding production of nuclear energy. In the heated debate on the question now going on in many countries, opposition is voiced by scientists and public opinion on several points. Dominant among these are the environmental risks relating to waste disposal, radioactive leaks, and other accidents. Risks of theft and malevolent diversion of fissionable material by terrorists and criminals play a smaller but still agonizing role. The danger that an international black or gray market might be organized is adding to the worries about proliferation of nuclear weapons. The main concern for disarmers is, however, still the risk that governments may decide to use the abundantly available fissionable material for systematic production of nuclear weapons, openly or under the guise of peaceful use of nuclear explosives.

The threatening political picture was evoked at the 1974 General Assembly by Senator Stuart Symington, speaking as the United States delegate. He informed the world that the United States stockpile of nuclear weapons was equivalent to 615,385 Hiroshima bombs; this estimate may be increased to more than a million when the Soviet capacities are added. In addition, he estimated that by 1980 "close to one million pounds of plutonium will have been produced worldwide in electric power reactors, enough to manufacture over 50,000 nuclear explosive devices."[36]

This estimate is more or less corroborated by studies made in the United States and other countries. SIPRI has compiled a table of the production of plutonium, annually and accumulated, from 1970 (9,000 and 20,000 kgs respectively) to 1980 (80,000 and 350,000 kgs respectively). About a third of that production will occur in hitherto non-nuclear-weapons countries. That would be enough for some 50 bombs per week in these countries, calculating that 10 kilograms of plutonium is more than enough for a nominal (20-kiloton) bomb, or 100 per week if one finds it possible to manage with 5 kilograms. Some thirty countries in 1980 will have the capacity to produce some such devices on their own.[37]

Access to plutonium is, of course, not the whole story. What are the real risks involved? First, fissionable materials like plutonium and highly enriched uranium are in themselves extremely poisonous. While much attention has been given to the damage that can be caused by nuclear bombs due to radiation from fallout, astonishingly little discussion has been devoted to the fact that nuclear material, even nuclear waste, can be used directly as a radiological weapon. It can be made to function as a weapon in many ways, even through large-scale dispersion of it in open air.

> A variety of ways to disperse plutonium with timed devices are conceivable. These would allow the threatener to leave the area before the material is dispersed. . . .
>
> Unlike other poisons, however, plutonium can be used either as a poison or as explosive material. Accordingly, a threat using a plutonium dispersal device could conceivably be followed by a threat involving plutonium used in a nuclear explosive.[38]

The next rung on the ladder of risks relates to the question of whether the fissionable materials can be used for producing a crude explosive device "in the kitchen," as has been asserted. Agreement is now converging that it can be done, even clandestinely, if requirements are set low enough, neither yield nor reliability being of great concern.[39] The diversity of opinion is probably due to the lack of experience: the nuclear-weapons powers started from the outset on a program for building a nuclear arsenal, for which they knew that great resources, both technological and financial, would be available. The risk relating to homemade bombs is, of course, more immediate as a terrorist ambition than it is of a military establishment, although in some cases countries in certain adversary situations might want to show off a threat even with a single bang.

Our main problem lies higher in the production chain, as further steps in the complex nuclear fuel cycle are usually considered necessary for bomb manufacture for military arsenals of any size. In the early days, only nations which had advanced rapidly in nuclear energy production and from the outset had nuclear-weapons production in mind built plants for the subsequent processes of uranium enrichment and the separation of weapons-grade plutonium. More countries are now obtaining capabilities for the crucial further processing of the double-purpose fissionable materials. While the chemical reprocessing of plutonium is relatively complicated, it has not been a closely guarded secret. It is even conducted in the private sector in some countries.

SIPRI points out that plants or even laboratory-size facilities for chemical separation of plutonium exist or are coming into being in several countries outside the nuclear-weapons club. India used plutonium to explode a nuclear device derived from reactors constructed for its energy programs. India has a plutonium separation plant. A similar picture is evolving in regard to enrichment of uranium through gas diffusion, ultracentrifuge jet nozzle, or other techniques, including laser, now being installed and/or experimented with in several countries.[40]

Some recent developments seem ominous: West Germany selling Brazil a practically complete nuclear cycle—Brazil having uranium on its own soil—and France's plan to provide Argentina, South Korea, and Pakistan with plutonium-extraction plants. The Shah of Iran is also in the buyers' market. Governments who have at their command some fairly considerable reactor programs, with the spin-off production of plutonium and reprocessing facilities with perhaps some capacity to produce highly enriched uranium, have the material options for production of nuclear weapons. At the same time, they would have the technological manpower well prepared. The risk grows that, in the future, countries devoid of these opportunities would take recourse to black market offerings. This possibility was strongly emphasized at the expert preview conference on NPT with descriptions of several scenarios for unauthorized acquisition of nuclear material.[41] An international black market in nuclear materials similar to the narcotics trade looms on the horizon as a new horror. That it could be organized and utilized by insurgents and terrorists makes the picture even more terrifying.

All these developments, present or potential, have not rendered the multilaterally negotiated but imperfectly formulated and implemented NPT any more promising as a brake on nuclear proliferation. Or, to put the conclusion into a more positive vein: what is urgently needed is comprehensive, universal, extremely vigilant controls, particularly of the critical elements in the fuel cycle, those which carry the options for bomb fabrication closer and closer.

So far, the arguments have been marshaled according to the probably limitless technical *capabilities* for nuclear-weapons proliferation. Nothing has been said about the politically decisive *intentions* to turn to production of such weapons. Which countries might take this fatal turn is a question that must be constantly examined and judged in relation to highly diverse situations.

That Germany and Japan are under treaty-bound obligations not to acquire nuclear weapons has been a stroke of historical luck.[42] Both these countries have now piled up much prestige and economic benefits by having forsworn nuclear armaments; it seems unlikely that they would divert their assets to an independent nuclear arsenal even if they believed in the French position of not being convinced of protection by the U.S. nuclear arsenal.

Among the United States' Western European allies there was in the 1950s and 1960s far-reaching debate about a regional nuclear-weapons system. Mostly it was envisaged as being based on a combination of British and French nuclear forces and, later, sharing even with Germany. The idea of a Multilateral Force (MLF) was at one time encouraged by the United States; among its proponents was Henry Kissinger and among the opponents Robert McNamara, who was a foe of any independent nuclear forces, existing or prospective. After the conclusion of the NPT and particularly since the European Nato allies have joined it, the idea has become dormant. On the other hand, there is and has been no public debate on the issue of independent acquisition of nuclear weapons among the allies of the Soviet Union in Eastern Europe. Their reliance on Soviet willingness to defend them with nuclear weapons in case of a nuclear attack is probably as solid as their fear that any such warfare might lead to total subjugation, perhaps even the disappearance of their national independence.

Among nations outside formal alliances, the most dangerous situations relate to those geographically and historically paired constellations of political adversaries: Israel and the Arab states, particularly Egypt; India and Pakistan; South Africa and black Africa, and—although prestige is probably a stronger motivation than the desire to threaten—Argentina and Brazil. No political prophesy will be made here, but it must be strongly underscored that an important dynamic factor is the chain-reaction pattern. If one link in the international concordance breaks the de facto nonproliferation bond, a grave risk of a run towards nuclear weapons is in the offing.

One element effecting any national decision on the nuclear-weapons alternative is the difficulty of holding back the national military establishment if it sees the chance to acquire new weapons capabilities. The emergence of a sixth, seventh, or nth nuclear-weapons power would certainly invite others to follow suit. The NPT tenuous paragraph on the right of withdrawal in case "extraordinary events . . . have jeopardized the supreme interests" of a country is open to various interpretations.

All risks are not connected to developments within hitherto

non-nuclear-weapons countries. The inherent danger of the super-powers' deployment of nuclear weapons around the world in allied countries and foreign military bases, provides those who want to follow with invidious arguments. The superpowers seem to have forgotten that they will have to pay a certain price if they want to stop further proliferation of nuclear weapons by other nations.

7. The Prices to Pay

To stop the proliferation of nuclear weapons, other countries must be prevented from acquiring them while more and more of these weapons must be wrested from the hands of their present possessors. How—at this late hour?

This can only be done if the "haves" pay the price they should have paid from the beginning to make the other nations satisfied with being "have-nots." Major political decisions are necessary to remedy the obvious failure to win adherents to the NPT among the crucial threshold nations. First and foremost, the superpowers must cease the nuclear arms race as they solemnly pledged to do in NPT, Article VI. In addition, the Treaty obligations must be balanced. There are several prices that must be exacted in the form of im-provements of NPT rules in order to make them more equitable and more effective.

The first political payment should be a grand gesture of historical significance: the nuclear-weapons powers—jointly, bilaterally, or unilaterally—*should give a pledge never to attack non-nuclear-weapons powers with such weapons.* Some modification of this requirement would be necessary in cases where non-nuclear-weapons powers cooperate with their allied nuclear-weapons powers in actual nuclear warfare. This pledge is so directly connected with the es-sence of the NPT that many hoped it would be offered at the NPT Review Conference. It should be offered as a substitute for the empty Security Council resolution on so-called Security Assurances of 1968 (Chapter VI, Section 5). The formulation then was in terms of offering assistance in cases of attack. Now it is a question of out-lawing the attacks.

Exactly this point was made during the Security Council debate on the Security Assurances by the four non-nuclear-weapons mem-bers, Algeria, Brazil, India, and Pakistan, who together with France abstained on the 1968 vote. The Assurances were only declarations of intent and [those] were uncertain because of the existence of the veto. Also, they were discriminatory because applicable only to Parties to the Treaty on Non-Proliferation, and they did not establish an acceptable balance of obligations since if non-nuclear States forswore nuclear weapons for defense, the nuclear powers should in return renounce the use or threat of use of such weapons against them.[43]

There is another, less obvious objection to positive guarantees or promises of protection. It is the risk that the nuclear powers may want to ascertain the purity of the non-nuclear-weapons status of a protected country, claiming the right to question, to examine, and perhaps to interfere. The questionable value of such security guarantees may be expressed in more general terms. As I stated at the outset of the debate on what was then called the "nondissemination" issue:

> In the context of our present negotiations on the issue of non-dissemination of nuclear weapons, our main concern remains that of demanding some corresponding sacrifices on the part of nuclear and non-nuclear countries alike. This requirement of some kind of "compensation" does not amount, however, to any claim to obtain an "inducement" for our adhering to a treaty in the form of any guarantees, any promises, or protection by the nuclear Powers against nuclear attacks or even against "nuclear blackmail." Sweden is willing in principle to play its part when a nondissemination agreement is reached, without raising demands for any such guarantees—being, as a matter of fact, doubtful as to their desirability.[44]

The Swedish Government has taken the stand of no protection under any pretexts. Like its nonalignment, that stand is traditional and firmly based upon principles.

The clamor for a solemn pledge about non-use of nuclear weapons was renewed during the preparations for the NPT Review Conference 1975.* A proposal suggesting that the Depositary Governments solemnly undertake "never and under no circumstances to use or threaten to use nuclear weapons against non-nuclear-weapons Parties to the Treaty whose territories are completely free from nuclear weapons"[45] was also made at the NPT Conference in a statement by the Swedish delegation and in a draft resolution formally submitted.

---

* At the expert preview conference in 1974, I strongly appealed for such a pledge, a view that found support from many sides. *NPT: Paradoxes and Problems*, p. 5.

The move met with as cold a *nyet* as a no. In the Final Declaration there is but a faint and unclear echo of something having been proposed, with no commitment other than a reiterated reference to general UN principles about refraining from the use of force:

> At the Conference it was also urged that determined efforts must be made especially by the nuclear-weapons States Party to the Treaty, to ensure the security of all non-nuclear-weapons States Parties. To this end the Conference urges all States, both nuclear-weapons States and non-nuclear-weapons States to refrain, in accordance with the Charter of the United Nations, from the threat or the use of force in relations between States, involving either nuclear or non-nuclear weapons.[46]

Despite discouragement, new efforts must be made. They could be pursued along two different lines.

First, the pledge cited above would be of sufficient importance to usher in a new era of goodwill; it might well deserve to be introduced in the spectacular setting of a World Disarmament Conference (Chapter XI, Section 2). It would correspond in large part to what the Chinese have requested as a condition to their participation in such a Conference. This would allow them to enter disarmament negotiations as a responsible party. France also makes such a pledge a condition for joining disarmament talks. In a speech made in October 1974 President Giscard d'Estaing confirmed this stand, which was then echoed in a French statement to the General Assembly. The request for political guarantees that countries abstaining from nuclear weapons shall not be attacked with such weapons must now be vigorously pursued in the United Nations.

Such a pledge would be intended primarily to bolster the sense of security and of fairness to the non-nuclear-weapons states. If they themselves would rally to such a pledge as part of a universal move by all states, it would serve to still apprehensions on the part of their neighbors that some nations with advanced capabilities may be undertaking clandestine preparations to go nuclear. This would be of great psychological and political value.

The second line to pursue—indeed, it is a virtual ultimatum—is the promise, in Article VI of the NPT, to negotiate for an early cessation of the nuclear arms race. The superpowers must be brought to realize that they are losing prestige and credibility, that they can have no leverage against further proliferation if they do not immediately proceed seriously to agree on restraints.

The reduction in quantities of nuclear arms and/or the means of delivery has been the main, though largely unfulfilled, objective of SALT, but it is simply not enough in the eyes of the non-nuclear-weapons majority. Reduction of the number of strategic weapons is not of direct concern to the majority of nations in the world. To avoid further proliferation it is far more important to renounce advances in the quality of nuclear weapons.

To immediately signal a willingness to stop testing—in the atmosphere and underground and over international territory, be it land or water—would be a gesture capable of winning confidence among adherents and potential adherents to the NPT. While this readiness to stop testing must be forcefully demonstrated at an early date, the actual closing of test series and test sites may have to follow some gradual negotiated timetable (Chapter VII).

The blessings of qualitative disarmament, i.e., a restraint on new weapon technology, would help to relieve the political insecurity and psychological anguish of the peoples of the world. A sacrifice on the part of the superpowers to give up additional refinements of their nuclear weapons is the very key to a future of greater security in this world. It would not even be a real sacrifice. The present nuclear overkill capacity is way beyond what could ever be used, and freezing the competition for new varieties of such arms would serve to keep the reliance on mutual deterrents stable. Mankind must feel reassured that there are no further surprises in store of ever more deadly arms (Chapter V).

But can we know anything about the effectiveness of these politically decisive moves, the nonattack pledge, the cessation of testing? Would they induce would-be possessors of nuclear weapons to join the league of abstainers? To state it in a negative way: without these concessions other nations can lay all the blame for the fearful trends of today on the superpowers, appearing as they do to be utterly unreasonable. The price indicated is one that could serve as the portal to a new era of security.

8. Make IAEA Safeguards Meaningful

Beyond the fundamental discrimination allowing total liberty of possessing and developing nuclear weapons and explosive devices to one group of countries and total denial of that liberty to another group, there is a triple set of unfair rules incorporated in NPT. These refer to transfer, to IAEA controls, and to the promised preferential treatment of fellow parties to the treaty. Moreover, the so-called peaceful nuclear explosives are an additional issue (Chapter VII).

   a.   Safeguards on All Transfers.   Those who joined the nuclear club before 1 January 1967 are free to *transfer* between themselves both nuclear weapons and the related nuclear explosive devices as well as to "assist, encourage, and induce" each other to acquire and manufacture such paraphernalia for weapons purposes. These transfers also include the right to import nuclear fuel, source material, and equipment from any country.

   The NPT Review Conference of 1975 devoted much time to urging that more stringent rules be applied to exports of nuclear material and equipment from supplier countries, but only applied to exports to non-nuclear countries. In the Final Declaration more than two pages are devoted to means of strengthening the safeguards which are to accompany such exports, per se a worthwhile endeavor. But no reference is made to safeguards in relation to imports of basic materials into nuclear-weapons countries.

   Unfortunately, the non-nuclear-weapons countries cannot realistically be expected to retaliate. Even to arrive at a joint refusal to deliver any source material to those nations which produce nuclear weapons would require a cohesion within the non-nuclear group which cannot be mustered. The nuclear powers are to some degree dependent on such deliveries: France on Niger and some other African states, the United States on Canada, the Soviet Union on Czechoslovakia. Such dependency may become more important when the large deposits of lower-grade uranium to be found in many different countries including Sweden become commercially interesting. Deliveries of heavy water and even of plutonium to nuclear states are under no restriction; these could, however, hardly be affected by joint boycott action. In any case, initiatives to organize a boycott are lacking.

   A modest rectifying measure within the NPT framework which would seem self-evidently justified would be to place *all transfers* of fissionable material and equipment under the same controls of the IAEA, irrespective of what is the present or presumed status of the importing nation, whether it is inside or outside the nuclear-weapons club. During the NPT negotiations this proposal was pursued by the Swedish delegation with a view not only to the risks of proliferation but with concern for fairness to compete on an equal basis in the growing market for reactor plants, equipment, and source material:

The most effective and the most balanced solution would be a universal and obligatory submission to safeguards of *all* nuclear industry of *all* Parties to a Treaty and of *all* transfer of nuclear materials, principal nuclear facilities, and certain specialized equipment for *all* nuclear purposes from, to and between *all* Parties.[47]

The next year, as the negotiations drew to a close, I complained with great regret and some bitterness that the superpowers' joint draft laid down no conditions on the exports to nuclear-weapons powers of fissionable material, equipment, etc. for military or peaceful nuclear programs:

We maintain that this is a serious limitation in the scope of the treaty, in fact it is a loophole by which non-nuclear-weapons States may without even knowing it themselves, be aiding a military nuclear program.[48]

To remedy this would certainly be a minimum compromise. For the nuclear-weapons countries controls could begin with *imports* of sensitive material and equipment and gradually be extended to include existing domestic installations and resources within the international safeguard system.

b. Safeguards on All Nuclear Facilities in All Countries. A more satisfactory step, of course, would be to make the obligatory rule on safeguards universally applicable. Prescribed in Article III, this rule applies to only installations within the non-nuclear countries. An amendment, only a slight revision, substituting "all States" for "non-nuclear-weapons States" in the rules on safeguards would rectify that second glaring inequality in the NPT.

A practical argument against placing all nuclear installations under IAEA safeguards has been raised because of the tremendous burden in terms of labor, costs, and inconveniences the great number of inspections would entail, but ways out of this difficulty are now being found. The international system of controls was not originally designed to cope with the widening scope of problems primarily caused by the expansion of nuclear-power generation. One reform is already on its way as IAEA is seeking to simplify its rules by reducing the number of physical inspections, undertaking them as random surprise checks. Permanent control is to be achieved through (a) national systems of self-control and (b) international accountability for the total flow of sensitive material for different purposes, using the IAEA's materials-accountancy system as the basic verification measure.[49]

This clearly facilitates the application of a positive and forward-looking reform which would place the handling of nuclear material, including that for military purposes in all countries, on the same footing in regard to controls. The partial approach, offered by Britain and the United States, that IAEA safeguards should be applied to their countries, excepting plants of "national and security significance" is meaningless, as military and civilian uses of fissionable material would be interchangeable. All installations must be included and can be with the new technical systems of IAEA. As long as nuclear weapons are legitimately produced in some countries, it would suffice for them to indicate what portion of what material goes to that destination—which is hardly much of an incursion.

Open accounting for all nuclear material, including the military flow, is now more acceptable than before; secrecy is no longer of the essence, at least for the routine production of greater quantities of established types of weapons, and that is where the bulk of the material goes. A change in the present practices would also be an important corollary to the recommendations made throughout this book for a reduction of secrecy.

This invitation to allow such an improvement in this Treaty of their own making is addressed to those members of NPT who are nuclear-weapons powers. I call it an invitation, as the Depositary Powers have been given veto rights in regard to this Treaty. The suggested amendment could be introduced very simply and submitted at any time, according to Article VIII, not waiting the five years between Review Conferences. The question is open: who will be the sponsor? Who will work to enlist the necessary support, to constitute a majority once the amendment is set in motion?

c. Internationalization of Processing Plants. An addendum to the above proposal would be to concentrate the most rigid controls at crucial checkpoints in the nuclear fuel cycle, at the separation and enrichment plants where plutonium and uranium are processed; they become susceptible to being diverted to weapons production.[50] But control alone is not the answer. A solution that a few years ago might have seemed utopian is now an increasingly practical reality: international management, or at least coordination of these most critical phases of the nuclear fuel cycle. Considerations of these possibilities, presaged by individual experts, surfaced in the international 1974 expert conference, which was a precursor to the NPT Review Conference.[51]

This idea was given some attention at the NPT Review Conference in 1975, although the main emphasis was on studies rather than recommendations. It was stated that "regional or multinational nuclear fuel cycle centers may be an advantageous way to satisfy, safely and economically, the needs of many States." The Parties to the Treaty were urged to cooperate with the IAEA, providing where possible

> economic data concerning the construction and operation of facilities such as chemical reprocessing plants, plutonium fuel fabrication plants, waste management installations, and longer term spent-fuel storage, and assistance to the IAEA to enable it to undertake feasibility studies concerning the establishment of regional nuclear fuel cycle centers in specific geographic regions.[52]

Such nuclear fuel cycle centers for obvious reasons should be under IAEA safeguards, as is the case with some cooperative European undertakings currently under construction. Just because it is vital that no uncontrolled weapons material gets out of national centers, the Regional Centers should not be limited in their activities to countries which are Parties to the NPT. Other countries may not be willing to participate in the centers under such a rule, but by all means everybody should be made welcome.

d.   No Exceptions from Control on Political Grounds.   There has been a third form of discrimination in the implementation of the NPT. Preferential treatment to States that are Parties to the Treaty was, in Article IV, held out as inducement to join the NPT. The implication was that nuclear assistance, whether in the form of reactors, enriched nuclear assistance, or technological know-how, would go only to States that are Parties of the NPT. The Treaty itself, however, does not stipulate this as a strict requirement. It only obligates exporters to require importers to submit to IAEA controls.

The actions of several suppliers have recently begun to run counter to both the stricter (to export only to NPT members) and the more lenient (to request IAEA controls) requirements. The largest supplier of all, the United States, has made several deviations from those rules. In 1974 it offered preferential treatment to two nonmembers of NPT, Egypt and Israel, by promising delivery of reactors. Neither NPT adherence nor acceptance of IAEA safeguards was made a condition. When the demand for IAEA safeguards was later made by the United States, both the prospective recipients declined the offer—at least so far nothing has materialized. Though in this case the recipient countries balked at the safeguard requirements, it remains true that such unconditional offers contravene the spirit if not the letter of NPT and are an affront to loyal adherents of the NPT.

Nuclear-weapons states should certainly not be allowed to choose their customers according to political motivations using different rules about safety. Only one criterion should be valid, one IAEA standard, equal for all. The very serious questions of principle involved were summed up at the 1974 preview conference of experts. Without naming individual countries, the report states:

> Parties to the NPT in a position to supply nuclear assistance should discontinue a practice which has the effect of discriminating *against* the non-nuclear-weapons States that have become Parties to the NPT.
>
> There was discussion whether this practice is in violation of Article III. Opinions have been expressed on both sides of the issue, but no matter which opinion is correct, the practice is inconsistent with the purposes of the NPT. It serves as a disincentive to States joining the NPT. It also tends to undermine the effectiveness of the safeguards system itself.[53]

The matter was also touched upon at the NPT Review Conference, although only peripherally. The Final Declaration expresses the wish for adherence with no explicit prohibition or warning to those who deviate:

> The Conference recommends that, in reaching decisions on the provision of equipment, materials, services, and scientific and technological information for the peaceful uses of nuclear energy, on concessional and other appropriate financial arrangements, and on the furnishing of technical assistance in the nuclear field, including cooperation related to the continuous operation of peaceful nuclear facilities, States party to the Treaty should give weight to adherence to the Treaty by recipient States.[54]

Any categorical requirement about NPT adherence seems now to have lost out. Several suppliers have followed the path of least resistance. The NPT seems to be totally disregarded in such transactions. West Germany—now a party to the NPT but not a nuclear-weapons power—signed a $4 billion agreement in July 1975 giving Brazil, a non-NPT member, virtually an entire nuclear industry, including reactors and equipment to process, enrich, and recycle uranium. The agreement did, however, contain a proviso that Brazil conclude a safeguards agreement with IAEA. France, a non-NPT member but a nuclear-weapons power, is proposing to sell nuclear fuel reprocessing facilities to South Korea, Pakistan, and Argentina, all non-NPT members. A sale to South Korea—at present the tinder box of Asia—was concluded evidently without full international safeguards control.* The Shah of Iran is also making bids to buy crucial elements of the nuclear fuel cycle. It will be interesting to note later whether the fact that Iran has signed and ratified NPT makes any difference.

Differential treatment of NPT and non-NPT Parties is a moot point; what is imperative is whether there is a formidable barrier against any receiver country turning to producing atomic weapons.

With NPT now in much disrespect and its practices in great disarray, a new opportunity must be sought to vindicate the only full-fledged solution: all recipients of nuclear equipment or material, all nations with any nuclear programs, whether NPT Members or not, whether nuclear-weapons powers or not, must submit the totality of their relevant activities to IAEA safeguards in a nondiscriminatory way. An urgent proposal to this effect should be taken up in the United Nations and in the Geneva Disarmament Committee.

Such a solution might decide the future proliferation or not of nuclear weapons. A crucial point is India's categorical position in favor of an all-or-nothing solution, reemphasized in 1974 in the United Nations. It might almost be read as an ultimatum from the new aspirants in the threshold countries:

> Now, as we have explained India's view in regard to verification, inspection, and a system of safeguards, it should be clear that we are in favour of universal, functional, and nondiscriminatory safeguards which apply to all, whether they are nuclear-weapon States or non-nuclear-weapon States, and that they apply to all programs. It is not possible for us to agree to a system of verification and inspection which would be applicable to the peaceful activities of non-nuclear-weapon States only; or, at best, applicable to the peaceful activities of all States, while leaving open the military activities of nuclear-weapon States.[55]

This, to my mind, is a straightforward challenge: are the nuclear-weapons powers willing to pay the price of cooperation?

Comprehensive application of IAEA safeguards in all countries

---

* The latest news is that the deal is off, owing to strong United States pressure (*International Herald Tribune*, 3 February 1976).

is absolutely necessary, though it can no longer be expected that all countries will join NPT. Naturally, there can never be any guarantee that all the nations in the world will cooperate. Unfortunately, the NPT provides no means to discipline wrong-doers. Some restraining power might barely be possible, to be exercised by the concurrence of all supplier nations along IAEA lines.

A universal adherence to IAEA standards must be understood as being beneficial to all. In all bilateral dealings the value of checks on the other partner must be realized. With the expansion of nuclear industry, IAEA safeguards are indispensable, and if they were accepted the awkward NPT might be forgone. But if the nuclear-weapons powers want to keep NPT alive they must be willing to negotiate anew. If they are sincere about stopping the spread of nuclear weapons, they must themselves be willing to do what is required to achieve this goal. Otherwise, nothing will help us. But then they should be forced to make a clear confession about their lack of care.

e. A Future of Nuclear Cooperation. A total solution for nuclear control would require a return to the Oppenheimer-Lilienthal plan for international control of the whole nuclear field (Chapter III, Section 3). National monopolies are most to be feared—the quite farsighted proposal of international management of fuel-cycle centers is crucial in this connection.

But international control could go even further. The IAEA's safeguards division with a data bank on the flow of nuclear material could be the basis of a common international householding of nuclear energy to the benefit of all.

Such future steps have recently been recommended by the Swedish delegation to the Geneva Disarmament Committee, beginning July 1974. My successor there, Inga Thorsson, resubmitted this thinking to the General Assembly:

> In the long-term perspective, we see the need for some system of international management of fissionable material, as in the future no exclusively national solutions to this management problem will be adequate and satisfactory. We do not underestimate the difficulties in elaborating such a system and achieving its general acceptance by States, but the direction of our work should be made clear now.[56]

The IAEA is already available and may be given the resources to become the banker for fissionable material and for technologies, as was once planned. Such international management by an inter-governmental agency would seem to be the only long-term solution. It might operate through having deposits in different countries, all under license and all subject to inspection. Atomic Energy Commissions in various countries would then be expected to pool their resources and their experts. Ideally, in the future when reduction of nuclear weapons becomes effective, the IAEA could and should be the recipient of transfers of fissionable material released from dismantled weapons and from stocks of materials previously earmarked for military purposes. This would provide a more egalitarian access of all countries to these sources of energy.

The idea of the IAEA as a nuclear banker may seem novel but it will come to seem more realizable, not primarily through debates on the risk of weapons proliferation but because of general worry about the proper husbanding of nuclear energy resources. This concern will undoubtedly come to figure more and more prominently in the increasingly heated debates between proponents and opponents of the expansion of production of nuclear energy. There is a swelling tide of concern about dangers inherent in the problems of waste disposal, accidents, and terrorist activities in relation to the development of nuclear industry and technology, both for energy and for explosion purposes.

Such was the reasoning behind the 1974 Swedish proposal:

> It is our convinced view that the international community must take a hard look, now, at these problems; for let us not close our eyes to the effects of national efforts towards energy self-sufficiency through, *inter alia*, rapidly growing nuclear power programs. One such effect is, as we all know, the ensuing and awesome increase in plutonium production, creating nuclear explosive capabilities with the spread of nuclear technology, and opening possibilities for nuclear blackmail and nuclear violence.
>
> We would be seriously and probably calamitously lacking in responsibility towards the peoples of the world, both present and future generations, if we did not make every effort to check and control nuclear explosives technology as well as to prevent the many obvious dangers to the environment that accompany an increase in the stocks of plutonium.[57]

Let us hope that international forces, nuclear and non-nuclear, will join together to stop proliferation of weapons and to protect a deteriorating environment—that this urgent challenge to the future will soon be reflected in the actual policies of all governments.

9. Nuclear-Weapons-Free Zones—
Voluntary, Not Imposed

Present trends point in the direction of rapid proliferation of nuclear weapons in more and more countries (Chapter VI, Section 5). This irrational course does not serve the national interests of the as yet nuclear-weapons-free countries. Nuclear weapons are really no asset for lesser powers, in spite of what has been said by the superpowers about their value.

All countries would be better off if they would agree not to possess nuclear weapons. The rationale supporting the idea of voluntarily self-organized, nuclear-weapons-free zones is one of fostering cooperation among the countries of a given region[58] to prevent further nuclearization and of reaching agreement with the nuclear-weapons powers that they will give firm assurance to never use nuclear weapons against a nuclear-free zone nor deploy any such weapons on these territories or in these seas.

This principle was put forth to the General Assembly in 1961 in the Undén plan (Chapter VI, Section 3). Two concepts were used interchangeably, one for a nuclear-free club, the other for contiguous nuclear-free zones. In either case the cooperating States would fortify each other by agreeing to keep their countries nuclear-free, thus stemming the tide of proliferation. Unfortunately, the Undén plan did not sufficiently emphasize the concomitant necessity of receiving assurances from the superpowers not to threaten or attack any nuclear-free zone.

The establishment of nuclear-weapons-free zones would facilitate programming for the peaceful use of nuclear energy. Some regions could participate in the establishment of nuclear fuel cycle centers (Chapter VI, Section 8), reach cooperative arrangements for verification and control, and thereby decrease suspicions among themselves as neighbors. They might eventually expand their cooperation to mutual restraint on the acquisition of conventional weapons (Chapter V, Sections 2 and 3). All such action would lessen tension and make still wider economic and political cooperation possible.

Such regional voluntary cooperation would be in every country's interest. The essential thing is that it can be the result of independent action and need not be imposed from outside. There is reason for a series of regional disarmament conferences as well as the international one. As late as 1973, I entertained hopes that steps would be taken then to establish nuclear-free zones, particularly in the large underdeveloped regions of the world; I further hoped that such action would be followed by regional cooperation to limit the arms race even more. Sadly, later developments have made such hopes seem less and less realistic. Instead of devoting a planned chapter to the analysis of such prospects and proposals, I am, in the main, restricting myself to a few remarks centering on the problem of establishing nuclear-free zones.

There are several explanations for the lack of progress in regional initiatives for disarmament. One factor is the competition of the superpowers to line up lesser powers economically, politically, and militarily. And among the lesser powers there has been markedly less will to act collectively in the disarmament field than in the economic field, where they have been able to join in the demand for a New Economic World Order.

Everywhere there are jealousies and assumed national interests preventing collective action for keeping down the arms race. In some regions there have been wars between neighboring countries and, more commonly, disputes which it is feared might lead to wars. The idea creeps in of balancing actual or potential adversaries. Some countries are obviously tempted to acquire nuclear weapons. The risk of proliferation itself nurtures such strivings, as shown by the sparring betwen Israel and the Arab countries and between India and Pakistan.

The idea of nuclear-weapons-free zones has now and then reappeared in the United Nations. The moves in 1974 to reintroduce the issue began with a partisan tinge, as the sponsors were Egypt, Iran, and Pakistan (Chapter VI, Section 10). But the ensuing resolution, introduced as a practical compromise by Finland, was that a comprehensive study should be undertaken of the question of nuclear-weapons-free zones "in all its aspects."[59]

The study, under the auspices of the Geneva Disarmament Committee, was completed late in 1975.[60] It contains a wealth of information and painstaking analysis of the historical background; it accounts for all official proposals; it covers relations to international law and with international organs such as IAEA.

However, there are no specific recommendations for the establishment of nuclear-free zones nor any recommendations as to precise rules. A pragmatic and flexible approach is recommended. The report is, unfortunately, so pragmatic that analysis of the political obstacles created by superpower policies and military alliances was avoided. The main body of the report refers to some experts as being of one view, or most experts as having another view. Therefore, the study has remained inconclusive on the vital points.

But this corresponds to political reality as it now is. At the 1975 NPT Review Conference the issue of nuclear-free zones was not on the agenda, and it was made sufficiently clear that a non-attack pledge could not be exacted from the superpowers in return for a country's pledge to remain nuclear-free (Chapter VI, Section 7).

Today, there is only one successful example of a treaty for de-nuclearization and complete demilitarization of a region. This treaty covers the Antarctic.[61] Outside political skirmishes, and practically unnoticed by the mass media, a regional plan for its demilitarization was introduced at the end of the 1950s. The Antarctic Treaty was signed in December 1959 by Britain, France, the Soviet Union, and the United States together with eight other States which had declared their interest. It was later signed by five others.

Signers of the Treaty forsake territorial claims and prohibit claims to sovereignty by any other State. All deployment of military forces and weapons is prohibited. Specifically, nuclear explosions and disposal of radioactive wastes within the region are forbidden. The territory of the region is freely accessible to the contracting States and they can construct installations for scientific purposes which are open to observers from other Parties.

The Antarctic thus has become the one region in the world where there are no arms, except for personal self-defense, no military secrets, and no need of spies, where thousands of experts work together in intensive peaceful coexistence. But it is a region without countries and boundaries, without governments, without inhabitants.

This singular example of success underlines that timing is of the essence. Countries and regions still free from nuclear weapons and outside military alliances with nuclear-weapons powers must act in time. If they become allied to one of the nuclear-weapons powers, and if some are permitted to establish bases and deploy nuclear weapons, self-organized cooperation for nuclear-free status will be prevented.

10. In the Several Regions

a. *No Bright Prospect for Europe.* Unfortunately for the development of the issue of nuclear-weapons-free zones, the interest, particularly of the superpowers and their military allies, focused from the beginning on Europe. It has been the most sensitive region, where the idea is not practical in the foreseeable future. Nuclear-weapons-free zones should be more feasible in the less developed regions, where the danger of proliferation is now threatening alarmingly.

During the debate in 1961 in the General Assembly on the Undén plan (Chapter VI, Section 3), the spokesman for the United States, in his criticism of the proposal, demonstrated his country's concern with the possibility of confrontation in Europe:

> The United States opposed the draft resolution on the ground that the proposal sought to shift the emphasis entirely to non-nuclear Powers receiving nuclear weapons on their territory on behalf of any other country, and thus to prejudice existing defensive arrangements. The conditions which created the need for defensive arrangements would have to be removed before those arrangements could be terminated.[62]

The Soviet Union, which for geographical if no other reasons has less interest in insisting on deploying nuclear weapons in the territories of its own East European Allies, could afford to take an even stronger line than Undén's proposal, which had reference only to the future.

> The Soviet Union regarded the text of the resolution as weak and not sufficiently categorical, and objected to the words "in the future" which appeared in the sentence "to refuse to receive in the future nuclear weapons on their territories on behalf of any other country."[63]

There is a long history of suggestions and proposals to establish not only nuclear-weapons-free zones but demilitarized zones as well, to straddle the confrontation line in Europe.[64] In contrast to the Undén plan for voluntary nuclear-free zones, these proposals were all conceived basically as imposed, following the tradition that victorious nations after a war prescribe to the defeated terms of peace, often restricting their freedom in the military field. The plans discussed all centered around the question of the remilitarization of Germany.

This prolonged debate came to a climax at the Geneva Summit Conference in the summer of 1955[65] when the British Prime Minister, Anthony Eden, in his introductory speech, rather loosely presented an idea of a "demilitarized zone between the East and West" (often

referred to thereafter as the "Eden plan"). Its lack of clarity, however, led to a number of contradictory statements which then led the
West to proclaim officially that there was no question of favoring any
plan for creating a neutral zone in Germany or elsewhere. Eden
himself denies that it was ever a plan.[66]

During this period the Russians expressed interest in some kind
of rearrangement of the military-political situation in Central
Europe. Molotov had mentioned, in connection with conditions for
unifying Germany, that there might be agreement about "forces and
armaments in Germany and neighboring countries together with a
form of supervision to control them."[67] At the Geneva Conference
Marshall Bulganin, then premier of the Soviet Union declared:

> The Soviet Government is of the opinion that our eventual objective
> should be to have no foreign troops remaining on the territories of
> European states.[68]

It is rather poignant to read those words today.

The Rapacki plan, originating in the framework of imposed
solutions, presented to the United Nations in 1957, provided for
a nuclear-weapons-free zone comprising Poland, Czechoslovakia,
East Germany, and West Germany.[69] It had a semblance of being
voluntary as Poland offered itself as a candidate for nuclear-
weapons-free status and was supported by the other two countries
belonging to the Soviet bloc. Interestingly enough, the sponsors of
the plan also offered to allow quite far-reaching measures of control
and inspection in their territories. Unfortunately, one of the countries envisaged as a member was not free to take such a step; there
were already United States nuclear weapons installed in West Germany. On the other hand, West Germany was the only sponsor to
have by treaty accepted a prohibition against the acquisition of its
own nuclear weapons. The Rapacki plan failed, as all similar plans
will do as long as military alliances restrict the freedom of action of
lesser European powers. Later, similar plans have been progressively
more modest in scope.

Even if the nuclear weapons were eliminated from Europe,
continental Europe, or any smaller zone in Central Europe, the
newly nuclear-free states would still be in danger of nuclear weapons
being used against them so long as they remain allied to a superpower.
A nuclear-free status for a group of countries in Europe would
presuppose the dissolution of the military alliances. With all the

scissions within the two blocs (Chapter II, Section 7) this is not in prospect.

Not even the Nordic countries can declare themselves to be a nuclear-free zone, as President Kekkonen of Finland has suggested several times since 1963. His idea was to "remove the Nordic countries from the sphere of speculation caused by the development of nuclear strategy and insure that this area will remain outside international tension."[70] None of the four main Nordic countries (Iceland excluded) has nuclear weapons on its soil in peacetime and they have all ratified the NPT, forswearing the independent acquisition of nuclear weapons. But Denmark and Norway, as NATO allies, are bound to accept deployment of nuclear weapons in case of war. And Finland is a member of the Finnish-Soviet Friendship and Assistance Agreement (1948). Only Sweden is wholly "nonaligned in peacetime, aiming to remain neutral in case of war," as the policy is defined.

Clearly nuclear-weapons-free status is going to be difficult to obtain. Moreover, no country inside a military alliance can insist on a right not to be bombed—a major purpose of belonging to a nuclear-free zone—if its superpower ally participates in nuclear warfare. Thus, as candidates for a nuclear-weapons-free zone in Europe there remain only a few nonaligned countries, too scattered to entertain plans to create a region.

In recognition of these hindrances, no proposal for nuclear-free zones was presented at the recent European Security Conference. Rumania, a country where no foreign troops are stationed, included mention of the matter in its submissions which also contained requests that disarmament be made a subject of the negotiations, a desire expressly shared by Yugoslavia. However, the Final Act (signed by thirty-five High Representatives in Helsinki, 1 August 1975) contains no recommendations for disarming or denuclearizing Europe.[71] Neither has the question of nuclear-weapons-free zones in Europe been taken up at the Vienna negotiations between the two military alliances on mutual force reductions (MBFR). (Chapter II, Section 6).

With the system of military alliances in existence and the militarization of both Germanies achieved, a nuclear-weapons-free zone in Central Europe is hardly feasible. Had the superpowers been willing it could have been made a reality twenty years ago. A Europe insulated from the superpowers' warfare might have emerged instead of the present Europe of nuclear nightmare (Chapter II, Sections 3–6).

b. Some Progress with Latin America. A pioneer attempt to establish a nuclear-weapons-free zone has been made in Latin America, in large measure due to the constructive work of Alfonso García Robles of Mexico, an indefatigable leader of disarmament endeavors in the United Nations. Latin America also has the advantage of a unique position. Though remaining in the interest sphere of the United States, a position on the whole uncontested by the Soviet Union (Chapter II, Section 8), it is not formally militarily allied to it, nor are there military alliances among the Latin American states.

The Tlatelolco Treaty of 1967 with eighteen members was concluded "for the prohibition of nuclear weapons in Latin America."[72] It debars

> the testing, use, manufacture, production, or acquisition by any means as well as the receipt, storage, installation, deployment, and any form of possession of any nuclear weapons. . . . The parties should conclude agreements with the International Atomic Energy Agency (IAEA) for the application of safeguards to their nuclear activities.

In regard to coverage, the number of adherents has risen to twenty, but the three large nations of Argentina, Brazil, and Chile have signed, but not ratified, the Treaty. Brazil has ratified, but hedged its adherence with so many interpretations that for its part the Treaty has not entered into full force. The main point of divergence is that Brazil, like Argentina, insists that peaceful nuclear explosions be permissible under the Treaty.

Cuba's refusal to join also diminishes the coverage of the Tlatelolco Treaty. Cuba justifies its abstention by the demand that the United States remove its military installations at Guantánamo Bay, which serves nuclear submarines, contaminating Cuban territory with these terror weapons. In addition, Cuba reiterated as late as 1973 in the General Assembly that its reservation also reflected its opinion that the United States illegally occupied territories in Panama and Puerto Rico.

In order to secure cooperation and respect from outside powers two important Protocols were annexed to the Treaty. Under Protocol I, non-Latin American States responsible for territories within the region were to apply the statute of military denuclearization to these. This has been consented to by Britain and the Netherlands, but not by France and the United States.

One important point is that the Treaty Parties have begun to obtain from nuclear-weapons powers assurances that nuclear weapons shall not be used against them. Still, complete adherence by all nuclear-weapons powers is not yet secured for the crucial Protocol II, which pledges

> to respect the statute of military denuclearization of Latin America as defined in the Treaty, not to contribute to acts involving a violation of the Treaty, and not to use or threaten to use nuclear weapons against the Parties to the Treaty.

The political conflict between Cuba and the United States seems to be the stumbling-block here, as the Soviet Union refuses to subscribe to the request in this Protocol as long as the Guantánamo base is not removed, a very sensitive point on account of the Cuban missile crisis of 1962. Protocol II has, however, secured the important signatures of Britain, the United States, France, and China. It would be appropriate to remind the Soviet Union of its promise, which, according to official UN history, was made early on in the debates on nuclear-weapons-free zones that it "would respect the denuclearized status of the territory of even a single country if the Western Powers would also do so."[73] At the time of signing, China made stringent demands on its fellow nuclear powers regarding transportation of nuclear weapons through Latin America. Transshipment of nuclear weapons might be used as a pretext for introducing nuclear weapons into the zone, as has lately been pointed out by a Soviet writer in the semiofficial Russian periodical *International Affairs*.[74]

Hopes have been kindled that Latin American cooperation could be extended from the nuclear-weapons-free-zone concept to a joint decision to reduce the levels of conventional armaments, at least in so far as foreign imports are concerned. Eight Latin American nations signed an agreement in December 1974 at Ayacucho, Peru, to limit armaments and stop buying offensive weapons altogether. The money saved could be used for economic and social development. That agreement was signed by representatives of Peru, Chile, Bolivia, Ecuador, Venezuela, Argentina, Colombia, and Panama. Brazil, the continent's largest economic and military power, remained outside.

However, no cancellation of arms orders or reductions in military spending have yet been recorded. SIPRI, often confirming press stories, continually reports the heavy outlays on large arms and sophisticated weapons such as jet combat aircraft, aircraft carriers, destroyers, frigates, corvettes, cruisers, submarines, tanks, and missiles.[75] Actual developments have shown increased militarization.

The Tlatelolco Treaty has a positive value as a model for other regions to follow in regard to both its tight structuring as a legal instrument and its organizational framework. But as long as coverage is incomplete it does not reassure the world that nuclear-weapons aspirations are quenched. The hesitant positions of Argentina and Brazil, coupled with their refusal to adhere to the Non-Proliferation Treaty, create stark misgivings.

   c.   An Agenda for Africa.   A strong group of African nations was first to make known to the United Nations its plans to establish all of Africa as a nuclear-free zone.* This plan received the approbation of the entire world community. That was in 1961, the year after France had exploded a nuclear device in the Sahara and the same year that the Undén plan had been set forth in the General Assembly. A plan to set Africa nuclear-free has been on the books of the UN ever since. One wonders why there has been hardly any progress.

The original African draft resolution proclaimed Africa's inviolability and expressed the wish that Africa should not be drawn into the superpower struggle, that nuclear and ballistic weapons tests not be conducted on African territory, that bases and launching sites not be permitted. All foreign powers were asked to respect the continent as a nuclear-free region. Though the African resolution was accepted by a large majority, the same problem that plagued the Swedish resolution prevailed: the Soviet Union voted for the resolution, but the United States, Britain, and France contended that it "interfered with an over-all approach to disarmament" or anyway could not be "effectively controlled."[76]

Since then the Africans have been strangely passive, although the resolution has been put forth several times. Hopes were raised anew after the resolution, sponsored by non-Arabic African states, was again presented in 1974. It reiterated:

> call upon all States to respect and abide by the declaration [on the denuclearization of Africa] issued by the Assembly of Heads of State and Government of the Organization of African Unity.[77]

---

* No clear demarcation of "Africa" has been made in these contexts. The major body of interested delegations belong to central, "black" Africa, but Egypt and North African members have from time to time participated in initiatives.

The resolution was again reviewed in 1975. This time it was introduced by the Nigerian representative. He directly referred to South Africa's nuclear capabilities, as well as its refusal to adhere to the NPT or to place its installations under IAEA control. This time no one abstained or voted against the resolution. There is obviously a growing sense of South Africa being a firebrand. But what practical measures for implementing the resolution will be taken?

There has been no indication that any of the countries active in these resolutions would themselves attempt to acquire nuclear weapons. The dangers, if any, clearly come from the outside. The nuclear-free issue could be utilized as part of the larger thought complex including anticolonialism and antiracism. With sympathy from the world majority, Africans could move full speed ahead to exact a formal pledge of nonattack from all nuclear-weapons powers. This would provide a valuable *cordon sanitaire* for Africa. They should demand assurance from the only technologically advanced country in the region, the Union of South Africa. In this context, the exclusion of South Africa from international deliberations cannot be in the best interest of its neighbors. The principle of universality of the United Nations is one of great practical value, not least in disarmament contexts.

Delegates to the Organization for African Unity could research suggestions that could be made in order to lower the levels of armaments in the region and keep out those of foreign powers. Are there any stocks of biological or chemical weapons for which a call for withdrawal should be made? Could arms imports to various countries in the region be made the object of a multilateral study, with the hope of lowering military outlay? Are there prestige weapons such as supersonic fighter planes which African countries could jointly agree to forgo? Might there even be a chance to go ahead with negotiations on balanced and mutual force reductions? The relatively poor African countries should find it profitable and appealing to take bold steps towards regional demilitarization. That would help to consolidate a continent previously fragmented by European colonialism.

These are sample queries. If a forward-looking proposal were made by the African countries to set up an African Commission of Arms and Disarmament, it would add considerably to make more dynamic and modern the image of Africa.

d.   Other Regions.   There has been no other regional progress comparable to that of Latin America or even Africa. There has, however, been no dearth of proposals for nuclear-weapons-free zones in several other parts of the world. The comprehensive study by the Geneva Disarmament Committee on the subject lists several such proposals besides the ones here detailed.

One proposal concerning the Balkan States was initiated by Rumania in 1957, suggesting an "area of peace in the Balkans, free of foreign military bases."[78] In 1959 the Soviet Union reformulated the proposal for making the Balkan peninsula a region of peace, without missiles or nuclear weapons. Later in 1959 the Soviet Union formally proposed that a nuclear-weapons-free zone be established, comprising the Balkans and the Adriatic. Rumania has returned to the question several times, recommending in 1972 that a special conference of Balkan countries be called. In the meantime, the whole Mediterranean area has been encompassed by a similar suggestion of the Soviet Union, submitted through the Geneva Disarmament Committee in 1963, specifying that the area should be declared a zone "free of nuclear missile weapons."

I have two political comments to make. One is that there must be more concerted action by the several countries concerned on their own accounts if they want to be successful. The second is that superpower involvement—amounting to alliance relationships (NATO, with Greece and Turkey, WTO, with Bulgaria and Rumania, and both the United States and the Soviet Union to an indeterminate degree in the Middle Eastern countries)—impedes any such self-organized activity, even if, as is evident in this case, a will exists for a region to free itself from nuclear weapons.

Such a will is not likely to exist or to be sufficiently shared in the Middle East, although to tie those countries to a nuclear-weapons-free zone and peaceful co-existence is most urgently needed. In 1974 Iran proposed the formation of a nuclear-weapons-free zone in the Middle East. With Egypt as co-sponsor, the recommendation was brought to the vote in the United Nations and adopted by a majority of the General Assembly.[79] Among the positive votes, as in 1975, were those of all five nuclear-weapons powers. However, there were "buts." *But* what should constitute the region has not yet been circumscribed; there is not even a kernel of sure adherents. *But* Egypt demanded as a prerequisite the accession to the NPT by all states of the region. *But* Israel abstained on the vote, advising that the way to achieve progress was through direct consultations among the states in the region. The question is whether the region wants to be nuclearized rather than denuclearized—a question that is ominous for the whole world.

There are other regions where greater peacefulness reigns and where the superpowers have less direct interest and influence. One such area, including Australia, New Zealand, and a considerable part of the Pacific Ocean, is possibly ripe for an attempt at self-organized cooperation for remaining nuclear-weapons-free. Such an effort will surely touch on many of the most acute problems besetting the world's oceans (Chapter III, Section 7).

The Indian subcontinent should also be ready to become nuclear-free. The traumatic experience of colonialism was followed by the partition into India and Pakistan; since then new wars have been fought between them. There are now three independent states vitally concerned to safeguard an uneasy peace: India, Pakistan, and Bangladesh. Each of them is, however, presently turning inward to its enormous domestic difficulties, climaxed by tragic assassinations as in Bangladesh and drastic curtailment of political freedoms as in India.

In 1974 there was a debate in the General Assembly, initiated by Pakistan, on a nuclear-weapons-free zone in South Asia. India submitted an alternative draft. Despite positive interest in the substance of the issue, both from states in the region and from nuclear-weapons states, the two resulting resolutions[80] were inconclusive, a situation repeated in 1975. India reacted negatively to the proposal's having been introduced by Pakistan without prior consultation with India, arguing that the essence of a nuclear-free zone is that it should grow out of the collective will of the countries concerned.[81]

Efforts have been made to get the whole Indian Ocean declared and maintained as a Zone of Peace. The issue was put on the General Assembly agenda in 1971 by Sri Lanka (Ceylon). A resolution was approved declaring "the Indian Ocean a zone of peace for all time." It called on the great powers to halt further escalation of their military presence in the Indian Ocean, "conceived in the context of great power rivalry."[82] An Ad Hoc Committee was also set up which conducted negotiations among the littoral states. The resolutions, however, have been reintroduced year after year without any success in sight.

In reality, things have moved in the opposite direction. The voting pattern foreshadowed the difficulties to come. The first, basic, resolution was approved by only sixty-one Member States, while no fewer than fifty-five abstained, among them both superpower blocs. While China voted for the resolution and is a member of the Ad Hoc Committee, the four other nuclear-weapons states have stood aloof. This pattern was repeated in the 1975 round.

During these very years both superpowers have fiercely stepped up military activities in the Indian Ocean. The United States has been in the spotlight because it has acquired an island from Britain, Diego Garcia; it was pretended that the island was uninhabited when actually its inhabitants had been evicted; plans are to make it a full-fledged naval base. The island commands a strategic position, being almost equidistant from India and East Africa and with possibilities of good observation of traffic to and from the Persian Gulf. While the Department of Defense actively promotes the expansion plans, opposition in Congress has so far been strong enough to prevent full implementation.[83] Such use of Diego Garcia would be in blatant contradiction to UN declarations on the matter of the Indian Ocean and the interests of lesser powers. Opposition to this move is motivated in part because it would likely lead the Soviet Union to increase its military presence there and even to feel justified in asking for equal facilities. So far the Soviet Union has reportedly only a communications facility near Berbera in Somalia. The United States, on the other hand, has a much larger facility close to Asmara in Ethiopia, besides Diego Garcia.[84]

Vigorous new protests have come from many countries in the region, from important coastal states like India and Sri Lanka, from Australia and New Zealand, and recently from Iran. The prospect of keeping the Indian Ocean a Zone of Peace is obviously dependent on how much leadership and pressure the nations of the region can muster.

To an outsider it would seem that any action would be more successful if it were taken step by step, concentrating first just on nuclear weapons. As an initial measure, nonaligned states in the region might refuse port facilities to vessels carrying nuclear weapons, a prohibition that Japan is beginning to do its utmost to enforce (Chapter II, Section 8). Refusal of bunkering and communications facilities to military vessels in general and hindering the deployment of antisubmarine detectors (Chapter II, Section 7) might be further steps. The Indian Ocean is dotted with islands somewhat less than the Pacific Ocean; these were inherited as part of old colonial empires or are purchasable from them, as was Diego Garcia. But the littoral and hinterland states of the Indian Ocean are no less than thirty-six in number, and their interests are widely splintered and cooperation is not strongly developed among them. Still, to work for the Indian Ocean and the countries around it to become a nuclear-free zone would seem more promising a target than to aim for its immediate transformation into a totally non-military Zone of Peace, as no other ocean is.

CHAPTER VII

Closing the Loopholes for Nuclear-Weapons Testing

1. The False Alibis: Thresholds and Verification

A total ban on tests of nuclear weapons has been understood to be for more than twenty years the cardinal measure for stopping the nuclear arms race. It would radically curtail the qualitative competition among the nuclear-weapons powers while erecting a next to categorical bar against newcomers acquiring these weapons. Even if transgressions cannot be totally excluded, tests can hardly be concealed, an asset not equally available in regard to many other proposed disarmament measures. And no other disarmament measure has been so widely and strongly supported by the important near-nuclear-weapons states.

The failure to achieve the comprehensive test ban (CTB) is indeed tragic (Chapter III, Section 6). It has partly been obscured by the false pride of having achieved a partial test ban in 1963, the Moscow agreement "Banning Nuclear Weapon Tests in the Atmosphere, in Outer Space, and Under Water," which actually legitimized the continuation of testing underground. No steps towards a comprehensive agreement, as promised in that Treaty, have been taken despite powerful criticism and constructive proposals elaborated in great technical detail by lesser powers, such as Canada, Japan, and Sweden.

Two recent developments have made success seem more distant than ever. One is the confusion brought about by the glorification of peaceful nuclear explosions. Many underdeveloped countries have been allured by this. The issue was introduced into the negotiation machinery through the Non-Proliferation Treaty and has since served to block progress.

The second is the disgraceful conspiracy between the two superpowers to set a ceiling for permitted nuclear-weapons tests so ludicrously high that it strangles all attempts to reach international agreements on a total ban. Moreover, in the bilateral agreement no ceiling was set on peaceful nuclear explosions to begin with. The hope of stemming the product improvement of nuclear weapons and hindering their proliferation has thus been dealt a fatal blow.

No knowledgeable participant in the disarmament negotiations can be beguiled into believing that the Threshold Ban Treaty which resulted from the 1974 summit meeting of United States and Soviet leaders means progress towards slowing the development of nuclear weapons. The limit of 150 kilotons which it sets for military tests has nothing to do with earlier discussions about the setting of a very low threshold. The new limit is ten times higher than any earlier suggestions. A device of that high a yield would only be relevant to the production of thermonuclear bombs. The majority of Soviet and United States explosions examined over a period of years have been well below the new limit.[1] The Indian explosion of May 1974 was somewhere near fifteen kilotons.

There have been earlier suggestions (by Egypt in 1965, by India in 1966, and up to this day by Japan) in the Geneva Disarmament Committee that a test ban might temporarily exclude tests of seismic magnitudes 4.75, roughly corresponding to a fifteen-kiloton explosion in hard rock. A motive for this is the difficulty of monitoring even the weakest seismic events and determining whether they are natural earthquakes or man-made explosions. The superpowers have been opposed to any such ban, confirming this at the 1973 General Assembly, approximately six months before they made their surprising move of negotiating the Threshold Ban Treaty.[2]

One must ponder this open disclosure of the superpowers' intention to go on developing their already overeffective nuclear-weapons systems. They are forgoing solely those test explosions of extraordinary strength, which from a military point of view were becoming uninteresting. Officially, they congratulate themselves and each other on this "important" or "significant" step forward. No criticism has been heard from inside the Soviet Union. The American Academy of Arts and Sciences was frank beyond what tact usually allows:

> The ultimate mockery at the summit was the "threshold test ban." Here is an agreement that, in the guise of restraint, permits underground explosives equivalent to 150,000 tons of TNT. That is ten times larger than the bomb that obliterated Hiroshima, and larger than almost all the tests conducted by the United States and the Soviet Union in recent years.[3]

The most reasonable course would be to call off nuclear-weapons tests tomorrow, even without conditions of mutuality. Continued testing is a disservice to all serious disarmament efforts. So is the bilateral Threshold Ban Treaty. Its credibility is so low that it may not even be ratified by the United States Senate. Repeated attempts have been made in the Senate to get a test ban accepted. Pleading for such a resolution in 1973, Senator Edward Kennedy cited a statement of mine, "Only a ban on further testing can stop the competition for qualitative proliferation, that is, the quest for product improvement which is the most dangerously destabilizing element in the arms race."

He followed up my words with his own statement:

> since the Partial Test-ban Treaty was signed, we have been obligated to negotiate a permanent ban on all testing. Yet the record of the past ten years is one of flagrant disregard for that commitment.

In 1975 he pursued the matter, introducing a resolution signed by twenty senators:

> We believe a CTB is far more in our interest than the proposed threshold agreement, an agreement which is set so high (150 kilotons) that it seems to have been drafted by arms developers rather than arms controllers.[4]

Though this agreement from a disarmament point of view is just one more of chiefly "cosmetic effect," there has lately been added (April 1976) a deal to place even the "peaceful" nuclear explosions below the same ceiling. In this context a contribution of genuine value has been made. The Soviet Union, formerly recalcitrant to allow such inspections and the one most eager to proceed with nuclear engineering works, will admit inspection at the sites of the peaceful explosions. This furnishes a valuable exchange of experiences and is an important expression of confidence.

But the terms agreed upon certainly do not stretch to any control of nuclear-weapons tests. Yet we know that such verification is fully feasible down to extremely low values and, in practical terms, to the whole spectrum of events which promote weapon development. It is high time to lay to rest the bogeyman that a comprehensive test ban is impossible because verification methods cannot guarantee a 100 percent assurance that no clandestine test would go undetected.

Any difficulty of verification has always been in regard to uncertainty only about very low-yield tests. This margin is continually being reduced by progressive scientific developments in detection and identification, if seismological means of verification from a distance are taken into account. The controversy remaining refers to tests between less than one up to twenty kilotons and depends on the method of execution. Some margin of error will exist, as teleseismic signals below a magnitude of four on the Richter scale may never be distinguishable from background noise (Chapter III, Section 6).

New technologies for verification continue to reduce the margin. Increasingly sensitive instruments have been developed, which when in array significantly improve observability. In addition, national stations in many countries are joining to form an extended detection club as it was initiated by Sweden in the middle 1960s, cooperating with rapid data exchange. Information collected from more and better-placed stations makes possible compound calculations based on a combination of criteria. The probability of underground explosions being discovered could be kept sufficiently high and the probability of an earthquake being mistaken for an explosion kept sufficiently low by the application of decision theory.[5] This knowledge is promising, as the effectiveness of a verification system ought to be measured by its capability to *deter* would-be violators of an agreement, not by abstract perfectionism. (For the philosophy, method, and machinery of control, see Chapter X.)

The superpowers have no reason to question the reliability of verification of a test ban; they have at their command a network of seismological observation facilities and, in addition, capacity for global surveillance by satellites using remote sensing instruments of increasing refinement. These cameras can ascertain human activities around suspected test sites; even the subsidence of craters can be photographed from satellites. These means of observation, tolerated by both superpowers as unobtrusive, certainly should assure the security of those possessing all monitoring paraphernalia. This would argue for the conclusion of a comprehensive test ban at once. Because satellite observations can hardly distinguish between weak and strong explosions, they do not serve any compromise using a "threshold" differentiation of tests.

Along with the bogeyman of nonverifiability from a distance, the United States demand for on-site inspections must be laid to rest. The unreliability of this method of obtaining incontestable evidence is now recognized (Chapter III, Section 5). To castigate the United States for lack of sincerity, in one of my last speeches in the Geneva Disarmament Committee, I summarized some of the unanswered questions regarding inspections:

> We would also request . . . that the United States, being the proponent of such measures, gives us an up-to-date evaluation of the effectiveness and limitations of such inspections. I think of the speed and precision with which a site for inspection can be selected, of the technical methods to be used at the site, of the modalities for such undertakings, and also of the precise definition of what would constitute conclusive evidence of an illegitimate explosion or otherwise. I would also ask for a reply, after so many years, to my question about the exact meaning of "a number of obligatory inspections." Should all Parties to a Treaty have the right to ask for the agreed number of inspections—whatever that magic number may be—and should each party have the obligation to submit to such inspections, thus multiplying the number of *inspections* by the number of *Treaty Parties*? This should not be belittled as some kind of humorous question: if we are invited to join a multinational treaty, we must know what our rights and duties are. I might also add that any bilateral concept of adversary inspection can, in our opinion, not be accommodated in a multilateral agreement.[6]

2.   "Peaceful" Nuclear Explosions—a Tenuous Link

The long and woeful tale of test-ban negotiations is not nearing a happy end. What has lately served to block the negotiations machinery is what goes under the name "peaceful nuclear explosive devices" (PNE, sometimes PNED). The potential economic benefits of extracting mineral wealth or digging huge canals and ports with the aid of nuclear explosions have been oversold in a way similar to the earlier overselling of radiation risks of nuclear tests.

The pretense that some nuclear explosions would be permissible if they would be for peaceful purposes only makes the whole question of PNEs the connecting link between the proliferation and the test-ban issues, or, to be more specific, between the Non-Proliferation Treaty with its Article V and a Test-Ban Treaty, whether Partial as now or the prospective Comprehensive one. Article V of the NPT promised that the benefits from any peaceful applications of nuclear explosions would be made available to the non-nuclear-weapons parties to the Treaty at low cost (Chapter VI, Section 4). It also stated that:

> Non-nuclear-weapons States party to the Treaty shall be able to obtain such benefits, pursuant to *a special international agreement or agreements*, through *an international* body with adequate representation of non-nuclear-weapons States. Negotiations on this subject *shall commence* as soon as possible after the Treaty enters into force. [Italics added.]

The Treaty did enter into force in 1970, but no negotiations have taken place. No special agreement or agreements have been concluded. No international body has been appointed. The failure to solve these outstanding problems has retarded all attempts to discipline nuclear developments and the spread of nuclear power. The Indian nuclear explosion of 18 May 1974, claimed to be for peaceful purposes, is a telling case in point.

Two preliminary questions have to be answered: what is the difference between peaceful and nonpeaceful nuclear explosions? What is the real value of the right for nuclear-weapons powers to continue to conduct such peaceful explosions if it entails the sacrifice of a comprehensive ban on nuclear testing?

The truth, to be kept firmly in mind, is that there is no distinction possible between nuclear explosive devices for military or for civilian purposes, one for bombing some place on earth and one for engineering work to mine or excavate it. All nuclear devices are potential bombs, and of a destructive force way beyond conventional explosives. The sole difference that can be claimed is the doubtful one of intent.

In practice circumstantial differences will appear at the later steps of disposition. These would be in regard to the degree of weaponization, the detonating procedure, the types of casing (for careful emplacement in engineering projects or for firing by military delivery vehicles), and the nature of the custodians, be they civilian or military authorities. However, in the early phase of R&D no difference appears, and typically, the cost of such development of nuclear devices has been carried on military budgets.[7]

The crucial step on the ladder towards manufacture of nuclear weapons is testing. It would be a practical impossibility to prohibit earlier stages such as accumulation of knowledge through research. The critical role of testing is obvious in all fields of military innovation. Tests ordinarily are the first observable actions that can be subjected to verification (Chapter X).

The near-identity between nuclear explosives for peaceful and for military purposes becomes of great significance in two important respects, proliferation and verification. They pose identical and still unsettled problems. An agenda on peaceful nuclear explosions today must be formulated in relation to both the Non-Proliferation Treaty and the existing Partial (PTB) as well as the prospective Comprehensive (CTB) Test-Ban Treaty.

To obtain a perspective on the supposed economic benefits of the peaceful use of nuclear explosions, we must look into the material-technical question: what would they be used for, once the testing of them was completed? Not much attention had been drawn to the possibility of using nuclear explosions for nonmilitary purposes before September 1968 when a report was delivered to a United Nations conference in Geneva on the peaceful uses of nuclear energy. Considerable optimism, bordering on euphoria, was then raised about the economic benefits possible from deep mining of ores and gas, excavation of canals, and the like. The most enthusiastic view was probably that of Edward Teller and his collaborators:

> The tremendous release of concentrated energy in a nuclear explosion can have application in the worlds of commerce and science.[8]

There is a certain irony in the fact that the superpowers have reversed their respective positions, with the Soviet Union now being more desirous and the United States more lukewarm about PNE.[9] A fair summation of the situation was made by the Soviet Academician V. S. Emelyanov:

> The possibilities of using nuclear explosions for civil purposes have been studied mainly in the United States and the Soviet Union. Both countries have been examining the feasibility of using nuclear explosions for exploiting oil and gas deposits, for opening up ore fields, for building water reservoirs in arid regions, for earth-moving operations in canal construction, and so on. In the United States the Plowshare Program was established to implement a number of such projects; the Soviet counterpart is "The Programme of use of commercial underground nuclear explosions." Such studies have so far

been largely theoretical, and although much useful data has been obtained from test explosions, none of the projects under investigation has yet reached the stage of wide and practical application. The advantages of using nuclear explosions for such projects lie chiefly in saving labour and therefore money. However, the danger of subsequent radioactive contamination of the environment is very real; the problem of designing a "clean" explosive has still not been solved. It is concluded that, at present, peaceful nuclear explosions are advisable only for exceptionally urgent problems which cannot otherwise be solved.[10]

What Emelyanov did not touch upon is the tug-of-war that has been going on about PNE that hinges on the question of discrimination. The attitudes of the non-nuclear-weapons states oscillate with the evaluations of potential benefits. Either we believe, as in the early period of enthusiasm, that PNEs might yield tremendous economic advantages and therefore that the lesser powers should be given an equal share in these techniques for advanced development, or we think that the present mode of pessimism is justified and that the nuclear-weapons powers could thus easily renounce PNE in order to prevent clandestine weapons testing.

Because the Partial Test-Ban Treaty forbids any nuclear explosions other than underground, however, only one of the several uses proposed for PNE can be contemplated, namely for *mining* operations at great depth. Yet the risk of harmful environmental effects would be vastly greater for such peaceful explosions than for military tests. The numbers of explosions involved would be greater, multiplied by factors of ten, perhaps a hundred. If gas or oil or minerals in any quantities were extracted by nuclear mining, the explosions would not occur as some odd, single phenomenon. They would emit masses of radioactivity. Already in underground tests considerable venting occurs. Senator Kennedy, in the previously quoted press statement asserted that "about one-fifth of our tests have vented, sending radioactive particles into the air." When such debris crosses national boundaries, it is a violation of the Partial Test-Ban Treaty. Although such violations occur, the nuclear-weapons Parties to the Treaty seem to treat them with mutual indulgence. Other nations, in particular Japan and Sweden, have raised objections through diplomatic channels when the winds have carried radioacivity to them.[11]

An even more serious radioactive threat would result from the use of PNE for *excavations*, the moving of great quantities of earth for digging canals or changing the course of rivers. The venting of radioactive debris from the craters would then be a major hazard, the extent of which may be seen from the analysis made of the nuclear costs of digging a sea-level Panama Canal: some 300 nuclear explosions with yields ranging up to 15 megatons would be required.[12]

Adding to the danger of radioactive fallout in the atmosphere is the danger of nuclear explosions destroying the earth's ozone layer. When in 1974 the director of the United States Arms Control and Disarmament Agency, Dr. Fred Iklé, examined this ominous possibility, he did so in relation to the potential effects of nuclear war. The implications, however, are the same for other nuclear explosions, the scale only having to be revised from case to case.

> The potential depletion of the ozone layer by nuclear explosions is a discovery that arms control officials believe adds an awesome element to the destructive effects of a nuclear war.
>
> An immediate implication of the discovery of ozone effects, Mr. Iklé suggested, is to reinforce the effectiveness of nuclear deterrence, since a nuclear power would know that it was perhaps ordaining the destruction of mankind if it resorted to nuclear weapons. But in the longer range, arms control officials hope that the discovery can contribute to disarmament by demonstrating the self-destructiveness of nuclear arsenals.[13]

PNE constitutes an unquiet legal-political knot, truly Gordian, not likely to be undone except with a cutting sword. If "peaceful" nuclear explosions should become more than experiments, cratering would in all probability be condoned and explosions not limited to tightly confined mining shafts. Yet to concede any right of venting presupposes a change in the Moscow Treaty. For such amendments the lesser powers possess what could amount to a veto: the votes of a majority of the more than 120 States Party to that Treaty would have to consent.

Thus, the non-nuclear-weapons powers are for once mighty. They can, if they stand together, decide the fate of "peaceful" nuclear explosions. The only changes to the Partial Test-Ban Treaty they would want to agree to would be to eliminate discrimination. Today's bizarre situation is that if a ban on only peaceful nuclear explosions were obtained, the nuclear-weapons powers could conduct them under the guise of nuclear-weapons tests.

3.   The Most Dangerous Loopholes

The similarity between peaceful or military nuclear tests explains why the question of PNE has been made such a center of superpower gaming. The political overtones of the subject will be a major theme in my treatment, as they have gone largely unnoticed through the years.

Since both superpowers have come to agree with the experts that the economic value of nuclear explosions for civilian engineering purposes is still quite uncertain, there must be other reasons for not giving them up. After all, a temporary moratorium while the subject is under study would otherwise make sense. It now appears that the superpowers' refusal to enter into the stipulated NPT negotiations on special agreements for the regulation of PNE was to shield the conduct of "peaceful" nuclear explosions. They wanted testing capabilities secured from limitations which are or might be placed on the testing of nuclear weapons. In short, they wanted a loophole.

This political intention became manifest in the Moscow 1974 Threshold Ban Treaty between the superpowers as they astutely only prescribed that engineering applications of nuclear explosions must be conducted at separate locations from those sites which are to be specified as weapons test sites.

The two superpowers indulge in doubletalk, confessing that "it is *not possible to distinguish* between the technology of nuclear devices for peaceful engineering purposes and that for nuclear weapons," but that "it is important to develop a set of agreed procedures for peaceful explosions, as and if they become technically and economically feasible, *to distinguish them clearly* from weapons tests and make sure that they would not be used for weapons purposes."[14]

Evidently, hope that the two governments might work out "agreed procedures" was held out to satisfy the military and pacify the public before the belated, modest bilateral restriction on testing of nuclear weapons and other devices with higher yields than 150 kilotons enters into force. What would it mean for the international situation and multilateral negotiations if they tried to win sanctioning of this bleak prospect of large latitudes for testing in Geneva or the United Nations? Is it to serve as any model for India and others to follow? This is a most serious question.[15]

4.   An International Approach

To cope with the problems surrounding potentially beneficial nuclear explosions requires an international body to handle requests for such services as set out in NPT, Article V. The nonaligned delegations forcefully criticized non-action in this direction both in the Conference of Non-Nuclear Powers held in Geneva in 1968 and in the Geneva Disarmament Committee the same year.

A comprehensive test ban was to be achieved by (a) in principle prohibiting all nuclear explosions, and (b) making exceptions possible for some nuclear explosions for specified peaceful purposes. To assure nondiscrimination, the decisions on such exceptions should be taken by the aforesaid international body and not by the nuclear-weapons powers. For a long time the non-nuclear-weapons powers have pressed for such a solution.

> Canada and Sweden maintained that an underground test-ban treaty would have to include provision for specific permission for each peaceful nuclear explosion under an international regime for the peaceful utilization of nuclear energy. India agreed that the underground test ban was directly linked to the issue of peaceful explosions and that the two should be considered together. In its view, total prohibition of nuclear explosions must apply to all States, nuclear and non-nuclear. Peaceful explosions would then be permitted under a separate international regime.[16]

That question of nondiscrimination was of paramount interest to the non-nuclear-weapons states. Behind this arguing for international decision-making in regard to peaceful nuclear explosions, there was a strong feeling that the interests of technologically less-developed countries should be given due consideration. I voiced that concern before the closing of the debate on Article V in the Non-Proliferation Treaty:

> a reassurance should be given to all nations, and particularly to the nations in dire need of more speedy economic development, that the opportunities of *all* nations to avail themselves of the possible benefits of such a new technology as the application of nuclear explosions to major civil engineering projects would in fact be equal. Only a truly international regime, allowing for international decision-making in regard to permission to undertake explosions and for executive supervision of them in whatever country they occur, would give such an assured equality. It is not possible to admit as a permanent fea-

ture of the world's future that some countries, because they are militarily advanced, would also have direct access to important economic and technical benefits of new technologies that others would be able to obtain only in an indirect way.[17]

In the absence of negotiations to internationalize nuclear power, the desire to preserve the right to undertake peaceful nuclear explosions has grown stronger in many countries eager for development. A British expert recently analyzed the problem:

> It is hardly sufficient to contend, however justly, that PNEDs still offer no genuine "benefits"; failure to negotiate multilaterally on this subject, or even to disseminate widely enough much of the data on which judgements must be based, can only promote unfounded sympathy for Indian and Brazilian insistence that the "benefits" exist, but that nuclear-weapons States are cynically intent upon withholding them from others.[18]

But once again the superpowers' gaming has been successful. At the Review Conference for the Non-Proliferation Treaty, held in Geneva in May 1975 (Chapter VI, Section 8), they succeeded in getting through a "reinterpretation" of the requirement in Article V about "a special international agreement or agreements" to handle matters concerning peaceful nuclear explosions "through an international body with adequate representation of non-nuclear-weapons states." It now seems as if no more action will be taken, but that is against the agreed treaty. A special international agreement was to be entered upon. Some confusion might linger in the minds of a reader as to the meaning of agreement or agreements. But when the treaty was negotiated the legal distinction was clearly made by the United States delegate:

> This language contemplates a basic agreement defining the functions of the appropriate international body and holds open the possibilities of a series of separate international agreements dealing with particular projects.[19]

At the same meeting the Soviet delegate explained that the basic agreement would deal with principles and procedures and would be worked out with very broad participation of non-nuclear-weapons states.

The NPT Review Conference, obviously led by the superpowers, took upon itself to resolve:

The Conference considers the IAEA to be the appropriate international body, referred to in Article V of the Treaty, through which potential benefits from peaceful applications of nuclear explosions could be made available to any non-nuclear-weapons States.[20] *

This can be only half of the story. The nonaligned states, especially Mexico and Sweden, have held that a separation of functions must be made between the executive and the decision-making bodies. The primary need is for a proper division between a licensing authority which would have the power to permit explosions and the responsibility of assuring that they were for nonmilitary purposes, and a managing agency which would assure that rules concerning technical feasibility and health safeguards are strictly followed.

The International Atomic Energy Agency (IAEA) possesses excellent capabilities to handle the technical part. The Agency should be given all legal and administrative means to build up the necessary structure for performing these functions and services.[21]

The former, policy-oriented part has receded far into the background. Only an impartial authority, however, can solve the vexing question as to who shall have the right to undertake nuclear explosions, the devices themselves being inherently double-purpose, peaceful or military. For the decision-making authority, a locus must be sought where political responsibility can be exerted according to an agreed legal process which forces nuclear explosions under a licensing system (Chapter X, Section 2).

The relationships have been very succinctly stated by my successor to the CCD, Under-Secretary of State Inga Thorsson. A highly important role is preserved for IAEA, but she calls for another licensing authority:

> The technical feasibility of a particular project, its economic, health, and safety aspects, should be evaluated by the International Atomic Energy Agency. The over-all advisability of the project should in our view be determined by a political international body. This body should also have the authority to license such a project. When it comes to the execution of the project the International Atomic Energy Agency again would have an important role to play in arranging for and controlling the actual explosion.[22]

As matters now stand, there would be no point to international negotiations according to NPT's Article V, if they do not lead to the

---

* Note that the NPT formal restrictions about application to States Party to the Non-Proliferation Treaty is not maintained.

transfer of PNE services from the nuclear-weapons powers to an international body. It would be dangerous to foreclose a truly effective solution by some ad hoc compromise at this stage, when the only politically available step now would probably leave the nuclear-weapons powers free from any international regulation. Some delay is inevitable anyway and the IAEA can profitably use it to study the technical aspects. The Geneva Disarmament Committee, CCD, which has to consider the political aspects, can well afford to hold out.

A major question remains: is it not really best if all nations, rather than just Parties to NPT, agree on the permissibility of nuclear explosions? Is the NPT a necessary or a redundant intermediary in regard to IAEA safeguards? (Chapter VI, Section 8.)

While IAEA is continuing its studies on the utility and feasibility of PNEs, the negotiating process must continue. A moratorium on peaceful nuclear explosions might be a bargain. It would be a step in the right direction, a signal more than a sacrifice by the superpowers who are having second thoughts on the value of such explosions. Such a moratorium on testing *weapons* was urged by Resolution 3257 (XXIX) in the General Assembly in 1974, but there was no corresponding resolution on peaceful testing! The superpowers should be asked forcefully to stand ready to offer, through either bilateral agreements or unilateral declarations, to forgo nuclear-explosion projects, at least for the duration of the IAEA study.

5. *A Test Ban Without Loopholes*

A comprehensive test ban continues to figure as a goal in the rhetoric of the superpowers. Their sincerity must nevertheless be questioned. The Soviet proposal to the 1975 General Assembly to "take the final step" and agree on a total test ban was hedged in by the requirement that all states and "all nuclear-weapons powers" must agree—an unrealistic contingency[23] (Chapter VI, Section 2). Furthermore, the ban would not apply to tests carried out for peaceful purposes.

The superpowers do not seem to fear, or even much care, about the risk of proliferation of nuclear weapons being kept open by underground testing (Chapter VI, Section 2). They have shown no willingness to curtail their military options except to limit weapons-test explosions to 150 kilotons. This demonstrates once again a general truth of fundamental importance for disarmament negotiations: only when the arms race has reached a point where some type of bomb or delivery vehicle is obsolete or further weapons development has lost any military usefulness to the superpowers will a gesture of "disarmament" or arms limitation be made.

This insight makes the outlook for an agreement on a Comprehensive Test Ban dim indeed. Nonetheless, in the United Nations the non-nuclear-weapons powers, led by the nonaligned nations, must keep up the fight. Despite their commanding a majority, however, it often takes on a character of a *danse macabre*. In 1974, for about the fifteenth time a resolution was passed, now by a majority of ninety-five, with Albania, China, and France voting against and thirty-three countries abstaining, among them the Soviet Union and the United States with their close military allies, that the General Assembly:

> *Condemns* all nuclear weapons tests, in whatever environment they may be conducted;
>
> *Reaffirms* its deep concern at the continuance of such testing, both in the atmosphere and underground, and at the lack of progress towards a comprehensive test-ban agreement;
>
> *Emphasizes* once more the urgency of concluding a comprehensive test-ban agreement;
>
> *Reminds* the nuclear-weapons States of their special responsibility to initiate proposals to this end;
>
> *Calls upon* all States to refrain from the testing of nuclear weapons, in any environment, pending conclusion of such an agreement.[24]

The language was no milder in 1975. On the occasion of the NPT Review Conference, an attempt was made by some nonaligned delegations to get an even stronger commitment by tying the ban on nuclear testing to the number of Parties to the Non-Proliferation Treaty (Chapter VI, Section 5). The idea was, in brief, for a moratorium: all nuclear tests should be suspended for ten years as soon as the number of the NPT Parties reached one hundred—there were then ninety-seven—and prolonged for three more years any time five additional members joined the NPT.[25] This initiative was valuable for exerting pressure and interesting as a new device, but it did not succeed in forcing the nuclear-weapons powers to bend. But the struggle must not relent. The salient point is that all nuclear explosions, whether military or peaceful, must be encompassed in one and the same decision and covered in one and the same legal document. The loopholes of underground testing must be closed.

As India gave us an alarming reminder that peaceful explosions might be used for weapons development, it seems worthwhile to listen to its suggestions for a constructive, nondiscriminatory solution.

> We can make a beginning in controlling the nuclear arms race by agreeing on a comprehensive test ban. We feel that there is no justification or excuse for continuing nuclear-weapons testing. . . . Only in the context of a complete cessation of all nuclear-weapons tests could consideration be given to the possibility of concluding an agreement on the regulation of underground nuclear explosions for peaceful purposes to be signed by all States. The accompanying system of international safeguards which will have to be devised should be based on objective, functional, and nondiscriminatory criteria. It should be universal in application.[26]

A more pragmatic approach than asking for an immediate cessation of all testing, however, may have to be sought. To achieve that purpose some timetable must be used. Not even statesmen leading great nations can easily win approval for the closing of ongoing test series and all the operating test sites at once.

Consideration of such practical realities has inspired the Swedish delegation to the Geneva Disarmament Committee to present a draft treaty on a Comprehensive Test Ban with two outstanding advantages: (a) verification by challenge, including local inspection by invitation, whereby an accused Party has the possibility of clearing itself of charges of violation, and (b) three protocols which allow different time delays for the coming into full force of the ban (Chapter X).

The main idea behind this timetable approach is that the major *decision* to agree on stopping all nuclear explosions should be taken in the immediate future, but the *implementation* of the various steps stipulated in the protocols could be tuned to the conditions to be set for certain modalities, including the international regulation about decision-making and management of nuclear explosions for peaceful purposes.[27] As one of the architects of this proposal, I am eager to invite specific rejoinders with suggestions for improvements in the structure of this draft treaty.[28]

Under the draft treaty proposed by Sweden, the parties would undertake to "prohibit, to prevent, and not to carry out any underground nuclear-weapons test explosion or any other underground nuclear explosion" at any place under their jurisdiction or control. There were specific provisions to facilitate such a decision. First, the treaty would be fully operative for each nuclear-weapons power only after a certain number of months from its entry into force, "during which period any nuclear test explosions shall be phased out in accordance with provisions laid down in Protocol I, annexed to this treaty." The reason given for the proviso was that abrupt discontinuance of testing might create practical difficulties.

Next, specific provisions would allow for exceptions in case of "nuclear explosions which are carried out for construction or other peaceful purposes and which take place in conformity with the separate Protocol II annexed to this treaty." The protocol dealing with this exemption might alleviate the Partial Test-Ban Treaty's rules against venting, if it were desirable to facilitate peaceful uses of nuclear explosives.

Finally, much emphasis was laid on a full and open exchange of information as the basis for verification:

> Each State Party to this Treaty undertakes to cooperate in good faith in a effective international exchange of seismological data in order to facilitate the detection, identification, and location of underground events." Provisions [in this respect were to be] laid down in the separate Protocol III, annexed to the Treaty.[29]

For obvious reasons not all signatories to the Treaty need sign all protocols in regard to the phasing out of ongoing tests.

The more active phase of "verification by challenge" was described in the Swedish draft treaty:

> Each State Party to this Treaty undertakes to cooperate in good faith for the clarification of all events pertaining to the subject matter of this Treaty. In accordance with this provision, each State Party to the Treaty is entitled
>
> (a) to make inquiries and to receive information as a result of such inquiries,
>
> (b) to invite inspection on its territory or territory under its jurisdiction, such inspection to be carried out in the manner prescribed by the inviting Party,
>
> (c) to make proposals, if it deems the information available or made available to it under all or any of the preceding provisions inadequate, as to suitable methods of clarification.
>
> Each State Party to this Treaty may bring to the attention of the Security Council of the United Nations and of the other Parties to the Treaty, that it deems another Party to have failed to cooperate to the fullest extent for the clarification of a particular event.[30]

The world stands at the crossroads. The nuclear-weapons powers are responsible for refusing to conclude an international agreement on banning nuclear tests. The cost of their refusal is enormous, and it might become unbearably high by actual proliferation of nuclear weapons. The risk that more countries may acquire nuclear weapons is potentially a higher cost, even to the superpowers, than some unforeseen breakthrough in weapons technology that might be achieved by clandestine testing after a treaty is signed. Here the interests of the few who want to continue their tricky gaming stand against the interests of all peoples of the world.

CHAPTER VIII

Outlawing the Use of Cruel Weapons and Methods of Warfare

The growth of armaments is cancerous, spreading always into new places, appearing in new variants, infecting political, social, and economic institutions ever more deeply. The most radical cure is the surgical one: eliminating all armaments, except agreed minimal forces for police protection, border defense, and UN peace functions. The goal of General and Complete Disarmament has, however, not been universally accepted. Instead, in continuous negotiations (and in this book) the aim is the more modest but at the same time more urgent one of *removing* or *reducing* the quantity of specific weapons from the armories and *blocking* deadly new developments in the qualitative arms race.

There is a second possible approach, the prescriptive one: to lay down rules restricting the *use of weapons*. This chapter is devoted to outlawing the use of weapons which cause unnecessary suffering and those indiscriminate methods of warfare which cause destruction to civilians as well as soldiers, civilian property as well as military. The aim of international humanitarian law is to uphold human rights even in warfare, to reduce cruelty, and to protect the civilian population.

This second approach is the more traditional one. Almost a hundred years ago at the Hague Conferences, the rules of war were modified and codified succinctly even if the terms today sometimes seem quaint. These rules, the Hague Law of War, were binding on all governments. The General Protocol of 1925, banning the use of chemical and biological warfare, is the latest follow-up of this tradition so far (Chapter VIII, Section 2, and Chapter IX). With each successive war, from World War I, these humanitarian rules of war have become increasingly outmoded and disregarded. Yet the revulsion against the cynical disrespect of humanitarian considerations displayed in modern warfare and weapons development has for some time given rise to efforts to modernize and reinstate the rules of war. These efforts have involved the United Nations and the International Committee of the Red Cross (ICRC). Their apex was a Diplomatic Conference on the Reaffirmation and Development of International Humanitarian Law Applicable in Armed Conflicts (CDDH), called by the Swiss Government.*

Our era is fortunate in possession of the valuable heritage of an agreed-upon system of international laws and customs for the conduct of warfare. With all its imperfections, the system sets a firm frame of reference which is undisputed. In the latter half of the last century, when representatives of governments started to meet and lay down legal rules for armed conflicts, they already had an old juridical, ethical, and cultural tradition to build upon. From time immemorial, rules to limit the horrors of warfare have been proclaimed.[1]

1. The Emergence of International Laws of War

Efforts to introduce humanitarian restraints into the conduct of war have ancient roots in the history of mankind.

Historically, people have believed that completely lawless war, without any restraints than those imposed by lack of resources and techniques, had serious disadvantages for both parties to a conflict. Even in ancient civilizations there are examples of prohibitions against the poisoning of water sources and the razing of forests. Such rules of war, imposed for obviously practical reasons were

---

* Between the Geneva Protocol of 1925 and the present activities should be noted the work resulting in the four Geneva Conventions of 1949, centering on the protection of war victims. They will not be dealt with in the following, nor will the related large body of provisions, in force or under negotiation dealing with prisoners of war and wounded, with protection of medical facilities, etc. Neither will be taken up the question of the responsibility of individual government officials, officers, and soldiers for conduct in violation of rules of war, the kind of atrocities which have been so much in the foreground of public attention since the Nuremberg trials. The analysis in this book will be restricted to issues which have a direct bearing on disarmament.

early combined with stipulations of a humanitarian nature. Some
of the oldest known treaty rules are agreements on the treatment of
prisoners of war, concluded in Egypt as far back as 1400 B.C. Another example of farsighted ancient rules is the Manu Law of India,
dating from about 500 B.C., which forbids the use of poisons and
other weapons which were considered unjustly inhumane.

The influence of various religions on the conduct of war is also
evident at an early stage. The rules introduced by the Saracens
about A.D. 600 for the regulation of warfare, considered to be the first
systematic code of international law, were based directly on the
Koran. These old rules forbade, for instance, the use of incendiary
weapons, poisoning wells, and devastating forests; they were aimed
at upholding humanitarianism and chivalry in warfare. The earliest
Christians were totally against the taking of life. Later the Church
manifested a desire to establish humanitarian rules for the conduct
of war. Two of the more famous interpreters of Christian views on
warfare were St. Augustine (354–430) and St. Thomas Aquinas
(1225–1274). The ethical debate on what constituted a just war
long continued in the Catholic Church and among philosophers.

Though there was much overt praise of chivalry during the
Middle Ages, wars were conducted with extreme barbarity. Women
and children were not spared. Conditions appear to have been
particularly terrible in states of siege; a number of special launching
devices and weapons of great cruelty were developed, among them
several varieties of incendiary weapons. This caused the Catholic
Church to intervene time and time again, from around the year
1000, in attempts to limit the use of such arms. At the Lateran
Council in 1139 Pope Innocent II denounced instruments of
war which launched projectiles, but he was overruled by advocates
of "military necessity." Towards the end of the fourteenth century
the Church also played a part in the establishment of rules in
England concerning the behavior of combatants towards prisoners
of war and civilians. However, such visionary attempts to establish
rules for international conduct, prohibiting use of certain types of
weapons, remained mostly ineffective.

At the beginning of modern times, the conceptualization of international law was greatly advanced through the work of Hugo Grotius,
a Dutch jurist and statesman (1583–1645). He was influenced by
natural-law philosophy and wrote under the shadow of the bloody
Thirty Years' War, one of the most uninhibitedly plunderous of all.
Often regarded as the father of modern international law, Grotius

sought criteria that might justify war, and posed questions about prisoners of war, terror attacks, plunder, collective punishment, and illegitimacy of useless injury.[2]

The rationalistic-ethical opposition against war and its brutality was deepened considerably through the writings of a long line of philosophers of the Enlightenment in the seventeenth and eighteenth centuries. Pacifistic doctrines were elaborated by Rousseau and the Encyclopedists in France, by Bentham in England, and most thoroughgoingly of all by Kant, who wrote a treatise on eternal peace.[3] In turn, the confluence of such important cultural influences as Enlightenment philosophy and liberalism together with traditional religious-ethical precepts led to a new international ethical ideology. The trend was considerably stronger in Great Britain and the United States than on the European continent, partly because of their more protected geographical location and safer distance from wars, but also because both continued to rely on professional armies and endeavored to discipline them. Europeans first experienced a different kind of war with Napoleon's people's armies; later von Clausewitz enunciated positive justifications for warfare without mercy.[4]

As the rapid evolution of the technology of weaponry made wars increasingly savage, there developed in the mid-nineteenth century a heightened awareness of the need to restrain cruelty. The Crimean War (1854–1856) moved Florence Nightingale to work for improving the lot of the wounded. Henri Dunant's humanitarian propaganda campaign a few years later, leading to the foundation of the Red Cross, was prompted by the same awakening. The 1864 Geneva Convention on the amelioration of the conditions of wounded soldiers in the field became the first in a series of international agreements, conventions, and declarations which were gradually widened in scope from helping the victims of war to regulating the conduct of conflicts. The Civil War in the United States—another example of a shockingly bloody and devastating war—led President Lincoln to be the first to issue, in 1863, a national military legal code for the conduct of war.[5]

In 1868, under the aegis of Czar Alexander II of Russia, seventeen nations representing the "civilized world" met in St. Petersburg. The result of that meeting was the Declaration of St. Petersburg, which prohibited the use on land or sea of high explosives in projectiles weighing less than 400 grams. These new projectiles were far more damaging to humans than earlier generations of weapons had been, and their only legitimate purpose was to put an enemy soldier out of action.

Though the delegates to St. Petersburg drew much inspiration from Lincoln's code, the United States was not represented at the meeting. Nor was the United States present at a subsequent conference which issued another Declaration from Brussels in 1874. Although the Brussels Declaration was later superceded by the Hague Conferences of 1899 and 1907, it is worth mentioning here the main stipulation: "the laws of war do not allow belligerents an unlimited power as to the choice of means of injuring an enemy." Of special note also is that the declarations of both St. Petersburg and Brussels "were largely the work of military men."[6]

The fundamental principles of the St. Petersburg Declaration have remained the tenets of all subsequent efforts to legislate rules for armed conflicts. The Declaration set forth:

> That the *only* legitimate object which States should endeavour to accomplish during war is to *weaken* the *military* forces of the enemy,
>
> That for this purpose it is *sufficient* to *disable* the greatest possible number of men,
>
> That this object would be *exceeded* by the employment of *arms* which *uselessly* aggravate the *suffering* of *disabled* men or render their death inevitable,
>
> That *the employment of such arms would, therefore, be* contrary to the laws of humanity.[7]

But wars went on, and the technological development of new and more potent weapons continued. In many quarters strong indignation was being voiced that the rules of war were neither sufficiently comprehensive nor binding. More decisive steps were needed to contain the twin evils of warfare and weapons development. This general tenor led Czar Nicholas II of Russia to instigate the first of the Hague Conferences in 1899. He invited all governments represented at the Imperial Court to meet to consider "a possible reduction of the excessive armaments which weigh upon all nations," and to attempt to curb "the progressive developments of existing armaments."[8]

The second Conference was held in 1907. Twenty-six nations participated in the Conference of 1899 and forty-four in 1907. Though both Conferences failed of their ambitions to halt the increase of arms by mutually agreed limitations of arsenals and the further development of new weapons, there were substantive agreements on the uses of arms and methods of warfare that could be considered legitimate to armed conflict and those that must be prohibited on humanitarian grounds.

More than ten Conventions were agreed upon at the Conference of 1907. Of these, the most important was Convention IV, "Respecting the Laws and Customs of War on Land," and the Annex to it, "Regulations Respecting the Laws and Customs of War on Land," which was largely an incorporation of the earlier corresponding Convention of 1899.

In the Preamble to this 1907 Convention, it was stated as a principle that if armed conflicts occured between the signatories to the Convention they would keep up "the desire to serve, even in this extreme case, the interests of humanity and the ever progressive needs of civilization." Another part of the Preamble, often called the Martens clause after one of the delegates, set forth that the fundamental principles of the Conventions had general validity as international customary law:

> Until a more complete code of the laws of war has been issued the high contracting Parties deem it expedient to declare that, in cases not included in the Regulations adopted by them, the inhabitants and the belligerents remain under the protection of the rule of the principles of the law of nations, as they result from the usages established among civilized peoples, from the laws of humanity, and the dictates of the public conscience.[9]

One chapter in this 1907 Convention dealt with "Means of Injuring the Enemy, Sieges, and Bombardments," which provides excellent groundwork for our time in three important prohibitions:

> Article 22. The right of belligerents to adopt means of injuring the enemy is not unlimited.
>
> Article 23. In addition to the prohibitions provided by special Conventions, it is especially forbidden:
>
> a) To employ poison or poisoned weapons; . . .
>
> e) To employ arms, projectiles, or material calculated to cause unnecessary suffering; . . .
>
> Article 25. The attack or bombardment, by whatever means, of towns, villages, dwellings or buildings which are undefended is prohibited.

Within a short time twenty-five countries—most of Europe, the United States, some Latin American and Asian nations—had ratified this Convention. It should be noted that though many nations were at that time still dependencies, they remain bound by the ratifications of the colonial powers of Britain, France, and Holland. China signed the Convention of 1899 which, in regard to the articles quoted, is essentially identical to that of 1907.

Three prohibitions with significance for our time were the subjects of declarations at the 1899 Conference. The first, astonishingly perspicacious, prohibited the discharge of projectiles and explosives from the air, by balloon. This proscription was included in the 1907 document with an additional phrase "[by balloon] or by other new methods of a similar nature."

The second of these prohibitions dealt with "asphyxiating gases"; the third with expanding bullets, often called dum-dum bullets. Neither of these two were reaffirmed in 1907, chiefly because of opposition from the United States.

The three prohibitions were not, however, a total loss. They remain valid. The first to become updated and widely accepted was the one prohibiting what was once spoken of as asphyxiating gases.

During World War I, the use of incapacitating gas by both sides on the Western Front aroused widespread indignation and was solemnly condemned in the Versailles Peace Treaty. Gas warfare came to be regarded as particularly abominable. Endeavors were made to establish a binding total ban on the use of this type of weapon. These efforts were crowned with success through the acceptance of the 1925 Geneva Protocol on the prohibition of the use of chemical and bacteriological weapons.

The articles in the Geneva Protocol succinctly prohibit the use in war of "asphyxiating, poisonous, or other gases, and of all analogous liquids, materials, and devices" as well as "bacteriological methods of warfare." The Protocol has been ratified or acceded to by nearly a hundred nations, including all military and politically important states. Japan only acceded in 1970, however, and the United States, which had fifty years earlier been instrumental in authoring the original agreement and had signed the Protocol, in 1974.

Lack of ratification by some countries might not have been a calamity if the rules had been strictly observed by all.[10] The Protocol is recognized as forming a part of international customary law, binding on all, regardless of signature. This character of the Geneva Protocol as binding *towards all* was reaffirmed by action of the General Assembly in 1969 (Chapter VIII, Section 2. See also "A Personal Note.")

This Protocol of 1925 remains the last formal agreement under international law dealing with the use of specified weapons. The Geneva Conventions of 1949 contain important rules for the treatment of protected groups of persons, as well as wounded soldiers and prisoners of war, but they do not contain any stipulations on the use of specific weapons or means of warfare. However, the principles of the rules of war have been repeatedly affirmed. In 1946 the General Assembly unanimously confirmed them along with the Nuremberg Principles, announced in connection with the Nuremberg trials of war crimes. Among the crimes held punishable under international law, Article VI (b) is of particular relevance to this chapter. War crimes were designated as:

> Violations of the laws or customs of war which include but are not limited to, murder, ill-treatment or deportation to slave-labour or for any other purpose of civilian population of or in occupied territory, murder or ill-treatment of prisoners of war or persons on the seas, killing of hostages, plunder of public or private property, *wanton destruction of cities, towns or villages, or devastating not justified by military necessity.*[11]

In 1954 the International Law Commission submitted a Draft Code of Offenses against the Peace and Security of Mankind, which was "noted" but not formally "affirmed" by an almost unanimous General Assembly. Some of its condemnatory formulas closely relate to the issue of concern here, for example, Article 2, paragraph 10: "Inhuman acts by the authorities of a State or by individuals against any civilian population," and, a general reference to the old body of rules, paragraph 11: "Acts in violation of the laws or customs of war." When this proposed code was discussed in the General Assembly practically all the delegations that took a stand in the matter accepted the formulated principles as part of international law.[12]

The system of laws and customs internationally accepted as part of international law—until superseded by some newer and better ones—provides us with a powerful common denominator for judging the use of certain weapons or warfare methods as permissible or impermissible. The principle rule is that they can be used legitimately only to put enemy soldiers out of action. What goes beyond that objective is judged to be excessive; thus whatever cannot be limited to military objectives is condemned. This consensus covers the two principal categories of rules, namely against weapons which can cause "unnecessary suffering" to human beings and against targets of "indiscriminate warfare," that is, the attacking or devastating of the human environment involving civilian populations.

By applying these cardinal rules we can live with the seeming paradox that although all weapons are cruel, some are more cruel than others; just as, although all war is inhumane, some warfare methods are more inhumane than others.

The condemned weapons and methods of warfare have continued to be used time and again in spite of all these valiant efforts to introduce legal constraints. The conduct both of World War II and the Korean War provide examples of blatant violations for which responsibilities are widely shared. The same is true of more localized wars, such as in Bangladesh and Vietnam.

What is then the purpose of underscoring that a fair degree of consensus exists about what tools and methods may not appropriately be used for warfare? The purpose is to try to push back military claims and to strengthen the restraints dictated by common public morality.

2.   Modern Warfare Violates International Law: The Case Against Use of Chemical Weapons

Rules of war should be formulated to relate stringently to the current state of weapons technology and warfare strategy. As such adaptation has long been lagging, modernization of international humanitarian law is urgently needed. Ethical principles basic to all rules of restraint and the explicit regulations established in our own cultural era should be respected as valid and compulsory. They should also be interpreted by responsible governments as applying to new generations of weapons and warfare techniques which once were proscribed no matter in what form.

Unfortunately, the ugly truth is that the restrictions agreed to have been and are being violated, sometimes in such a gross manner that our era might come to earn the epithet "the age of neobarbarism."

Chemical weapons—lethal and harassing nerve gas, tear gas, herbicides—belong to the category of impermissible tools of war. The actual use of some of them is a record of frightening destructiveness that has gone far beyond the confines of codified international law. Together with biological weapons they are explicitly banned by the Geneva Protocol, and they were condemned in sufficiently *clear language* from the earliest attempts to humanize the conduct of war (Chapter VIII, Section 1). These cumulative efforts to prohibit gas and bacteriological warfare resulted in a body of international customary law which was solemnly affirmed by the United Nations in 1969.[13]

The words of the Preamble to the Charter of the United Nations about the untold sorrow which war has brought to mankind twice in our lifetime evoke the memory of World War I and its gas clouds, first gathering over the battlefield of Ypres. It is fitting to recall here the toll of death and lifelong suffering just by mentioning the bare figures: more than 90,000 dead by gas warfare among the estimated 1,300,000 casualties.[14]

Even after that horrible experience and the 1925 Geneva Protocol agreement to avoid the like ever after, history records several instances, though sporadic and not sometimes well-documented, of the use of chemical weapons, harassing and lethal. (The respect for biological weapons has functioned more completely as an inhibition against their use.) When Italy attacked Ethiopia in 1935–36, Mussolini did not hesitate to break the Geneva Protocol by ordering his air squadrons to spray huge quantities of fatal mustard gas over the unprotected enemy. It is estimated that of the total Ethiopian army casualties of some 50,000, perhaps 15,000 were due to chemical weapons. When Italy stood accused before the League of Nations of such inhumane warfare methods, the first defense was denial but the second was an attempt to excuse itself by maintaining that the Geneva Protocol did not prohibit the use of chemical weapons "in reprisal against other illegal acts of war." The Italians accused the Ethiopians of atrocities, including "systematic use of dum-dum bullets."[15] Thus are opportune interpretations of one or another of the Laws of War made according to circumstance and interest. Other reports of chemical warfare have come from the Japanese war against China 1937–1945. SIPRI concludes that chemical warfare can be militarily advantageous only if the enemy is unprotected against it (Chapter VIII, Section 6).[16]

No concealment was possible after the use of chemicals became massive in scope. After President John Kennedy authorized them for field operations in Vietnam in 1961, the weapons were deliberately planned, tested, produced, transported, and sprayed in gross quantities—tons upon tons. As a result of this gigantic application no legal pretext could defend these activities from the charge of premediated chemical warfare. The resulting devastation, of such wide scope, requires that such use be characterized as brutally inhumane warfare.

The excuse was that only nonlethal means were used—mostly antiplant agents and tear gas—and that these were not covered by the Geneva Protocol. But the UN adamantly rejected this by action in 1969 which affirmed that the prohibition in the Geneva Protocol was all-inclusive. Vietnam demonstrated that such action could only be effective against a population that could not afford protection.

The vast devastation brought onto Indochina by chemical warfare cannot be pictured by naked figures alone. Here is the conclusion of an expert who has made several study trips to these battlefields.

> One of the most distasteful aspects of the war in the eyes of the world was the massive United States chemical warfare program with antiplant agents, both to deny forest cover and to destroy crops. . . .
>
> Vast areas of forest, largely in South Vietnam, were sprayed with herbicides, in particular during 1966–1969. . . . All told, more than four million acres were sprayed, representing 10 percent of South Vietnam. The resulting herbicidal damage has been monumental. . . .
>
> About a quarter of South Vietnam's fourteen million acres of dense upland forests have been sprayed at least once. Particularly in the multiply sprayed areas, ecological debilitation has been severe. . . .
>
> Of the somewhat more than one million acres of coastal mangrove forest . . . at least 25 percent and probably more has been chemically destroyed. . . .
>
> What may be less readily apparent is that [the antiplant agents] have also raised havoc with the faunal component. Wildlife cannot survive without food or shelter, both of which are largely derived, directly or indirectly, from the plant life of the area. . . .
>
> Nor have domestic animals been immune to the effects of bombing and herbicides, especially when these were used in the intentional crop destruction program, aimed at denying food to the enemy. That program was carried out largely in the highlands of South Vietnam where, I have estimated, enough food was destroyed to feed 900,000 people for a year.[17]

This report concentrates on antiplant agents which have a much greater damaging effect on the civilian population than tear gas. "Defoliation" may sound harmless, but it is severe indeed when the wide acreage is considered and when, as the United States National Academy of Science points out, some of the damage caused will take more than a century to be repaired. Also highlighted by the Academy, in its painstakingly detailed study,[18] was the even more inhumane crop destruction program—temporary fields, swiddens, customarily cultivated by the highlanders, were classed as forests and destroyed.

Chemical warfare in Indochina perhaps may not qualify as genocide, but it definitely deserves to be called ecocide. It entailed a malevolent destruction of the environment and was used in conjunction with such warfare methods as area bombing (Chapter VIII, Section 5). After all, the crops would have given food to human beings. The possibilities of quite new dimensions of effective warfare against food crops and fauna point towards a fearful new dimension of food denial warfare against some technologically less advanced country. While the massive application in Vietnam was made by a technologically superior power against poor and defenseless people, the chemical weapons might, if condoned, become the poor people's future weapons. Cheap and simple to produce as they are, they might be used even by some less developed country as anticrop weapons and lead to systematic wars of starvation against neighbors who are desperately dependent on their harvests and their grazing and hunting grounds.

The reaction against chemical warfare in Vietnam was massive. The criticism voiced by other nations in the United Nations has been mentioned (See "A Personal Note"). Members of the scientific community in the United States should be praised for vigorously expressing alarm. Some Senators and Congressmen began to raise strong cries of concern. Some of the nonmilitary personnel in Vietnam also feared that farmers and other sectors of the local population were being alienated and pacification programs undermined.

Under this manifold and growing pressure of disapproval and dismay, President Nixon ordered curtailment of the chemical warfare at the end of December 1970. The impact of the scientists' strictures is underscored by the fact that the announcement coincided with the meeting of the American Association for the Advancement of Science at which the preliminary results of its extensive field study was reported.[19] Ethics and science can make a strong team, and even more so when political leaders join in.

The final blow to chemical warfare as a United States policy was administered in connection with hearings of a Committee of the House of Representatives, May 1974, and hammered in later that year when urged by the powerful statements of Senators Fulbright, Humphrey, and Nelson, the Senate unanimously approved a resolution consenting to the ratification of the Geneva Protocol.[20]

The war in Indochina has now passed into history and that country has finally ratified the Geneva Protocol. No more admonitions may be necessary for people and nations to take a firm stand against chemical warfare. This should give encouragement to the disarmers that a turning point has been reached and that efforts can and must from now on be directed towards eliminating the very weapons whose use has lost all respect (Chapter IX, Sections 5–7).

Still, one more duty remains to be performed in the legal domain. As long as there was doubt about its rules being upheld the Geneva Protocol had to be kept intact as sacrosanct. There is still reason not to meddle with its structure nor even with its somewhat antiquated terminology, but a kind of housecleaning is in order, as a variety of reservations has been attached to it by some adherent governments. The great majority have made no reservations or qualifications. This is particularly true of many of the old nations with peaceful traditions which were early signatories and of the encouragingly great number of nations who have ratified the Protocol during the last few years, after what might be called a successful membership drive within the United Nations.

Some governments have made reservations which restrict the interpretation of the Protocol to a ban on first use only of biological and chemical means of warfare. Several important countries like Britain, France, the Soviet Union, and Israel have made reservations about retaliation being permissible, even in cases of attack against allies. The same governments often make the reservation that they need only abstain from biological and chemical warfare with other Parties to the Protocol. The United States retains the restraint of first use, thus permitting retaliation, but it has not restricted its obligation only to Parties. A checkerboard of formal obligations where anomalies and shifting interpretations abound has been created.

How could accusations be properly addressed—if unlawful use should once more be reported? I raised this question in the General Assembly:

> How are "allies" defined nowadays, so as to justify a BC attack on a country that may have a more or less clearly recognizable "ally" which misbehaves?[21]

There are many examples of complicated and rather incongruous interpretations from which to choose. For instance, Czechoslovakia reserved freedom of action should any State or its allies fail to respect the Protocol, but Poland, not having done the same, would still be kept to its non-use obligation.

The time would seem to have come when a systematic appeal should be made

> to proceed also to a pruning of some of the ungraceful encumbrances which . . . make the picture of the true applicability of this international instrument such an unclear one.
>
> Some 60 of the 90 Parties have felt that they are able to abide by the Protocol without any reservations. Why then not the remaining third?[22]

Such supplementary action is now necessary so that the Protocol will stand out clearly as being what the United Nations has affirmed it to be: international law against the use of all biological and chemical means of warfare, valid for all nations in the whole world community.

3.   The Case Against Use of Dum-Dum Bullets

Another example of widespread violation of the rules of war is the modern antipersonnel, small-caliber projectiles, often of a high-velocity type. They are especially injurious, having the same effect on the human body as dum-dum bullets. Towards the end of the nineteenth century it had become increasingly common for the armed forces of the major powers, particularly in the colonial wars, to use unevenly jacketed or soft-nosed bullets which flatten when entering the human body and thus tear up the flesh, causing large wounds. They uselessly aggravate suffering and are contrary to the law of humanity. By means of realistic portrayals of the effects of dum-dum bullets, public opinion became aroused and this type of weapon was proscribed through several of the early Laws of War (Chapter VIII, Section 1).

Nevertheless, such unnecessarily cruel weapons are still widely used. The M-16, the main rifle used by the United States Army in Indochina, now incorporated into the armories of several countries throughout the world, is not the only example. There is a host of guns of many different national origins which have the same or similar wounding effects far beyond the capabilities of the rifles that were common up to the end of World War II. There is a great measure of agreement among the experts that such new rifles, with a high velocity on impact, should be classified as being "of a grossly inhumane nature, both on account of the serious injuries they inflict on human beings and because of the great strain these injuries impose on military medical services."[23]

Recent studies attribute the especially injurious effects not only to the velocity factor but also to the caliber and shape of the bullet and include several types of projectiles of varying designs as being inhumane.[24] There appears so far to be no inhibition against ordering and deploying them in military practice, no recall of prohibitions against their use. Regarding the M-16 rifle and similar weapons, the United States might use the excuse that it did not become a Party to the Hague Convention IV:3 of 1899 which adopted their ban. But in the preparatory work the United States delegation "had pressed for the adoption of more stringent limitations: 'The use of bullets inflicting wounds of useless cruelty, such as explosive bullets, and in general all kinds of bullets which exceed the limit necessary for placing a man hors de combat should be forbidden.' "[25]

In any case, the duty to follow humanitarian law is not dependent upon verbatim formulations or signature to a specific legal instrument. These principles are accepted as customary international law, binding towards all, signers and nonsigners alike.[26]

Small-caliber projectiles have been singled out here because they fit so closely into the explicitly forbidden category of dum-dum effects, which certainly can cause unnecessary suffering. Other types of antipersonnel ordinance must be judged as indiscriminate: cluster or fragmentation warheads with multiple bomblets, flechettes, many antipersonnel land mines, delayed-action and treacherous weapons, all of which are abundantly present in the contemporary arsenals of many nations, together with incendiary weapons like napalm (Chapter VIII, Section 4).

Here is a description from a perspicacious study of the actual situation compared with international law, written by Lawrence C. Petrowski:

> A variety of weapons used in Vietnam might also be questioned as causing unnecessary pain and suffering, therefore challenging the basic humanitarian principles underlying the law of war. One such weapon is the cluster bomb unit (CBU), a metal container dropped from aircraft and opening in mid-air to release many small bombs, grenades, or other munitions over a wide area. CBU's can also carry the so-called Lazy Dog, a drum of steel pellets dropped from a plane and exploding at about 6,000 feet to spray men and equipment below

with a deadly buckshot effect. A variation on Lazy Dog includes a weapon consisting of several hundred baseball-size explosives which detonate on impact and spray hundreds of pellets in all directions. In some cases, the pellets may be coated with napalm-like material, causing them to stick to whatever they hit.

. . . concentration on the questionable humanitarian nature and arbitrary application of American and allied weapons [is not] meant to intimate that the Viet Cong and perhaps North Vietnamese have not made use of weapons equally arbitrary in their firepower and equally inhumane in the suffering they cause, despite the fact that they are often more primitive. Bamboo stakes at the bottom of a grass-covered pit, or steel spikes driven through a piece of wood and concealed point up in a rice paddy are not weapons that necessarily seek out the enemy, nor do they wound or kill with a minimum of suffering.[27]

It should be emphasized that the laws on armed conflicts do not raise the question of the legitimacy of war as such. What is here in focus is the condemnation of combat practices that strike civilians and combatants alike. As regards the legitimate aim of putting the enemy soldier hors de combat, there is a quite clear order established: if a combatant can be put out of action by taking him prisoner, he should not be injured; if he can be put out of action by disabling him, he should not be killed; if he can be put out of action by light injury, he should not be gravely injured.[28] From the military point of view the evaluation is somewhat different. Their optimum would sometimes seem to be: cripple but not kill, so that for each wounded soldier two would be needed to carry him away. Even this remains an argument for not seeking maximum injury.

Thanks to the rules of war we are on quite safe ground, without having to go through the exercise of defining what would be "necessary" suffering, if we condemn some suffering as "unnecessary." The violation of this principle is the graver when attacks are made under grossly inequitable conditions where protection for one side is minimal and medical aid nearly totally lacking.

The prosecutor's case is further strengthened when it is demonstrated clearly that modern weapons technologies by present-day military planners are aimed at *increasing* the pain effects. SIPRI has drawn the unavoidable conclusion:

In the age of "total war," *the clean-bullet concept of disablement appears to be no longer acceptable to the military* of at least some of the major powers.

Emphasis is now placed on increasing lethality and *permanent* incapacitation. This may be achieved in essentially two ways: *a large explosive-type wound* or a *burn*. It is significant that it is precisely these two means of disablement that were prohibited by the St. Petersburg Declaration.[29]

4.   The Case Against Use of Napalm

Napalm was extensively used towards the end of World War II to make incendiary weapons more effective; in so doing, the effective pain from burns caused unnecessary suffering. But incendiary weapons have been used since time immemorial. The Bible relates how Samson affixed firebrands to the tails of foxes and released them among the cornfields of the Philistines.[30] Technological developments gradually perfected the use of burning oil, incendiary powders, and sophisticated mixtures which were then weaponized in more perfected equipment as flame throwers, flame projectors, or incendiary artillery, until in World War II the airplane became the prime means for mass delivery of incendiary bombs to devastate whole cities. In this section, however, the characteristic use of incendiary weapons as antipersonnel weapons will be considered first, following in the other categories of cruel weapons, condemned by the Laws of War.

Several chemical formulas have been employed in incendiaries. White phosphorus long held the lead for causing grave damage. It is highly poisonous, and burning phosphorus cannot be extinguished by water. The burns caused have certain characteristics:

> Because the particles of white phosphorus are usually distributed by an explosive charge, these particles may penetrate deeply into the skin. Secondly, the phosphorus may continue to burn for hours, and, in some cases, days, until it is neutralized by some means. For these reasons, phosphorus burns tend to be made up of small deep lesions.
>
> Thirty years ago any toxicity of phosphorus in burns would probably not have been observed since severely burned patients usually died. Since World War II, the treatment of burns has improved considerably, with the result that the death rate in the best modern conditions has decreased. With this decline in mortality the severity of white phosphorus burns compared with wounds from other burning substances has become apparent from a number of recent studies.[31]

A new burning compound of U.S. origin, napalm (the patent was applied for on 1 November 1943), made its appearance at the end of

World War II. It was soon used in overwhelming quantities in bombing raids. Napalm proved its effectiveness first in Europe in connection
with the D-Day invasion to push back the Germans. Thereafter, it
was used in enormous quantities in the Pacific theater of war.
"United States military experts concluded that napalm bombs were
most effective against human targets and in addition had a terroriz-
ing effect."[32] There can be no doubt about the abominable effects of
weapons like napalm against human beings. A special UN report
summarizes the medical effects as follows:

> Whether mortal or not, napalm injuries . . . may be intensely painful,
> both when they occur and during some or all of the subsequent
> period.
>   Recovery from burn injuries is slow, and during most of the
> period the patient remains in great pain. Napalm and white phos-
> phorus burns are likely to leave him deeply scarred and disfigured for
> the rest of his life.[33]

The characteristic casualty effects of napalm are described first
in regard to burn wounds:

> Napalm is spread in clumps of burning jelly, which may burn for up
> to some 10–15 minutes at temperatures exceeding 800° C, depending
> on the composition . . . it has been demonstrated that the tissues
> beneath the burned area remain above the normal temperature for
> five or six minutes after the fire is quenched. This causes further
> tissue damage and local thrombosis and necrosis spreads rapidly in
> the first hours and days, the wound becoming easily infected.
>   Because of the high burning temperature and extended burning
> time of thickened gasoline fuels, burn wounds resulting from them
> are typically deep and extensive. . . . According to . . . reports . . .
> some two thirds of the victims have total areas of burn of up to 25
> percent of the body surface area and one-third have burns of more
> than 25 percent.[34]

To this primary effect can be added a whole catalogue of others:
heatstroke, pulmonary burns, carbon monoxide poisoning, oxygen
starvation, shock, physiological complications, infection. To sum
up what this means to human beings under varying social conditions:

> Exceptional medical resources are required to prevent and treat
> burn wound sepsis, resources which are unlikely to be immediately
> available in an embattled area.
>   It may be concluded that extensive tactical use of napalm in the
> Pacific theatre in World War II, in Korea, in Indochina and else-

where has resulted in a high mortality amongst the persons affected. . . .

Those who survive the initial infliction of serious burns are faced
with a great variety of potentially fatal complications over a period
of weeks or months. . . .

The majority of victims whose lives are saved are faced with
varying degrees of physical disability, characterized by ugly scars
and contractions . . . napalm burns rapidly affect the underlying
muscles, tendons, and bones which greatly complicates the surgical
problems. Reconstructive surgery to treat such conditions requires a
long series of operations over several years and is unlikely to be available to ordinary people in most societies in wartime conditions.[35]

The reaction against the use of incendiary weapons has taken
on poignancy only in very recent years, when the voices of civilians
and of lesser powers have, through amplification in the United
Nations, begun to make themselves heard above the clamor of military
considerations. Several resolutions in the General Assembly have requested action to restrain the use of incendiary weapons and studies
to support such action. At the 1968 International Conference on
Human Rights held in Teheran, the Secretary General of the
United Nations was asked to study steps to secure the better application of existing humanitarian international conventions and rules in
all armed conflicts. In October 1972, the Secretary General's report
*Napalm and Other Incendiary Weapons and All Aspects of Their
Possible Use* was published. Likewise, the International Committee
of the Red Cross devoted a chapter to Incendiary Weapons in its
report of 1973 on *Weapons that may Cause Unnecessary Suffering
or have Indiscriminate Effects,* as well as in its 1975 report, *Conference of Government Experts in the Use of Certain Conventional
Weapons.*

The UN report highlights how, during and after World War II,
an enormous increase in the production and use of more and more
sophisticated, more and more devastating, pain-producing incendiary weapons has occurred. They can be delivered by most weapon
systems: aircraft, artillery, naval ordinance, armored vehicles, and
by individual soldiers. They can be of an intensive type or a scatter
type.[36] The characteristics of the most well-known incendiary
weapons, the oil-based napalm and the pyrophoric white phosphorus
are such that they might well be dealt with in the category of mass
destruction weapons rather than conventional weapons. The most
widespread use of them is through large-scale bombing, and the major

question of their justification will be dealt with in connection with terror bombs (Chapter VIII, Section 5).

These studies have shown how prevalent such weapons are in contemporary arsenals, and the detailed descriptions of the excessive injuries which have been inflicted on multitudes of humans through their use in recent wars ring with condemnation. The very word "napalm" has become loaded with horror in the minds of people all over the world, although incendiaries containing white phosphorus are probably worse and may even act as a poison. In its home country, the United States, napalm has been at the center of a protest among young people, causing its producer, the DOW Chemical Company, to report loss of profits from the uproar.[37]

The summary conclusion from the UN report on incendiaries contains an accusation against the participation by scientists and technicians:

> The rapid increase in the military use of incendiary weapons, especially napalm, during the past thirty years is but one aspect of the more general phenomenon of the increasing mobilization of science and technology for war purposes. New weapons of increased destructiveness are emerging from the research and development programs at an increasing rate.
>
> Alongside [with this development] the long upheld principle of the immunity of the noncombatant appears to be receding from the military consciousness. . . . It is . . . essential that the principle of restraint in the conduct of military operations, and in the selection and use of weapons, be reasserted with vigour. Clear lines must be drawn between what is permissible in time of war and what is not permissible. Incendiary weapons, in particular napalm, are already the subject of widespread revulsion and anxiety, and because they are weapons of great destructive potency, they are a fitting subject for renewed efforts of this type.[38]

The issue of prohibiting incendiary weapons altogether is now under active consideration by the Diplomatic Conference on Reaffirmation and Development of International Humanitarian Law Applicable in Armed Conflicts, which is holding its so far quite promising meetings at repeated intervals in Geneva. Several expert studies have been instituted. Its decisions are not yet final and the interim report[39] is marred by the anonymous assignation of views expressed by several delegations, while some delegations hold a different view. Since the issue at that Conference is whether to prohibit such a staple commodity of most arsenals as incendiary weapons, it is understandable that some government delegations hesitate to express themselves categorically. The heart of the matter is nevertheless revealed, even if unwillingly. It is the public aversion to this inhumane way of making war:

> Another delegation . . . stated that the military in its country regarded napalm as the ideal weapon for close support, but that in view of the suffering it caused and the attitude of public opinion the military had to make a sacrifice and to forgo its use—and for that matter, the use of flame throwers.[40]

Some delegations to the Diplomatic Conference are ready to take a firmer stand. A working paper, originally submitted by the delegations of Austria, Egypt, Mexico, Norway, Sweden, Switzerland, and Yugoslavia, contains the basic proposals for the coming concluding debate on incendiaries. (See Section 7 for summary of proposals.)

> There is an important body of opinion which maintains that the military value of incendiary weapons is rather low. The effects seem to be the greatest where the use is most questionable, namely, against residential areas and against unprotected persons.[41]

Does it not follow that these weapons, regarded with special aversion, are clearly covered by existing prohibitions against weapons causing "unnecessary suffering" and have indiscriminate effects? The situation is apparently not crystal-clear. Different governments choose different interpretations as exemplified by the Italians in the Ethiopian war (Chapter VIII, Section 2). Also, the texts of the various Declarations and Conventions dating from the turn of the century do not define incendiaries comprehensively. The St. Petersburg Declaration prohibited the use of small incendiary projectiles for land warfare. A commission of lawyers, meeting in the Hague in 1923 to formulate more explicit rules for Hague Conventions, attempted to incorporate incendiary projectiles into the prohibitions. These had, during World War I, begun to be used "by or against an aircraft."[42]

Concentrated international attention began to be directed to incendiaries at the ill-fated League of Nations Disarmament Conference held in Geneva in the early thirties. The British expressed a strong view that incendiaries were already covered by established rules of international law when in 1933 they listed as, among other things being embodied in that law, "the use of all incendiary weapons."[43] Nonetheless, the Conference found it desirable to formulate explicit prohibitions against the use of incendiary weapons (in the vocabulary of the time divided into the categories of projectiles and flame-throwers). Strong opposition was voiced against "appliances such as flame-projectors designed to attack not objects but persons," on account of "the cruelty inherent in the use of these appliances, which cause suffering that cannot be regarded as necessary from a military standpoint."[44] A precise formula was submitted by the British Government in a draft convention, containing provisions concerning incendiary as well as chemical and bacteriological warfare. Despite some reservations, the draft was approved by consensus as a basis for a future convention. But, alas, it never came up for a final decision (Chapter III, Section 2). An Article 49 had been proposed to lay down the rules:

> The prohibition of the use of incendiary weapons shall apply to: (1) The use of projectiles specifically intended to cause fires . . . (2) The use of appliances designed to attack persons by fire, such as flame-projectors.[45]

Only now, several cruel wars later, in the wake of the untold sorrow of casualties caused by incendiaries in the millions, does the international community seem to be prepared to discuss the prohibition of their use (Chapter VIII, Section 7). It is now up to the disarmers to follow this up and meet the challenge of eliminating napalm and similar incendiary weapons from all arsenals.

5.   The Case Against Terror Bombing

The most massively inhumane deeds in the wars of this generation have resulted in the horrors brought on by bombing. This kind of warfare stands condemned by the 1907 Hague Conference which upheld the immunity of civilians to such attacks. Article 25 reads:

> The attack or bombardment, by whatever means, of towns, villages, dwellings, or buildings which are undefended is prohibited.

Millions of bombed victims, killed or maimed or rendered homeless, bear eloquent witness to the disdain for humanitarian rules and principles applicable in war, that began in World War I, became a systematic policy in World War II, and continued ever more recklessly in the Korean and Vietnam Wars. Undefended buildings have certainly not been spared, nor villages, or any kind of human habitat, not even hospitals.

The revolt against such outrages has been slow in coming, but now the world is beginning to look back in anger. The Swedish Prime Minister, Olof Palme, made a forthright statement on the occasion of the United States Christmas bombings of Hanoi, 1972.

> We should call things by their proper name. What is happening today in Vietnam is a form of torture. There can be no military justification for the bombing. . . .
> . . . The fact is that people are being tormented, that a nation is being tormented in order to humiliate it, to compel it into submission to force. That is why the bombing is an outrage. There have been many such outrages in modern history. They are often associated with names—Guernica, Oradour, Babi Yar, Katyn, Lidice, Sharpeville, Treblinka. Violence has triumphed. But history has condemned those who were responsible. Now there is another name to add to the list—Hanoi, Christmas 1972.[46]

The Pope denounced the United States action and the churches offered prayers for the victims of the terror bombing of residential quarters of Hanoi and other densely populated parts of North Vietnam. The raids killed and wounded thousands of innocent people, destroyed their homes, churches, pagodas, schools, hospitals. Governments all over the world gave vent to their dismay over this stepping-up of United States aggression. In Europe the smaller nations were most outspoken in their condemnation, as were Canada and many Third World countries.

Vietnam was not the beginning. Palme did not include in his litany the names of London or Dresden or Tokyo or many of the other great population centers bombed in World War II and the Korean War. Still, the historical record should be set straight. Guernica—Hitler's gift to Franco in April 1937—was the first shock of this kind to the world. In one day a whole town was destroyed by waves of foreign aircraft. Until then, the general public had hardly observed what a departure was under way from the ethical values codified by the Hague Conferences. While the law of armed conflict does not allow indiscriminate bombardment, with its implied mass murder of civilians, this new technological toy of the air evidently had provoked military temptations. The Germans began using their Zeppelin fleet: in 1916 nine Zeppelins attacked an English town—to the military benefit of killing fifty-nine people. These experiments went on during World War I, and the Germans valued their field experiments of the Spanish Civil War.[47]

Admittedly international regulations concerning air warfare are insufficiently specific—and no wonder—for flight was only in its infancy in 1907, the time of the last Hague Conference. Since air forces began to prove their worth in World War I, no efforts to outlaw any of their activities have succeeded. However, in 1923 an international commission of lawyers was formed to draft rules specifically relating to aerial warfare. Their Article 22 states:

> Air bombardment for the purpose of terrorizing the civil population, of destroying or damaging private property not of military character or of injuring noncombatants is prohibited.[48]

There was one more brave attempt to prohibit bombings. In September 1938, on the very eve of the new world war, the League of Nations without a dissenting vote adopted a British resolution against bombing of nonmilitary targets. Its first principle was forthright enough: "The intentional bombing of civilian population is illegal." Following this up, President Roosevelt on 1 September addressed a last minute appeal to all governments participating in the war, asking them to declare that under no circumstances would they submit civilian populations to air bombardment. Some official replies were positive; the British Government committed itself, the Germans just noted "the command."[49] The acts soon spoke differently.

Defiance of the strictures against bombing of civilians was there from the beginning. The Germans were to blame for air raids, during the very first days of the war in September 1939. They struck indiscriminately—not only military targets but population centers such as Warsaw. Not much later the Russians bombed hundreds of targets in Finland including the capital of Helsinki during the so-called Winter War of 1939–40. German bombings increasingly took on less of a military and more of a terroristic character: April 1940, Norwegian cities; May 1940, Rotterdam. There were no signs of any legal or moral inhibitions.

Greater caution marked the early phase of the bitter feud between Germany and Britain. At first both governments concentrated bombing raids on places were there were some military objectives, although highly inaccurate targeting resulted in indiscriminate bombing. Even in the early days of the dramatic Battle of Britain the Luftwaffe, seeking to secure control of the air space, struck first against British ships and naval installations, air bases and airplane industries, while the Royal Air Force defended the air space in the fight against invasion.

Somewhere in the ensuing exchange of aerial attacks there occured an ominous turning point. I can only call it a mutation of public morality which ever since seems to have condoned even the most wanton mass murder of civilian populations from the air. There is no doubt that the historical turning towards making terror bombing of civilians an intentional policy came in the European war of the 1940s.

What happened to sanction such bombing must be made clear. "Megamurder" is the term that has been coined by a respected former colleague of mine in disarmament negotiations, General E. L. M. Burns of Canada. He tells the story of how the strategy of terror bombing to destroy Germany came to be accepted against the opposition of many in Britain who knew about it. The public throughout was kept in the dark, made to believe that

> [the] bombing was still directed against militarily justifiable targets, such as submarine and aircraft production plants, transportation key points, and synthetic oil works.[50]

Considerable controversy has surrounded the interpretation of how the ethical mutation happened and the distribution of blame. Summarizing the data objectively reveals:

(a) that Hitler in early August 1940 launched the main offensive for his hurried plans for an invasion of Britain and also dropped some bombs on London;

(b) that Churchill on 20 August 1940 paid the never forgotten tribute to the brave defense of Britain by the RAF heroes;

(c) that five days later the RAF bombed nonmilitary, nonindustrial targets in Berlin;

(d) that the Luftwaffe in September launched the full rage of its blitz against London and Coventry.

The number of civilians killed reached the tens of thousands. According to Churchill the blitz against London, despite all its horror, in a sense saved the RAF and thus Britain—because the Germans bombed civilian targets the fighter bases and communication centers needed for continuing the war were spared.[51]

British strategic plans to exploit the weakness of German air defense and carry the air war to the enemy in huge bomb attacks on its population centers matured gradually. The strategy for the Bomber Command reached a climax with the concentration of the bomber force against the enemy's weakest points: "the morale of the civil population and the inland transportation system."[52]

The policy of area bombing was developed in increasingly close cooperation between the British and American air forces; daylight precision bombing was largely done by the USAF, night area bombing by the RAF. The new policy was sanctioned at the Casablanca Conference in January 1943:

> Your primary object will be the progressive destruction of the German military, industrial, and economic system, *and the undermining of the morale of the German people* to a point where their armed resistance is fatally weakened.[53]

The worst raids were Hamburg, 1943, and Dresden, 1945. The total number of German civilians killed by air attacks has been estimated to be above one million.[54]

The deeply disturbing story of the transformation of war into the megamurder of civilians, flagrantly countermanding the rules of war, is in many ways utterly incredible. General Burns, who has most courageously set out the story, underscores the ethical argument:

> "Undermining morale" sounds a nice, gentle, persuasive way of waging war until one realizes that it means killing civilian men, women, and children indiscriminately, destroying their dwellings and burning and suffocating them by tens of thousands.[55]

It seems not to have helped that fact-finding surveys of bombing effects have since cast grave doubts on the military benefits derived from such ghastly costs. Scientific surveys have confirmed that the mass bombing had been a strategic mistake, while precision bombing of aircraft factories and oil refineries had been effective.[56] Albert Speer, Hitler's Minister of Production, when asked after the War about the effects of bombing, concluded:

> The attacks on the synthetic oil industry would have sufficed . . . to render Germany defenseless.[57]

Even Churchill had a later twinge of conscience:

> The destruction of Dresden remains a serious query against the conduct of Allied bombing. I am of the opinion that military objectives must henceforward be more strictly studied in our own interests . . . I feel the need for more precise concentration upon military objectives, such as oil and communications behind the immediate battle-zone, rather than on mere acts of terror and wanton destruction, however impressive.[58]

If costs and results are compared terror bombing is certainly not rational. More fundamentally, it goes against international humanitarian law and is condemned by our consciences. Although the Nuremburg Principles formulated at the end of World War II included explicitly among war crimes the "wanton destruction of cities, towns, or villages or devastation not justified by military necessity," no such verdict has officially been pronounced on the exchange of massive air raids among the main combatants in World War II. They had all sinned too much to dare accuse the others. As the leading Nuremberg prosecutor explains:

> Aerial bombardment had been used so extensively and ruthlessly on the Allied as well as the Axis side that neither at Nuremburg nor Tokyo was the issue made a part of the trial.[59]

The policy of intentional bombing raids against civilian targets was pursued in the Korean and Vietnam Wars, despite the shattering experience of such a war in Europe. With each new war the illegal and unethical practices[60] have been implemented on an ever greater scale. This is true not only of the increasingly massive bombing of civilians but also of the use of ever more injurious bombs. Bomb warfare is a collective term, bombs allowing for many variations. Chemical weapons are mostly spread by zonal bombardment and so fall under a double violation, of the Geneva Protocol and of indiscriminate methods of warfare (Chapter VIII, Section 2). Many cruel antipersonnel weapons are most often delivered by air, for example, fragmentation bombs and flechettes (Chapter VIII, Section 3), as are the massively used napalm and other incendiary weapons (Chapter VIII, Section 4). (This delivery of several condemnable means of warfare by air is one reason why they should be dealt with in conjunction when new rules are codified against them.) It is rarely realized to what a large extent terror bombing has employed incendiary rather than conventional weapons. This is true of two major onslaughts at the very end of World War II. The attack on Dresden killed at least 135,000, perhaps 300,000 people.[61] The attack on Tokyo, 9–10 March 1945, was conducted entirely with incendiaries and left in its wake a greater number of dead than either of the two nuclear attacks on Hiroshima and Nagasaki five months later.

The Korean War and the Vietnam war provide horrendous examples of how the techniques of mass murder engulf the ever more helpless civilian populations. An example of such violations of the rules of war in Korea, formally committed under the auspices of the United Nations, is the area bombing of Pyongyang with incendiaries. During the Korean War the number of civilians killed grossly exceeded the number of soldiers killed (Chapter I, Section 6, b).[62]

The area bombing in Indochina was even more systematic and "successful." From 1965 to mid-1972 the United States dropped seven million tons of bombs—twice the quantity of bombs dropped by the Allies in World War II on all fronts. The final figures of casualties are not yet revealed, but we know that civilians killed and wounded are to be counted by the millions, with many more millions of refugees. How many dams, dikes, schools, hospitals, and temples have been hit has not been officially divulged. However, the question of statistics is not crucial for drawing conclusions. That war was enormously costly, with the heaviest burden falling on innocent men, women, and children.

War through bombing now encompasses a new objective— which can hardly be called an enemy: the human environment. Bombing is not only concentrated on cities and other population centers, but it wrecks terrible devastation to the countryside as well. Again, several methods are used. For deforestation and crop destruction, chemical means of warfare have been used. Other methods of area denial include scraping land and forests bare by companies of giant tractors. Bombing, however, remains the major method, creating craters beyond counting. A recent United States investigator reports that aspect:

By Pentagon admission, more than 15½ million *tons* of munitions of all kinds were expended by the United States against Indochina between 1965 and 1973. This may have been more than the total munitions previously expended by man in all of his past wars. . . .

Other calculations show it to represent an incredible 124 pounds per second for the entire eight-year period or the equivalent in explosive energy of 570 Hiroshima or Nagasaki bombs—one every six days!

Although all of Indochina was affected to some extent, South Vietnam was by far the major recipient of U.S. largesse.

No type of habitat seems to have been spared from craterization, including forests and swamps, fields and paddies. Indeed, the most important ecological aspect of the United States bombing and shelling

program in Indochina—aside from its sheer enormity—was the nature
of the most usual target. The many crater fields I encountered, particularly in South Vietnam, almost always seemed to be far from any
obvious military objective, as if the target were the land itself.[63]

But let us turn from the conclusions of scientists on the strategy
of devastation to that of a lawyer. A well-known French specialist
writes:

> This strategy of devastation cannot be justified either by military
> necessity or by arguments based on the particular character of
> guerilla warfare.[64]

The willful violation of the international humanitarian law did
not prove very profitable from a military or political point of view,
even for the mighty United States. Premonitions of this outcome,
together with moral qualms, were expressed quite early, as a memo to
Henry Kissinger in 1969 attests:

> The North Vietnamese surprised many observers, and confounded
> many predictions, by holding the North together and simultaneously
> sending ever increasing amounts of supplies and personnel into the
> South during three and one-half years of bombing (as of 1969). It is
> clear that the bombing campaign, as conducted, did not live up to
> the expectations of many of its proponents. With this experience in
> mind, there is little reason to believe that new bombing will accom-
> plish what previous bombings failed to do, unless it is conducted with
> much greater intensity and readiness to defy criticism and risk of
> escalation.[65]

To the lessons of World War II about the questionable military
value of submitting civilian populations to terror bombing can now
be added another about the probable nonprofitability of using these
methods even in circumstances of war against underdeveloped
countries. A study—prepared for the Senate Committee of Foreign
Relations in 1972:

> calls into serious question the efficacy of strategic and interdiction
> bombing against a highly motivated guerilla enemy in an underde-
> veloped country.[66]

And my colleague, Hans Blix, who has made a thoroughgoing
legal analysis of bombing policies, draws a conclusion with a strong
tenor of common sense:

> There are, moreover, serious doubts as to whether morale and
> allegiance can be pulverized by bombs.[67]

This conclusion as to the militarily nondecisive, or outright unsatisfactory, effect of area bombing has been generally drawn for the whole of Indochina. The war in Indochina should teach us all the great historical lessons which we didn't take to heart after the gruesomeness of World War II:

> Somehow we failed ourselves to learn the lessons we undertook to teach at Nuremburg and that failure is today's American tragedy.[68]

It should be the last great lesson needed in order to get new laws to express a new ethic for air warfare.

6. *The Inegalitarian Character of Unethical Warfare*

Prohibitions against the use of certain cruel weapons and methods of warfare, in addition to the goal of reducing armaments generally, are designed to limit the options for military actions and the devastation and the torments of eventual wars.

Before analyzing what is being done to moderate man's inhumanity to man, added emphasis must be given to the deep problem of the unequal status of parties to actual or potential military conflicts. To try to resuscitate any notion of parity in weapons, as was once instituted in the chivalric rules of duels, would be romanticism. Nevertheless, one aim of all agreements on disarmament or arms limitation should be to reduce the gaps in military strength, in technological sophistication of arms, and in protective devices and services.

The discriminatory aspect of a lack of protective equipment has been exemplified repeatedly in regard to chemical weapons, incendiary weapons, terror bombing. The UN report on napalm demonstrates how modern warfare has a typical downhill effect: an increasingly inegalitarian character for people who are poor and technologically less developed:

> Burn injuries differ from the wounds commonly caused by conventional weapons in the exceptional difficulty of their *medical treatment*. In conflict areas where medical resources are modest, casualties from incendiaries such as napalm have little chance of receiving effective medical aid.[69]

The report gives an example of the costs in terms of medical services and supplies needed for treatment of wounded:

It may be estimated that the requirements for treating a thousand wartime casualties having 30 percent burns would include 8,000 litres of plasma, 6,000 litres of blood, 16,000 litres of Ringer's lactate solution (a balanced salt solution), 250 trained surgeons and physicians, and around 1,500 skilled attendants. Each patient would require a hospital bed for anything up to four or five months. The degree to which the area in which the casualties occur, or to which they might be transported, can fulfill these requirements determines the proportion of the casualties that could be expected to survive. Success would be proportional to the facilities and supplies available. Even in the developed countries, the requirements would be difficult to mobilize on any scale; in the developing countries they might be far beyond available resources.[70]

Such vast outlays necessary for the treatment of the wounded bring to mind the call for greater compassion for them made by Henri Dunant, Swiss founder of the Red Cross and a major instigator of the 1864 Geneva Convention. Though his efforts were inspired by the sight of wounded in the slaughter of Solferino, the mercy of his vision should now be directed towards the plight of the people in poor countries suffering under wartime conditions.

All technological innovations work to the disadvantage of the poorer, less developed countries. In Indochina and in the Middle East one or both of the superpowers have taken the opportunity to test out some new weapons systems demonstrating that technological developments favor the militarily all-too-mighty powers. Still newer weapons are in the offing. In the attempt to modernize international humanitarian law, care must be taken to have new weapons included (Chapter VIII, Section 7).

The discriminatory effects of war need not depend on a considerable superiority in means of warfare. Even when the technological gap is not so wide, as between two more or less poor countries, war between them still tends to become marked by increasingly unfair competition and take on the character of "downhill" war.

These tendencies to increased discrimination, accompanied by increased cruelty, take on a serious importance in civil wars or revolts for independence. For the first time these are being scrutinized at the Diplomatic Conference in Geneva (Chapter VIII, Section 7). Guerilla warfare, predominantly a poor people's way of waging war or staging revolts, has called forth advanced counterguerilla warfare techniques on the part of several nations. Some of these are comparatively advanced militarily and possess technological superiority, sometimes provided as part of military aid from richer nations (Chapter V, Section 2). Counterguerilla or counter-insurgency warfare has proven to be particularly inhumane in its treatment of civilian populations. It is one more example of the discriminatory character of war between unequals.

Are wars between equals to be avoided in the future, leaving the discriminatory type prevalent? A French specialist, General André Beaufre, says yes, spelling it out against the background of downhill fighting:

> Counterguerilla warfare is unhappily very familiar, as the frequent accompaniment of the process of decolonization . . . an overwhelming material superiority of modern military forces over the guerillas tends to foster policy based on purely military decisions . . . the use of all these increasingly powerful modern weapons can mean subjecting the general population to almost inhuman stresses. With these massive and often blind techniques, counterguerilla warfare comes to look more and more like a war against the population, the opposite of its declared objective.
>
> Personally, I believe that more subtle methods—and more political ones, as I have mentioned—are the only ones which will achieve re-sults. Failing that, counterguerilla warfare is simply an extremely costly means of postponing political solutions which will impose themselves sooner or later.

His main prophecy stands out, somber and cynical:

> The idea of conventional war between adversaries of technically com-parable strength is luckily not very realistic.[71]

7. Updating the Humanitarian Laws

Opposition to the modern forms of unethical warfare has been slow in evolving. Now, at last, a resistance movement seems to be under way. A few years ago several nongovernmental organizations, bodies of scientists, and the governments of some nonaligned nations got the General Assembly to start moving towards effectively outlaw-ing inhumane and indiscriminate weapons. An International Confer-ence of Human Rights, convened by international but nongovernmen-tal organizations in Teheran in April–May 1968, called upon the Secretary General of the UN and the International Committee of the Red Cross (ICRC) to study "steps which could be taken to secure better application of existing humanitarian conventions and rules in all armed conflicts," as well as the need for additional rules. Both the United Nations and the ICRC quickly took various steps in the desired direction.[72] From the outset the endeavor was to encompass in this new codification all the various forms of cruel weapons and indiscriminate warfare methods, except for chemical and biological weapons, which have been dealt with in the traditional setting of the Geneva Protocol (Chapter VIII, Section 2). To this there has been added the category of new weapons, the as yet undeveloped generations endangering the future.

Initially, the steps taken met with considerable opposition. The United States, then in the midst of the Vietnam War, used great skill and energy to avoid having the issue raised. The Swedish delegation, among others, tried to exert as much pressure as a non-aligned but technologically advanced nation can, at the Teheran, the United Nations, and the Red Cross meetings. Sometimes there was even resistance against studies being undertaken. Or, when studies nevertheless were decided upon by the majority, some nations were not prepared to have their experts participate. When the Secretary General effectuated the requested study on napalm, I noted:

> It appears that despite the wide support given to the proposal for the study it did not prove possible for the Secretary General to secure assistance from governments on a broad basis, as it would have been desirable to have had participants also from the technologically advanced states in Western Europe and North America. This did not prove possible. The Swedish Government did what it could to assist the Secretary General by sending an expert.[73]

To provide ammunition for a continuation of this humanitarian fight, an interdepartmental committee was appointed by the Swedish Government (Chapter VIII, Section 1), of which I became the chairman. Our pressure continued in the national forums for a diplomatic conference. I testified in the United Nations:

> Our memories are now painfully clear of the immense suffering brought by modern methods of war and modern weapons. This awareness should help, indeed make it mandatory, for governments to go to the conference with humanitarian ambitions that also match their own long term interests. Given such a determination the conference could result in rules which would significantly alleviate the sufferings in the all too numerous armed conflicts which our world community and world organization fail to prevent. . . .

It is, of course, the use in recent conflicts of particularly cruel or indiscriminate weapons, like napalm and other incendiary weapons, pellet bombs, high velocity small arms, delayed action weapons, and so on, which has aroused the world's conscience to the need for reversal of a development toward more and more inhumane warfare methods affecting both soldiers and civilians. This development of weapons, which are actually being *used,* has too long lacked our attention, while we have mainly—but vainly—devoted it to the nuclear weapons, which have not been used.[74]

Gradually the opposition has mellowed and a considerable spirit of cooperation has evolved. The stage is now set for a thorough-going reconsideration of humanitarian rules for warfare. The positive attitudes of the majority prevail. The negative attitudes manifested by the United States and some of its allies are no longer politically one-sided, as the Soviet Union is becoming more and more recalcitrant the closer the discussion comes to proposals of material content. The decision-making body is the Diplomatic Conference on the Reaffirmation and Development of International Humanitarian Law Applicable in Armed Conflicts, convoked by the Swiss Government (Chapter VIII, Section 1). Its work is being supported by expert meetings called by the International Committee of the Red Cross, especially by the Conferences of Government Experts on Arms, Lucerne, June 1974, and Lugano in the spring of 1976.[75]

The draft protocols as prepared by the International Committee of the Red Cross are a highly ambitious attempt to make humanitarian considerations prevail. The rules proposed are radical, particularly the demand that the civilian population be protected not only against cruel weapons (as are soldiers) but against air bombardment.[76]

There has been one important omission: neither the draft rules nor the discussions at the Diplomatic Conference address themselves to nuclear weapons. Those weapons, being the cruelest megamurder arms of all, should naturally fall under a general prohibition of area bombardment or attacks against civilians or indiscriminate methods of warfare, however the phenomenon is to be described. But at earlier Red Cross Conferences a specific ban against any use of them had been discussed in vain. It may seem illogical, but neither reason nor the political will of the majority of nations is enough to wrest these most powerful weapons from the minority of most powerful nations.

The Diplomatic Conference has been working with four main

committees, each one comprising representatives of all participating States. Of these, Committee III, dealing with Civilian Population, Methods, and Means of Combat, and the Ad Hoc Committee on Conventional Weapons are of especial concern to this treatise.[77] Decisions taken by one of the Committees amount to what is known as acceptance in a first reading.

It is still too early to predict what the total and final outcome will be in regard to detailed and specific prohibitions. The basic rules agreed to by consensus are nevertheless a triumph worthy of much more public attention than has hitherto been bestowed upon them. What remains to be accomplished depends on vigilant attention by all those who genuinely care about disarming the reign of violence.

Article 33, adopted by consensus, sets out the Basic Rules:

> In any armed conflict, the right of Parties to the conflict to choose methods or means of warfare is not unlimited.
>
> It is forbidden to employ weapons, projectiles, and material and methods of warfare of a nature to cause superfluous injury or unnecessary suffering.

This is something that all conscientious citizens ought to learn by heart! The wordings have been the subject of a careful study of definitions. The term "methods or means of warfare" was preferred to the term "methods or means of combat" to meet the possibility that "combat" might be narrowly interpreted. Also the phrase "superfluous injury or unnecessary suffering" was chosen to substitute for various terms used in previous Declarations and Conventions, including the normative French term, *maux superflus*.[78]

Article 34, likewise approved with consensus in a first reading, lays a new obligation on governments:

> In the study, development, acquisition, or adoption of a new weapon, means, or methods of warfare a High Contracting Party is under an obligation to determine whether its employment would, under some or all circumstances, be prohibited by this Protocol or by any other rule of international law applicable to the High Contracting Party.

This virtual embargo on harmful new weapons is more welcome than the attempt by the Soviet Union to launch a separate international treaty against as yet unknown and unspecifiable weapons of mass destruction. Most of the nations capable of producing new weapons of mass destruction abstained on a recent vote regarding the Russian proposal in the General Assembly, notably the United States, Israel, and some NATO countries.[79]

Prescriptions dealing with safeguarding the interests of the civilian population and its protection from indiscriminate bombardment are elaborated in Articles 43 to 47 and have already been adopted in a first reading. The main rule is spelled out in Article 43:

> In order to ensure respect and protection for the civilian population and civilian objects, the Parties to the conflict shall at all times distinguish between the civilian objects and military objectives and accordingly shall direct their operations only against military objectives.

Definitions as to who is a civilian and what is to be understood by the civilian population are amplified in Article 45 and by a cover-all rule in Article 46:

> The civilian population and individual civilians shall enjoy general protection against dangers arising from military operations. To give effect to this protection, the following rules, in addition to other applicable rules of international law, shall be observed in all circumstances.

The cardinal issue then became area bombardment, the object of several specific rules. Article 46, 1. and 3., indirectly condemn warfare practices from Guernica to Vietnam:

> The civilian population as such, as well as individual civilians, shall not be made the object of attack. Acts or threats of violence which have the primary object of spreading terror among the civilian population are prohibited.
> . . . Indiscriminate attacks are prohibited. Indiscriminate attacks are those which are not directed at a specific military objective; or those which employ a method or means of combat which cannot be directed at a specific military objective, or the effects of which cannot be limited as required by this Protocol, and consequently are of a nature to strike military objectives and civilians or civilian objects without distinction. Among others, the following types of attacks are to be considered as indiscriminate.

3 (a) makes the prohibition explicit:

> An attack by bombardment by any methods or means which treats as a single military objective a number of clearly separated and distinct military objectives located in a city, town, village, or other area containing a concentration of civilian objects.

This is underlined as a moral imperative what has been said repeatedly in this book and in current political debate about condemning mass bombardment. In addition, Article 48, also adopted by consensus, spells out a stark general rule against attempts at war by starvation, followed by a detailed command:

1. Starvation of civilians as a method of warfare is prohibited.

2. It is forbidden to attack, destroy, remove, or render useless objects indispensable to the survival of the civilian population, such as foodstuffs and food producing areas, crops, livestock, drinking water installations and supplies, and irrigation works, for the purpose of denying them as such to the civilian population or to the adverse party, whatever the motive that produced that purpose, whether to starve out civilians, to cause them to move away, or any other motive.

An awareness of a new kind of public morality is evident in the prohibitions against environmental warfare, highlighted in Article 33:

3. It is forbidden to employ methods or means of warfare which are intended or may be expected to cause widespread, long-term, and severe damage to the natural environment.

It is stressed even more by Article 48 (b) that:

Care shall be taken in warfare to protect the natural environment against widespread, long-term and severe damage. Such care includes a prohibition of the use of methods or means of warfare which are intended or may be expected to cause such damage to the natural environment and thereby to prejudice the health or survival of the population.

However, the interpretation of what constitutes "widespread, long-term and severe damage" is still the subject of some dispute. This is partly because there is a "panoply of bodies concerned with one or another aspect of environment and war."[80]

An initiative was taken in the General Assembly in 1974 by the Soviet Union for a Convention to prohibit environmental and climatic modification "for military and other purposes incompatible with the maintenance of international security, human well-being and health." This line was followed in the negotiations at the United Nations, in the Geneva Disarmament Committee, and at a meeting of experts in Geneva, August 1975. The scope of the convention was delimited to deal only with actions with hostile aims. Peaceful actions having side effects on the environment are the domain of the UN Environmental Program. Some confusion was created at the end of August 1975 by the United States and the Soviet Union presenting a joint formal proposal to the United Nations without regard to the handling of the same matter in the Diplomatic Conference. The two texts are now at variance on a point which may seem small but could well be important: the substitution of *or* for *and* in the central phrase about the damage from which the environment should be protected. The United States-Soviet text, without the implications of the change having been explained, reads:

> Not to engage in military or any other hostile use of environmental modification techniques having widespread, long-lasting *or* severe effects as the means of destruction, damage, or injury to another State Party.[81]

Banning the use of specific categories of conventional anti-personnel weapons has not yet been achieved. This subject had not been submitted to scrutiny since the last Hague Conference of 1907. A basic document for the coming meetings is a working paper of 7 February 1975 which was submitted originally by some non-aligned and later subscribed to by a large number of delegations. It set out definite proposals in regard to all the categories which the Diplomatic Conference's Ad Hoc Committee had already dealt with in the form of an exchange of views. The texts proposed refer to:

I. INCENDIARY WEAPONS

Incendiary weapons shall be prohibited for use. This prohibition shall apply to:

> the use of any munition which is primarily designed to set fire to objects or to cause burn injury to persons through the action of flame and/or heat produced by a chemical reaction of a substance delivered on the target. Such munitions include flame-throwers, incendiary shells, rockets, grenades, mines, and bombs.

II. ANTIPERSONNEL FRAGMENTATION WEAPONS

> Antipersonnel cluster warheads or other devices with many bomblets which act through the ejection of a great number of small calibre fragments or pellets are prohibited for use.

III. FLECHETTES

> Munitions which act through the release of a number of projectiles in the form of flechettes, needles, and similar are prohibited for use.

IV. ESPECIALLY INJURIOUS SMALL CALIBRE PROJECTILES

It is prohibited to use small calibre projectiles which are so designed or have such velocity that they:

a) break or deform on or following entry into a human body, or

b) tumble significantly within the human body, or

c) create shock waves which cause extensive tissue damage outside the trajectory, or

d) produce secondary projectiles within a human body.

V. ANTIPERSONNEL LAND-MINES

Antipersonnel land-mines must not be laid by aircraft.[82]

Agreement on these subjects is without doubt more difficult to wring from those governments who are mindful of what their arsenals contain and what their military authorities demand. Some progress is nevertheless to be expected, as the majority in the United Nations is now supporting demands for steps forward. Recommendations in the General Assembly have come to center on napalm and other incendiary weapons, a real campaign stretching over several years by several delegations, mostly from the nonaligned nations. In 1975, for the first time, a resolution carried by consensus in the General Assembly.[83] It noted with satisfaction the work of the Diplomatic Conference on napalm and on weapons which generally might be deemed to be excessively injurious or have indiscriminate effects. More than symbolic importance should be attached to the change in the agenda item for the General Assembly deliberations in coming years, from the narrower one of napalm to the broader one of "Incendiary and other specific conventional weapons which may be the subject of prohibitions or restrictions of use for humanitarian reasons."

The work can, and must, go on. As soon as the *use* of certain weapons has been made the subject of agreed restrictions, the attention of disarmers should be called to the possibility of agreeing on their *elimination*. This new leaf on the disarmament agenda has already been turned in regard to chemical and biological weapons (Chapter IX). There is every reason first to extend the consideration of elimination to incendiary weapons, closely related as they are to chemical ones, and then to other excessively injurious weapons. The restriction of trade in and production of such weapons also belongs on an urgent disarmament agenda for conventional weapons (Chapter V, Section 3).

The prize is high, for disarmers to win and for weaponeers to lose. Military arsenals, procurement plans, and development programs would have to undergo considerable changes if the options to use high-velocity, small-caliber weapons, some types of fragmentation bombs, napalm, etc. are to be denied the military. If we succeed in restoring the ethical principles of not bombing civilian populations or their means of livelihood, it would amount to a whole new dimension in the art of air warfare—a tremendous retraction of military free choice. We should bear in mind that military and political leaders only a hundred years ago had agreed that "the rules of war do not allow to belligerents an unlimited power as to the choice of means of injuring an enemy." It is just such unlimited power that the military of our time in so many countries has come to usurp. The world must now turn back to that earlier principle. Admittedly, it is a long and arduous task, but there is no other way.

Peoples everywhere are beginning to revolt. They would revolt even more if they were not mislead by their governments. Much publicity is given to military needs, often under the emotionally laden guise of national security and the threat to survival, and much less to civilian needs and the rights of people. Popular concern must start to function at all levels. If the international councils are not immediately sensitive to public pressure, it must be because not enough pressure is built up at the national levels. Where are the churches? Where are the teachers and the scientists? Where are the workers' organizations? These groups can, when they do speak up, have great effect.

8. *An Agenda for Each Nation*

International negotiations cannot per se mend the ways of national governments. Or, to turn the burden of responsibility around, national governments can change their rules and purge their arsenals without waiting for international agreements.

Agreements of a global character are valuable in so far as they encompass both technologically advanced and less advanced nations, limiting the discrimination of downhill war. Agreements of a regional character would be especially valuable as they could establish a kind of equality between neighbors, guaranteeing fair practices even if conflict breaks out.

Reforms at the national level are in order for three different fields of operation. The most important is, which weapons to produce or procure. As the military planners have not proven to be the best guardians of humanitarian principles, they should be supervised by a group of civilians in as many countries as possible. National committees should screen military plans from the point of view of the rules of war.[84] Even if not established within an official framework, citizens' groups should create themselves. This would create an active, effective pressure.

Such a task is consonant with the obligation now laid on governments by Article 34 in the new draft laws on International Armed Conflicts (Chapter VIII, Section 7). The first duty of such committees would be to scrutinize existing weapons in the nation's armed forces to decide from the humanitarian point of view which should be weeded out, withdrawn immediately, or at least not replaced. Next, the consent of citizens should be solicited before any production of new weapons is permitted to start. Special attention should be given to alternative weapons systems or weapons construction with the same or only slightly reduced military value. In accordance with the principles set forth in this book, this screening should be made public, any differences to be settled after public debate.

A second level of activities, also open to public scrutiny, would be concerned with field manuals and military textbooks. The Secretary General of the United Nations, in an early report on the subject, "Respect for Human Rights in Armed Conflict,"[85] stressed the importance of compiling and circulating field manuals from Member States. Existing manuals present striking divergencies in the attention they give to the rules of war and in the insistence on compliance with international rules of conduct. It is encouraging to learn that the military manual of one big European country, the Federal Republic of Germany, already contains a ban upon area bombardment.[86]

Manuals, however, present only that picture which is considered suitable for external observation. The real test of use must be made on a third level, that of the actual instruction in the use of weapons, on the obligatory restraints regarding methods of warfare.[87] What are individual soldiers taught about the rules and principles of humanitarian consideration? How are the officers indoctrinated? How many hours are devoted at each level of training to the international rules of war? What textbooks on that subject are available? What do even field commanders really know about the Laws of War?

An international digest and survey would be highly desirable, not to shame those who disregard the ethics of military pursuits but to raise standards by the process of emulation. That process might be greatly stimulated if the General Assembly would pass a resolution calling for periodic reports on improvements of military ethics to be submitted by individual governments. A progressive white list—not a black list.

CHAPTER IX

Eliminating Biological and Chemical Means of Warfare

1. No Possession of Weapons When Use Is Outlawed

The term "mass destruction weapons" denotes those whose use has mass effect. They are understandably regarded as especially barbarous. Their use cannot be limited to single targets. They spread death, destruction, and devastation to wide areas, hitting civilian as well as military targets. Often their effect lasts for prolonged periods of time. It has become customary to group together weapons under the acronym A, B, C—atomic, biological, chemical, for they constitute the top echelon of terror arms.[1]

Chemical and biological means of warfare have a special claim on the attention of disarmers. Their use is already prohibited by international law; their elimination must now be ordered by arms limitation agreements. To possess, produce, test, and stockpile weapons which are in principle never to be used is an exercise in redundancy.

The prohibition against chemical and biological weapons has age-old antecedents anchored in the laws of war, later modernized by the Geneva Protocol and affirmed by the United Nations to be international law (Chapter VIII, Section 2). Efforts to follow through with prohibitions against the possession and production of such weapons were initiated in the 1960s by groups of scientists and citizens, by governments in the General Assembly, and by the

Geneva Disarmament Committee. This has led to the publication of a very lage number of studies—especially numerous in United States scientific publications—to official reports by the United Nations and the World Health Organization, and to a thoroughgoing analysis and extensive bibliography in a six-volume publication by SIPRI.[2]

Consistency requires that disarmament negotiations continue the process of outlawing CB-weapons from the point to where the Geneva Protocol and its ratifications have brought the international community. There are also some special reasons, perhaps somewhat cynical, to hope for progress in this field. Experience has taught us that governments are more prone to renounce weapons when they are understood to be of questionable military value, either because they are becoming obsolescent or because they are dangerous in handling or have a boomerang effect. These characteristics certainly apply to CB-weapons. Their production and storage may even invite theft by terrorists.

If the next-to-no value of CB-weapons is now recognized by governments, why have they not voluntarily eliminated them? This has happened in some cases (Chapter IX, Section 4), but the military authorities in some countries, usually the strong ones, have been reluctant to renounce CBW capabilities, maintaining that such arms may be needed for retaliation. This argument, however, is seriously flawed. Even if there remains a risk of CB warfare by some belligerent power, despite the existence of the general prohibition, a retaliation need not be rendered in kind. Any attacks would probably be on a battlefield where other weapons are available. Those nations in possession of nuclear weapons obviously have a superior capacity to retaliate, but their main strength lies in their general capacity to deter any rash actions. They would not realistically need CB-weapons as a middle rung on the escalation ladder. All nations, not least the lesser powers, must fear that the very possession of a CBW capacity may draw the threat of such warfare upon them.

True security from CB-weapons can only rest on building up *protection* against possible attacks by such weapons. For that kind of defense-readiness considerable research and technical knowledge about the effects of CB-weapons is indispensable, as well as is a massive deployment of protective devices—early warning systems to detect attacks, techniques for decontamination, medical services equipped to administer countermeasures, physical equipment (gas masks, shelters, protective clothing). Such a high level of preparedness is hardly attainable for other than the technologically and economically advanced countries, but one conclusion is obvious: this kind of preparedness for defense is not threatening to anybody.

Protection against CB attacks may even act as a deterrent if it makes an offensive prohibitively costly. SIPRI uses as an illustrative example the situation in Sweden, where the issuing of CB protective equipment to the armed forces and to the civil defense branch of the total defense effort is particularly extensive:

> A concept that underlies the Swedish approach to CB defense is the view that an enemy can be deterred from initiating CBW by the excessive costs of overwhelming a well-developed protective array. Thus sufficient antichemical protection is given to Swedish combat troops, as well as to the civilian population, to make it probable that the weight of the CW attack which an enemy would have to mount in order to achieve worthwhile results would be uneconomical in terms of manpower and material.[3]

2. The Meandering Course of Negotiations

Negotiations for elimination of chemical and biological means of warfare were so late in coming in a purposeful and sustained way because such chemical weapons as herbicides and tear gas were being used in ample quantities in Vietnam (Chapter VIII, Section 2). When moves were made towards the end of the 1960s to start more active negotiations on CB arms-limitation agreements,[4] the Western side tried to veer them only to consideration of the B-weapons. There the countenance of guilelessness could be upheld.

In one way it was a step forward when in 1968 the British delegation at the Geneva Disarmament Committee submitted a working paper proposing the "early conclusion of a new Convention for the Prohibition of Microbiological Methods of Warfare" and "calling for a ban on the production of microbiological agents on a scale which has no independent peaceful justification."[5] In another way, however, it was a step backward for it built a barrier against a more comprehensive prohibition to encompass both B- and C-weapons. Everybody knows, and should admit, that chemical weapons are the more important to be banished as they have been repeatedly used on a grand scale and are stocked in giant arsenals.

Here began another act of the gaming maneuvers characteristic of disarmament negotiations, which followed a familiar course.[6] The nonaligned countries stood against a limitation of only B-weapons which would set back the clock; B- and C-weapons belonged together as the Geneva Protocol had grouped them. This nonaligned position about the inseparability of B- and C-weapons prohibitions received strong support through the expert report produced in 1969 after a request from the General Assembly the previous year.[7]

The British persisted, however, in their one-sided approach. On 10 July 1969, they submitted a draft convention according to their earlier outline. When the matter was brought up in the UN General Assembly, the United States and some of its military allies (Canada, France, and Japan being exceptions) were shown to be ready to make concessions only on B-weapons. The majority position to outlaw the production and possession of both B- and C-weapons got a strong push forward when the Soviet Union, as so often, grasped that the majority attitude was a popular one in world public opinion. Together with eight other socialist countries it submitted a draft convention, comprehensive in scope but vague in tone. This proposal of 19 September 1969 envisaged a "convention on the prohibition of the development, production, and stockpiling of chemical and bacteriological (biological) weapons and on the destruction of such weapons."[8]

The negotiations in the Geneva Committee were, however, drawn out over several years. The main bone of contention, joint versus separate treatment of B- and C-weapons, called for considerable detailed argument and technical documentation by the nonaligned members.[9] It may look like an academic dispute carried on with excessive stubbornness, but its underlying motivation was the premonition, based on such bitter experiences as the Partial Test-Ban Treaty of 1963, that a half-measure, once accepted, would never be completed (Chapter III, Sections 5 and 6).

That was exactly what happened. Drama was as usual provided by the duel of the superpowers. The game they played followed a familiar scenario, designed to reduce the comprehensive scheme for CB disarmament to rather innocuous rules. The United States refused to include the C-weapons and mobilized much technical expertise and diplomatic skill to demonstrate the impossibility of prohibiting them; while at the same time it upheld the fiction that an agreement confined only to B-weapons was of an "intermediate" character. The Soviet Union on 30 March 1971 in a kind of graceful concession to the impatience of public opinion suddenly abandoned its own, and the majority's, approach in favor of the United States minimal solution.

Such complicity served to secure the acceptance of one more

treaty hailed as a sign that the disarmament negotiations were producing results. Disappointment and frustration were strong on the parts of those delegations, mainly from nonaligned nations, who had worked indefatigably to achieve something more important. The Russian move came just two weeks after the Swedish delegation had tabled a proposal for a comprehensive convention on prohibiting production and storing of both B- and C-weapons, with a built-in time sequence.[10]

The main motivation for our tenacious attempts to get chemical weapons eliminated was, of course, the risk of legitimizing chemical warfare by forbidding only the production of biological means. That was a real risk, at the time of the Vietnam War. We worried, as I stated at the Geneva Disarmament Committee:

> Last year we agreed to a partial Sea-Bed Treaty (General Assembly Resolution 2660 (XXV), annex; CCD/318) limiting the prohibition to denuclearization. It may be early to show impatience there but, again, the information about plans for extended military uses of the sea and the sea-bed is ominous indeed. So here I ask, what would be the effective result in regard to chemical armaments should they be excluded from a new partial treaty? . . . Here an unavoidable question of truth and conscience arises and I must put this question directly to the two superpowers. If they now agree not to enter upon a ban on chemical weapons, while I believe that all the rest of the world is ready for the complete elimination of all chemical and biological weapons, what kind of future is then opened up? Will the result not be to legitimate proliferation in regard to chemical weapons, from nerve gases to kill people to defoliants to kill their food crops?[11]

A frank answer was never given. The United States for a long time asserted that the means of chemical warfare, which they so lavishly used in Indochina (harassing gases and herbicides), were not weapons. The Soviet Union preferred to keep silent.

3. The Inglorious Fate of the B-Weapons Convention

After some more contortions, a narrow Treaty was agreed upon at the 1971 General Assembly, the Convention on the Prohibition of the Development, Production, and Stockpiling of Bacteriological (Biological) and Toxin Weapons and on their Destruction.[12] Requirements for verification and control had been abandoned.* The Convention was opened for signature in April 1972, but considerable difficulties came in the way of its entering speedily into force. This occurred only on 26 March 1975. The main reason for the delay was that the major Parties, the Depositary Powers, withheld their own ratifications for nearly three years while waiting for the United States to ratify the Geneva Protocol. Other signatures and ratifications were also comparatively slow in coming in.

Some aspects of this B-Weapons Convention indicate danger signals for the future, indicating pitfalls to be avoided in international treaty-making. The main shortcomings, due to political pressures and compromise deals, are the selection of Depositary Powers, the nonverifiability of implementing Treaty obligations, and, finally, the role given to the veto powers in the Security Council.

The designation of three nuclear-weapons powers, the United States, the Soviet Union, and Britain, as Depositary Powers is in itself remarkable. It is part of the superpowers' pattern for overlordship. There is no tenable, logical, or material reason for this designation. The BW Convention does not deal with nuclear weapons; all countries in the world are potentially capable of procuring B-weapons. France is the Depositary Power for the Geneva Protocol, which, as it prohibits their use, constitutes the basis for any following legislation for elimination of CB-weapons. Even if France were not available this time (Chapter IX, Section 4) there could have been a new path made by recommending the United Nations or its Secretary General as the most universally suitable Depositary Power. It would have been a novel departure in the disarmament field, though this approach is used, for example, in the 1971 Convention on Psychotropic Substances.

Of greater importance is the unsatisfactory treatment of the verification problem in the present BW Convention. As no control measures were prescribed, there is in essence no assurance that it will be implemented. There might at least have been a requirement to report measures taken to comply with the Treaty, for example, diverting production facilities to peaceful purposes. For the sake of promoting openness, it might also have been desirable to have

---

* Toxins had been included in the later stage of the negotiations by the demand of Sweden (CCD, 20 July 1971). This is a valuable addition, not least because toxins form a link with chemical weapons; it now became explicitly stated that they are included under the prohibition if they are synthetically developed, the text referring to "toxins whatever their origin or method of production."

had an accounting of the types and quantities of agents and equipment available for research for protective and prophylactic purposes.

The absence of any measures or machinery for verification in the BW Convention, strikingly different from the case of NPT (Chapter VI, Section 8), makes the handling of complaints about breaches of Treaty obligations to the Security Council most inadequate. There is no intermediate ground for preliminary work, no assembling of data that might help to allay or confirm suspicions. There is not even a recommendation that national means of control be used (Chapter IX, Section 5).

This Convention has unfortunately opened a door to discriminatory treatment of its adherents. The Treaty has become enclosed within political shackles because of stipulations in Article VI that complaints, raised about breach of obligations, must be lodged with the Security Council (Chapter III, Section 2). Even the decisions to initiate an investigation on the basis of a complaint is made dependent on unanimity by the permanent Members of the Security Council.

Of course, had the permanent Members of the Security Council been willing to give up the veto regarding decisions which refer only to the initiation of investigations and to let such questions be treated as procedural, the menace of discrimination could have been avoided.[13] A better course would have been what the nonaligned disarmament delegations have been fighting for so valiantly: to follow a verification procedure of gradually increasing strictures, to begin with requests for information, and to continue, if need be, with preliminary inquiries by an objective body prior to lodging an accusation with the UN body which has the right to take punitive action (Chapter III, Section 2, and Chapter VII, Section 5).

The two superpowers, especially the Soviet Union, wanted to tie up the BW convention with the Security Council. As a result, a resolution for the Security Council's formal acceptance of its control duties was drafted. This was worse than a blunder. The resolution itself became a victim of procedural snag. A draft Security Council resolution was submitted on 25 April 1972, but it has had to be shelved, since China made clear it would veto this authorization decision. One is reminded of the old saying about somebody tumbling into a grave he has himself dug. This nonacceptance by the Security Council was one of the reasons for the delay in the Convention's entering into force. It heightens the doubts about its value.

When raising the query about the discriminatory implications of the Security Council taking responsibility for investigations of verification and control, I had intimated what has since proved to be a fact. Some countries might not be willing to adhere to the convention because the veto powers and their allies and friends might be able to go scot-free while other countries might have to answer any inquisitive query as to their development and possession of B-weapons.[14] The overriding concern is, however, not one of national pride, and still less one of wanting to preserve clandestine BW capabilities. But the warning signal must be taken to heart so that similar failings should not be allowed to mark a CW convention, if it ever comes to be.

Luckily an opportunity exists to remedy the situation. The three Depositary Powers have not, as in the NPT, monopolized the right to approve amendments. These can be accepted by a majority. If a majority wants to exercise this power, it should move to obtain the result that was lost in the negotiations—the institution of a verification procedure including preliminary inquiries and objective fact-finding investigations which would serve to clarify doubts and suspicions prior to a formal complaint.[15]

My proposal is that concerted action be taken in the immediate future by a group of States, Parties to the BW Convention, to amend Article V in order to spell out the verification procedure; this should include a well-defined mandate to undertake preliminary investigations by the Secretary General or some specially assigned international body. If pressure is needed behind such a move, it could use the form of the standing invitation to call a Review Conference.[16]

Such action, to establish a more flexible, more objective, less discriminatory pattern of verification, clearly separating the fact-finding stage from the political considerations and judiciary powers of the Security Council, may seem overzealous in relation to the ban on biological weapons, but it would be a valuable exercise, a rehearsal for the more stringent control rules and verification opportunities which must be part of an international ban on chemical weapons.

4.   Renouncing CB-Weapons—Treaty or No Treaty

Several governments answering the call of enlightened public opinion for more rational, ethical, and humanitarian considerations, have proceeded either before or in connection with the negotiations to renounce CB-weapons. Most striking was the November 1969 decision by the United States to close the facilities for production of B-weapons at Fort Detrick and Pine Bluff and turn them over to medical research (Chapter VIII, Section 2). On the other hand, the United States possesses copious stockpiles of chemical weapons, including tens of thousands of tons of the most modern toxic nerve gases. Deployed in many parts of the world, they are sufficient to exterminate entire populations.[17]

The Soviet Union, the only WTO country with an independent CBW capability, has always chosen to remain silent both about stockpiles and plans for closing production facilities of B- and C-weapons. When notifying the Geneva Disarmament Committee of its ratification of the BW Convention in 1975, the Soviet Union announced that it "did not possess any biological agents or toxins."[18] The Convention requires destruction of stocks within nine months after its entry into force (Christmas 1975), but no country except the United States has given notification of such an act of destruction of B-weapons. Knowledge about the availability of C-weapons in the Soviet Union would be of even greater interest. It is assumed that the Soviet Union has full operational capacity for chemical warfare,[19] but its government has not given information on the size of such capacities and has "offered no comment on the assessments publicized in the West."[20]

Several of the lesser powers made early unilateral decisions to renounce B- and/or C-weapons. In March 1970 Canada declared complete renunciation of B-weapons and stated that it did not possess any C-weapons and did not intend to procure them "unless these weapons should be used against the military forces or the civil population of Canada or its allies." The Swedish government made an unconditional unilateral commitment on 29 April 1970 to neither possess nor allow acquisition of B- or C-weapons. The Yugoslav government in September 1970 stated that it had none and did not intend to develop B-weapons.

The list of nations who have ratified the BW Convention includes the Eastern European countries, several in Latin America, including Brazil, and India and Pakistan. Ominously, in some of the world's danger spots such as Israel and its neighboring Arab countries, ratification has yet to be achieved. Nor has China adhered.

The position of the major European nations is of particular interest, since they participated prominently in various acts in the negotiations. The British representative said as early as 1969 that

> as successive British governments have made very clear, we have never had any biological weapons, we do not have any now and have no intention of acquiring any.[21]

In 1973, as a preliminary to ratification of the BW Treaty, the House of Commons passed a biological weapons bill making it punishable up to imprisonment for life to commit an offense against the Convention. However, the position on C-weapons is not nearly so definitive. According to SIPRI, the United Kingdom maintained a substantial stockpile of chemical weapons until about 1957 "when the last of it was dumped into the Atlantic Ocean."[22]

The French government acted with exemplary haste after the BW Convention was concluded. Finding itself unable to adhere formally to a treaty which was not the comprehensive CBW one it wanted, and having boycotted the Geneva Disarmament Committee, in 1972 France outlawed once and for all the manufacture of biological and toxin weapons. Its position on C-weapons is, however, less clear.

West Germany in accordance with its postwar settlement must abstain totally from BC-weapons as well as nuclear arms.[23]

What blurs the picture of "renunciations" is that allies, at least in Europe, are able to rely on considerable deployment of United States chemical warfare supplies. Stores of chemical weapons exist in Western Germany, for example, but they belong to the United States forces stationed there.

Like France, China has neither voted for nor signed the BW Convention. Its position on CB mass destruction weapons is unclear. A guess might be that humanitarian arguments against their use are given due weight, but that some arguments based on the pride of independence and the fear of outside attacks may speak for retaining certain retaliatory capabilities. China is a Party to the Geneva Protocol but holds to the condition of reciprocity (Chapter VIII, Section 2).

Quiet can be expected to settle down over the question of biological weapons. They are among the least significant for military capabilities. It would be less than gracious in conclusion not to place a positive value on the BW Convention. It is the one true disarmament measure agreed upon in that it requires total elimination, even destruction, of stocks.

5. *Any Hope to Eliminate C-Weapons?*

The ambition of disarmers to achieve wholesale prohibition of procurement and possession of all chemical and biological weapons is being cut down bit by bit. First, the ban covered only the militarily less significant B-weapons. Thereafter, attempts were made to narrow the scope of a CW Convention so that it would include only certain categories of chemical warfare agents. Several proposals for a ban to cover only lethal C-weapons, especially highly toxic nerve gases, are still being actively pursued in the Geneva Disarmament Committee.[24]

Early on there were premonitions that this road might come to be chosen, when similar attempts were made to interpret the Geneva Protocol as not being all-inclusive. But the majority view prevailed that the ban on use of CB-weapons is to be applied to the total spectrum. No dividing line was recognized in the gamut of chemical substances which can be employed as warfare agents (Chapter VIII, Section 2). The a priori position is that a ban on production must also include all means of chemical warfare, whether lethal, only more or less incapacitating, or capable of destroying the means of human livelihood.

With chemical weapons a second classification, of great importance in comparison with the degree of potential damage, which technically means toxicity is the extent to which chemical substances may serve legitimate civilian purposes. The fact is well known that many substances widely used in industry, for example, in plastics production, can also be used for manufacturing weapons.

Recognition of the multipurpose character of some chemical agents has become a main feature of all debates on a Convention to eliminate C-weapons. It has gradually become standard practice to distinguish between chemical agents as single-purpose military, single-purpose civilian, or double-purpose military-civilian. This facilitates a practical approach, but it does not give the key to the construction of an international agreement.

The search for a systematic formula led me, as Swedish delegate, to suggest early in the negotiations that the single-purpose military chemical agents be under a rule of unconditional surrender. For the double-purpose agents I urged conditional prohibition or prohibition with partial restraints, and totally exempted the single-purpose civilian agents.

The relevant question is connected with the purpose of their production. In that respect a crucial difference makes itself felt in regard to certain agents production of which is possible for peaceful purposes as well as for warfare. . . . Biological agents obviously lend themselves practically wholesale to unconditional prohibition. . . . Unconditional prohibition is also possible for a long series of chemical agents.

The road divides at a certain point, however. That is related to the fact that some specific chemical agents have a legitimate use in peaceful activities which would have to be recognized in any future convention. With that problem in mind we have to discuss the need for a separation into two categories of prohibition, what I have called unconditional and conditional prohibitions.[25]

This nomenclature—single-purpose military, single-purpose civilian, and double-purpose civilian-military—is now widely accepted. It has made it possible for many delegations to join on principle the proposal that a CW Convention should consist of a general agreement to eliminate all chemical weapons, though details can be elaborated in special annexes or protocols. This procedure is somewhat similar to the one suggested in the Swedish draft of a nuclear test-ban treaty (Chapter VII, Section 5).[26] In the CW context, various provisions may enter into force at separate times and be the object of periodic revisions while the main ban remains intact.

However, negotiations are not proceeding single-mindedly towards the goal of a comprehensive but composite CW Convention. As has become customary, the two superpowers are in collusion, playing the game to get a partial solution accepted which bans only the top echelon of most lethal nerve gases. During President Nixon's visit to Moscow in the summer of 1974, a joint communiqué from the summit meeting announced that "the United States and the USSR agreed to consider a joint initiative in the Conference of the Committee on Disarmament with respect to the conclusion, as a first step, of an international convention dealing with the most dangerous lethal means of chemical warfare."[27]

Alas, this is once again only a paper formula. The superpowers could have decided then and there to renounce and destroy these dangerous weapons. Participants in the multilateral negotiations, where an international convention on chemical weapons is high on the agenda, have since repeatedly asked for information as to details but waited in vain to see a superpower draft.

The joint United States-Soviet "initiative" is not only a partial solution, but as such it is probably a superfluous act. There already exists on the books of the international community a widely agreed recommendation to "refrain from any further development, production, or stockpiling of those chemical agents for weapons purposes which, because of their degree of toxicity, have the highest lethal effects and are not usable for peaceful purposes." It is true that it is not a convention but a United Nations resolution, establishing a moratorium "pending agreement on the complete prohibition of the development, production, and stockpiling of chemical weapons and on their destruction."[28] One hundred one members voted yes, among them the Soviet Union, none was against, and 10 abstained, among them the United States. Though Washington has been unwilling to bind itself for even a moratorium, it has advised the Geneva Committee that no nerve gas has been produced since 1968. As is known, some of the old stocks have been destroyed.

But the crucial question is not whether there are further additions to the extant overkill CW capacity. It is whether any nation, especially the superpowers, has any plans to totally destroy the frightful stocks. On this point the Moscow communiqué was silent. This one aspect now needs urgent attention. Existing stocks of chemical weapons are regarded by citizens of other countries with dismay, as a threat, and by nationals of the countries possessing them at least with shame.

It is not enough to wait, hoping that stockpiles of chemical weapons will be destroyed in accordance with a future CW Convention. In the climate of compromise now apparently settling over the CW negotiations, an ugly possibility has cropped up: a partial ban may forgo the destruction rule and only prohibit further production of certain chemical means of warfare. There have been indications that the United States at least would prefer such a course.[29]

What the United States seems to want—and Russia probably welcomes—is to retain chemical weapons. The argument is that they might be needed for retaliation or deterrence so long as it is not fully certain that verification can reveal clandestine activity.

Such a stacking of the cards cannot be tolerated. The lesser powers, as defenders of nondiscrimination, have cause to issue strong warnings. A nonaligned memorandum of 1973 underscored the need for destruction of stocks.[30] Discrimination between those asking for the right to retain chemical weapons and those not having the right to produce them is particularly cruel. I emphasized the warning, with stronger arguments:

> If it were contemplated, for instance, to make a treaty partial by proclaiming a ban only on production, i.e., new production, while delaying the elimination of existing arsenals, that would amount to a freeze of the monopoly situation for the haves, while leaving the have nots to run all the risks. . . . It has been said that chemical warfare so far, at least after the first World War, has always implied "shooting downhill." Therefore a partial solution of that kind would blatantly disregard the interest of weaker nations.[31]

There is considerable fear that the old story will be repeated of preserving the interests of the stronger nations. If reduced to a rule of no-further-production, such a partial CW Convention would leave the haves as *beati possedentes* of stocks of even the most lethal nerve gases, making that monopoly safe for so long as they refuse to bow to the will of the majority who want possession as well as production to be banned absolutely.

To fill in the details of a comprehensive CW Treaty is indisputably very complicated. It has been tempting to simplify matters by concentrating on the most toxic agents. Over the years, much excellent technical work has been done in and for the Geneva Committee on determining the physiological effects of toxicity categories. This has been done by Japan, the Netherlands, Sweden, the United States, and West Germany. Canada, in one of the latest working papers, has sought agreement on measurement of lethality while clearly admitting that if any single criterion is adopted several agents of military significance would not be included among those prohibited.[32]

All arguments which center on the chemical substances as such, however, miss the important point of whether they are usable for manufacturing *weapons*. So, the various chemical substances must be evaluated in terms of *weapons purpose*.[33] Providentially, the most toxic nerve gases—such as Sarin, Soman, Tabun, and mustard gas—belong in the category of single-purpose warfare agents. They do not serve any civilian purposes. At the other end of the scale, there is a large number of chemical compounds which serve only peaceful ends. In-between there is an ominous dual-purpose category—the manifold phosphorus, phosgene, and hydrogen cyanide compounds on which large sectors of modern industry are based. These can be utilized for lethal warfare.

A breath of fresh air has now blown renewed life into the Geneva

Committee's work on CW. Great gratitude is due the Japanese delegation, which early in 1974 submitted a draft convention on the Prohibition of the Development, Production, and Stockpiling of Chemical Weapons and their Destruction.[34]

The proposal has characteristics long sought: it proposes an immediate commitment to complete chemical disarmament, using the weapon potential criterion for the treaty as a whole; an annex would deal with phased implementation of the ban on individual agents according to the categories of unconditional or conditional prohibitions. A less satisfactory feature is that the annex leaves open two alternatives. One version would list only those agents to be banned obligatorily, and permit all others temporary exclusion from the prohibition. The second would make prohibition total and exemptions would be granted only to substances specifically listed. Further, in a separate paper, the Japanese have suggested that the chemical agents obligatorily banned in the first alternative should be selected on the basis of toxicity, in a way satisfying those who want the prohibitions to cover only supertoxic chemicals.

Nonetheless, the Japanese draft is of such value as a basis that work ought to proceed urgently on its completion. The problem of initially blacklisting warfare agents might be solved by combining the two alternatives, establishing one list of mandatory bans and one list of exemptions for the time being. Such a suggestion has been made by the Swedish delegation in an attempt to organize and synthesize the various approaches to a CW treaty. The suggestion is supported by a technical model for the solution of the dilemma.[35] It illustrates

> what the combination of the concepts of conditional and unconditional prohibitions and annexed lists of exempted and absolutely prohibited chemical warfare agent production might look like when a treaty comes into force [and] . . . how possible changes, after a number of years and after continued negotiations, e.g., at future review conferences, might result in a treaty which is comprehensive from all practical points of view. The annexed list of exemptions has [then] diminished, and the list of absolutely prohibited chemical warfare agent production has grown as large as might be possible from a practical point of view.[36]

The question of dependable verification, a serious stumbling-block in all disarmament negotiations, applies to chemical weapons. Naturally, if on-site inspection of munitions, pertinent military equipment, training, etc. could be accepted, the verification problem could probably be satisfactorily solved. This not being the case, painstaking work has to go on to find nonintrusive, but still reasonably effective, verification methods. This is extremely difficult but not altogether impossible even in the CW field. Agreeing to treaties without verification provisions, however, seems as implausible as on-site inspection.

Accordingly, the Japanese draft treaty's phased approach hinges very much on the gradual perfectibility of verification methods. The degree of verification feasibility would influence the establishment of a list of chemicals to be unconditionally banned and facilitate the gradual moving up of all others into that category. However, this may be asking for more verification than is actually needed, thus risking strangling an effective ban. There is urgent need for a broad and general prohibition of chemical warfare agents, even if only in the form of a gentlemen's agreement, while letting verification methods mature gradually. Or, in SIPRI's words:

> Verification is certainly essential to deter treaty violations or to enable their timely detection, but its stringency should be commensurate with the importance of the weapons banned. The [opposite] principle that the scope of weapon limitations should be closely related to the possibilities of effective verification could block progress in any disarmament negotiations if applied with uncompromising inflexibility. It would have made impossible, for example, the conclusion of the Biological Convention.[37]

Fortunately, there now exists an ample battery of practical verification methods which are increasingly acceptable also to the two delegations which suffer most from political inhibitions. These methods vary: wider openness, declassification of data, special techniques such as monitoring effluents from production facilities, the scanning of scientific and technical literature and production and trade statistics, controls at the national level, reports, preferably obligatory, to be made public and submitted to an international agency.[38]

Some verification methods are worthy of particular emphasis because of political considerations. First among them is the growing possibility for reliance on national means and distant, nonintrusive ones like checking on training and field manuals. More technically refined methods are being worked out, such as sampling of air particles and reconnaissance by aircraft and satellites.[39]

Second among these is amplified verification, the reliance on several detection techniques in a multipronged approach. This would be of particular importance in cases where suspicions existed, and it would help to avoid the situation of a nation, on the basis of imperfect knowledge by outsiders, being falsely accused of having trespassed Treaty rules.

> The way of circumventing the problem of false alarms would lie in the insight and acceptance of the fact that each verification method is in itself a weak instrument that only in exceptional cases can give a straight answer, and that normally provides incomplete answers. Thus, there should be no reason to look upon a single result as an alarm, but rather as part of the continuous information procedure that has to be provided for on national and international levels.[40]

Thirdly, there is an encouraging increase in national legislation which directly and indirectly bears on chemical warfare agents when dealing with poisons and dangerous uses of chemicals in industry and agriculture.[41] The apex of this approach is contained in proposals, to which Soviet experts have lent much support, for establishing national committees, reporting in a standardized manner to an international agency.

The Japanese draft proposes the establishment of a special International Verification Agency. I strongly maintain that such an agency should deal not only with chemical weapons, but have multiple functions (Chapter X, Section 6).[42] An agency, receiving information, storing it in a data bank, and competent to undertake fact-finding investigations if desired by parties to a treaty, is the most effective way to prevent discriminatory treatment by the Security Council (Chapter IX, Section 3). The memorandum of 1973 by ten nonaligned CCD-delegations also requested such a solution: "International measures of verification should be performed by a qualified and independent international control organ."[43]

With the firm basis laid by the Japanese draft and the technical-theoretical jungle now cleared by many excellent contributions, I can see no reason for delays in concluding a CW convention, except a lack of political willingness. A recent General Assembly resolution[44] affirmed that there now exists a sufficient basis for an early conclusion of a comprehensive CW ban, generously—or falsely?—promised in Article IX of the BW Convention. It is up to the delegations who represent the majority of nations to clinch the issue without waiting for the superpowers.

More and more encouraging aid from the outside is becoming available for the task, ostensibly so delicate, of establishing the original lists of unconditional and conditional prohibitions for various chemical substances. Chemicals once used freely in industry and agriculture are being increasingly questioned by health experts and environmentalists, the dispute over the value of DDT being perhaps the most obvious example. At the negotiating table in Geneva, I tried to show a glimmer of hope on the horizon:

> Luckily, we could, at least to a certain extent, probably be aided . . . through the fact that in later years some of the substances used, for instance, as herbicides and pesticides have actually been found to have such considerable negative side effects, involving short- or long-term risks to the health of man, animal, or useful vegetation, that they have been put under stringent regulations. Although such prohibitory regulations belong under the competence of national legislation and differ considerably from country to country, we should internationally be able to strive gradually towards agreement that such agents which are generally excluded from civilian use would be automatically included in a [CW] treaty of unconditional international prohibition.[45]

Certain conventions have already been agreed upon by other members of the United Nations family, the World Health Organization and the Food and Agriculture Organization. The *Codex Alimentarius*, dealing with recommendations for permissible toxicity levels in regard to food additives, shows one way to open the doors. The UN Environment Program's work to list and computerize data on dangerous toxic chemicals shows another. Much technical and legislative work is going on at the national level. The key to progress is here as always: research and information available to the world at large.[46]

The work on a CW Convention must be expedited. In order to put pressure behind it and at the same time mobilize wider cooperation among all specialized groups dealing with harmful chemical substances, my practical suggestion is that a Conference on Harmful Chemicals—a high-level, joint-expert meeting—be called, preferably by the United Nations in cooperation with various intergovernmental agencies. The immediate task should be to consider the appropriate listing of chemical warfare agents and evaluate available methods of verification. But the assignment, like the expertise, should include bordering fields, the desired result being a set of recommendations for practical implementation of prohibitory rules, relating to both production and trade, including international transfers of all kinds of harmful chemicals. For this purpose, in addition to experts on chemistry from research institutions and industry, jurists and patent and trade experts from national agencies should be included. Such work is clearly needed prior to the establishment of a verification agency. It cannot wait. It also would be wider in scope than the expert meetings organized by the Geneva Disarmament Committee. Therefore, we eagerly look forward to a UN Member sponsoring such a conference. Its rationale would be to rid the world of all the excuses and obstacles in the way of eliminating chemical means of warfare; its supreme goal would be to prevent mankind from poisoning itself.

6. A New Shock—Binary Weapons

Those who follow technical discussions in military publications with their puzzlelike bits and pieces have long been aware of the technical possibilities of producing chemical weapons of a new type which almost defies present means of verification. These are called binary chemical weapons.

The duty of drawing international attention to these dangerous developments fell once more to the Swedish delegation,[47] in bitter wisdom that once a weapons system is introduced, it is extremely difficult to pry it loose from vested interests. The most promising time for action against a weapons system is in its very early phase, preferably before it goes from blueprint to prototype; at least before it is authorized for production.

> Our experts on chemical weapons have recently come to be much worried by plans to produce lethal nerve gas by a new method—a so-called binary form—which might escape all attempts at control. Two nonlethal components would be produced and even loaded into a shell in two separate containers. The components might only be brought to mix when the shell is fired. In this way the moment of *use* would coincide with the moment of *production* of a chemical weapon, i.e., a composite gas with lethal characteristics.[48]

If not stopped, this development may well undermine all previous attempts to lay chemical means of warfare under a ban. A critic, as competent as outspoken, warns about the negative aspects. His over-all conclusion is that the costs, conceived in financial, environmental, and security terms, would greatly outweigh the benefits. Whatever the validity of this conclusion, the factors on which it is based need careful and dispassionate assessment before the binary program should be allowed to advance to the point of no return. That point is clearly imminent, for the present time is one in which the interests vested in the program are on the verge of a massive increase.[49]

Behind the development of binary weapons are not only the narrow ambitions of the armed services, but the rapidly aging, post-war chemical munitions which are becoming dangerously corroded or obsolete in relation to their delivery systems. By 1985 the entire stockpile of filled munitions will have outlived its life.[50] To the world at large this is a real challenge: to agree to destroy all chemical weapons and not to produce any new ones, or, at a minimum, to let the present ones die of old age. If this is done, all of them will be eliminated in ten years, cleansing the world of one of the most awful of its technological aberrations.

These facts should be a challenge to the political leaders of the superpowers not to give in to the military interests, who might make the senescence and obsolescence of the old chemical arsenals an excuse for starting up a whole new generation of weapons with binary chemicals. Perhaps the financial arguments could be a stopper; the costs for the United States have been estimated by the Department of Defense to run towards $2 billion.[51] Choosing disarmament instead reduces the cost to nought, or just to the cost of detoxification.

The risk of proliferation is another negative factor which should carry some weight. The reduced danger of handling this new type of chemical weapon might in itself increase the risk of production and use by more countries. The risk of their acquisition for terrorist activities is thus considerably heightened. The ability to steal or buy fairly innocuous chemical components in the market and combine them into deadly weapons according to the binary technique would significantly augment the scope of guerilla groups to threaten governments and for governments of small, poor countries to threaten their neighbors.

Munitions-fabrication capabilities have already proliferated rather extensively around the world, not least to India, Egypt, and Israel. The only impediment that can be placed in the way of a corresponding proliferation of binary production capabilities is nondissemination of the data from which design specifications can be drawn up. But much is already available from the United States patent literature; and it is inevitable that once large-scale fabrication of binary munitions gets under way in the United States, there will be a rapid dissemination of still more data. Stringent security precautions may delay this process. But time and human ingenuity are against them.[52]

The risk that binary chemical weapons may proliferate is, however, a specter with a time-lag. At present we have to be concerned rather with the discriminatory effects which are inherent in this kind of technological race. The gap will widen between the advanced military powers, the potential early possessors of this new chemical weapon system, and all others, who are so much weaker in protective devices and health services.

Another very serious consideration of binaries relates to the ever present problem of verification. Components not yet brought together to constitute a weapon are a particularly hard thing to prohibit. They are not yet weapons, and as such are not covered by prohibitions.[53]

Delegates as well as experts participating in informal meetings in the Geneva Committee have been particularly preoccupied with this difficulty of subjecting binary weapons to control methods. The one verification technique which might catch the binaries is monitoring of economic data on production of chemicals. This would cover components employed in the binary option, or unwarranted quantities of agents defined as dual-purpose which could be detected.[54] Field and training manuals could be examined for instructions on handling of binaries as munitions (Chapter VIII, Section 8). Fortunately, one of the components used in the binary process has no commercial applications, and verification of its nonproduction is feasible and crucial.[55]

Once more the challenge is for the opposing forces to exert pressure. They must influence political power to stop the development of binary weapons. Again, watchful criticism is gathering strength in the same quarters usually in the vanguard. The contributions by American scientists are particularly worthy of honorable mention. Political repercussions in other countries against a new generation of chemical weapons must be taken seriously. Many delegations in the Geneva Committee, and many more supporting them, represent a worldwide reaction of alarm and consternation over United States plans to produce binary chemical weapons. Awareness of this alarm is sometimes expressed in Washington by governmental officials. In Congressional hearings on chemical warfare policies, for example, a representative of the State Department said that

> any effort to expand the size of our stockpile overseas or to increase the number of sites at which we have chemical weapons deployed would run into very serious political difficulties, diplomatic difficulties. . . .[56]

A Finnish expert, prominent in this field, hammers home this lesson:

> For binary weapons to be effective as a deterrent in Europe, they should be stockpiled in Europe. It is a big mistake if the U.S. Army believes that it will be able to replace its 6,000-ton Hanau stockpile in West Germany with binary munitions without a major political outcry in Europe.[57]

An expression of the political resistance against any such deployment in Europe, not only of binaries but of all chemical weapons came in 1969, from Willy Brandt, then Foreign Minister of West Germany. It is milder than an outcry but firm enough to be heard in Washington as well as around all the negotiating tables dealing with the European affairs:

> Should the American Government . . . come to the conclusion that withdrawal of the American supplies of chemical weapons from the Federal Republic of Germany was desirable, I would have nothing against it. Such an American decision would certainly not endanger our security. I don't need to make myself plainer.[58]

These warnings have echoed in the American Congress, which would be responsible politically for the decision to embark on production of binary weapons, thus undercutting all strivings to get agreement on a ban on chemical means of warfare. Several hearings were conducted in 1974; on 6 August 1974 the House of Representatives killed budget plans for binary nerve gas production. But continued vigilance is certainly needed, as no hard and fast decision has stemmed the development work. The risk is that military requests will be renewed for production of these frightful binary weapons.

The terrifying prospect of a future with uncontrolled binary chemical weapons has been increasingly worrying the negotiators in the Geneva Disarmament Committee. The Soviet government, when asked what was entailed in its recent initiative to get new mass destruction weapons prohibited before they were on the ledgers of arsenals, mentioned specifically that "binary chemical weapons are the most dangerous type of chemical weapon with which any contemporary army can easily be armed."[59]

The main imperative is to block the prospect of chemical warfare by blocking technological innovations. The situation is too dangerous as it is.

7.   *A Stepladder Approach to Prompt Action*

The aim of CW negotiations must be to agree immediately on a commitment to prohibit totally production of chemical means of warfare, although a number of chemical substances can only gradually be phased out. Some delays must be foreseen both for the listing of unconditionally prohibited chemical compounds and for planning verification. Of course, the needed time to work out specific details of the implementation scheme should not be used as an excuse; the over-all and binding decision should be taken with all possible haste.

The misgivings about the superpowers' lack of political will to conclude a comprehensive CW convention and the danger that the Soviets will once again connive with the United States and settle for a partial treaty, as they did in their 1974 Moscow initiative, makes it necessary to debate a radically new approach. The majority of nations, who overwhelmingly desire and need a prohibition against production and stockpiling of chemical weapons, could take the matter into their own hands and conclude such an agreement right away. If the others prefer to stand aside, they will have to carry a next-to-unbearable burden of blame in the eyes of the world. But if that reflects the true situation, why not make it manifest?

A modification of this approach could also be tried to overcome delays. A different timetable, for speedier action, could be planned if the phasing out of prohibited agents was coupled, not to the various *substances* being listed as ready for full prohibition and verification, but to the onset of various production *activities*. I am taking the liberty of proposing that all those nations impatiently waiting for the green light from the superpowers make it their responsibility instead to plan a strategy for immediate decision, but phased implementation, first banning certain obnoxious, clearly distinguishable activities, while allowing subsequent implementation for others.[60]

The first order of business ought to be the ousting of chemical means of warfare from any *deployment abroad*. The burden of verification at this step is singularly light. It would be a duty for the countries involved with present or intended deposits of such weapons to report on them. This step has already arisen as a lively issue in Japan. It could be raised as a political issue at intra-European deliberations—if some European governments mustered the courage to make demands as Japan did in order to achieve the removal of nerve gas from Okinawa (Chapter II, Section 6).

Next would be to forbid all *transport*, except to incinerators, of chemical means of warfare. A new international Law of the Sea could forbid all passage over international waters, and an international convention could proscribe passage over land belonging to treaty parties. In this case, verification would not pose great obstacles as transport of such contaminated wares requires considerable care in handling and protective measures, making them highly visible.[61]

A third step in order of feasibility and verifiability would be *destruction of stockpiles*. This would be a test of national willingness to give up military capabilities. As an example, the destruction of B-weapons and some C-weapons in the United States ought to be given wide publicity. International observers should be invited to watch the bonfires, without this implying that they would know if all stocks were destroyed. Due account must be taken for the time required to destroy C-weapons. Some are near indestructible and some will require great patience to learn how to destroy.[62]

As a gesture to demonstrate goodwill, the measures thus far envisaged could begin immediately. Weapons envisaged in this phase would be those already in arsenals, those falling under the Geneva ban on field use, including tear gas and herbicides (Chapter VIII, Section 2), and those proposed for unconditional banning on the CW Convention list. Activities such as training in the use of such weapons and preparation of manuals describing them should cease at once.

The fourth important move would be to ban explicitly *trade* in chemical warfare agents. Careful study would be required for this as trade in dual-purpose agents and binary components may be difficult to circumscribe.

Fifth would be to ban all *production* of chemical warfare tools, such as all kinds of canisters, casings, and equipment, including the manufacture of prototypes, the setting up of production facilities, and similar activities. These can probably be verified relatively easily. The prohibitions on production of the CW-agents themselves would then encompass all activities in the experimental and manufacturing processes. The number of chemical compounds would be the main target of production prohibition. Under the future convention these would be progressively classified as warfare agents. Stockpiling them would fall away, being fruitless when destruction and nonproduction are already prescribed and faithfully implemented. Verification of stockpiling is deemed to be extraordinarily difficult without inspections. Therefore, this prohibition should initially be only lightly emphasized.

Sixth would be to prohibit *testing* C-weapons. SIPRI has helped to enlist considerable cooperation of specialists in this area and the results are quite encouraging. Detection of weapons tests is a fascinating field, to the technically minded as challenging a vocation as work for production of murderous weapons could ever be.[63]

The seventh and last prohibition should cover *research*. However, the freedom necessary to scientific pursuit makes wholesale prohibition undesirable. Establishing selective prohibitory clauses would hardly seem feasible, at least not without much work on definitions and delimitations. I wish to turn the demand for international cooperation in the field of R&D towards a positive task: exchange of information on techniques and practices to increase protection of both soldiers and civilians against potential CW attacks.

Such a new phased strategy requires initiatives by governments; but behind governments stand groups of concerned citizens, in particular, scientists. This is where we all come in. As citizens of the world we must watch for any new developments where military ambitions threaten to overtake what is the common, long-range ideal of building for peace and protecting human beings.

CHAPTER X

Verifying Disarmament and Internationalizing Knowledge

1. The Obnoxious Role of the Control Issue

Without any doubt, the request for tight control, on the one hand, and the stubborn unwillingness to accept verification by direct means of inspection, on the other hand, have been stumbling-blocks in the disarmament negotiations up till now.* The United States has from the beginning been pressing for far-reaching controls as a precondition for its preparedness to enter into agreements of any military significance. The Soviet Union, on its part, has consistently declined to accept inspections within its territory when any agreement has been under active negotiation. Only in some ideal state of a totally disarmed world did the Soviet Union express a willingness to accept a profusion of inspections.[1]

Behind their outwardly often fierce disagreements, however, there has always been a secret and undeclared collusion between the

---

* This juxtaposition of "control" and "verification" indicates the sense in which the term "control" must be used in arms regulation contexts. To make the term "control" synonymous instead with the limitation or regulation of armaments—as in the American usage of "arms control"—leads to nothing but confusion. (See Preface.)

A slight difference of meaning attaches to the two terms "control" and "verification." Even if they can often be used interchangeably, "control" refers more generally to rules allowing developments in regard to treaty obligations to be followed, while "verification" is more specifically concerned with the methods used for ascertaining facts about compliance.

superpowers. Neither of them has wanted to be restrained by effective disarmament measures. (Chapter III, Section 6; Chapter IV, Section 6; Chapter VI, Section 7; Chapter VII, Section 1; and Chapter IX, Section 3).[2] A deep distrust exists, of course, between the governments of the superpowers. In the United States the feeling that the Soviet government cannot be trusted is deep-rooted. There is no reason to believe that the feelings of those responsible for the policies of the Soviet Union towards the United States are any different. The Soviet government has often felt free to launch broad proposals for disarmament, which serve to keep its masses and intellectuals convinced that it stands for peace, ending the arms race, and general disarmament. It can safely rely on the United States to raise demands for controls, which the Soviet Union can then decline to accept. Thus agreements are prevented. And so the gaming and the arms race continue.

2.   The Need for Controls

The purpose of control is to assure that disarmament agreements will not be broken secretly. The historical record, indeed, confirms that clandestine violations of agreements are not often committed. In the armaments field they have hardly ever occurred in peacetime. Accusations are heard from distrustful Americans that the Soviet Union violated the nuclear-weapons test moratorium from the end of the 1950s to 1961. But there can be no violation if there is no formal agreement. In this case, the United States had indicated its intention to resume testing. And the bang was certainly no secret.

India's recent nuclear explosion is even less an example of a "violation." For twenty years India had worked assiduously for a ban on all nuclear-weapons testing. It had not accepted the Non-Proliferation Treaty and lead the nations that protested the partial, discriminatory character of the Treaty. India assured the world that its 1974 nuclear explosion was for peaceful purposes—an assertion that cannot be contested or verified, as the only distinction between such a test and a weapons test is the difference in intention (Chapter VII, Section 2). Again, the explosion was not kept clandestine.

Breaches are more likely to be open than clandestine. An example from the postwar period is the prohibition in the Korean armistice against introducing improved weapons to the territory; this was openly violated first by North Korea, and then "the United

States promptly became aware of the violation and responded in kind."[3]

Though undesirable, a different method of circumventing hindersome prohibitions is also detectable. For example:

> The record of Japanese and German violations of the Washington Naval Arms limitation Treaty of 1922 also suggests that, although violations of a disarmament agreement can occur, *secret* violations are not particularly likely. While the Germans and the Japanese made some attempt to conceal their naval building programs, most of their efforts were devoted to devising ingenious variations of those vessels prohibited under the treaty—variations that would fall outside the letter of the prohibition.[4]

As some critics point out, it is true that the ultramodern weapons might be more easily concealed:

> Up till the Second World War the military preparations of one's neighbors, if they were to be dangerous, were bound to be obvious. The building of strategic railways, the training of manpower, the redeployment of heavy industry, all the measures needed for the creation of an effective war machine, were not activities which could be entirely concealed from the world outside. Germany's so-called "secret" rearmament between the wars was no secret to the French Deuxieme Bureau or to the intelligence service of the United Kingdom.[5]

Nor, I would add, was Germany's rearming prior to World War II secret to any trained and inquisitive journalist. In fact, it was openly discussed in the British Parliament.

On the other hand, if the deployment and production of weapons have become more difficult to observe from outside, the means of detection have also become vastly more effective. Not only has organized spying, on both sides, been kept up, but many new means of accurate monitoring from a distance have been added. These are by-products of the arms race. Satellites are a prime example; others include radar and acoustic devices such as sonars, for marine surveillance, the examination of emissions (of radioactivity or chemical substances), and the analysis of telecommunication signal frequencies. Regrettably, the most effective of these monitoring devices, like the satellite systems, are now monopolized by the two superpowers. Yet it is significantly the superpowers' resistance on the issue of controls that leaves the disarmament negotiations floundering or resulting in less than effective treaties.

The use of new, more powerful means of close observation from a distance has been tacitly accepted and tolerated by both sides. Eisenhower's Open Sky proposal of twenty years ago, although never formally agreed upon, is nevertheless in full operation over our whole globe (Chapter III, Section 4). When the two superpowers concluded their first strategic arms limitation agreement, SALT I, control clauses were left out because the two governments knew that breaches or deviations could not be kept secret.

New technological developments should considerably lessen the mutual distrust of the superpowers and decrease the need for verification by intrusive methods such as inspection in loco. A clear understanding of this fortunate situation was brought out by the then chief United States negotiator at SALT I, Gerald Smith, during Senate hearings to confirm his appointment:

> I think that in any international arrangement some rule of reason must apply, and if you start in saying something has got to be not only foolproof but knaveproof and 100 percent verifiable, I would suspect you wouldn't reach many agreements. But I think if you have adequate assurances that agreements are substantially being lived up to that ought to be a pretty good criterion.[6]

Generally, when a government has negotiated a disarmament or nonarmament agreement, and worked to get it tailored as much to its wishes as mutuality permits, it is fair to expect that it does not harbor intentions of secretly breaking the agreement. A political commitment to abstain from certain weapons is itself a reliable guarantee, whether supported by mutual controls or not. From a rational point of view, the clamor for controls is usually exaggerated, serving to conceal unwillingness to enter agreement on limitation of armaments.

As violations can hardly remain secret, they raise essentially political problems. In the United Nations, the veto right of the five permanent Members of the Security Council would rarely allow any collective sanctions to be enforced against such breaches. It is also difficult to envisage what kind of penalty could be meted out by an international organ, or what punitive expeditions set afield. The risk that a transgressor runs is mainly the one of political reaction; other parties will then find reasons to abrogate the Treaty. In arms-regulation treaties, there are often provisions for such withdrawal, mostly using the formula "that extraordinary events . . . have jeopardized the supreme interests of a country."

Nevertheless, the question of controls remains a live issue in all negotiations in the disarmament field. The argument in favor of rules of control or verification which I hold to be most important is for increased openness, promoting the sharing of knowledge both among governments and within the general citizenry (Chapter VIII, Section 8). More openness and less secrecy would decrease the need for controls and help to reduce the shameful reliance on various types of clandestine spying. In addition, it would help create an atmosphere of trust, favorable to disarmament agreements (Chapter X, Section 5).

3. Control Requirements According to Scope and Character of Agreements

The issues relating to control are often befuddled because of confusion between requirements for General and Complete Disarmament and for more limited agreements. The lingering influence of ideas about the need for a foolproof system is clearly irrational, for the goal of total disarmament has been abandoned.

At the beginning of the 1960s, disarmament negotiations ambitions were very high, aimed at a state of world affairs where all nations were disarmed and the United Nations was to collectively police the world society. In preparation for the work of the Geneva Disarmament Committee, the superpowers reached agreement on important guidelines for the negotiations on General and Complete Disarmament. These are generally called the McCloy-Zorin Agreed Principles, which were approved in 1961 by the General Assembly. The sixth of the Agreed Principles reads:

All disarmament measures should be implemented from beginning to end under such strict and effective international control as would provide firm assurance that all parties are honoring their obligations. During and after the implementation of general and complete disarmament, the most thorough control should be exercised, the nature and extent of such control depending on the requirements for verification of the disarmament measures being carried out in each stage. To implement control over the inspection of disarmament, an *international disarmament organization* including all parties to the agreement should be created within the framework of the United Nations. This international disarmament organization and its inspectors should be assured unrestricted access without veto to all places as necessary for the purpose of effective verification.[7]

When the Geneva committee began work in 1962, the superpowers presented parallel proposals in great detail as to how the radical goal of General and Complete Disarmament should be attained by stages, according to a preset timetable (Chapter III, Section 4).[8]

The two programs were not only very similar as to their general structure, but set great store on a control and verification system to guarantee the security of nations once the complete disarmament was achieved. Similar weight was placed on control of the single disarmament measure, far more restricted in scope, which they discussed at about the same time, the test ban. Such reports as the expert study on that verification system provide examples of the irrational strivings for unnecessary perfectibility of control methods (Chapter III, Sections 5 and 6).

What now looks like an overzealous concern with controls was typical of the situation during what I would call the halcyon days of disarmament studies, in the transition from the 1950s to the 1960s. A great number of academic publications reported the untiring search, particularly in the United States, for the perfection of methods of control. One book is sufficient testimony, intelligently written by competent researchers as it was, to a frame of mind that now seems quite strange and remote. Its very title, *Security in Disarmament*, eloquently reveals the reliance on strict surveillance to create trust. The two editors, Richard Barnet and Richard Falk, in introductory articles, warned against overreliance on techniques of control.[9] But several chapters in the book so emphasize the building up of requirements for security through inspection that it appeared that disarmament would require a world police state.[10] Fortunately, this trend has all but abated.

It was unfortunate that ideas about achieving a watertight system of controls tended to obfuscate thinking about the control methods necessary or desirable for the partial and collateral disarmament agreements which have been, and are now, discussed as a more practicable way of proceeding than the holistic approach of General and Complete Disarmament. Today, it is increasingly understood that controls must relate to specific conditions, differing from case to case.

The first demonstration was made in the initiative of the non-aligned members of the Geneva Committee to move rapidly towards a very simplified, but sufficient and practicable, system of verification for a ban on nuclear-weapons testing (Chapter III, Section 6). With the means of detecting and identifying nuclear explosions effective then and still more perfected today, no verification by inspection is needed for a credible comprehensive test ban. Local inspections to allay suspicions are less effective than observations from a distance. However, the control of production and storage of chemical weapons is more difficult, and one is understandably anxious to devise methods which are incisive enough to track what happens inside civilian chemical plants (Chapter IX, Sections 5 and 6).[11]

Much attention to the issues of controls has not led to any commonly shared clarification about the function of controls, what sort and degree of controls are needed, when controls should set in, what should be controlled, by whom, and by what methods.

The common practice when constructing disarmament proposals for negotiation has been to build into the treaties different control rules, apparently chosen ad hoc without any systematic analysis of effectiveness or comparison with measures prescribed in other treaties. These variations regrettably often put control under different machinery.

Sometimes references to control are so abstruse as to make succinct interpretations impossible, thus inviting different interpretations of what control clauses in already signed and ratified treaties really mean. For example: Article III:5 in the Sea-Bed Treaty states: "Verification . . . may be undertaken by any State Party . . . or through appropriate international procedures within the framework of the United Nations and in accordance with its Charter." Does that allow the Secretary General to mount an investigation? The wording was introduced to accommodate both a positive—Western—and a negative—Russian—answer.

The totally unsystematic character of varying demands for control springs clearly to the eyes when the pattern is set out in illustrative diagram form as was done for my article "The International Control of Disarmament" in *Scientific American*, October 1974. The information was originally prepared for and presented in a Swedish Working Paper to the Geneva Disarmament Committee.[12]

4.   Ex Post and Ex Ante

To sort out the vexatious issues of control and verification, the question should be answered: what is the function of verification in relation to disarmament treaties? I would argue forcefully that the main function of verification is to deter violators of an agreement, not to track down violators in order to prosecute them. Thus, assum-

ing it is desirable to ensure faithful observation of treaty obligations, the practical question is how to construct verification methods
which can be applied from the outset so clearly, openly, and as far
as possible automatically that they serve as a constant warning to
would-be violators that clandestine adventures will not succeed. I
would call this the *ex ante* approach. Previously, far too great an
emphasis has been placed on verification methods which could be
used to secure evidence of a possible violation after suspicion had
arisen and on this evidence to bring the culprit to court. This I
would call the *ex post* approach.

In the ex post, or after-the-event approach, the main emphasis
has been on police and prosecutor functions to keep parties accountable. Evidence would have to be so strong that it would hold
up before a judiciary authority. Thus, the accused party preferably
should be caught red-handed in the act of violation, or should have
left behind indisputable material proof—hence the insistence on
obligatory inspections. The reasoning goes that only a guaranteed
foolproof system for after-the-event verification would allow enough
trust to be engendered for an agreement to be concluded. This is
still the position of the United States in regard to some important
treaties, including the crucially important total ban of nuclear-
weapons tests. The Soviet Union will not permit inspections within
its territory, when it is not a question of complete disarmament. As
a result of this stalemate, negotiations have for decades just been
treading water. Still, we know that the supposed issue of contention
is not a real issue, because the inspections proposed do not provide
the certainty of collecting foolproof evidence (Chapter III, Section
6).

In an ex ante, before-the-event approach, methods of control
and verification should function to prevent violations, deterrence
before detection. Sufficient likelihood of disclosure would act as a
deterrent to any party attempting to violate a treaty obligation.
Such methods already exist in the highly developed systems of current and continuous observations from seismic stations and satellites
to verify a test ban.

Verification is no substitute for trust. The sincere willingness of
all parties to a treaty to honor their obligations should be the
basis for concurrence. In relation to a nuclear-test-ban treaty, it
would be reasonable now to accept the small margin of uncertainty
that lowest-yield tests might go undetected. In uncertain cases, a

strategy of no response could be employed, saving response for cases of more certainty. The risk of nondetection would be minimized by the factor of deterrence, as it would be known with mathematical accuracy what the chances are that one violation would be detected and how much greater the risk of detection of numerous violations. This scheme is clearly more effective than to attempt to get irrefutable proof after a suspicion has arisen—and to then decide how to react.[13]

In practical terms, solutions to these seemingly theoretical riddles do not present great difficulties. The merit of the before-the-event approach is that it can motivate the first steps, though on somewhat shaky ground. It would allow confidence tested by experience to grow gradually.

The type of control and verification which relies on police surveillance and aims at a verdict by judicial authority must be avoided as far as possible for the sake of not poisoning the international climate. The Swedish delegation has designed a largely voluntary control procedure, called verification by challenge. It relies on the interest of a party under suspicion "to free itself through the supply of relevant information, not excluding an invitation to inspection by an outside party or organ," as I briefly described the concept in 1966. "It is easier to prove your own innocence than somebody else's guilt."[14] The official presentation of the method may be taken from the UN sourcebook on disarmament:

> Sweden proposed an arrangement referred to as "verification by challenge," under which a party suspected of having conducted an underground test, in violation of the treaty, would be expected voluntarily to offer clarifying information to allay suspicion, the assumption being that the suspected party would itself be vitally interested in establishing its innocence. An "invitation to inspection" might be forthcoming spontaneously in some instance and under pressure in more severe cases of doubt. If such a challenge went unheeded on several occasions, other parties to the treaty would acquire the right to withdraw from it. . . .
>
> The threat of withdrawal might induce the accused party to offer clarification of the suspected event, or if the accusation persisted, to invite inspection. The system of "verification by challenge" would be useful whether or not obligatory inspections were invisaged in the treaty. If obligatory inspections were envisaged, "verification by challenge" would help reduce the size of the unresolved problem, and if inspection were not envisaged, it would help resolve suspicions.[15]

In this scheme of verification by challenge, or challenge and response, the sanction of *publicity* is relied upon as being of considerable efficacy for deterrence.

5. *Dismantling Secrecy*

For either the ex post or the ex ante approach to function efficiently, a precondition would be more information about armaments as well as disarmament. As this knowledge became available, more reliance could be placed on the ex ante approach to verification. In turn this would provide more rational reasons for governments to reach agreement on disarmament and more hope for the viability of such agreements.

Towards the end of World War II, Niels Bohr suggested that the way to deal with the problem of nuclear arms was to abandon the secrecy surrounding the technology of nuclear explosions. Edward Teller, who is not given to believing easily in a thorough change in the ways of the world, quoted Bohr and indicated that a possible path was "a gradual and well-planned abandonment of all secrecy concerning technical and scientific facts."[16] As the spread of knowledge is unavoidable, that is not the main factor limiting nuclear-weapons production or improvement. Teller argued that a policy of openness must be actively pursued:

> We should at the same time exert as much pressure as we possibly can on every nation in the world that they likewise permit complete freedom for the flow of information. At the present time some technical facts are subject to secrecy in many nations. We should try by every means to reverse this trend toward secrecy. Every additional secret is an obstacle to the free collaboration and the eventual union of nations. A strong and widespread condemnation of all practices of secrecy may in the long run have a strong effect even on those countries which value this form of security most.[17]

Openness is the primary tool for verification of disarmament (Chapter X, Section 6). However, to be practical and acceptable it must be a request for a scaled process. Immediately accessible to verification by the international community are scientific and technological data available through publications and other media. In the middle, which would gradually be made to expand its open sectors, belong facts available from national budgets, trade and production statistics (Chapter V, Section 2 and 3), satellite observations of civilian and military resources in other countries, and so on. Closer in, military interests will certainly shield information about each nation's own weapons strength, deployment of forces, and similar arrangements of immediate concern, although the policy of secrecy is now beginning to be breached, for example, by the European Security Conference agreement about prior notification of and invitations to observe maneuvers.

National policies of openness must be coupled with an honest desire by every country to provide its citizens with accurate information, such as what has begun to occur in relation to nuclear weapons, particularly strategic missiles. The governments of the two superpowers now have sufficient knowledge of each other's capacities, derived chiefly from satellite observations, that they can conclude agreements without requiring intrusive controls. Missiles numbers are also openly discussed (Chapter III, Section 7). This knowledge thus also becomes available to their own nations, representing a tremendous advance in comparison with the hysterical guesses at the time of the debate on the missile gap and other "gaps."

Still, this valuable new openness about strategic missiles has not led to agreements on reducing them or even less on freezing their qualities. The continued superpower gaming in SALT is related to the less-than-straightforward governmental dialogue with the public which is extremely tightly controlled by authorities on the Soviet side. In the United States Congressional hearings and leaks to the media provide much information. Indeed, the Soviet Union gets much of its own information about United States military planning through these open channels. However, neither United States citizens nor the Congress is sufficiently well informed of the significance of United States knowledge about Russia's military capabilities to stop the game of frightening the public with projections of threatening growth in Soviet strength. Neither is enough information being spread to call the bluff about the need to increase its own strength and to have bargaining chips. Thus, overreaction continues. The citizens are never effectively told that the main risk of nuclear weapons is in higher quality rather than in higher quantity, and in the development of new weapons. Silence and secrecy still reign almost supreme in this area.

More openness is also in line with the cultural trends of our time, for information is flowing in ever fuller streams within and among our societies. This also makes secretiveness about foreign policies and military activities less likely to succeed. The time is at hand for a purposive change towards greater openness. The general public within our countries will then increasingly function as watchdogs so that disarmament agreements are respected.[18]

More and more the world might be rid of the shameful reliance on espionage, deceit and covert actions by so-called "intelligence" agencies. With the advance of technical means of observation from a distance we ought to be able to cease to use human beings as spies. They are regarded as despicable people when they are found out. Their shady existence should not be tolerated any more as respectable. A new policy of open information should help to erase this blot from our civilization. The key to control of disarmament is the construction of universal confidence based upon the cumulative process of shared information.

6. International Verification of Disarmament

Some verification of disarmament and some monitoring of armament developments take place without being institutionalized. All nations are able to follow to a degree what happens elsewhere, although the superpowers have the greatest capacity for acquiring such knowledge. But the world community cannot rest secure. There is still too much uncertainty. Too many verification needs are unfulfilled and many more have to be satisfied if and when desirable disarmament agreements are to be reached. The international responsibility for verification of disarmament therefore must have an organized forum.

The history of disarmament negotiations is punctuated by proposals for the creation of an international agency for controlling disarmament. The McCloy-Zorin Agreed Principles insisted that the implementation of disarmament measures in a Treaty on General and Complete Disarmament should "from beginning to end" be under "strict and effective international control" through "an international disarmament organization" (Chapter X, Section 3).

The two draft treaties, presented in the beginning of 1962 by the superpowers, followed these lines (Chapter III, Section 4).[19] They differed on several points in regard to inspection and control methods, but not on either the need for international control or on the establishment of an International Disarmament Organization, IDO. In both drafts, the international control agency's composition, function, and services were extensively detailed. The IDO's role was foreseen rather early in the course of the disarmament process. The Soviet Union wanted it to begin operating as soon as disarmament measures are initiated, which was not much different from the United States formulation to establish it upon the entry into force of the Treaty. In the painfully protracted, but unproductive, negotiations on the comprehensive treaty drafts, which continued for some years in the Geneva Disarmament Committee, not much attention was devoted to this organizational matter. And then plans for General and Complete Disarmament faded away.

The idea of a jointly organized verification agency has, however, come back time and again in the international discussions and negotiations. When the nonaligned nations in the Geneva Disarmament Committee took the initiative to switch, rather brusquely, to collateral disarmament agreements on measures for immediate implementation, the kind of international agency they proposed to verify nuclear-weapons tests, in particular seismological data (Chapter III, Section 6), had a very different character. It was to be a commission of scientists to receive, process, and report all information, to cover the one field only, to have no policing function, and, as I later suggested on behalf of the Swedish delegation, possibly to be set up on an interim basis before an agreement was reached.[20] Voluntary cooperation in the form of a detection club for monitoring nuclear explosions by seismological methods has come close to functioning as such a preliminary, interim, scientific verification agency (Chapter VII, Section 1).

After the bold plans for systematization in the beginning of the 1960s had capsized, the development of verification ideas grew in relation to specific needs. So it was with the nonaligned initiative for international monitoring of nuclear explosions. The attempt to check the flow of fissionable material in the 1950s led to the establishment of IAEA, a control agency. From the conclusion of the Non-Proliferation Treaty, IAEA's functions have been expanded from the original supervision of general safeguards to a more exacting verification role, as specified in that Treaty and valid for its adherents, whether as exporters or importers of fissionable material. IAEA is also preparing to execute control tasks in relation to peaceful nuclear explosions (Chapter VI, Section 8, and Chapter VII, Section 4).

Later initiatives have focused particularly on the need to verify the prohibited production and stockpiling of chemical means of warfare. In 1972 the delegations of the Netherlands, Sweden, and Yugoslavia made separate but similar proposals in the Geneva Disarmament Committee for setting up an international institution to monitor the rather extensive verification network which was considered necessary to chemical disarmament.[21] The idea was supported by ten of the Committee's nonaligned members in a memorandum in the spring of 1973. Clearly separating their demands from the question of formal complaints to the Security Council, they stated:

> International measures of verification should be performed by a qualified and independent international control organ to be designated by the State Parties, and the results should be made available to all parties on an automatic and fact-finding basis.[22]

I broadened the suggestion by proposing that an international verification agency should encompass all aspects of disarmament control and monitoring, in whatever field an agreement was envisaged, and that it should be set up immediately to accelerate work on disarmament agreements.[23] The Netherlands delegation largely supported this approach, submitting a Working Paper on an International Organ for the Support of a CW Convention and other Disarmament Agreements. As the title indicates, however, it continued to keep the function of monitoring centered on chemical weapons and did not particularly favor what it called an embryonic IDO.[24] The trend of the debates within the Geneva Disarmament Committee has continued to concentrate almost entirely on verification of a prohibition on chemical weapons whose control is both needed and difficult.

A breakthrough occurred with the proposal submitted in the spring of 1974 by the Japanese delegation, in the form of a complete draft convention against production of chemical weapons (Chapter IX, Section 5).[25] It gave not only a most practical and thoughtfully prepared approach to the whole subject of a CW ban; it has also been widely acclaimed as a solid basis for the ensuing negotiations.

Since the Japanese draft convention deals with verification, incorporating the best ideas from earlier attempts and giving considerable powers to an International Verification Agency, I believe we may, at last, have a proposal that stands a fair chance of success. For that reason I want wholeheartedly to endorse it. If a beginning can be made in one field, chemical means of warfare, we should gratefully acknowledge that any beginning is a good beginning. Consequently, I want to amalgamate my suggestions for a verification agency with the plan presented by Japan.

Four major points vis-à-vis any international verification organ have to be resolved. They concern structure and powers; scope of functions; status as independent or attached to some existing organ; and establishment date. These points are pertinent to a comparison of the substantive formulas proposed in the three basic proposals, the Dutch, the Japanese, and the Swedish. The very first step should be to call an expert group to scrutinize the various implications of the three proposals and advise on the most feasible solution for an organizational form for an institution of disarmament control.

The primary problem in the structuring of a verification agency is whether it should serve only one treaty or several. The Japanese proposal is for the agency to deal with C-weapons only. Article VI states that the purpose is "to promote the realization of the provisions of this Convention." The Dutch working paper suggests membership in the organ would function best in the context of a CW convention only. Otherwise, there are difficulties:

> Taken as the nucleus of an international disarmament organization with future responsibilities also in other fields, the Organ should be open-ended. Rights and duties of individual members, except for the right of speech, would then have to be limited and determined by their adherence to the treaties (or their review conferences) which specifically provide for certain tasks of the Organ.[26]

The Swedish proposal supports this wider interpretation, and I have spelled out in concrete detail how such a multilayered structure, serving the varying constituencies of different disarmament treaties, would operate.[27] An important creative innovation would be the central role of the review conferences. This presupposes eliminating the irrational reliance on "Depositary Powers" which has allowed nuclear-weapons powers to have authority over the several treaties. That system has proved to have very harmful effects, as exemplified both in the B-Convention and the Non-Proliferation Treaty (Chapter IX, Section 3, and Chapter VI, Section 5). Having the International Verification Agency to call review conferences for checking on and possibly amending various disarmament agreements would create a pattern of one verification agency servicing different constituencies, as these legally competent bodies are varyingly composed by parties to individual treaties. Regional treaties might come to utilize the services of the agency as a joint secretariat.

The second point to discuss is the scope of functions. The Dutch proposal gives few definite guidelines, mentioning specifically only the duties to update the CW treaty annexes, which set forth the unconditionally and conditionally prohibited chemicals and to observe the destruction of existing chemical stockpiles. Conversely, the Japanese draft sets forth extensive duties in Article VI, of which the three first are:

> to analyze and evaluate periodic reports and statistical and other documents or information submitted by each State Party; to request explanation and conduct inquiries; to conduct inspection.

The Japanese list of projected duties of a verification agency tallies with the Swedish proposal, including the machinery for conducting verification by challenge. The Japanese proposal is weakest regarding general clearinghouse functions, but this problem will have to be solved between this new agency and the others. As of today, SIPRI, as part of its work, fills most preverification needs. In the future, it is possible that the UN Secretariat will have expanded resources for documentation. Much hinges here on suggestions to come from the 1976 review of UN work in the field of disarmament "improving its existing facilities for collection, compilation, and dissemination of information on disarmament issues."[28]

But the work of a verification agency, politically sensitive as it is but crucial for the credibility of disarmament agreements, can never be placed directly under the UN, not the Secretary General or the Security Council. Such an agency would require the prestige of scientific objectivity and a status of fearless independence. I emphasize that the role of the Security Council is only as the ultimate judge of violations, not an intermediate station. The separation of investigative and jurisdictional functions, relegating them to different organs, must be clear and explicit. Such a separation should be the basis of the system, as was also proposed in the nonaligned memorandum of April 1973.[29]

The status of an International Verification Agency would depend on two conditions sine qua non: that it be intergovernmental and that it be independent. The Dutch and the Japanese proposals both take these conditions for granted, without describing precisely the character and the location of such an agency in the international organizational framework. While strongly emphasizing the independent character, but taking into consideration a number of practical desiderata, I would suggest an intermediate position, not one as independent as that of the Specialized Agencies, like WHO, but neither one totally dependent on the central organs of the United

Nations. The best parallel is probably the semi-independent status of the UN Environmental Program (UNEP). A relatively high degree of independence is singularly needed for an organ whose whole respectability and usefulness hinges on its objectivity and freedom from political shackles. Like the IAEA, it should report directly to the General Assembly.

To succeed, an International Verification Agency would need strong leadership and a director with considerable prestige, competence, enthusiasm, and drive. It also would need sizable funding in order to undertake work of recognized importance to Member States. Studies in depth should be made of forward-looking programs in the disarmament field. The agency further would be called upon to investigate contested cases. These functions must not be allowed to falter for lack of funds; even such an expensive monitoring apparatus as satellite observation must not be out of reach. While the proposals hitherto officially submitted have not considered the problem of financing, it must be tackled from the outset. This should be done immediately by the preparatory study commission mentioned above, together with the mapping out of a work program making possible a step-by-step expansion of responsibilities. Even if such an agency initially would be concentrating on verifying just one treaty, the one on chemical weapons, the experience would be well worth it.

Neither the Dutch nor the Japanese proposals have suggested a date for establishment, evidently assuming this would be decided in due course once the convention banning production of chemical weapons is ready for signature. This is a serious mistake. After the completion of the preparatory study, a decision should be made to set up the agency immediately, on an interim basis. The agency should function as soon as possible as an instrument to accelerate the negotiations on agreements. A nucleus of temporary personnel could be assembled under the director from basic staff already within the UN agencies concerned, adding outside experts on a pro tem basis. Such an agency, even when only embryonic, should be able to demonstrate its worth in relation to the disarmament agreement selected as its first responsibility, thus inviting additional tasks.

When I suggest that such an agency begin operation soon, it is in the conviction that such a beginning could be fairly easily made in regard to the CW Treaty. A quorum would be available in the General Assembly for a majority resolution on the first two steps: the immediate instigation of a study and planning group and an agreement in principle to set up an International Verification Agency on an interim basis. It must be strongly underscored that there is no need to wait for anything but the initiative to bring a majority together.

Though there has so far been a reluctance to take any steps without the concurrence, or the sponsorship, of the superpowers, this reluctance should now be overcome. As the first treaty on C-weapons does not deal with nuclear weapons, its viability is not dependent on the nuclear-weapons powers. The lesser powers have the ability to stem the proliferation of means of chemical warfare. And that is enough basis for the decision to agree on an international convention and for the mounting of an intergovernmental cooperation for verification. A convention to ban the production of chemical weapons is a good start. I would even say that it is a godsend for strong initiatives to be taken by the majority of nations in the disarmament field.

The management of an International Verification Agency, as it expands its activities beyond the ban on chemical weapons, should not work in isolation. A constituent feature would be cooperation with other agencies, specialized in various fields. For its more inquisitive tasks of verification, in cases where doubts or suspicions have been expressed, where field investigations may be required, these might well be farmed out to various specialized bodies such as WHO, WMO, IAEA, or to ad hoc expert groups to be appointed after consultation with the competent sectorial agencies. For example, it should be examined whether the Earth-Watch system, set up by the UN Environment Program for global monitoring of pollution and other environmental risks, could not be utilized for international disarmament verification needs. A similar scanning of possibilities for simultaneously satisfying collateral needs should be made in relation to some of the powerful national systems, using satellite systems for observations of various kinds. The representative of the United States held out the promise at a UN Working Group on Remote Sensing of the Earth by Satellites, that United States data might be released regularly for international use.

> If, after examining the cost and other factors involved, the need for an international distribution center or centers of some kind should become apparent, its character defined and, at a later date, its establishment agreed, the United States would undertake to provide a master copy of the data we receive from our experimental satellite program and to do so on a timely basis.[30]

Some encouraging moves towards greater international participation in space activities, at least in regard to the use of earth sensing and broadcasting satellites, are now being made in the United Nations. Its Committee on the Peaceful Uses of Outer Space in 1975 recommended that action be taken towards a UN Satellite System to service member nations. A reliability study should be made on a possible structure for coordinating such a system, the costs and other requirements, including financing. This must include an examination of how the stations in various countries could participate and what the benefits accruing to various countries would be. The Committee has also explored the possibility of establishing regional data centers in the near future. Support for such programs also comes from the newly reorganized European Space Agency, which now has greater resources for participation in space activities with both hardware and programs. So far, these plans envisage only earth resource studies such as crop inventory, but they also imply encroachment on the near-monopolies of the superpowers over space activities.[31]

International access to data from satellite monitoring will come to be an absolute necessity for a truly serious work of verification of disarmament agreements, and also a valuable early warning on changes in the world's armament picture and the deployment of military forces. While it may sound overambitious to raise these issues now, the world community should not remain forever the poor relative when it comes to acquiring knowledge vital to safeguarding international peace and security.

So much attention has here been bestowed on an International Verification Agency because the time is ripe for a bold initiative at the international level. Rightly, however, what is envisaged is not so much an agency for verification purposes as a system, built on national as well as international responsibilities. Even when advocating the establishment of a verification system over a wide vista of disarmament measures, I emphasized that it must be part of a comprehensive scheme organically and hierarchically built up from the national to the international levels:

> The broad base of such a structure must be the national means of detection and verification that are organized within countries not only for internal purposes (for the control of poisonous chemical agents, weapons production, and the like) but also for monitoring events abroad by remote observation (by means of seismological stations, analysis of radioactive particles in the air, and so forth).[32]

The Japanese proposal likewise places the fundamentals of verification on the national level. Article V lists the four duties of the national organ or organs to be set up by the various member governments:

(a) observation as well as supervision of the national activities related to the subject matter of this Convention; (b) collection of statistical and other information thereon; (c) preparation of periodic reports to the International Verification Agency; (d) cooperation with the International Verification Agency such as presentation thereto of requested statistical and other documents or information, and acceptance of inspection.[33]

The mentioning of inspection raises a moot question which needs further negotiations; the Swedish draft treaty for a comprehensive test ban, which in a very similar fashion sets out the model for verification by challenge, speaks of inviting inspections only as a mode of cooperation.[34] There is evidently a growing acceptance of the idea of national controls, coupled with duties to report to an international body. One such signal of considerable interest was given in the Geneva Disarmament Committee in a working paper in 1974 by the Soviet Union and six other socialist states. The one-sided reliance on national means of detection, habitually kept up by the Soviet bloc delegations, has given way to some understanding that international cooperation on a voluntary basis would be valuable for verification of compliance with a convention on production of chemical weapons. The working paper outlined a quite comprehensive system of internal control, based on national committees. Domestic legislation would provide for their reporting to the governments and also for possible publication of such reports for general information. The information in turn could be used for international exchange. The analysis of statistical data and research results in open publications considerably broadens the opportunities for sharing such information internationally.[35]

A significantly more active form of international data exchange, presupposing an international committee to furnish guidelines for comparable and standardized national reporting, was indicated in a paper by three Soviet scientists to a SIPRI symposium in 1972; the idea has since reappeared in the Geneva negotiations.[36]

Plans for national controls and international exchange of verification data in relation to the CW Convention have been advanced within many countries. Both the United States and Sweden have submitted to the Geneva Disarmament Committee fairly extensive reports on such activities in relation to chemical substances. The same national-international combination is valid for other controls, for example, of cruel weapons (Chapter VIII, Section 8. See also Section 5 above).

There should be no doubt that if an International Verification Agency is given the capacity to handle a data exchange, there would be a spate of information forthcoming. Such an opportunity would enable us to know more about how far chemical means of warfare are controllable, which in turn would add credibility to a disarmament agreement that is just waiting to be born (Chapter IX, Section 5).

Again, other disarmament agreements could use the same verification agency for monitoring needs. This might first apply to the comprehensive test ban, for which international cooperation exists in the form of the voluntary exchange of data through the detection club. The Swedish draft treaty for a comprehensive test ban projects the formalization of such an exchange; the modalities would be spelled out in an annex or protocol to the main agreement.[37] And the Soviet delegation to the Geneva Committee has formally pledged its cooperation in such an international data exchange, once a treaty on a comprehensive test ban is signed.[38]

But it must be stated as a *praeterea censeo*: monitoring activities and institutional arrangements for verification and surveying of arms regulation can proceed even in the absence of formal treaties. More than that, such activities might well stimulate the formal disarmament agreements which are long overdue.

7. *Internationalization of Knowledge*

Many positive interests favor international access to and distribution of relevant information. I have here stressed how knowledge could deter cheating on disarmament agreements. In addition, there are two important groups who would reap great benefits from a reduction of military secretiveness. One group constitutes the scientifically and technologically less advanced countries. The other is the world republic of scientific workers.

Scientific research on the whole is to some 98 percent pursued in laboratories and universities of the rich countries. It predominantly serves their interests. In turn, about half of that work is devoted to military research (Chapter V, Section 5).

A sharing of technological progress is not only generally proclaimed as an international duty by the United Nations, it is also
prescribed in several disarmament treaties. The Japanese draft for
a convention on chemical weapons sets great store on such a sharing
of knowledge. It is also specifically embedded in the Antarctic
Treaty, Article III, the Outer Space Treaty, Articles I and IX–XIII,
the Non-Proliferation Treaty, Article IV, the preamble to the Sea-
Bed Treaty, and the Biological Weapons Convention, Article X.

What is not usually known is how little is achieved because so
much of this research is restricted by military secretiveness, or how
many civilian applications of new technologies are military in origin.
The scientific explosion is a hallmark of the postwar era. Even World
War II was largely fought by application of already known technologies. Philip Noel-Baker reminds us:

> It is already difficult to remember that in May 1945, when Hitler's
> Germany surrendered, there were no nuclear weapons; no ballistic
> missiles except Hitler's rudimentary V2; no aircraft that could travel
> faster than 400 m.p.h.; no bomber with a range of more than 1,000
> miles. There were no nuclear-powered submarines or surface vessels;
> the conventional torpedo was still the deadliest weapon of naval war.
> Potent new poison gases had been prepared by German chemists,
> but Hitler's subordinates, already conscious of defeat, had success-
> fully prevented them from being used. Both sides had arsenals of
> "biologicals," but dared not risk the general opprobrium and the
> strategic hazards which their employment would have meant. Broadly,
> up to the day when Hitler fell, the war had been fought with im-
> proved versions of the conventional weapons which the First World
> War had produced.[39]

Nuclear science, electronics, aeronautics, materials research,
particularly in the fine structure of metals, data processing by com-
puters, solid-state physics, hydrodynamics, oceanography, and space
science are examples of remarkable recent progress which burgeoned
under the impetus of military research after the War.

This progress has been simultaneous with the new era of decolonization that revealed the needs of the Third World. And these
countries' needs for development warrant no restatement here, nor
does the connection between their economic underdevelopment and
the underdevelopment of their science and technology (Chapter V,
Section 5).

What then is the share of the poorer nations in the technological heritage going to be? This is a problem ready for a major confrontation. It is already beginning within the framework of the discussions of a New Economic Order, where the representatives of the disadvantaged countries are taking the lead for achieving greater justice. I leave this major subject with a reference to the UN report on *Disarmament and Development*, 1972, where the connection between economic development needs and the waste on armaments is spelled out, pointing just to Research and Development work as the fatal nexus.

Here I want to highlight one dominant feature that augurs for continuation of the conditions of inequity and discrimination. Certain of the new macrotechnologies are not only demanding a very high research level, but they require so much in terms of advanced and costly equipment that it actually prohibits their being mastered by nations other than the most advanced ones. The inherent discrimination is best exemplified in the unequal access to the deep oceans and to outer space. The extraordinary resources possessed by the superpowers can be turned into both military and civilian advantages. This justifies our constant worry about their threatening world hegemony.

How to make the international community a shareholder in the most expensive and advanced systems is admittedly a very knotty problem. In regard to the oceans, with their riches declared as the "common heritage of mankind," the matters are being aired at consecutive sessions of the UN Law of the Sea Conference, although the part of the ocean space which was to be freely shared is meanwhile being dramatically narrowed by nationalistic aspirations of coastal states to expand the area of their jurisdiction.[40]

The monopoly held by the technologically most advanced nations is even more fixed in regard to the satellites. Their capacities indicate risks for both economic and cultural hegemony by the superpowers. They are the ones who can track the existence of and changes in the earth's resources, of such crucial importance for development. They are also the ones who can reach all corners of the globe with rapid communications, in sounds and pictures, thus creating a capacity for conditioning all our thinking.

Access to all knowledge, not only the most advanced, must be internationalized. How far the lesser powers can proceed to win influence over the management of ocean-probing and space-dominating activities remains to be seen. So far, the representatives of the lesser nations have not been too successful or even outspoken in defending their interests within the various UN organs dealing with these problems.[41]

As the research and development resources of the world are now distributed and utilized, they seem to constitute a built-in factor that mankind will forever be divided into have and have-not categories of nations, and that the detrimental effects on the weaker will, in relative terms at least, grow with each year. Therefore, the claimants for development within a new economic world order should join up with the disarmers as the most natural of all supportive partners. The open release of information should be one of their primary demands.

Science itself is harmed by the present lack of freedom of information. The cross-fertilization of ideas, so necessary for progress, should not be stopped by bureaucrats at national or even agency boundaries. The secretiveness claimed by military considerations is holding back much valuable scientific work. It obviously creates a personal and professional dilemma, experienced in varying degrees by individual scientists, when national agencies use their discretionary power to keep scientific results "classified" and hidden and thus stifle the natural flow of information.

Attempts have been made to organize scientists for a defense of their freedom of research. Many sense that they are being misused to work for destructive rather than constructive purposes. "Codes of ethics" have from time to time been suggested. The Pugwash movement tried to lay down rules parallel to the Hippocratic oath for doctors. At its twenty-second conference in Oxford in 1972 a working group recommended a "Pledge for Scientists" based on the following text, which is similar to one suggested by the Norwegian Academy of Sciences:

> I will not use my scientific training for any purpose which I believe is intended to harm human beings.
> I shall in my work strive for peace, justice, and the betterment of the human condition.[42]

This is not the place to dictate a new morality for scientists in the various fields. But we should all, as citizens of the world, be aware of the need to free ourselves from the shackles of military secretiveness.

CHAPTER XI

In Conclusion

1. Looking Back

The nuclear arms race between the two superpowers continues unhampered. Competition for ever more destructive technologies is steadily accelerating. A frightening new momentum is spreading nuclear-weapons capabilities to more and more countries. And conventional arms of ever greater military effectiveness are being acquired by all countries, particularly in regions where conflicts are brewing. Truly it is no exaggeration to say today that "unless significant disarmament measures are soon achieved, it is difficult to see how catastrophe can be avoided."[1]

The mounting dangers are of cataclysmic dimensions. Rationally, all peoples have a common interest in stopping this insane development. Yet the world finds any will towards resolutely halting the arms race faltering. Why? How have attempts to take serious action on disarmament become so frustrated?

As this book shows, a major responsibility falls upon the two superpowers, who are so blindly driven by their desire for world hegemony. Even granted their perception of a needed deterrence, they could unilaterally begin to reduce their nuclear weaponry without losing real power (Chapter IV, Section 2). Indeed, the closing of the current competitive phase would make them militarily more secure, and the saving of resources would make them economically and socially stronger. But so far they have refused to take any major steps.

Other nations also share the responsibility to varying degrees, especially the other three nuclear-weapons powers. And all nations sin by their silence on the madness of the arms race and by participating in the militarization of the world in their humbler way.

Vested interests always play a crucial role in politics. In foreign policies they are less controlled by criticism than in domestic policies, where knowledge of the relevant facts is greater and more broadly dispersed in the population and where conflicting interests and adversary views are more easily mobilized. In every nation suspicions against foreign nations can be aroused in the name of threats to national security. Of primary relevance to disarmament are the vested interests of the military and of business concerns engaged in arms production, often bolstered by the trade unions and those engaged in military research and development, whose careers and employment give them a stake in continued production and technical advance. Behind it all is the competitive spirit of our civilization (Chapter I, Section 4, and Chapter V, Section 5).

It is tempting to throw all the blame upon the politicians and the leading world statesmen who should know better than to engage in an arms race as if possessed by what might well be diagnosed as "terminal psychosis." But there is a mutual interdependence between the political leaders and public opinion. If the people are subverted by the vested interests in a militaristic-national direction—remaining ignorant of and therefore vulnerable to propaganda—the political leaders are only too apt to give expression to what they feel "goes over well at home." Thus they fortify "public opinion" and soon become prisoners of their own propaganda.

This set of observations relates primarily to democratic nations where political power depends upon elections. In a recent public opinion poll in the United States, only 37 percent thought government spending for military defense should be reduced; 52 percent did not share this opinion.[2] How people in the Soviet feel is not known.

The truly astonishing fact is that people all over the world have become conditioned to live on unconcerned about the steadily increasing risk that holocaust might suddenly destroy us all and our civilization. Only in Japan has a lasting anxiety persisted, rekindled time and again by "Hiroshima anniversaries." Otherwise postwar history has only for brief periods and in a few countries witnessed some perturbations of the public calm. A groundswell was caused after the Bikini megaton blast in 1954 hit the Japanese fishing boat *Lucky Dragon* with radioactive debris. Prominent scientists seized the occasion to mount a protest movement against the atomic bomb, especially in Britain, where it was unsuccessful, and in Sweden, where it scored success (Chapter III, Section 5). A certain uneasiness, mostly in political circles and among alert citizens, has at times been aroused in West Germany. In the middle fifties a maneuver called "Carte Blanche" illustrated what a so-called limited war would mean in terms of casualties and suffering (Chapter II, Section 6). Information on the realities implied by a nuclear exchange over Europe has since been tuned down, and practically all Europe has accepted, in a false euphoria, compliance with the horrible prospects for their continent.

It is as if we have all been conditioned to go on living with the threatened dangers to our lives and our civilization, as we live with the inevitable personal catastrophe of our own death, attending in an unconcerned way to daily duties and pleasures. The difference is that while individuals can do little to alter their ultimate fate, a collective nuclear suicide can be prevented by effective agreements on arsenals and warfare methods (Chapter IV, Section 4, and Chapter VIII, Section 5).

The lack of concern is the result not only of our opportunistic inclination to turn our attention away from disagreeable thoughts, but also of reckless and systematic propaganda by the vested interests and their obedient servants among politicians, governments, military and foreign policy bureaucracies, and even captive scientists. The mass media serve as megaphones for this propaganda while blacking out our knowledge of facts and rational reasoning. The director of SIPRI, Frank Barnaby, summarizes in a recent information booklet:

We have learnt to live with nuclear weapons. We have become mentally paralyzed by the rhetoric of the arms race, in which horror weapons are given innocent sounding names—like Bambi and Hound Dog, euphemisms for nuclear missiles. We have become inured to violence—impersonal, automated violence. Our moral judgement has been impaired by the apocalyptic calculations of scholars and strategists—how many million deaths would be "acceptable" in a nuclear war, how much more megatonnage is needed for superiority, and so on. We have been misled by absurd statements about the possibility of a "limited" nuclear war, of "damage limitation," of the political "value" of overkill, and so on.[3]

Disarmament interests have nowhere had strong organizational backing. Peace organizations everywhere lack strength both in numbers of participants and in resources. Politicians do not need to give in to their pressures. On account of their weakness, they are often forced to speak in generalities and unable to act in unison on specifics.

Those scientists who dare to stand up against official propaganda have little influence for the opposite reason: their protests are directed only at particular aspects pertaining to their specialties, while the general conclusions which should come from bringing together all of this knowledge are not drawn. This is just as true in the United States, where many concerned scientists have come forward. The biologists stand up against the use of biological weapons, the meteorologists against climatic war, the environmentalists against ecological destruction. Only in regard to nuclear weapons has the core group of atomic physicists been joined by larger groups in drawing attention to the general dangers from nuclear developments and the heedless race for more and better nuclear weapons.

The peace research institutes, which are rapidly becoming established in many places, often concentrate upon problems of "strategic" importance—as viewed from the point of view of one country or one bloc. Some lose themselves in model-building abstracted from the acute dangers implied in developments of the international arms race and from the practical questions that are perpetually being decided by politicians. Others, by focusing their attention on the ultimate problem of whether human aptitudes for aggression are innate or socially determined, render little guidance for actual policy. The leaders of institutes or groups for peace research occasionally confess privately that should they devote their work more directly to problems of armaments and the arms race, they would risk not receiving any funds from government sources or from foundations anxious not to fall away from the official line.

International organizations in the peace research field are beginning to be formed, but at present they serve mostly as a meeting ground for scholars interested in research methods. More of an exchange of views on substantive issues is organized by the Pugwash movement, which brings scientists from the two blocs together. This is a very worthwhile seminal activity, inspiring and providing mutual support to individual scholars who often work as pioneers in their countries. Collectively, a position is taken against the continued arms race and sometimes against participation in the further development of specific arms,[4] but only in a few cases, such as chemical weapons, has there been multinational cooperation on research projects. The Pugwash meetings too often produce generalized statements marked by the political desire not to favor either side. They are marred by too respectful an attitude towards the partial and ineffective agreements actually reached on some disarmament matters. The per se quite laudable efforts made in the many Pugwash meetings and workshops suffer most of all, however, from the lack of a decent amount of publicity by the mass media. Thus they largely lose whatever influence they might have in pressuring for a change of policies.

Civic movements, otherwise quite powerful, have been remarkably weak on the arms race, at both the national and the international level. This holds true for both the trade union and the cooperative movements, which in the time of the League of Nations were strong supporters of disarmament negotiations (Chapter III, Section 1). The illusory but widespread argument that reductions in arms production would cause unemployment has probably been a paralyzing factor. This problem has not been squarely debated and false views refuted by circumspect studies of alternative uses of both the work force and the brain power (Chapter V, Section 4).

The religious movements have not as yet had much of an impact for creating peace or against preparing for war. Lately, the World Council of Churches and the Vatican have demonstrated greater interest. The latter has urged the United Nations to work for "transforming national security and its military instruments into an international security."[5] And the World Council of Churches has recently issued a strong appeal to remind the churches of their duty "to resist the temptation to fall for a false sense of either powerlessness or security." Its Central Committee is now asked to see to it that disarmament is made a main assignment for the World Council.[6] The real test, however, will be whether this task is passed from the national church bodies down to the local parishes and members of various congregations.

I have painted a sad and not very promising picture of public apathy. How can this unfortunate passivity of peoples, popular movements, organizations, political parties, and finally governments be changed into realistic and rational concern?

2. A World Disarmament Conference

For many years the idea of a world disarmament conference has been launched and relaunched, winning support particularly from the nonaligned countries dissatisfied with the lack of practical results from the resolution-making in the UN General Assembly and the inconclusiveness of the negotiations in the Geneva Disarmament Committee.

The calling of such a conference was seen as a spectacular event that would force attention on disarmament as a truly urgent task and bring together governments and peoples for a new beginning. The result of the conference, it was hoped, would be the start of an effectively sustained process along an agreed course of strategy that would not end until a satisfactory state of General and Complete Disarmament was reached. This is still in principle the generally accepted goal, professed even by the superpowers. The two of them have parted, however, in the face of actual proposals for calling the conference. The only nuclear-weapons power unconditionally in favor has been the Soviet Union (Chapter VI, Section 7). The result has been a stalemate in the debate and no prospect so far of a conference.

Representing the Swedish Government, I myself have argued the case for calling such a conference now that China is finally allowed to take its rightful place in the United Nations. I have insisted, however, that in order to prevent it from ending in failure, certain substantive agreements should be reached in advance by the nuclear-weapons powers and that they must commit themselves to entering the negotiations with a real willingness to halt the arms race.

I now definitely call for two politically crucial agreements, two Principal Security Guarantees, to be cleared in advance. The first one is a pledge not to be the one to initiate any act of nuclear warfare. The second is a pledge not to attack any nuclear-weapons-free country with nuclear weapons.

Commitments to these pledges have repeatedly been requested by China as a precondition for its participation in a world disarmament conference and are essential if Chinese collaboration in substantive multilateral negotiations is to be secured. Without having formulated it as a condition for taking part in a disarmament conference of world scope, nonaligned countries have urgently made the same plea (Chapter VI, Section 7).[7]

When viewing the problems of a world disarmament conference

in the present political situation, I have advocated in this book that more states give these crucial initiatory pledges. The demand was rightly directed first to the superpowers. But it should also apply to other countries possessing nuclear weapons, specifically those outside the stringencies of the NPT. In addition, pledges should be made by other countries, at least enough to give a conference significant importance. The intentions would be to lay to rest suspicions that "threshold countries" are acquiring nuclear-weapons capabilities, and generally to reduce anxieties between neighboring countries.

It has sometimes been argued that such pledges are superfluous because the United Nations Charter already binds all members to abstain from the use of armed force, "save in the common interest," because several General Assembly and Security Council resolutions more or less explicitly condemn the recourse to nuclear weapons, or because unanimously adopted resolutions approve the idea of general and complete disarmament.[8] But much water has gone under the bridge since agreement on the United Nations Charter was reached between the founding members, and General Assembly resolutions of this general character have a doubtful relevance as international law. What is now required is firm and specific pledges by individual governments, prepared to follow these up with ratification. Such fresh pledges cannot so easily be swept away as empty "commitments in words."

The first pledge has often been discussed as a "no-first-use" principle applying only to the two superpowers. So far they have refused to make such a commitment. The refusal is, as practically always, most explicit on the side of the United States. It was strongly reiterated by former Secretary of Defense James R. Schlesinger: "We have never indicated that we were prepared to renounce the option of first use"—the first use of nuclear weapons even against an attack with conventional ones.[9] The de facto position of the Soviet Union is the same, exemplified by what is known of its nuclear-weapons strategy and its scenarios for massive attacks in Europe (Chapter II, Section 4). The prospects of the pledge being accepted by the superpowers are now dim indeed, but someday they must come to realize their accountability for the present rush towards nuclear-weapons capabilities around the world. Only if, and when, that occurs will other countries be strongly motivated to proffer their pledges.

The second pledge is the security guarantee for non-nuclear-weapons states and is a *quid pro quo* for proposals for nuclear-weapons-free zones. Its urgency has been strongly underscored in this book in connection with the rapid-proliferation risks. I have untiringly called for it as the political price to be paid to the non-nuclear-weapons powers for their refraining from participating in the nuclear arms race:

> The political price, perhaps the only one which should legitimately be called "a price," would be a grand gesture of historical significance: the nuclear weapon powers—jointly, bilaterally, or even unilaterally —should pledge never to attack nonnuclear weapon powers with such weapons.[10]

Except in the special case of the Latin American nuclear-free zone (Chapter VI, Section 10), this has been unacceptable to both of the superpowers. Some accommodation of its terms would have to be agreed upon for states which form part of an alliance with a nuclear-weapons state, e.g., that the proposal be more precisely formulated to apply only for peacetime. Thus it could be extended to countries who have no nuclear weapons on their territories so long as no ally of theirs takes recourse to nuclear weapons. In addition, a primary provision should be that these countries ratify the NPT about nonacquisition of nuclear weapons under their own control.

It continues to be my definite opinion that these two principal security guarantees constitute the pillars of confidence needed to hold open the gateway to a world disarmament conference. Such a conference could then proceed to true negotiations. It could begin by setting the agenda and timetable by which commissions could work out, with the aid of experts, solutions for the substantive issues and the conditions under which the continued work could be turned over to existing negotiation machinery. The conference itself would need only intermittent sessions for checking progress and redirecting the work.

Without the principal preliminary agreements there is scant hope of results coming from a world body of nations meeting to discuss the disarmament issue. We have recently had several experiences of worldwide conferences, insufficiently prepared politically and diplomatically, which ended up in empty rhetoric or confrontation. Nobody who has labored in the disarmament negotiations can wish to have the cause of arms regulation poisoned by that type of world conference assembling—the all but certain result unless the groundwork of confidence is laid by previous agreements to abstain from first use of nuclear weapons and to guarantee to the non-nuclear-weapons countries security from the threat of nuclear assaults.

For the sake of argument, let us assume that the two pledges were given or that there was a firm indication that they would be forthcoming. What would the agenda look like? It could be based on the wealth of proposals made in the course of previous negotiations in the Geneva Disarmament Committee and the UN General Assembly. These have been analyzed and expanded in the specialized chapters of Part Two of this book, which outline an Active Disarmament Agenda. The agenda must give priority to the most decisive aspects of arms regulation, even if only in a preliminary way by laying down guidelines.

The following examples are not meant to indicate a time sequence, but rather to suggest an order of priority.

1. *Quantitative disarmament of nuclear weapons and their delivery vehicles* by sharp curtailment of both strategic and tactical arsenals. Aim: agreement on de-escalating towards a minimum deterrent (Chapter IV, Section 6).

2. *Qualitative disarmament of nuclear weapons* by total cessation of further development of such weapons, both strategic and tactical, as well as of further development of their delivery vehicles. Immediate action: a comprehensive test ban to fasten the padlock on the ongoing proliferation of nuclear weapon types and on the spread of nuclear weapons to additional countries. Agreeing on a time-limited moratorium might be a first step (Chapters VI and VII).

3. *Similar quantitative as well as qualitative disarmament of conventional weapons* by mutually balanced reductions of arms production and by regulating and restricting trade in arms (Chapter IV, Section 4, and Chapter V).

4. *Prohibition of production, stockpiling, trading, and deployment of chemical weapons* (Chapter IX).

5. *Prohibition of the use as well as the production of cruel antipersonnel weapons*, i.e., weapons characterized as causing "unnecessary suffering" (Chapter VIII, Sections 3, 4, and 7).

6. *Prohibition of indiscriminate warfare befalling civilian populations, as well as prohibition of environmental warfare* (Chapter VIII, Sections 5 and 7).

7. *Agreements on demilitarization of ocean space*, not only prohibiting installations of certain weapon categories but also regulating the deployment of tracking, refueling, and other devices for military purposes (Chapter III, Section 7).

8. *Agreements on eliminating foreign bases*, withdrawal of tac-

tical nuclear weapons from foreign territories, and prohibiting passage through foreign territorial seas.

These give but a rough outline. They should be filled out to constitute a systematic list of goals and priorities. Running through all the categories is a demand for cutting off not just the quantitative but the qualitative continuation of all arms races. This is not only an eminent way to establish a reign of security in the world. It would also make possible a massive transfer of innovative capacities from military to peaceful purposes, thus promising the greatest spur to development that the world could have. It would be the only truly important contribution that could be made towards closing the gap between the technologically advanced minority of countries and the underprivileged majority.

3. Bypassing the Superpowers?

The pressure for disarmament measures has continually been kept up by states not aligned to the two superpowers. In some instances they have been joined by individual states who are members of the major military alliances. But both in the Geneva Disarmament Committee and in the Assembly the strength of the disarmers has been the allegiance of the nonaligned. Their number has recently been greatly expanded as new nations liberated from the colonial yoke have joined the United Nations and, almost without exception, defined themselves as nonaligned.

The clamor for some progress towards disarmament should thus gain in strength. And even if for the time being it does not seem realistic to assume that the superpowers will agree to the two principal security guarantees and that, therefore, a meaningful world disarmament conference could be held, disarmers cannot give up their efforts. The situation is too serious to permit a defeatist attitude.

Up to this very moment we nonaligned powers have been too submissive, restricting our efforts by assuming that we can act only when we can get the two superpowers to agree, between themselves and with us. Often our efforts have been spent as intermediaries trying to knit together whatever minimal agreement seems possible. The result has been either total failure or some incomplete and ineffective treaties under the label of disarmament.

What are the real possibilities open to the lesser states, the non-nuclear-weapons states and more specifically the nonaligned states, for carrying forward initiatives to stifle the arms race? Indeed, what would an agenda look like if it were established by the lesser states acting on their own without waiting for the concurrence of the mighty nuclear-weapons states?

Such an agenda must, of course, renounce the illusion that it will be possible to force the superpowers to disarm their arsenals against their will. In the case of nuclear arms, that means a major lacuna. Thus SALT will continue as hitherto, stalled in its bipolar postures, although sharper criticisms from the outside are in order.

But there is ample scope for a number of initiatives that the lesser states could vigorously take on their own. In the first instance, the majority which we are able to muster in the General Assembly should be used much more effectively to bring about some *structural changes* in the handling of disarmament issues at the international level.

Some improvements are needed in the consultation machinery for the substantive negotiations which we will want to continue in co-operation with the superpowers. There is need for a new pattern of rotating chairmanship for the important Geneva Disarmament Committee. This is a step which even the hitherto far too omnipotent "co-chairmen" may be ready to accept in the course of the overhauling of the UN disarmament machinery now in progress (Chapter III, Section 9).[11]

Another step, which can swiftly be taken on nonaligned initiative by majority decision in the United Nations, for which superpower accord may also become available, is to abandon the formula of choosing nuclear-weapons powers—the superpowers plus Britain— to be the depositary governments for treaties in the arms field as became the habit, for no real reason, in the 1960s, even in the case of such non-nuclear weapons as biological ones. International treaties should henceforth be deposited with the UN Secretary General, and more important regional treaties might well follow suit (Chapter X, Section 6).

By being more vigilant, lesser powers can also achieve rectification of the discriminatory rules which mar some treaties by allowing the permanent members of the Security Council to veto even preliminary, fact-finding investigations into the loyal fulfillment of disarmament obligations. This procedure has been criticized in regard to the Treaty on biological means of warfare (Chapter IX, Section 3). In future treaties, the lesser powers should exert that absolute power which in reality is theirs, to refuse to let any new veto rights be brought into play. They can prevent the superpowers from building veto barriers even against amendments in their role as depositary powers, as has sometimes happened, e.g., in the Non-Proliferation Treaty (Chapter VI, Section 7).

Among the imperative reforms for improving machinery is the revitalization of the UN Disarmament Commission. The purpose should be to give time for more penetrating consultations than in the General Assembly sessions. It would also give all the member states ample opportunity for participation, unlike the negotiations in the Geneva Disarmament Committee, which restrict membership even as they allot a very generous time for their sessions. The sessions of the Disarmament Commission, comprising the whole UN membership, would not be an alternative to a world disarmament conference, but would serve to energize the consultations on disarmament within the already existing framework.

If lack of progress threatens to stultify these disarmament negotiations, other steps must be resorted to. Much more important measures than hitherto can be taken and much stronger pressures exerted on substantive issues by independent action of the great majority of non-aligned states. I wish to exemplify the avenues that lie open by listing four points which refer back to several proposals made in previous chapters. The order does not necessarily reflect priorities, but rather a possible time sequence, dependent on how speedily the suggestions can be made feasible for being carried out within the UN framework.

I. *Some actual arms limitation agreements* can be reached independently of the superpowers. The best example is one practically ready for implementation, the Treaty against the production, stockpiling, and testing of chemical weapons (Chapter IX, Section 7). It neither requires global coverage nor intrinsically stands in need of the concurrence of the nuclear-weapons states. A great number of countries are ready to forswear not just the use but also the procurement of chemical means of warfare. It is in the interest of the underdeveloped countries to do so, as chemical warfare so patently risks "downhill wars." They should remonstrate against the immorality of recourse to these horror weapons. If the superpowers and their most obedient allies turn out to be the only ones standing aside from such a treaty, so much worse for the judgment of them in the eyes of the world. Thus a treaty committing its parties to not produce chemical means of warfare or allow any deployment of such weapons on their territory would be quite important in itself, even if originally adhered to only by a core of dedicated nations. By means of clauses on regular review conferences and a majority rule for accepting amendments, it would hold itself open for improvements and adjustments in the light of accumulated experience.

II. *The decision to establish an International Verification Agency* can likewise be made in the United Nations by majority vote. It can at least be set up on an interim basis, e.g., in respect to chemical weapons and seismological detection from a distance of nuclear explosions. There is absolutely no reason to wait for compliance by the nuclear-weapons powers (Chapter X, Section 6).

III. *A number of exploratory and preparatory studies* can readily be instituted by a majority in the United Nations. Usually this would continue to take the form of authorizing the Secretary General to call on a group of experts, the experts sometimes being seconded by interested member states but sometimes being independent. This is a proven technique for moving matters forward, even if one of the superpowers boycotts the study (as in the very important report on napalm, Chapter VIII, Section 4). There are qualified experts available, not least because the scientific communities are taking a more and more active role in studies in the arms field. The technique can be applied in a much more systematic way in order to accelerate progress and build up pressure in one area after another. Not least should the purpose be to educate the people and the politicians by laying bare the facts about the unreasonable course of the arms race in such a way that the knowledge compels change. A few examples:

1. Accounting for deployment on "encroaching" devices in the oceans (Chapter III, Section 7).

2. Alternative constructions for size and mix of a "minimum deterrent" (Chapter IV, Section 6).

3. Comprehensive account of systems applied or proposed for control and comparative analysis of military expenditures (Chapter V, Section 3a).

4. International survey of activities relating to conversion plans for alternatives to weapons production (Chapter V, Section 4).

5. Survey of rules and practices for transfer of war matériel in relation to the international neutrality rule (Chapter V, Section 3b).

6. Scheme for international reporting on how "cruel weapons" are handled in national manuals and training schemes and, possibly, their presence in production statistics and in arsenals (Chapter VIII, Section 8).

7. Report on the state of the art of economic data monitoring for production of chemical weapons (Chapter IX, Section 5).

8. Elaboration of a scheme for factual surveying of the institutionalized activities of transnational political and military espionage (Chapter X, Section 5).

IV. *A disarmament conference of non-nuclear-weapons states can be held*. This decision can be made by the majority in the United Nations as was done for a similar conference in 1968.[12] I recommend this as a measure to be enacted if progress is too slow. Ideally, a number of the steps outlined above will be instituted after consultations between the members of the nonaligned majority in the Geneva Disarmament Committee, the UN Assembly, or the UN Disarmament Commission.

A disarmament conference of non-nuclear-weapons states, where the nuclear-weapons powers would have only observer status if they desired to participate, must be very carefully prepared, diplomatically and politically. This should be done by raising the crucial issues well in advance, seeking partners who share a positive interest, and then taking recourse to this ultimate measure in the face of enduring resistance against progress in disarmament on the part of the mighty minority.

The conference should benefit from the fact that its consultations could be held in a climate of understanding among like-minded participants. To ensure success, I believe it should clearly demarcate two quite separate subdivisions of its agenda: the first focusing on nuclear weapons in order to sharpen *the demands for nuclear disarmament* by formulating them in as specific terms as possible, e.g., relating to the test-ban issue; the second establishing *the detailed agenda for continuing persistent independent action* by the non-nuclear-weapons states along the whole disarmament frontier.

Here should rightly follow an additional agenda setting out some suggestions for independent action, by region this time. Rich possibilities for such decentralized action can well be visualized, starting with energetic implementation of schemes for nuclear-free zones. But for political reasons the prospects for any such joint, regional action in the direction of disarmament now seem so dim for the near future that I abstain from making any concrete suggestions (Chapter VI, Section 10).

4. Not Against the Superpowers

The lack of forward drive by the superpowers should not be an alibi for inaction on the part of the non-nuclear-weapons states. They need not lean backward in the multilateral negotiations, where they should continue to participate side by side with the nuclear-weapons powers. They should exert more critical pressure there and be less willing than hitherto to endorse partial, discriminatory, and ineffective treaties. They should also be prepared, however, to circumvent the superpowers and act independently when necessary. Whenever action along the agenda lines sketched above can be taken with the concurrence of one or both superpowers, that should of course be hailed as an advantage. But it should not be bought at the cost of watering down treaty terms. Rather, when full support is initially missing, the lesser states should be prepared to proceed on their own, always hoping that if their work is good and its results convincing, the superpowers might later join on one issue of arms regulation after another.

Disarmament is a common world interest, not least for the peoples in the lands of the superpowers and their all too silent military and political allies. My proposals for independent action are directed, on a deeper level, not against but for their true national interests. They are, however, directed against their present policies, which are headed for disaster. These policies are irrational from the national as well as the international point of view. And they are deeply immoral.

At bottom, an important element of every disarmament move must be educational, trying hard to spread correct and relevant knowledge. What is needed is, indeed, something of a conversion, and the hour for salvage is becoming late. This conversion must happen in the superpowers, where the main responsibility for the arms race lies. And such a conversion is possible.

This book is being published in the United States, and although its message is meant to be directed towards all peoples in the world, my hope for a hearing is very much focused on America. I have not hidden that I am critical of the United States' present official policy and the support it has acquired in public opinion there. But this can be changed. I know of no nation that is more capable of switching policy line. The whole history of the country is a history of conversions, sometimes going against reason and morality, but as I see it, most often moving towards better fulfillment of the American Dream. The basis for this extraordinary readiness for conversion is its Puritan heritage and its fierce insistence on being an open society.

Much of the factual basis of my analysis is derived from American sources: the open disclosures from government agencies, often squeezed out through questioning in Congressional committees; the regularity of leaks to the mass media, whose freedom to use what they come to know is protected by law and constitution; and the great freedom of scholars to speak out. To the national tradition belongs also the rather unique openness to criticism from foreign authors when they write out of a friendly understanding of what is fundamentally good in the country. This book, like so many others by foreign authors, will be accepted in the United States on its merits, though of course not without criticism. It will be permitted to exert whatever influence it can have by the force of its arguments.

I do not expect the book to be translated into Russian or other languages of nations in the Soviet bloc. This is only a reflection of the fact that the Communist countries are not open societies. In the fields covered in this discourse of mine great secrecy remains, as does an almost total absence of analytical, incisive public discussion of the issues. I want to believe, however, that the arguments in a book like this will be carefully weighed by those responsible for Soviet policy.

I have stressed the responsibility of the lesser states for taking independent action in the present deadlock on disarmament matters in order to keep up the pressure. But the superpowers cannot be compelled, against their will, to stop their nuclear-arms race or even to participate in other disarmament measures. Neither government, however, is independent of the disposition of its peoples, although this makes itself felt in different ways and degrees.

Devotion to peace is an ingrained ideal with deep roots in America. Yet the American people have never concretely suffered much in their numerous foreign wars. The United States emerged from two world wars, contributing decisively to winning both of them, without any destruction of its homeland, and actually each time richer than when it entered the war. This unique experience has influenced public thinking in a way that cannot be entirely comforting to the disarmers. It is, of course, understood, in an abstract way, that the next war will not leave America undestroyed and richer. But the truth about the carnage and devastation that war really involves is widely con-

cealed by all sorts of technical jumbling. It does not reach down to
the people as a realistic conception.

The situation is very different for the Russian people. They have
lived through tremendous sufferings brought to their land from the
beginning of World War I and again in World War II, with its tens
of millions dead, cities demolished, and economy so severely dis-
rupted that the reconstruction policies meant even longer years of
hardship. Russians from practically every walk of life will spend
hours and days telling you what they themselves and people in general
had to endure.

There is, undoubtedly, a greater abhorrence of war among the
people in Russia than in America. While popular opinion in the
United States has remained suspicious of any move to end the arms
race (Chapter IV, Section 3), in the Soviet Union the government
continually is forced to present its policy to the people as an ardent
striving against the tide of armaments and for peace.[13]

Against this background stands one similarity between the two
superpowers in regard to calling off the arms race: so much depends
upon leadership. In the United States courageous leadership is needed
to calm down a public opinion that has been worked up to blind
fear of being left behind in the arms race, while in the Soviet Union
no persuasion of the people is needed. There, ending the nuclear
arms race or, indeed, taking any other step towards disarmament as
well as real détente would be easily understood and welcomed as a
continuation of what is explained to be the nation's peace policy.

In this situation we should perhaps not feel entirely discouraged.
Old leaders may have become prisoners of the past and the positions they have taken. But as these last pages are being written,
leadership in both superpowers may pass into new hands. Once
before there was such a conjuncture, when Khrushchev and Kennedy
surged forward to power, followed by some moves on both sides
towards relaxation of tensions. They apparently borrowed strength
from each other and, although it soon led to disillusion, probed some
new steppingstones in pursuing agreement on a nuclear-test ban.
Will Brezhnev be followed by a hard-liner or a man willing to pay
heed to his people's deep desire for halting the arms race and
releasing resources for the needs of its citizens? Will the future president of the United States have the courage to move towards ending the
arms race and have the skill to carry the American public with him?[14]

Meanwhile, we disarmers have to persist in doing everything in
our power to campaign for public enlightenment. The present com-

petitive escalation of the arms race is a flagrant miscalculation. And it is endangering the security of us all. More security can only be assured by reversing the trend, by beginning and continuing to disarm and to demilitarize our societies.

Such a strategy of truth means, in the final instance, facing the arms race as the major intellectual and moral dilemma of our time. As it has been created solely by mankind, it lies within our power to solve it.

notes

Notes

Preface

1. Declaration in the Swedish Parliament, 22 October 1945. Italics added. English translation, Nils Andrén, *Power-Balance and Non-Alignment: A Perspective on Swedish Foreign Policy* (Stockholm: Almqvist & Wiksell, 1967), p. 46.

A Personal Note

1. Alva Myrdal, "The Game of Disarmament," *Impact of Science on Society,* vol. 22, no. 3 (July–September 1972), pp. 217–218.

PART ONE: THE FORCES BEHIND THE ARMS RACE

CHAPTER I
The Reign of Unreason

1. More detailed estimates are given each year in publications by Stockholm International Peace Research Institute (SIPRI) and the United States Arms Control and Disarmament Agency (ACDA). SIPRI's figure for world military expenditures in 1974 was $210 billion in constant 1970 prices; in 1973, it was $212 billion in constant prices, while in current prices for 1973, it was estimated to be $244 billion and for 1975 $280 billion. SIPRI, *World Armaments and Disarmament, SIPRI Yearbook 1975* (Stockholm: Almqvist & Wiksell, 1975), p. 121, and *SIPRI Yearbook 1976,* p. 127. ACDA estimates military expenditure for 1973 to have reached $242 billion in constant 1972 dollars and $270 billion in current prices. ACDA, *World Military Expendi-*

tures and Arms Trade 1963–1973, ACDA Publication no. 74 (Washington: U.S. Government Printing Office, 1975).

Important information is also available in a series of reports published in New York by the United Nations: *Economic and Social Consequences of Disarmament: Report of the Secretary General Transmitting the Study of His Consultative Group* (1962); *Economic and Social Consequences of the Arms Race and of Military Expenditures: Report of the Secretary General* (1972); *Disarmament and Development: Report of the Group of Experts on the Economic and Social Consequences of Disarmament* (1972); *Reduction of the Military Budgets of States Permanent Members of the Security Council by 10 Percent and Utilization of Part of the Funds thus Saved to Provide Assistance to Developing Countries: Report of the Secretary General* (1974).

2. *SIPRI Yearbook 1975*, p. 100. UN, *Reduction of Military Budgets*, p. 10, gives a slightly different version; the figure for global military expenditure is said to be "larger than the combined estimated product of the developing countries of South Asia, the Far East, and Africa combined, and much larger than that of Latin America."

3. The estimates for China are made by outside observers; China does not publish figures on defense forces or budgets.

4. *SIPRI Yearbook 1975*, pp. 120–143, and ACDA, *World Military Expenditures*, pp. 20–66. Comparisons with population and Gross National Product are given in this latter publication. The figure for the Third World has been updated according to *SIPRI Yearbook 1976*, pp. 150–173.

5. *Historical Statistics of the United States from Colonial Times to 1957* (Washington: U.S. Bureau of the Census, 1960). Quoted in Seymour Melman, *The Permanent War Economy: American Capitalism in Decline* (New York: Simon & Schuster, 1974), p. 137.

6. *SIPRI Yearbook 1975*, p. 97. Also see Frank Barnaby and Ron Huisken, *Arms Uncontrolled*, Stockholm International Peace Research Institute Series (Cambridge, Mass.: Harvard University Press, 1975), pp. 5 ff.

7. *SIPRI Yearbook 1974*, p. 123.

8. If war costs as such became lower after 1970, this did not apply to orders and plans for acquisition of equipment. U.S. military budget subtitles "Procurements" and "Research, Development, Test, and Evaluation" show continuing increase. Even for fiscal year 1976 (FY 1976) an increase of funds is requested "to provide real (noninflationary) growth in funding for the modernization and readiness of U.S. forces." U.S. Department of Defense, *Report of Secretary of Defense James R. Schlesinger to the Congress on the FY 1976 and Transition Budgets, FY 1977 Authorization Request and FY 1976–1980 Defense Programs, February 5, 1975* (Washington: U.S. Government Printing Office, 1975), p. I-24 and Appendix D, p. D-1.

9. Ruth Leger Sivard, *World Military and Social Expenditures 1974* (Leesburg, Va.: Institute for World Order, 1974), p. 12.

10. Barnaby and Huisken, *Arms Uncontrolled*, pp. 44–45. Cf. table 4 in *Ambio: War and Environment, A Special Issue* (Royal Swedish Academy of Sciences), vol. 4, nos. 5–6 (1975), p. 181.

11. See SIPRI estimate, *SIPRI Yearbook 1975*, p. 100. UN, *Reduction of Military Budgets*, p. 12, generalizes that aid equals only about 5 percent of

the sum devoted to military purposes. UN, *Disarmament and Development*, p. 4, cites that "Military expenditures of the countries which provide aid for development are estimated to be approximately 6.7 percent of their GNP, or 25 times greater than the official development assistance they provide." I chaired the Group of Experts who submitted that report, and I judge the more recent estimates to be idealizing the situation. Since the time of our calculations aid has continued to decrease globally—and the figures representing official assistance tend to exaggerate the generosity of the rich countries. The statistics, especially those of the United States, are juggled in that direction (Chapter II, Section 8).

12. UN, *Economic and Social Consequences of the Arms Race*, p. 33.

13. UN, *Disarmament and Development*, pp. 16, 21.

14. See David C. McClelland, *The Achieving Society* (Princeton, N.J.: D. Van Nostrand Co., 1961), and other books by the same author.

15. *SIPRI Yearbook 1974*, pp. 61–62.

16. UN, *Disarmament and Development*, p. 32.

17. UN, *Disarmament and Development*, passim.

18. UN, *Economic and Social Consequences of Disarmament*, passim.

19. Remarks by Senator Allen Ellender made in the debate on the U.S. Defense Budget 1973. *Congressional Record*, vol. 118, no. 6 (25 January 1972), p. S409. Quoted in Melman, *Permanent War Economy*, p. 362.

20. A "catalogue of [seven] sins" was presented in my statement before the General Assembly, First Committee, A/C.1/PV.1882, 2 November 1972, encompassing costs, economic and human, here treated separately (Sections 3 and 5), and the unbalancing effect of these costs on national security (Section 2).

21. See *SIPRI Yearbook 1968/1969*, pp. 359–380, on post–World War II armed conflicts and disputes. Cf. *SIPRI Yearbook 1975*, pp. 6–7. Also, see a specialized monograph by István Kende, *Local Wars in Asia, Africa, and Latin America, 1945–1969*, Studies on Developing Countries no. 60 (Budapest: Center for Afro-Asian Research of the Hungarian Academy of Sciences, 1972).

22. As elsewhere in this book, figures are only intended to illustrate magnitudes and trends. Actual attempts to provide more precise information result in highly varied estimates. The *Encyclopædia Britannica* (1964 ed., vol. 23) even gives different estimates in its overview article on war and in the specialized articles on World War I, World War II, and the Korean War, different categories of casualties being covered or not covered. See Lewis F. Richardson, *Arms and Insecurity: A Mathematical Study of the Causes and Origins of War* (Pittsburgh: Boxwood Press; Chicago: Quadrangle Books, 1960), for a classical analysis of the difficulty in ascribing causes of death to wars or other circumstances.

23. Tom Wicker, *New York Times*, 27 May 1975 (items 1–3); William H. Edward (Military & Veterans Affairs, National Urban League), Letter to the Editor, *New York Times*, 24 May 1975.

24. *Los Angeles Times*, 24 March 1974.

25. E. L. M. Burns, *Megamurder* (New York: Pantheon Books, 1967).

26. *Encyclopædia Britannica* (1964 ed., vol. 23) estimates the Korean

casualties at approximately 1 million soldiers killed in battle, and 4 million civilians killed.

27. UN, *Economic and Social Consequences of the Arms Race*, pp. 27–28. Italics added.

28. Philip Noel-Baker, private communication, 8 October 1973.

29. No wholly conclusive empirical studies have been forthcoming as to the extent and depth of such effects. A summary of international studies on "Violence in the Mass Media" was prepared by Otto Klineberg for a UNESCO publication on *Attitude Change*, with special reference to mass media. Recent experiments conducted by the Swedish Broadcasting Company, using three versions of a thriller in which the elements of violence varied from high to low, also suggest a contagion effect of aggression. Olga Linné, *The Viewer's Aggression as a Function of a Variously Edited TV-Film—Two Experiments* (Stockholm: Sveriges Radio, Publik- och Programforsknings-avdelningen, 1974), cited in Sveriges Radio, *Audience and Programme Research*, no. 2 (April 1975), p. 3.

30. Michael J. Harrington, "The Politics of Gun Control," *The Nation*, 12 January 1974, p. 41; *The Nation*, 23 February 1974, pp. 227–228.

31. Alan Newcombe and James Wert, "The Use of an Inter-Nation Tensiometer for the Prediction of War," *Peace Science Society (International) Papers*, vol. 21 (1973), p. 76.

CHAPTER II
The Superpowers' Game

1. Richard Nixon, address to a joint session of Congress, 1 June 1972, immediately on his return from Russia after SALT I. *Congressional Quarterly Almanac*, 92nd Congress, 2nd Session, 1972, vol. XXVIII (Washington, 1972), p. 74-A.

2. Jules Moch, *Destin de la paix* (Paris: Mercure de France, 1969), p. 211.

3. Herbert F. York, "Nuclear Deterrence: How to Reduce the Overkill," in Fred Warner Neal and Mary Kersey Harvey, eds., *Pacem in Terris III* (Santa Barbara, Calif.: Center for the Study of Democratic Institutions, 1974), vol. 2, p. 25.

4. *Ibid.*, pp. 23–24.

5. Jerome B. Wiesner and Herbert F. York, "National Security and the Nuclear-Test Ban," *Scientific American*, October 1964, p. 35.

6. *Ibid.*, p. 24. (N.B. Error in source: 10,000,000 is correct, not 10,000.)

7. Fred C. Iklé, *Can Nuclear Deterrence Last Out the Century?* California Seminar on Arms Control and Foreign Policy, Research Paper no. 20 (Santa Monica: January 1973), note 27, p. 35.

8. Paul H. Nitze, "The Strategic Balance Between Hope and Skepticism," *Foreign Policy*, no. 17 (Winter 1974–75), p. 136.

9. During the period before the idea of German reunification was de facto given up, with the remilitarization of West Germany and its alliance with NATO, there had been some plans for leaving Germany as a neutral state, possibly to be joined by other neutral European nations to form a neutral

belt stretching from the Scandinavian countries to Italy. Two main reasons could be advocated for such a solution: (a) that it was unhealthy that the hostile armies of the superpowers faced each other directly; and (b) that if the possibility ever arose for an Eastern satellite state to break away and win greater independence, it should have somewhere else to go other than into the opposite camp. Then the Hungarian revolt in 1956 might not have been interpreted as risking a new world war. Professor Arthur Schlesinger, Jr., has reminded me (private communication, 6 February 1976):

> Walter Lippmann in the late summer of 1947 [advanced a thesis in a series of articles] published later that year in book form under the title *The Cold War* [*The Cold War: A Study in U.S. Foreign Policy* (New York: Harper & Brothers, 1947)]. Here Lippmann, taking issue with Kennan's *Foreign Affairs* article on "The Sources of Soviet Conduct" [July 1947, pp. 466–582], argued that the proper goal of American policy should be to bring about the mutual withdrawal of non-European armies from Europe. He did no more than touch on the question of neutralization as such, but I think this could have been taken as an implication of his argument. The argument focused on Germany and did not include Italy or Scandinavia.
>
> I do not think, though, that Lippmann's book had much impact on American policy-makers, except for Kennan himself. You will recall that a decade later, in his Reith Lectures of 1957 [George F. Kennan, *Russia, the Atom, and the West* (London, 1958, BBC Reith Lecture, 1957], Kennan proposed more explicitly the neutralization of a unified Germany and perhaps of other countries in central Europe (cf. his *Memoirs*, vol. 2, 238 ff.) [George F. Kennan, *Memoirs: 1925–1950* (Boston: Little, Brown & Co., 1967].

Concerning attempts to establish nuclear-free zones in Europe, see Chapter VI, Sections 9 and 10.

10. There are great difficulties involved in any such comparison, depending on important asymmetries between the superpowers in composition of forces and also in regard to the difference in distances for bringing up reserves. When the whole of WTO strength is compared with NATO, there exist on the Eastern side rarely admitted weaknesses: Can the Soviet Union count on loyal support from its allies' military establishments? Or might it even have to deploy some of its own forces to keep the allies quiet?

According to Professor Robert Neild (private communication, February 1976):

> In the light of past revolts against Soviet hegemony in Eastern Europe— Albania and Yugoslavia have broken away, Austria and Finland have been let go, Hungary and Czechoslovakia have had uprisings put down only by Soviet invasion, East Germany and Poland have had uprisings put down by indigenous forces, Rumania is defiant—Soviet troops in Eastern Europe must be regarded partly as garrison troops, only partly as frontier troops, though the Soviet authorities must obviously claim that they are all frontier troops serving the purpose of defense against NATO. This has implications which are generally ignored, for calculations of the

balance of forces between the Warsaw Pact and NATO. Some divisions of unreliable Warsaw Pact countries are no threat to the West, nor are those Soviet divisions whose task it is to neutralize those divisions. At the extreme, if each non-Soviet Warsaw Pact division had to be neutralized by a Soviet division, the appropriate treatment when assessing the *net* forces facing NATO would be to subtract from the number of Soviet divisions in Europe the number of other Warsaw Pact divisions. The usual convention in the West is to go to the other extreme and add them all, thus giving the most alarming picture. An intermediate calculation, based on explicit political premises, is likely to be most sensible.

See Peace Research Institute, *Force Reductions in Europe*, SIPRI Monograph (Stockholm: Almqvist & Wiksell, 1974), for comparisons of the military balance. A further imponderable is in how far the U.S.S.R. might need their reserves for other borders.

11. Henry A. Kissinger, *The Troubled Partnership: A Reappraisal of the Atlantic Alliance*, Atlantic Policy Studies, Council on Foreign Relations (New York: McGraw-Hill Book Co., 1965), p. 111.

12. Gunnar Adler-Karlsson, *Western Economic Warfare 1947–1967: A Case Study in Foreign Economic Policy*, Acta Universitatis Stockholmiensis, Stockholm Economic Studies, New Series, no. 9 (Stockholm: Almqvist & Wiksell, 1968).

13. To obtain an overview of relevant Russian sources I have found the following useful: Leon Gouré, Foy D. Kohler, and Mose L. Harvey, *The Role of Nuclear Forces in Current Soviet Strategy*, Monographs in International Affairs (Miami, Fla.: University of Miami, Center for Advanced International Studies, 1974). Manne Wängborg, *Militär doktrin och politik i Sovjetunionen*, Försvar och Säkerhetspolitik (Stockholm: Centralförbundet Folk och Försvar, 1974); Nordal Åkerman, *On the Doctrine of Limited War* (Lund: Berglingska Boktryckeriet, 1972); Trevor Cliffe, "Military Technology and the European Balance," *Adelphi Papers*, no. 89 (London: International Institute for Strategic Studies, 1972); R. N. Rosecrance, "Can We Limit Nuclear War?" *Military Review*, vol. 38, no. 12 (March 1959), pp. 51–59.

14. A. Yé Yefremov, *Yevropa i ladernoe Oruzhiye* (Moscow: Voenizdat, 1972); translated in JPRS, *Europe and Nuclear Weapons*, 14 March 1973, pp. 329, 331; quoted in Gouré *et al., Role of Nuclear Forces*, p. 129.

15. Aratov, *Promlemy Mira i Sotsializma*, no. 2 (February 1974), p. 46, quoted in Gouré *et al., Role of Nuclear Forces*, p. 129.

16. David Packard, *Perception of the Military Balance* (prepared for the Europe-America Conference, Amsterdam, March 1973), quoted in Piet Dankert (Chairman of the Foreign Affairs Committee of the Dutch parliament), "Amerika's veiligheid is de onze niet" [America's security is not ours], *Internationale Spectator*, vol. 27, no. 12 (22 June 1973), p. 399 (author's translation).

17. Henry A. Kissinger, *Nuclear Weapons and Foreign Policy* (New York: Harper & Brothers, 1957), pp. 174–268.

18. "Second Edition: Limiting War: A Younger Henry Kissinger Interviewed by Mike Wallace," reprint of a pamphlet originally published by the

Fund for the Republic in 1958, *The Center Magazine,* vol. 4, no. 1 (January–February 1971), p. 56.

19. Henry A. Kissinger, "The Search for Stability," *Foreign Affairs,* July 1959, p. 548. Italics added.

20. Kissinger, *The Troubled Partnership, passim,* e.g. p. 181.

21. U.S. Department of Defense, *Report of Secretary of Defense James R. Schlesinger to the Congress of the FY 1967 and Transition Budgets, FY 1977 Authorization Request and FY 1976–1980 Defense Programs,* 5 February 1975 (Washington: U.S. Government Printing Office, 1975), p. III-2. Italics added.

22. *New York Times,* 24 April 1974.

23. Opinion polls have at various intervals attempted to measure trends in regard to "isolationism" in the United States. An account of the Gallop polls taken in 1971 and 1975 with identical questionnaires shows that, although the changes in attitude over time have been relatively small, the trend has been towards a decline in public support of military intervention. This demonstrates how little positive support any policy for the United States to become involved in the defense of other countries would have, with possible exceptions being made for the neighboring countries of Canada and Mexico. The willingness to send American troops to support a nation if it is actually attacked stood at 57 percent for Canada in 1975 (Canada was not included in the 1971 study) and for Mexico changed from 45 percent in 1971 to 42 percent in 1975. But for the allies in Europe and elsewhere the figures were "only" 37 percent for England on both occasions, moved down slightly for West Germany (from 28 to 27 percent), Japan (from 17 to 16 percent), and Taiwan (from 11 to 8 percent), and moved slightly up for Israel (from 11 to 12 percent). The willingness to send military supplies was generally stronger but also indicated a downward trend. ("Gallup Poll Finds Little Evidence of a Trend Toward Isolationism," *New York Times,* 5 May 1975.

24. Helmut Schmidt, *Defense or Retaliation: A German View,* trans. Edward Thomas (New York: Frederick A. Praeger, 1962), p. 76.

25. Helmut Schmidt, *The Balance of Power: Germany's Peace Policy and the Super Powers,* trans. Edward Thomas (London: William Kimber, 1971), p. 196.

26. *Ibid.,* p. 76.

27. Heinz Trettner, "Tactical Nuclear Weapons for Europe," *Military Review,* vol. 51, no. 7 (July 1971), p. 48.

28. Carl Friedrich v. Weizsäcker, ed., *Kriegsfolgen und Kriegsverhütung* (Munich: Carl Hanser Verlag, 1971), p. 10.

29. Herbert F. York, "The Nuclear 'Balance of Terror' in Europe," *Ambio,* vol. 4, nos. 5–6 (1975), pp. 203–208.

30. James L. Richardson, *Germany and the Atlantic Alliance: The Interaction of Strategy and Politics* (Cambridge, Mass.: Harvard University Press, 1966), p. 40.

31. Alva Myrdal, Massachusetts Institute of Technology interim report intended for later revision and publication.

32. Alain C. Enthoven, "U.S. Forces in Europe: How Many? Doing What?" *Foreign Affairs,* April 1975, pp. 513–532.

33. The United States proposal, as approved by the NATO Council of Foreign Ministers on 11 December 1975, was an offer to withdraw 1,200 of its 7,200 nuclear warheads deployed in Western Europe, together with the 29,000 men servicing them (out of a total of 300,000 troops stationed there). In return it was asked that the Soviet Union withdraw a complete tank army of 1,700 tanks and 68,000 men. The proposal was formally handed to the Russian delegation in Vienna on 16 December 1975, and no reply as yet has been given. For press news see, for example, *International Herald Tribune,* 17 December 1975. It should be noted that the negotiations on tactical nuclear weapons in Europe are part of the Vienna talks, not SALT.

34. York, "The Nuclear 'Balance of Terror' in Europe," p. 208.

35. *Ibid.,* pp. 203–204.

36. *Disarmament Conference Document CCD/PV. 620,* 9 August 1973, p. 13.

37. "U.S. Pledges Not to Develop 'Mini' Atom Arms for Battlefield," *New York Times,* 24 May 1974.

38. *James R. Schlesinger, Report to Congress,* p. III-2.

39. James R. Schlesinger, in a testimony before a joint meeting of two Senate Foreign Relations subcommittees headed by Senators Stuart Symington and Edmund S. Muskie, quoted in "Nukes in NATO," *Aviation Week & Space Technology,* 8 April 1974, p. 7.

40. Herbert Scoville, Jr., "Nuclear Explosives: Potential for Ecological Catastrophe," in *Air, Water, Earth, Fire: The Impact of the Military on World Environmental Order,* Sierra Club Special Publication, International Series no. 2, Office of International Environment Affairs, May 1974, p. 32.

41. W. S. Bennett, R. R. Sandoval, and R. G. Shreffler, "A Credible Nuclear-Emphasis Defense for NATO," *Orbis,* vol. 17, no. 2 (summer 1973), p. 465.

42. *Ibid.*

43. *International Herald Tribune,* 7 October 1975.

44. Quoted in Timothy W. Stanley, "The Military Balance," in John Newhouse, ed., *U.S. Troops in Europe: Issues, Costs, and Choices* (Washington: Brookings Institution, 1971), p. 45.

45. *Ibid.*

46. While Western Europe imports practically all oil from abroad, the United States is almost 60 percent self-sufficient and the Soviet Union more than 100 percent. Even if other fuels may in the future be substituted for oil for some purposes, liquid fuel is essential for the military. The political and military aspects related to oil are analyzed in great detail in Stockholm International Peace Research Institute, *Oil and Security,* SIPRI Monograph (Stockholm: Almqvist & Wiksell, 1974).

47. *New York Times,* 25 January 1975.

48. Henry A. Kissinger, "Critical Issues of U.S. Foreign Policy," *Dialogue,* vol. 2, no. 3 (1969), p. 7.

49. "Premier Chou En-Lai's Letter to All Government Heads, August 2, 1963," in *People of the World, Unite, For the Complete, Thorough, Total, and Resolute Prohibition and Destruction of Nuclear Weapons!* (Peking: Foreign Languages Press, 1963), pp. 7–8.

50. *Der Spiegel,* October 1973.

51. *SIPRI Yearbook 1975,* pp. 221 ff., cites a 30 percent increase of 1974 over 1973, and nearly a trebling from 1972 imports.

52. Changes over time as well as in trade patterns are important; they can best be followed in the consecutive *SIPRI Yearbooks.*

53. Many attempts in these directions should be given due recognition as well as the one decision on economic sanctions against Rhodesia, approved by the Security Council in November 1965 on account of the unilateral declaration of independence by Southern Rhodesia's leader, Ian Smith. United Nations, Security Council, *Resolution 216(1965),* 12 November 1965, and United Nations, Security Council, *Resolution 217(1965),* 20 November 1965.

54. Gunnar Myrdal, *The Challenge of World Poverty: A World Anti-Poverty Program in Outline,* Christian A. Herter Lecture Series, Johns Hopkins University School of Advanced International Studies (New York: Pantheon Books, 1970), pp. 310–385; and Gunnar Myrdal, *Against the Stream: Critical Essays on Economics* (New York: Pantheon Books, 1972), pp. 126–131.

55. Gunnar Myrdal, "The Equality Issue in World Development," in Nobel Foundation, *Les Prix Nobel en 1974* (Stockholm: Norstedt & Söner, 1975), pp. 263–281.

CHAPTER III
A History of Lost Opportunities

1. Philip Noel-Baker, *The Arms Race: A Programme for World Disarmament* (London: John Calder [Publishers], 1958).

2. The major international agreement reached at the Hague Conference of 1899, summoned by Czar Nicholas II to stave off the arms folly, was typically framed as a "Convention with Respect to the Laws and Customs of War on Land."

3. Philip Noel-Baker, privately circulated memo. Cf. Noel-Baker, *The Arms Race,* pp. 390 ff.

4. Such clauses applied to Austria, Bulgaria, Germany, and Italy in Europe and to Japan.

5. *United Nations Charter,* Article 27.

6. In the context of one treaty in particular, dealing with biological means of warfare, I have had to conclude that the veto totally distorts the verification pattern for checking on breaches of the treaty (Chapter IX, Section 3).

7. The disarmament negotiations were at first cast in two main commissions, namely:

> 1946 The Atomic Energy Commission, established by the General Assembly on the recommendation of a Moscow meeting in 1945 of the Foreign Ministers of Britain, the Soviet Union, and the United States. Membership: the eleven Members of the Security Council and Canada.
>
> 1947 The Commission for Conventional Armaments, established by the Security Council after a proposal by the Soviet Union. Same membership as the Security Council.

These two commissions were followed by:

1952 The Disarmament Commission, established by the General Assembly by merging the two commissions. Membership: in the beginning the same as the two commissions, later expanded until in 1958 it was made to encompass all UN members. It has not been reconvened since 1965.

1954 A Five-Power Sub-Committee, established by the Disarmament Commission, acting on the suggestion of the General Assembly to facilitate more intensive negotiations. Membership: France, the Soviet Union, Britain, the United States, and Canada. It met in private in 1954–1957, reporting periodically both to the Disarmament Commission and the General Assembly.

From 1958 Conference machinery became established by the major powers on an ad hoc basis as "linked to but not an integral part of the United Nations," the Secretary General being represented by a Personal Representative. Among such bodies:

July 1958 A Conference of experts to study the possibility of detecting violations of a possible agreement on suspension of nuclear-weapons tests. Membership: experts from four Western countries (the United States, Britain, France, and Canada) and four Eastern European countries (the Soviet Union, Czechoslovakia, Poland, and Rumania).

October 1958 A tripartite conference began work on a treaty on the suspension of nuclear-weapons tests. Membership: the Soviet Union, the United States, and Britain. Its work ended early 1962.

1958 A conference of experts to study possible measures helpful in preventing surprise attack met on the basis of an understanding between the Soviet Union and the United States. Membership: experts from five Western countries (the United States, Britain, France, Canada, and Italy) and five Eastern European countries (the Soviet Union, Czechoslovakia, Poland, Rumania, and Albania).

1959 The Ten-Nation Committee on Disarmament, established by decision of the Foreign Ministers of France, the Soviet Union, Britain, and the United States. Membership: the sponsors and Bulgaria, Czechoslovakia, Poland, Rumania, Canada, and Italy.

1962 The Eighteen-Nation Committee on Disarmament (ENDC), established according to an agreement in 1961 by the Soviet Union and the United States, endorsed by the General Assembly Resolution, *UN Document A/RES/ 1722 (XVI)*. Membership: same as the Ten-Nation Committee, meeting since 1959, with eight nonaligned members added, namely, Brazil, Burma, Ethiopia, India, Mexico,

Nigeria, Sweden, and the United Arab Republic. France has not been participating.

1962 The aforementioned tripartite committee of 1958 was transformed into a subcommittee of ENDC, on the initiative of the nonaligned members who refused to accept its ceasing to negotiate.

1968 A conference of Non-Nuclear-Weapons States, called by the General Assembly Resolution, *UN Document A/RES/ 2346 B (XXII)*.

1970 ENDC was expanded to twenty-six members by the addition of Hungary, Mongolia, the Netherlands, Japan, Argentina, Morocco, Pakistan, and Yugoslavia. Its name was changed to the Conference of the Committee on Disarmament (CCD).

1974 CCD was expanded by the addition of the German Democratic Republic, the Federal Republic of Germany, Iran, Peru, and Zaire.

The above drawn from: United Nations, *The United Nations and Disarmament 1945–1970* (New York, 1970).

8. UN, *The United Nations and Disarmament 1945–1970*, p. 12.

9. U.S. capabilities for production were, however, in an advanced stage. See George H. Quester, *Nuclear Diplomacy: The First 25 Years* (New York: Dunellen Pub. Co., 1970).

10. United Nations, *Atomic Energy Commission, Official Records, First Meeting, Friday, 14 June 1946* (New York, 1946).

11. Dean Acheson, *Present at the Creation: My Years in the State Department* (New York: W. W. Norton & Co., 1967), p. 123. This history is thoroughly documented in Richard G. Hewlett and Oscar E. Anderson, Jr., *A History of the United States Atomic Energy Commission*, vol. 1, *The New World 1939/1946* (University Park: Pennsylvania State University Press, 1962), pp. 427 ff.

12. Acheson, *Present at the Creation*, p. 154; italics in the original. The presentation was made by Dean Acheson and Vannevar Bush, the latter then serving as Director of the Office of Scientific Research and Development.

13. Rexford G. Tugwell, *Off Course: From Truman to Nixon* (New York: Praeger Publishers, 1971); see particularly Part 5 on Truman's "five mistakes": The Bomb, Disarmament Fumble, Containment, Korea, and Assisting the French in Indo-China, pp. 181–222.

Tugwell had been close to Roosevelt from the beginning and throughout his presidency. The tenor of his judgment is reflected in one condensed sentence: "It had taken only two years after Roosevelt's death, and with Truman's management, to turn two great victorious allied powers into aggressive enemies. Russia and China. . . ." (p. 203).

It is still a controversial issue how much American policies towards the Soviet Union changed after Truman's ascendancy to the presidency. Roosevelt had towards the end of his life been deeply disturbed particularly by the

Soviet Union's actions towards Poland. But in regard to the problems discussed in the text—on the dropping of the bombs in Japan and the American position towards internationalizing the controls of atomic power—I believe Tugwell's judgment stands.

14. The matter of sanctions had been discussed by the Acheson committee: "After careful analysis we had concluded that provisions for either 'swift and sure,' or 'condign,' punishment for violation of the treaty were very dangerous words that added nothing to a treaty and were almost certain to wreck any possibility of Russian acceptance of one." Acheson, *Present at the Creation,* p. 155.

15. For full text of the final and official Baruch statement, see UN, *Atomic Energy Commission, First Meeting, Friday, 14 June 1946.* Also, Chalmers M. Roberts, *The Nuclear Years: The Arms Race and Arms Control, 1945–70* (New York: Praeger Publishers, 1970), pp. 123–133.

16. Acheson, *Present at the Creation,* p. 155.

17. Such warnings were made repeatedly, e.g., by P. M. S. Blackett, see *Atomic Weapons and East-West Relations* (Cambridge: Cambridge University Press, 1956), pp. 90–92.

18. Roberts, *The Nuclear Years,* p. 17, quoted from a 1962 interview with American journalists.

19. Acheson, *Present at the Creation,* p. 152.

20. See UN, *The United Nations and Disarmament 1945–1970,* pp. 11–24, for a succinct and detailed description.

21. See *ibid.,* p. 50, for the connection between this and the earlier proposal.

22. *Ibid.,* p. 22.

23. *Ibid.,* p. 26.

24. *Ibid.,* p. 27.

25. *Ibid.,* p. 30.

26. *Ibid.,* p. 31.

27. *Ibid.,* pp. 38 ff.

28. William R. Frye, "The Quest for Disarmament Since World War II," in Louis Henkin, ed. *Arms Control: Issues for the Public* (Englewood Cliffs, N.J.: Prentice Hall, 1961, The American Assembly, Columbia University), p. 23. The comments refer particularly to 1951 but obviously are more generally valid.

29. A driving force—intellectually and politically—behind this move was the French representative, Jules Moch, who for many years was a stalwart fighter for disarmament. In his own book, *Destin de la paix* (Paris: Mercure de France, 1969), Chapter 5, "Le Temps de L'Espoir (1953–1955)," pp. 63–77, he does not claim enough personal merit, and I am glad to pay special tribute to him here and to deplore that later we have had for so long to forgo French input in the disarmament negotiations in the Geneva Committee.

30. UN, *The United Nations and Disarmament 1945–1970,* pp. 51 ff.

31. *Ibid.,* p. 55.

32. *Ibid.,* p. 56.

33. Moch, *Destin de la paix*, p. 72. For detailed analysis, see Jean Klein, *L'Entreprise du Désarmement depuis 1945* (Paris: Editions Cujas, 1964), pp. 79 ff.

34. UN, *The United Nations and Disarmament 1945–1970*, p. 58.

35. Rita Putins Peters, *The Politics of Nonaligned States and the Nuclear Test-Ban Treaty* (Boston: Boston University Graduate School, 1973), pp. 68 and 70.

36. UN, *The United Nations and Disarmament 1945–1970*, pp. 193–195.

37. "In conclusion, the Commission wishes to advance as its view that it does not lie in the interest of our country's security policy to acquire nuclear warheads." Translated from Swedish in *Säkerhetspolitik och Försvarsutgifter: Förslag om Försvarsutgifterna 1968/72* (Stockholm: Statens Offentliga Utredningar 1968:10), p. 139. It may be mentioned that I was a member of that commission for the analysis of the Swedish position; see George H. Quester, "Sweden and the Nuclear Non-Proliferation Treaty," *Cooperation and Conflict: Nordic Studies in International Politics*, vol. 5, no. 1 (1970), pp. 52–64.

38. The Report of the Conference of Experts to Study the Possibility of Detecting Violations of a Possible Agreement on the Suspension of Nuclear Tests is available in *UN Document A/3897*, 28 August 1958.

39. See Harold Karan Jacobson and Eric Stein, *Diplomats, Scientists, and Politicians: The United States and the Nuclear Test-Ban Negotiations* (Ann Arbor: University of Michigan Press, 1966), for the very intricate and very interesting story of all these meanderings.

40. See Peters, *Politics of Nonaligned States*, and Jacobson and Stein, *Diplomats, Scientists, and Politicians*, for the inside of this turn of events. I recall a dramatic dinner when hard pressure was brought on the British Foreign Minister, Sir Alex Douglas-Home, by the Ethiopian and Swedish Foreign Ministers; as a result, the idea to continue the labors in the sub-committee form became accepted by the nuclear-weapons powers.

41. UN, *The United Nations and Disarmament 1945–1970*, pp. 222–223. The original document bears the number ENDC 128.

42. *Documents on Disarmament 1945–1959*, vol. 2, *1957–1959*, Department of State Publication no. 7008 (Washington: U.S. Government Printing Office, 1960), pp. 1108–1109.

43. Jacobson and Stein, *Diplomats, Scientists, and Politicians*, pp. 395–396.

44. *Disarmament Conference Document ENDC/PV.64*, 1 August 1962.

45. *Ibid.*

46. UN, *The United Nations and Disarmament 1945–1970*, p. 200.

47. Jacobson and Stein, *Diplomats, Scientists, and Politicians*, p. 352.

48. *Developments in Technical Capabilities for Detecting and Identifying Nuclear Weapons Tests*, Hearings Before the Joint Committee on Atomic Energy, U.S. Congress, 88th cong., 1st sess., 5, 6, 7, 8, 11, and 12 March 1963,, pp. 312, 410, 511.

49. Testimony of William C. Foster, Director of the United States Arms Control and Disarmament Agency, in *Review of Renewed Geneva Disarmament Negotiations*, Hearings Before the Senate Committee on Foreign Rela-

tions, Subcommittee on Disarmament, U.S. Congress, 87th cong., 2nd sess., 1962, p. 10, quoted in Jacobson and Stein, *Diplomats, Scientists, and Politicians*, p. 388.

50. "Science and the Citizen," *Scientific American*, September 1962, p. 99.

51. Jacobson and Stein, *Diplomats, Scientists, and Politicians*, pp. 425 ff.

52. Senator Hubert H. Humphrey has admitted this in private interview with Rita Putin Peters; see her *Politics of Nonaligned States*, p. 204.

53. However, a model is already prepared if the Great Powers wish to combine the various suggestions made by the different nonaligned nations at the Conference:

> One could take as one's point of departure the proposal made by the United Arab Republic that first an agreement should be reached that the number of inspections should be chosen somewhere between four and five annually. You remember that the positions are: of the Eastern side— 2–3; of the Western—7.
>
> Then, one could proceed with the suggestions made by the Indian delegation that while the treaty, in its entirety, be worked out on the basis of permanency, the clause on number of inspections might be submitted to periodical re-examination. And then this could be clinched with the proposal by the Swedish delegation that the number of inspections be decided, not for one year, but for a longer period. If these elements are combined and applied, for instance, for a period of five years, there stands a proposal to start renewed negotiations on the basis of a range of twenty to twenty-five inspections for five years, and to proceed to negotiate further details.

From: Alva Myrdal, "The Status of the Nuclear Test Ban Negotiations," in *Disarmament Is Possible: A Report on the Special Session on Disarmament held at the Tenth General Assembly of the World Veterans Federation, Copenhagen, May 1963* (Paris: World Veterans Federation, 1963), pp. 49–50. For the diplomatic sequences in this negotiation drama, there are several sources available besides those mentioned. Two participants have given somewhat different reports, namely, M. Samir Ahmed, "The Role of the Neutrals in the Geneva Negotiations," *Disarmament and Arms Control*, vol. 1, no. 1 (summer 1963), pp. 20–32, and Arthur S. Lall, *Negotiating Disarmament: The Eighteen Nation Disarmament Conference: The First Two Years, 1962–64* (Ithaca, N.Y.: Cornell University, Center for International Studies, 1964). I rather subscribe to the first version.

54. *Congressional Record*, vol. 109, part 12 (15 July 1974), pp. 16790–91, quoted by Harold and Stein, *Diplomats, Scientists, and Politicians*, p. 462.

55. Jacobson and Stein, *Diplomats, Scientists, and Politicians*, p. 462. See also pp. 462 ff. for an account of the Washington epilogue to the Moscow Treaty and President Kennedy's eager activities to secure ratification. See also for this, together with a very detailed account of Kennedy's and his advisers' many turnings back and forth in the planning of the move, Arthur M. Schlesinger, Jr., *A Thousand Days: John F. Kennedy in the White House* (Boston: Houghton Mifflin Co., 1965), pp. 762–770.

56. *Documents on Disarmament 1963,* United States Arms Control and Disarmament Agency Publication no. 24 (Washington: U.S. Government Printing Office, 1964), pp. 251–256.

57. "We, the majority of the world's nations, who have no nuclear weapons and conduct no tests to acquire them, consider that we are facing a breach of promise on the part of the superpowers.

"Development work on nuclear weapons with the aid of testing continued unabated; four of the five nuclear-weapons states [except Great Britain] have over this ten-year period increased their rate of such testing, in terms both of numbers and of yields. Nuclear weapons abound, and new generations of them are constantly in the offing.

"This, then, is the result of ten years of experience of the partial test ban and more than ten years of waiting since the United Nations in a majority resolution had condemned all tests and asked that all such testing should cease immediately (United Nations, General Assembly, *Resolution 1762 A [XVII]*).

"While the date 5 August 1963 is recalled with partial rejoicing, the date 5 August 1973 must be marked as a day of mourning." From: *Disarmament Conference Document CCD/PV.619,* 7 August 1973.

58. Hugo Grotius, *Mare Liberum,* first published in 1609.

59. *United Nations Conference on the Law of Sea, Final Act A/CONF. 13/L.58. United Nations Conference on the Law of the Sea, Official Records,* vol. II (Geneva, 1958), includes as annexes the texts of the four Conventions, namely: the Convention on the Territorial Sea and the Contiguous Zone; the Convention on the High Seas; the Convention on Fishing and Conservation of the Living Resources of the High Seas; and the Convention on the Continental Shelf.

60. See UN, *The United Nations and Disarmament 1945–1970,* pp. 179 ff., for the early phase of these developments. See *Pacem in Maribus,* particularly vol. 5 (to appear in 1976), and Arvid Pardo and Elisabeth Mann Borgese, *The New International Economic Order and the Law of the Sea,* International Ocean Institute Occasional Papers, no. 4 (Msida, Malta, 1976), for the later phases and the work still under discussion.

61. *UN Document A/RES/2749(XXV):* the Soviet bloc abstained on the vote on account of divergent views on the desirability of international machinery.

62. United Nations, General Assembly, *Official Records, First Committee, 1527th Meeting,* 14 November 1967.

63. UN, *The United Nations and Disarmament 1945–1970,* p. 180.

64. *Disarmament Conference Document ENDC/228, The United Nations and Disarmament 1945–1970,* p. 180.

65. *UN Document A/RES/2660(XXV).*

66. Stockholm International Peace Research Institute, *Prospects for Arms Control in the Ocean,* SIPRI Research Report no. 7 (Stockholm: Almqvist & Wiksell, 1972), p. 16.

67. *Ibid.,* pp. 16–17.

68. Alva Myrdal, "Containing the Military Threats to the Oceans," *Pacem in Maribus V, 1976,* and Alva Myrdal, "Preserving the Oceans for Peaceful

Purposes," *Académie de Droit International, Recueil des Cours,* 1971-II, pp. 1–14.

69. SIPRI, *Prospects for Arms Control in the Ocean,* and *Tactical and Strategic Antisubmarine Warfare,* SIPRI Monograph (Stockholm: Almqvist & Wiksell, 1974).

70. *UN Document A/RES/3484 E (XXX).* France and Cuba abstained, and China did not participate in the vote on the Treaty.

71. *SIPRI Yearbook 1974,* pp. 317–318.

72. Myrdal, "Preserving the Oceans for Peaceful Purposes," pp. 9–10. Italics in original.

73. Stockholm International Peace Research Institute, *Strategic Arms Limitation, Part I,* SIPRI Research Report no. 5 (Stockholm: Almqvist & Wiksell, 1972), and *Strategic Arms Limitation, Part II,* SIPRI Research Report no. 6 (Stockholm: Almqvist & Wiksell, 1972). See also consecutive *SIPRI Yearbooks.*

74. For the exact wording of SALT I, see the texts of the agreements published in United States Arms Control and Disarmament Agency, *Arms Control and Disarmament Agreements 1959–1972,* ACDA Publication no. 62 (Washington: U.S. Government Printing Office, 1972), to which was added as an "insertion" the text of *Agreed Interpretations and Unilateral Statements.*

75. *SIPRI Yearbook 1975,* pp. 38 ff., and Barnaby and Huisken, *Arms Uncontrolled,* pp. 143 ff.

76. Communiqué of 24 November 1974, with Text of Agreement, published by the White House.

77. *SIPRI Yearbook 1975,* p. 423.

78. *Disarmament Conference Document CCD/PV. 572,* 27 July 1972.

79. Barnaby and Huisken, *Arms Uncontrolled,* p. 124.

80. United Nations, General Assembly Resolution, *UN Document A/RES/2602A (XXIV),* commented on in United Nations, General Assembly, First Committee, 4 November 1970, *UN Document A/C.1/PV.1750.*

81. *SIPRI Yearbook 1976,* pp. 423–468, status as of 31 December 1975.

82. They are emerging from the Strategic Arms Limitation Talks (SALT). The most important ones are:

The *Agreement on Measures to Reduce the Risk of Outbreak of Nuclear War Between the USA and the USSR of 1971,* for notification and exchange of information in case of accidental or unauthorized detonation of a nuclear weapon.

The *Agreement on the Prevention of Incidents on and Over the High Seas of 1972;* a Protocol was added in 1973.

The *Treaty on the Limitation of Antiballistic Missile Systems of 1972,* prohibiting nationwide deployments of ABMs or their components, and limiting the actual deployments; reduced to one each by a Protocol of 1974. (Chapter IV.)

The *Interim Agreement on Certain Measures with Respect to the Limitation of Strategic Offensive Arms of 1972,* placing certain temporary limitations on numbers and types of strategic offensive nuclear arms. The originally stated intention of this agreement, to arrive by 1977 at formal limitations and even reductions, has now been postponed until 1984 (Chapter IV).

The *Agreement on the Prevention of Nuclear War of 1973,* which moves in the direction but stops considerably short of a no-first-use arrangement; it provides for consultations in case of situations that appear to involve the risk of war between the superpowers.

The *Treaty on the Limitation of Underground Nuclear Weapon Tests of 1974,* prohibits the carrying out of underground nuclear tests having a yield exceeding 150 kilotons, to become effective 31 March 1976. Its effect on the prospect of disarmament negotiations must be judged as negative (Chapter VII).

From: *SIPRI Yearbook 1975,* pp. 543–546.

83. *Conference on Security and Cooperation in Europe. Final Act. CSCE/ II/C/9,* 1 August 1975.

84. Stockholm International Peace Research Institute, *Force Reductions in Europe,* SIPRI Monograph (Stockholm: Almqvist & Wiksell, 1964), with bibliographical references. See also the consecutive *SIPRI Yearbooks.*

85. *UN Document A/RES/3484 B(XXX).* The Chairman of the Committee, which is to report in the summer of 1976, is the Swedish Under-Secretary of State, Inga Thorsson.

86. UN, *The United Nations and Disarmament 1945–1970,* p. 117.

87. *UN Document A/RES/2602E (XXIV).*

88. *Disarmament Conference Document CCD/313 and UN Document A/RES/2661C (XXV).* The Resolution was approved by 106 votes, with 10 abstentions, the Soviet bloc (except Rumania) and France.

89. Alva Myrdal, "The Game of Disarmament," *Impact of Science on Society,* vol. 22, no. 3 (July–September 1972), pp. 217–218.

PART TWO: AN ACTIVATED AGENDA FOR DISARMAMENT

CHAPTER IV
Reversing the Arms Race

1. Private communication from Bertrand Russell.

2. SIPRI press release, 12 June 1975.

3. Herbert York, "Nuclear Deterrence: How to Reduce the Overkill," Fred Warner Neal and Mary Kersey Harvey, eds., *Pacem in Terris III,* vol. II (Santa Barbara, Calif.: Center for the Study of Democratic Institutions, 1974), p. 26.

4. See, e.g., Maxwell Taylor, *The Uncertain Trumpet* (New York: Harper & Brothers, 1960).

5. Fred Charles Iklé, "Can Nuclear Deterrence Last Out the Century?," *Foreign Affairs,* January 1973, pp. 266–285. Here quoted from a more complete version of the paper, published by California Arms Control and Foreign Policy Seminar, January 1973. This version is accompanied by a number of highly informative notes. Only Iklé's criticism of established doctrines is here in focus, not his apparent preference for turning towards a new selective, counterforce strategy.

6. York, "Nuclear Deterrence," p. 26.

7. Paul Doty, "Testimony Before the Committee on Foreign Relations, United States Senate, 12 September 1974," pp. 5–6 in Doty's manuscript.

8. York, "Nuclear Deterrence," pp. 27–29. Italics in original.

9. United States, *Congressional Record—Senate,* 17 January 1975, p. S462.

10. *Ibid.,* p. S463.

11. I have noticed that high United States officials, having dealt with defense and foreign policy matters, often become quite outspoken once they resign and join the critical experts.

12. Marshall Shulman, "Détente and Re-forming the World," *Worldview,* vol. 18, no. 6 (June 1975), pp. 34–35.

13. U.S. Department of Defense, *Report of Secretary of Defense James R. Schlesinger to the Congress on the FY 1976 and Transition Budgets, FY 1977 Authorization Request and FY 1976–1980 Defense Programs, 5 February 1975* (Washington: U.S. Government Printing Office, 1975), p. II-7.

14. *International Herald Tribune,* 2 September 1975.

15. Statement made in the United States Senate by Henry M. Jackson, 4 December 1973. Here quoted from his article "A SALT II Disarmament Plan," *War/Peace Report,* vol. 13, no. 1 (June 1974), pp. 8–11.

16. See, e.g., Gene R. La Roque and David Johnson, "Toward a Realistic Military Budget," (summary in) *Center Report,* vol. 8, no. 2 (April 1975); York, "Nuclear Deterrence," p. 31; G. W. Rathjens, *Paper to the 25th Pugwash Symposium,* 1975, summarized in *Pugwash Newsletter,* vol. 13, no. 2 (October 1975); and others in the same publication: Doty, "Testimony," p. 14, Herbert Scoville, Jr., "The Limitation of Offensive Weapons," *Scientific American,* January 1971, pp. 15–25.

17. Iklé, "Can Nuclear Deterrence Last Out the Century?," p. 15.

18. A draft for an Additional Protocol II to the Treaty on the Non-Proliferation of Nuclear Weapons proposed that the Depositary Powers undertake "as soon as the number of Parties to the Treaty has reached one hundred: to reduce by fifty percent the ceiling of 2,400 nuclear strategic delivery vehicles contemplated for each side under the Vladivostok accords, likewise the number of missiles which may be MIRVed, and then, each time ten additional states become members, reduce these ceilings by ten percent." See also Chapter VI under Draft Protocol I, Section 4.

19. United Nations, General Assembly, *Resolution 3261C(XXIX),* 9 December 1974.

20. United Nations, General Assembly, *Resolution 3484C(XXX),* 12 December 1975.

21. Stockholm International Peace Research Institute, *World Armaments and Disarmament, SIPRI Yearbook 1974* (Stockholm: Almqvist & Wiksell, 1974), pp. 103–122. See also *SIPRI Yearbook 1975,* pp. 311–377; *SIPRI Yearbook 1796,* pp. 11–14; and Stockholm International Peace Research Institute, *Stockholm Paper 5: Offensive Missiles* (Stockholm: Almqvist & Wiksell, 1974), pp. 29–33.

22. *SIPRI Yearbook 1975,* p. 39.

23. *Ibid.,* p. 38.

24. *Ibid.,* p. 604.

25. *Ibid.,* pp. 11–14, 38–46. In order not to take up too much space nor

risk falling into the pitfalls of technicalities, I refer the reader to the consecutive, watchful comments from year to year in the *SIPRI Yearbooks.*

26. *Ibid.,* p. 39.

27. *Ibid.,* p. 41.

28. Stockholm International Peace Research Institute, *Tactical and Strategic Antisubmarine Warfare,* SIPRI Monograph (Stockholm: Almqvist & Wiksell, 1974).

"The term 'antisubmarine warfare' (ASW) might in a way be slightly misleading, as the term refers to the whole field of surveillance, not restricted to attack each other, or to the use of submarines as launchers for strategic or tactical attacks against 'enemy' territory." Frank C. Barnaby, *Pacem in Maribus V,* 1976, pp. 94–96 (to be published).

29. Frank Barnaby, "Changing Nuclear Myths," *New Scientist,* vol. 69, no. 983 (15 January 1976), pp. 128–129.

30. Alva Myrdal, "Preserving the Oceans for Peaceful Purposes," Académie de Droit International, *Recueil Des Cours: Collected Courses of the Hague Academy of International Law 1971,* II (Leyden: Sijthoff, 1972), pp. 1–14. See also Edvard Hambro in the Norwegian journal *Lov og Rett: Norsk Juridisk Tidsskrift,* no. 4 (1963), pp. 167–171.

31. *Eighteen Nation Disarmament Conference Document ENDC/PV.202,* 28 July 1964. This was the major substantive speech, made after the Swedish delegation had welcomed the Gromyko proposal in the General Assembly First Committee, 30 October 1963.

32. *Ibid.*

33. *Ibid.*

CHAPTER V

Stemming the Conventional Arms Rush

1. No fixed boundary line can be drawn between nuclear and conventional weapons as several of the newer, most costly weapons systems are double-purpose. Missiles can be fitted with nuclear or non-nuclear warheads and are, up to short-range ballistic missiles, produced and sold as conventional.

2. *SIPRI Yearbook 1976,* pp. 16–20.

3. *International Herald Tribune,* 8 July 1975.

4. Bundesrat Bericht über die Sicherheitspolitik der Schweiz vom 27. July 1973, as quoted in *Neue Wege: Zeitkritische Monatsblätter* (Zurich), February 1974, p. 47 (author's translation).

5. *SIPRI Yearbook 1975,* p. 153 and chart 7.1, p. 150.

6. *Ibid.,* p. 195.

7. *Ibid.,* p. 196.

8. *Ibid.,* p. 152.

9. *Ibid.,* p. 191 and table 8B.2, p. 220. Latest figures in *SIPRI Yearbook 1976,* p. 16 and p. 138. The detailed SIPRI estimates are conservative. It should be recalled that they encompass only major weapons systems—tanks, aircraft, vessels, missiles—and only those transfers going to Third World countries. Further, they are based on actual deliveries during the year in question. These facts explain the seeming discrepancies in relation to figures presented

elsewhere. Official United States estimates are given in U.S. Arms Control and Disarmament Agency, *World Military Expenditures and Arms Trade 1963–1973*, ACDA Publication no. 74 (Washington: U.S. Government Printing Office, 1975), pp. 72–77. Its estimate for the world trade in arms was $8.7 billion in 1973, referring to total global sales and based on sales programs when purchases are contracted. Estimates currently rise sharply; a U.S. estimate for 1974, quoted in *SIPRI Yearbook 1975*, pp. 191–192, gives the totals for U.S. sales as $8 billion and for the Soviet Union as $3 billion. The U.S. estimate was raised to nearly $11 billion in August 1975. News media abound with more recent and ever more stupendously high figures for the world trade arms.

A basic source book, although the series ended in 1971, is Stockholm International Peace Research Institute, *The Arms Trade with the Third World* (Stockholm, Almqvist & Wiksell; New York: Humanities Press, 1971). The U.S. Arms Control and Disarmament Agency (ACDA) has also published a detailed report, although less analytical; its series also ended in 1971: *The International Transfer of Conventional Arms: A Report to the Congress from the U.S. Arms Control and Disarmament Agency*, U.S. Congress, Committee on Foreign Affairs, 93rd cong., 2nd sess., 12 April 1974. An older but more analytical study is Amelia C. Leiss *et al.*, "Arms Transfers to Less Developed Countries," *Arms Control and Local Conflict* (Cambridge: Center for International Studies, Massachusetts Institute of Technology, 1970), (C/70-1) vol. 3.

10. Stockholm International Peace Research Institute, *Oil and Security*, SIPRI Monograph (Stockholm: Almqvist & Wiksell, 1974), pp. 104–115.

11. *SIPRI Yearbook 1975*, pp. 198–203.

12. "Global Growth in Guns," *Time* Magazine, 11 March 1974, p. 87.

13. Derived from tables in ACDA, *World Military Expenditures and Arms Trade 1963–1973* (see note 9 above).

14. *SIPRI Yearbook 1975*, pp. 220–221. West Germany's sales to Latin America are larger than those of the United States. It exports submarines and high-speed boats to the Third World. European countries have on the whole sold more high-performance weapons than the United States.

15. The League of Nations' Preparatory Commission for the Disarmament Conference of 1932 made the recommendation for publishing military budgets in a draft convention, which was elaborated by a group of budget experts. The recommendation was tested on some budgets, the data obtained were analyzed, and a beginning of regular submission of budgets was made. See United Nations, *Reduction of the Military Budgets of States Permanent Members of the Security Council by 10 Percent and Utilization of Part of the Funds thus Saved to Provide Assistance to Developing Countries. Report of the Secretary General* (New York, 1974), *UN Document A/9770*, 14 October 1974, Annex II, pp. 15–16. In regard to reporting on arms production and trade, considerable work was also done by the League of Nations, supervision of such trade having been one of the recommendations already in the League's Covenant. Strong recommendations for both supervision of and publication about arms manufacture and trade were made by the French and American delegations. The *Statistical Yearbook of the League of Nations*

was first compiled in 1925; in its last edition of 1938 "it contained particulars of the international trade in arms and ammunition of 60 countries and 64 colonies, protectorates and mandated territories." SIPRI, *The Arms Trade with the Third World*, p. 94; section from pp. 86–100.

16. *Eighteen Nation Disarmament Conference Document ENDC/PV.156*, 29 August 1963.

17. *Disarmament Conference Document CCD/421*, 14 May 1974.

18. *Conference on Security and Cooperation in Europe Documents CSCE/ II/C/9*. Swedish proposals, made in a statement of 28 September 1973, were accompanied by detailed comments as to possible models. *Working Document CSCE/II/C/9*. The success has so far been minimal. No recommendation to this effect appeared in the *Final Act*, signed in Helsinki, 1 August 1975.

19. UN, *Reduction of the Military Budgets, A/9770*, 14 October 1974, p. 5.

20. United Nations, General Assembly, *Resolution 3463(XXX)*, 11 December 1975. 108 voted for, China and Albania voted against, 21 members abstained: the United States and its allies in NATO and the Soviet Union and its allies.

21. SIPRI, which in 1971 published its comprehensive study *The Arms Trade with the Third World*, is following it up with chapters in the consecutive yearbooks and is supplementing the information with its detailed *Arms Trade Registers: The Arms Trade with the Third World* (Stockholm: Almqvist & Wiksell, 1975).

22. Philip Noel-Baker, *The Arms Race* (London: John Calder, 1958), pp. 393–403.

23. This "Swedish profile" has been strongly advocated by Anders Thunborg, Chairman of the Swedish Parliamentary Commission, in *Doktrinutveckling och försvarsekonomi* [The evolution of doctrines and the economics of defense] (Stockholm: Swedish Ministry of Defense, 1973), pp. 54–56.

24. United Nations, *Disarmament and Development: Report of the Group of Experts on the Economic and Social Consequences of Disarmament* (New York, 1972), p. 24.

25. *Ibid.*, pp. 11–12.

26. Dieter Senghaas, "Arms Race by Arms Control," *Bulletin of Peace Proposals*, 1973.

27. U.S. Arms Control and Disarmament Agency, *The Economic Impact of Reductions in Defense Spending* (Washington: U.S. Government Printing Office, 1972), p. 3.

28. *Report of the Committee on the Economic Impact of Defense and Disarmament, July 1965* (Washington: U.S. Government Printing Office, 1965), p. 17.

29. U.S. Senate *Resolution S.1285*, 1969.

30. George McGovern, "Back to the Drawing Boards: Nth Round in the Arms Race," *Center Report*, vol. V, no. 2 (April 1972), p. 7. Italics added.

31. For Bofors, popularly symbolizing the Swedish war industry, the military component of its sales in 1973–74 was 17 percent; for SAAB, with its military aircraft production, 15 percent; for Kockums, producing i.a. submarines, 2 percent; for Volvo, with military vehicles, and LM Ericsson,

with electronics, 3 percent. *Försvarsindustriella problem* [Defense industry problems], Report Presented to the Defense Committee, Swedish Department of Defense, 1975. Recent reductions in defense orders have been compensated by other production and the normal rate of retirement of staff.

32. UN, *Disarmament and Development,* pp. 16–18.

33. *Ibid.,* p. 14. The 1972 UN Reports will be updated in 1976.

34. *Ibid.,* pp. 14–15.

35. *Ibid.,* p. 15.

36. *Ibid.,* p. 1. Italics added.

37. *Ibid.,* p. 14.

38. *Ibid.,* pp. 15–16.

39. SIPRI, *Resources Devoted to Military Research and Development* (Stockholm: Almqvist & Wiksell, 1972). See also *Program of Research, Development, Test and Evaluation, FY 1975,* U.S. Congress, 93rd cong., 2nd sess., 26–27 February 1974, raising the request to over $10 billion (instead of the $8 billion mentioned in the literature quoted above).

40. United Nations, Department of Economic and Social Affairs, *World Plan of Action for the Application of Science and Technology to Development,* Prepared by the Advisory Committee on the Application of Science and Technology to Development for the Second United Nations Development Decade (New York, 1971).

41. Frank Barnaby, "The Spread of the Capability to Do Violence: An Introduction to Environmental Warfare," *Ambio,* vol. IV, nos. 5–6 (1975), pp. 178–185, table 4, p. 181.

42. Quoted after Richard J. Barnet, *The Economy of Death* (New York: Atheneum Publishers, 1969), p. 9.

CHAPTER VI
Barring the Spread of Nuclear Weapons

1. For the debates, or even quarrels, inside the group of American and British experts on the "ethical" problems before and after the doors to bomb production were opened, see the valuable collection *Arms Control: Readings from Scientific American,* ed. and commentary by Herbert F. York, (San Francisco: W. H. Freeman & Co., Publishers, 1973). See also Herbert F. York, *The Advisors: Oppenheimer, Teller and the Super Bomb* (read in manuscript February 1975).

2. Henry D. Smyth, *Atomic Energy for Military Purposes: The Official Report on the Development of the Atomic Bomb Under the Auspices of the United States Government, 1940–1945* (Princeton, N.J.: Princeton University Press, 1945). This was the first official report, eagerly read also in the Soviet Union.

3. The American-British relations were for a long time puzzling. For examples of eyewitness accounts, see Leonard Bertin, *Atom Harvest* (London: Secker & Warburg, 1955), and Bertrand Goldschmidt, *L'Aventure atomique: Ses Aspects Politiques et Techniques* (Paris: Fayard, 1962). See also Margaret Gowing (historian of the British Atomic Energy Agency), *Britain and Atomic Energy, 1939–1945* (London: Macmillan & Co.; and

New York: St. Martin's Press, 1964), and Andrew J. Pierre, *Nuclear Politics: The British Experience with an Independent Strategic Force 1939–1970* (London: Oxford University Press, 1972). Autobiographical books by Dean Acheson, Vannevar Bush, General Groves (the leader of the Manhattan project), and many others including Winston Churchill give valuable glimpses of how this top scientific drama evolved. Official recording of the British contribution is available from August 1945 from the British Information Service and the corresponding Canadian Service, published as appendices to Smyth, *Atomic Energy for Military Purposes.*

4. Vannevar Bush, *Pieces of the Action* (New York: William Morrow & Co., 1970), p. 95: "There is a contention, perhaps just a myth, which Robert Oppenheimer often cited, that if one puts two scorpions in a bottle they will fight, but if they get into a position where each could sting the other, they will withdraw."

5. Pierre, *Nuclear Politics,* pp. 161–216. The earlier and later chapters are of interest for understanding British ideas for a semi-independent nuclear arms strategy.

6. Bertrand Goldschmidt, *L'Aventure atomique,* p. 116.

7. *Ibid.,* p. 96.

8. *Eighteen Nation Disarmament Conference Document ENDC/PV.222,* 10 August 1965.

9. Pierre, *Nuclear Politics,* p. 49.

10. *Ibid.,* p. 181. (House of Commons debate, March 1960, 618 H.C. Deb. col. 1135-9.)

11. After the Labour Party's victory in the 1974 elections, Gunnar Myrdal, Lord Ritchie-Calder, and I appealed to Prime Minister Harold Wilson to take the first step of renunciation of British nuclear weapons, but the answer was no (private communication). Wilson had previously, in 1964, promised "initiatives in disarmament." See Nicholas A. Sims, *Disarmament: An Analysis for Quakers* (London: Headley Brothers, 1967), p. 41.

12. Lawrence Scheinman, *Atomic Energy Policy in France Under the Fourth Republic* (Princeton, N.J.: Princeton University Press, 1965), p. 119.

13. See the official statement by the Government of the People's Republic of China, *People of the World, Unite and Struggle for the Complete Prohibition and Thorough Destruction of Nuclear Weapons!* (Peking: Foreign Languages Press, 1971). See also documentation on China's programs in *SIPRI Yearbook 1976, passim.*

14. Pierre, *Nuclear Politics,* p. 180, quoting *Disarmament and Nuclear War: The Next Step,* Declaration by the Labour Party and the Trades Union Congress, Transport House, 24 June 1959:

> Noting that Britain had a special responsibility as the third nuclear power and that it was in a unique position to persuade nations not yet in possession of nuclear weapons to desist from acquiring them, Labour proposed that every nation with the exception of the United States and the Soviet Union sign an agreement, preferably under the auspices of the United Nations, pledging itself not to test, manufacture, or possess nuclear weapons. This agreement would be subject to full and effective interna-

tional controls. If such an agreement could be negotiated, Britain would not only have to stop the manufacture of nuclear weapons but would also have to give up those in her possession.

15. Pierre's account continues with many specimens of radical reasoning, including this one by Richard Crossman: "How can we possibly prevent the Germans, the French, and every other nation in the alliance saying—'What the British demand for themselves we demand for ourselves?' The right to distrust the Americans cannot remain a British monopoly" (583 *Parliamentary Debates, House of Commons* 634 [27 February 1958]. Pierre, *Nuclear Politics*, p. 212.

16. United Nations, *The United Nations and Disarmament 1945–1970* (New York, 1970), p. 269.

17. *Ibid.*, p. 275. See *Eighteen Nation Disarmament Committee Document ENDC 158*.

18. United Nations, General Assembly, First Committee, *A/C.1/L.338*, 27 October 1965.

19. Detailed and up-to-date records of which States have entered into what kind of safeguards agreement with IAEA—the more stringent, comprehensive terms of agreements under NPT or the more lenient, partial regular IAEA agreements—are to be found in SIPRI yearbooks. For background information and explanations see *Safeguards Against Nuclear Proliferation*, A SIPRI Monograph (Stockholm: Almqvist & Wiksell; Cambridge, Mass.: MIT Press, 1975).

20. See *Eighteen Nation Disarmament Committee Document ENDC/215*, 8 February 1968, for author's criticism that the undertaking was not made part of the Treaty.

21. SIPRI press release, 19 May 1974. See also report by the International Atomic Energy Agency on *Activities Under Article IV of the NPT*, submitted to the Preparatory Committee for the Review of the Parties to the Treaty on the Non-Proliferation of Nuclear Weapons Conference, *Document NPT/PC.11/6*, 12 July 1974.

22. Anne W. Marks, ed., *NPT: Paradoxes and Problems* (Washington: Arms Control Association, Carnegie Endowment for International Peace, 1975), p. 5.

23. A number of lists of potential nuclear nations have appeared over the years. They are in agreement on at least fifteen States. Lloyd Jensen, *Return from the Nuclear Brink* (Lexington, Mass.: D. C. Heath & Co., 1974), p. 84. Mason Willrich and Theodore B. Taylor, *Nuclear Theft: Risks and Safeguards* (Cambridge, Mass.: Ballinger Publishing Co., 1974), p. 197, list twenty-nine as foreseen for 1980, Japan and West Germany with more installed nuclear power than Britain, the Soviet Union, or France. SIPRI gives the most recent enumeration of the countries which have had nuclear power reactors installed (nineteen at the end of 1974) or under construction (six more) or planned before 1980 (three more). At the end of this decade they will have a "total electrical generating capacity of about 300,000 MWE, about fifteen times the 1970 figure," all with an inevitable by-product of huge quantities of plutonium. *SIPRI Yearbook 1975*, p. 23.

24. E. L. M. Burns, *A Seat at the Table* (Toronto: Clarke, Irwin & Co., 1972), p. 208, referring to an authoritative White Paper on Defense, March 1964.

25. "In conclusion, the Commission wishes to advance as its view that it does not lie in the interest of our country's security policy to acquire nuclear warheads." Translated from the Swedish *Säkerhetspolitik och försvarsutgifter: Förslag om Försvarsutgifterna 1968/72* (Stockholm: Statens Offentliga Utredningar, 1968:10), p. 139. The author was a member of the Commission. For an analysis of the Swedish position, see George H. Quester, "Sweden and the Nuclear Non-Proliferation Treaty," *Cooperation and Conflict: Nordic Studies in International Politics,* vol. 5, no. 1 (1970), pp. 52–64.

26. They had been holding out, even if not on political grounds, to get EURATOM, a regional organization authorized to conduct the immediate verification, to be only indirectly accountable to IAEA.

27. SIPRI, *The Near-Nuclear Countries and the NPT* (Stockholm: Almqvist & Wiksell, 1972), a penetrating case-by-case study.

28. The author cannot refrain from quoting a question she posed nearly ten years ago to the consciences of Britain and France for the examples they set, which the world so lightheartedly seems to condone. Alas, their silence continues to be ominous:

> [We may admit] that "the titanic two . . . are in a special category in regard to nuclear weapons, as being responsible for [the] balance of deterrence. [But if all admit that it is desirable that no further states obtain nuclear weapons] what are the arguments for national control of nuclear weapons in the cases of the other three . . . nuclear weapons Powers . . . we must be aware that in [domestic] political discussions . . . at least in Europe, those who argue for production or acquisition of nuclear weapons, or at any rate for retaining the nuclear option, draw much of their support precisely from the argumentation in the [European] nuclear-weapons countries. . . .

From *Eighteen Nation Disarmament Committee Document, ENDC/PV.243,* 24 February 1966.

29. *Final Document of the Review Conference of the Parties to the Treaty on the Non-Proliferation of Nuclear Weapons, NPT/CONF/35/I–III* (Geneva, 1975).

30. *Ibid., NPT/CONF/35/I, Annex I,* Final Declaration, p. 8.

31. *Ibid.,* Annex II, Interpretative Statements, p. 33.

32. *Ibid., Annex III, Draft Resolutions.*

33. *Ibid.,* Annex I, Final Declaration, p. 1.

34. *Ibid.,* Annex I, Final Declaration, p. 4. The Chairman of the Review Conference, Inga Thorsson, stated, when narrating the story of the Conference to the Swedish Parliament: "It is no exaggeration to state that the Conference rather evolved to become a propaganda Conference for expansion of nuclear energy production in the world"! *Snabbprotokoll från utriksdebatten* [Record of foreign policy debate], 16 January 1976, p. 20.

35. For a detailed description of the alternatives see Willrich and Taylor, *Nuclear Theft* (see note 23).

36. United Nations, General Assembly, First Committee, *A/C.1/PV.1998,* 21 October 1974. Hiroshima is conventionally used as an off-hand measure of simple bombs; Nagasaki would be more appropriate as it was based on plutonium.

37. SIPRI, *The Nuclear Age* (Stockholm: Almqvist & Wiksell, 1975), pp. 79–82.

38. Willrich and Taylor, *Nuclear Theft,* pp. 26–27.

39. B. T. Feld, T. Greenwood, G. W. Rathjens, and S. Weinberg, eds., *Impact of New Technologies on the Arms Race,* A Pugwash Monograph (Cambridge, Mass.: MIT Press, 1971), pp. 137–138, where a discussion on this matter is reported as follows:

> I [J. Carson Mark] should like to mention a comment of Dr. Prawitz of the National Research Institute of Defense in Stockholm [FOA] . . . that a colleague . . . has become persuaded that he could produce a nuclear explosion from essentially any grade of reactor-produced plutonium that might be available. . . . I can only assume that by "nuclear explosion" [is meant] an explosion of at least three orders of magnitude more energy per pound than would be available from high explosives. . . . I have no reason to question such a conclusion, and I would like to warn people . . . that the . . . notion that reactor-grade plutonium is incapable of producing nuclear explosions [has] been dangerously exaggerated.

40. See SIPRI, *Nuclear Proliferation Problems* (Stockholm: Almqvist & Wiksell, 1974), pp. 93 ff. and 102 ff., for technical discussion and considerable details for individual countries.

41. Marks, *NPT: Paradoxes and Problems,* pp. 55–73.

42. The Federal Republic of Germany is committed by the Treaty of Brussels of 23 October 1954 "not to manufacture on its territory atomic, biological, and chemical weapons." Article 1, Part 1 of Protocol III (On the Control of Armaments) of 23 October 1954, modifying and completing the Treaty of Brussels of 17 March 1948 (211 *United Nations Treaty Series* 364). Neither the United States nor the Soviet Union are parties to this treaty. The Peace Treaties with Austria, Bulgaria, Hungary, Finland, Italy, and Rumania contain clauses prohibiting these States to possess, test, or manufacture nuclear weapons. From Eric Stein, "Impact of New Weapons Technology on International Law: Selected Aspects," *Recueil des Cours: Collected Courses of the Hague Academy of International Law* (Leyden: Sijthoff, 1972), note 76, p. 332.

43. *Yearbook of the United Nations, 1968* (New York: United Nations Office of Public Information, 1971), p. 21. In 1961 the United Nations had, in *General Assembly Resolution 1653 (XVI),* voted a declaration that any use of nuclear weapons violated the charter of the United Nations and was to be considered "as acting contrary to the laws of humanity and as committing a crime against mankind and civilization." This, however, cannot be considered a pledge, as only one nuclear-weapons power voted in favor, the Soviet Union with fifty-four other nations, while twenty voted against, including the United States and Britain; twenty-six abstained.

44. *Eighteen Nation Disarmament Conference Document ENDC/PV.222*, 10 August 1965.

45. *Final Document of the Review Conference*, Annex II, p. 11.

46. *Ibid.*, Annex I, pp. 9–10. When the Charter is referred to it may be noted that the 1972 resolution on permanent prohibition against the use of nuclear weapons is not mentioned, nor its many predecessors, e.g., in 1961, as it was accepted with a fairly narrow majority of votes, led by the Soviet Union as the sponsor (*General Assembly Resolution 2936 (XXVII)*.

47. *Eighteen Nation Disarmament Conference Document ENDC/PV.300*, 30 May 1967. (Italics added.)

48. *Eighteen Nation Disarmament Conference Document ENDC/PV.363*, 8 February 1968.

49. SIPRI, *Safeguards Against Nuclear Proliferation*.

50. Transfers from and activities at processing plants are now not submitted to IAEA control.

51. Marks, ed., *NPT: Paradoxes and Problems,* pp. 55–73. See editor's postscript, p. 14: "Enormous political and economic benefits, along with an equal reduction in the risk of nuclear weapon proliferation, can result from such arrangements." See also William O. Doub and Joseph M. Dukert, "Making Nuclear Energy Safe and Secure," *Foreign Affairs,* July 1975, pp. 756–772.

52. *Final Document of the Review Conference*, Annex I, p. 6.

53. Marks, ed., *NPT: Paradoxes and Problems,* pp. 8–9.

54. *Final Document of the Review Conference*, Annex I, p. 5.

55. United Nations, General Assembly, First Committee, *A/C.1/PV.2025*, 20 November 1974.

56. United Nations, General Assembly, First Committee, *A/C.1/PV.2000*, 25 October 1974. See also statement in United Nations, General Assembly, First Committee, *A/C.1/PV.2075*, 3 November 1975.

57. United Nations, General Assembly, First Committee, *A/C.1/PV.2000*, 25 October 1974.

58. Regions and zones are here used without delineation or even definition. For a more sophisticated treatment of the concept region, see Philip E. Jacob and Alexine L. Atherton, *The Dynamics of International Organization: The Making of World Order,* rev. ed. (Homewood, Ill.: Dorsey Press, 1972), Chapter 5.

59. *United Nations General Assembly Resolution 3261F(XXIX)*, 9 December 1974.

60. *Study of the Question of Nuclear-Weapon-Free Zones in All of Its Aspects,* Geneva Disarmament Conference Document CCD/467, 18 August 1975.

61. *The Implementation of International Disarmament Agreements,* (Stockholm: Almqvist & Wiksell, 1973, Stockholm International Peace Research Institute). See also ACDA, *Arms Control and Disarmament Agreements 1959–1972* (Washington: U.S. Government Printing Office, 1972, U.S. Arms Control and Disarmament Agency Publication 62).

62. UN, *The United Nations and Disarmament 1945–1970,* p. 264.

63. *Ibid.*

64. A good general survey of early plans is given by Philip Noel-Baker in *The Arms Race* (London: John Calder, 1958). A more complete account of the politically important postwar plans is given by Michael Howard, *Disengagement in Europe* (Harmondsworth: Penguin Books, 1958), pp. 26–38. *See also* memoirs by Dean Acheson, Anthony Eden, and Winston Churchill.

65. *Geneva Conference of Heads of Governments, 18–23 July 1955,* (cmnd 9543, HMSO 1955), p. 18.

66. Anthony Eden, *The Eden Memoirs:* Part III, *Full Circle* (London: Cassell, 1960), pp. 295–311.

67. *Ibid.*

68. Quoted by Howard, *Disengagement in Europe,* p. 36 (see Note 64).

69. The original Rapacki plan is presented in UN, *The United Nations and Disarmament 1945–1970,* p. 328. It had been preceded by a Soviet Proposal to the Sub-Committee of the Disarmament Commission of the United Nations in 1956 (*Official Records,* January to December 1956).

70. Statement by the Finnish delegation at the *United Nations General Assembly, First Committee, A/C.1/PV.1882,* 2 November 1972.

71. Conference on Security and Cooperation in Europe, *Final Act,* Document CSCE/11/C/9, 1 August 1975.

72. The Treaty and its two Protocols can be found in SIPRI, *The Implementation of International Disarmament Agreements,* pp. 19 ff.

73. UN, *The United Nations and Disarmament 1945–1970,* p. 327.

74. Y. Tomilin, "Nuclear-Free Zones: How to Make them Effective," *International Affairs* (Moscow), no. 8, August 1975, p. 71.

75. *The Arms Trade with the Third World* (Stockholm: Almqvist & Wiksell, 1971, Stockholm International Peace Research Institute), pp. 691 ff., and *Arms Trade Registers:* The Arms Trade with the Third World (Stockholm: Almqvist & Wiksell, 1975, Stockholm International Peace Research Institute.)

76. UN, *The United Nations and Disarmament 1945–1970,* p. 330.

77. *United Nations General Assembly Resolution 3261E(XXIX),* 9 December 1974. *See also 3471(XXX),* 11 December 1975.

78. *Disarmament Conference Document CCD/467,* 18 August 1975, pp. 16–17.

79. *United Nations General Assembly Resolution 3263(XXIX),* 9 December 1974.

80. *United Nations General Assembly Resolution 3265 A and B(XXIX),* 9 December 1974, and *United Nations A/Res/3476 A and B(XXX),* 11 December 1975.

81. For details see *Disarmament Conference Document CCD/467,* 18 August 1975, pp. 21–23.

82. *United Nations General Assembly Resolution 2832(XXVI),* 16 December 1971. The phrase quoted has appeared in several later resolutions. The latest resolution, *A/RES/3468(XXX),* 11 December 1975, is, however, more formal in character.

83. *Proposed Expansion of US Military Facilities in the Indian Ocean,* Hearings Before the Subcommittee on the Near East and South Asia of the Committee on Foreign Affairs, House of Representatives, Ninety-third Congress, Second Session; February 21, March 6, 12, 14, and 20, 1974, (Washington: U.S. Government Printing Office, 1974). In the Senate the fight against expansion is led by Senators like Culver, Mansfield, Kennedy, and Pell.

84. *SIPRI Yearbook 1975,* pp. 60–91.

CHAPTER VII
Closing the Loopholes for Nuclear-Weapons Testing

1. *SIPRI Yearbook 1975,* p. 409. See also new Swedish statement in CCD, 29 July 1976, now proposing a provisional limit of ten kilotons.

2. The Soviet delegate, who then praised the bilateral threshold treaty, three years earlier was quoted in the *Disarmament Conference Document CCD/PV.651,* 13 August 1974, as having said: "It must be admitted that such an approach would not provide a solution of the problem of banning underground nuclear-weapons tests, nor would it create more favourable prospects for progress towards its solution. We share the doubts of a number of delegations—Sweden, the United Arab Republic, Ethiopia, and the Netherlands—about the effectiveness of the 'threshold' approach as such. In particular we recognize the cogency of the arguments advanced by the representative of Sweden, Mrs. Myrdal, against the proposal to establish a 'threshold.' "

3. American Academy of Arts and Sciences, *Bulletin,* vol. XXVIII, no. 1, October 1974.

4. The first quotation is from the *Congressional Record,* Senate, 20 February 1973, p. S2761; the second [press release] from the office of Senator Edward M. Kennedy, 20 May 1975, entitled, Statement by Senator Edward M. Kennedy on Introducing a Resolution Urging the Negotiation of a Comprehensive Test Ban Treaty.

5. *Seismic Methods for Monitoring Underground Explosions,* Stockholm Papers 2 (Stockholm: Almqvist & Wiksell, 1969, Stockholm International Peace Research Institute). On application of decision theory, pp. 86–87. See also Ulf Ericsson, "Identification of Underground Nuclear Explosions and Earthquakes," FOA Reports, vol. 5, no. 8, December 1971 (Stockholm: Research Institute of National Defense).

6. *Disarmament Conference Document CCD/PV.600,* 12 April 1973.

7. Ulf Ericsson, "The Non-Controversial Use of Nuclear Explosions for Peaceful Purposes," *Cooperation and Conflict, Nordic Studies in International Politics,* vol. v, no. 1, 1970, p. 12. In this concentrated technical paper, a seven-point checklist is given; clear indications of military use appear at the end, the first listed indicate the possibility of concealing military applications, especially (a) to (c). The following are single or simultaneous purposes of nuclear-weapons tests:

(a) basic development of a nuclear explosive;
(b) refinement of existing nuclear explosives;
(c) proof testing of weapons in stock or of factory deliveries;
(d) system tests of the weapon, together with its delivery system;
(e) training of personnel designated to handle nuclear weapons in war;
(f) training of supporting troops;
(g) study of the effects on military targets.

8. Edward Teller, Wilson K. Talley, Gary H. Higgins, Gerald W. John-son, *The Constructive Uses of Nuclear Explosives* (New York: McGraw-Hill, 1968), p. 21.

9. ACDA, *An Analysis of the Economic Feasibility, Technical Significance, and Time Scale for Application of Peaceful Nuclear Explosions in the U.S.* (Ithaca: Cornell University, April 1975). The outlook resulting from this conscientious study is not promising from technical or economic points of view, the environmental risks are underscored; one state, Colorado, has introduced a constitutional ban on nuclear explosions.

10. V. A. Emelyanov, "On the Peaceful Use of Nuclear Explosions," *Nuclear Proliferation Problems* (Stockholm: Almqvist & Wiksell, 1974, Stockholm International Peace Research Institute), p. 215.

11. Observations in Sweden were reported by me in *CCD/PV.513,* 4 May 1971. For complete records, B. Bernström, *Radioactivity from nuclear weapons in air and precipitation in Sweden from mid-year 1968 to mid-year 1972* (Stockholm: FOA, 1974, Research Institute of National Defense). The occurrence of venting is rarely admitted by the testing powers. It is, however, a serious deficiency in the Moscow treaty, which was expected to close up radioactivity. President Kennedy was so keenly aware of this defect that he, before the Partial Test-Ban Treaty was concluded, would have preferred a comprehensive ban. In one year, September 1961 to September 1962, there were seventeen cases of discharge of radioactive debris into the atmosphere at one testing site alone. According to his historian Arthur M. Schlesinger, Jr., President Kennedy was ironical, "All the tests seemed to have proved was the need for more tests." *A Thousand Days: John F. Kennedy in the White House* (Boston: Houghton Mifflin Co., 1965), p. 763.

12. Herbert Scoville, Jr., "Peaceful Nuclear Explosions—An Invitation to Proliferation," in Anne W. Marks, ed., *NPT: Paradoxes and Problems* (Washington, The Arms Control Association, 1975, The Carnegie Endowment for International Peace), p. 48. The idea of using PNEs for a Panama Canal project is now abandoned. Scoville also reports on Soviet plans:

> The Russians have also reported on a proposed project to use nuclear explosives to dig the Pechora-Kama canal, which would connect the watersheds now flowing north into the Arctic with those flowing south into the Volga and Caspian Sea. The nuclear excavation could stretch over a distance of 65 kilometres and involve several hundred explosives with yields of 40 to 600 KT. The relatively sparsely populated area in which these explosions would occur, and the fact that the downwind fallout would pass largely over uninhabited areas of Siberia, may make such a project more feasible than similar projects proposed by the U.S. . . .

Nevertheless, the experience . . . suggests that some radioactive contamination will undoubtedly occur outside Russia, causing considerable
anxiety in Japan and elsewhere. *Ibid.*, p. 49.

13. *International Herald Tribune,* 7 September 1974.

14. *Arms Limitation Agreements—July 1974 Summit*, U.S. Arms Control
and Disarmament Agency (Washington: ACDA Publication 73, 1974), p. 3.
Italics added.

15. Scoville, "Peaceful Nuclear Explosions," p. 53.

> . . . the U.S. and the U.S.S.R. have provided themselves with the same
> 'peaceful' loophole that India has been criticized for using. Representatives
> of the two countries have been meeting to try to work out procedures for
> observing such tests to insure that they are indeed only for peaceful pur-
> poses. This will be extremely hard to do unless the nuclear explosives them-
> selves are to be inspected, an unlikely event because of the secrecy attached
> to their design. How can an observer at a detonation to release natural gas
> or to excavate a canal know whether or not it serves some weapons devel-
> opment objective?

16. United Nations, *The United Nations and Disarmament 1945–1970*
(New York: United Nations, 1970), pp. 244–245.

17. United Nations, General Assembly, Official Records, First Committee,
1564th Meeting, 9 May 1968.

18. Ian Smart, "Non-Proliferation Treaty: Status and Prospects," *NPT:
Paradoxes and Problems*, pp. 24–25. See also references to author's publications in Chapter VI.

19. United Nations General Assembly, First Committee, 31 May 1968.

20. *Final Document of the Review Conference of the Parties to the Treaty
on the Non-proliferation of Nuclear Weapons* (Geneva, 1975, NPT/CONF/
35/I), Annex I, p. 7.

21. Since 1968, at the request of the General Assembly, the International
Atomic Energy Agency (IAEA) has studied ways and means to establish,
within its framework, an international service for peaceful nuclear explosions.
It has promised the exchange of information, and technical panels have met
once a year to study these matters. It should be noted, however, that the
General Assembly Resolutions (see 2456 C [XXIII]) have only spoken of
"the establishment, within the framework of the International Atomic
Energy Agency, of an international *service* for nuclear explosions for peaceful purposes, under appropriate international control." Also the NPT Review
Conference "emphasizes that the IAEA should play the central role in matters
relating to the provision of *services* for the application of nuclear explosions
for peaceful purposes." *Ibid.*, Annex I, p. 7. Italics added.

22. *Disarmament Conference Document CCD/PV.647*, 30 July 1974.

23. Speech by Foreign Minister Andrei Gromyko in the General Assembly,
23 September 1975.

24. *United Nations General Assembly Resolution 3257(XXIX)*, 9 December 1974. The 1975 Resolution, 3466 (XXX), 11 December 1975, used much
lengthier language, and it referred to recommendations made at the NPT
Review Conference. There was an additional, to some extent competitive,

Soviet-sponsored Resolution, which passed with a much narrower majority. A/RES/3478 (XXX), 11 December 1975.

25. *Final Document of the Review Conference*, Annex II, Additional Protocol I, p. 4.

26. United Nations General Assembly, First Committee, 11 November 1974. A/C.1/PV.2016.

27. *Disarmament Conference Document CCD/348*, 2 September 1971, a revised version of Swedish working paper, ENDC/242, 1 April 1969. This draft treaty is published as an annex to UN, *The United Nations and Disarmament 1945–1970*, Appendix XIII, p. 490.

28. *SIPRI Yearbook 1972*, pp. 530–531.

29. *Disarmament Conference Document CCD/348*, 2 September 1971.

30. *Disarmament Conference Document CCD/348*, 2 September 1971.

CHAPTER VIII
Outlawing the Use of Cruel Weapons and Methods of Warfare

1. There is ample documentation, brought together by a Swedish Government Committee on humanitarian aspects on the rules of warfare, of which I was the first chairman. In 1973 it issued a report, *Conventional Weapons, Their Deployment and Effects from the Humanitarian Aspect: Recommendations for the Modernization of International Law* (Stockholm: Royal Swedish Ministry for Foreign Affairs, 1973). The continued work of the delegation is reflected in contributions by the Swedish delegation to the Diplomatic Conference, as well as to expert meetings under the aegis of the International Committee of the Red Cross. In all these deliberations as also in the United Nations work in this field Dr. Hans Blix has been very active and effective. See also his "Current Efforts to Prohibit the Use of Certain Conventional Weapons," *Instant Research on Peace and Violence,* vol. IV, no. 1, 1974; "Area Bombardment: Rules and Reasons," unpublished manuscript, 1975; "Human Rights in Armed Conflicts: Conflicting Views," *Proceedings of the American Society of International Law,* 1973.

2. Hugo Grotius, *De Jure belli ac pacis,* 1625.

3. Emanuel Kant, *Zum ewigen Frieden,* 1795.

4. Carl von Clausewitz called any introduction of a principle of moderation "an absurdity." Gerald J. Adler, "Targets in War: Legal Considerations," *Houston Law Review,* vol. 8, no. 1, September 1970, p. 7.

5. Telford Taylor, *Nuremburg and Vietnam: An American Tragedy* (New York: Bantam Books, 1971), p. 21, quoting *Instructions for the Government of Armies of the United States in the Field,* prepared by Francis Lieber, an emigrant from Germany.

6. Adler, "Targets in War," p. 8.

7. Dietrich Schindler and Jiří Toman, eds., *The Laws of Armed Conflicts* (Leiden: Sijthoff, Henri Duman Institute-Geneva, 1973), p. 96. Italics added.

8. *The Hague Conventions and Declarations of 1899 and 1907*, ed., James Brown Scott (Carnegie Endowment for International Peace, 1915, introduc-

tion. A main purpose of the Conferences was to reach agreement that international disputes be settled by arbitration. The Hague Permanent Court of Arbitration was established in 1899; later called the International Court of Justice, it is still in the Hague. *See also* Barbara W. Tuchman, *The Proud Tower: A Portrait of the World Before the War, 1890–1914* (New York: Macmillan, 1966).

9. Scott, *ibid.*, pp. 101–102.

10. *The Rise of CB Weapons*, vol. 1, *The Problem of Chemical Warfare* and *vol. III, CBW and the Law of War* (Stockholm: Almqvist & Wiksell, 6 vols., 1971, Stockholm International Peace Research Institute).

11. *United Nations General Assembly, Resolution 95 (I)*, 1946. Italics added.

12. Jorge Castañeda, *Legal Effects of United Nations Resolutions* (New York and London: Columbia University Press, 1969).

13. *United Nations General Assembly Resolution 2603 A (XXIV)*, 16 December 1969. Three governments voted against: the United States, Australia (which was participating in the Vietnam war), and Portugal (reported as having reasons to have a bad conscience because of chemical warfare in its African colonies).

14. SIPRI, *The Problem of Chemical and Biological Warfare*, vol. 1, pp. 125 ff.

15. *Ibid.*, p. 143.

16. *Ibid.*, pp. 322 ff.

17. Arthur H. Westing, "Indochina: Prototype of Ecocide," *Air, Water, Earth, Fire: The Impact of the Military on World Environmental Order*, International Series No. 2, Sierra Club, May 1974, pp. 19–21. *See also* detailed documentation in the collected work by J. B. Neilands *et al., Harvest of Death: Chemical Warfare in Vietnam and Cambodia* (New York: The Free Press, 1972).

18. National Academy of Sciences, *The Effects of Herbicides in South Vietnam* (Washington: National Academy of Sciences, 1974). This study was commissioned by the Secretary of Defense as directed by the Congress.

19. SIPRI, *The Problem of Chemical and Biological Warfare*, vol. 1, p. 170.

20. *U.S. Chemical Warfare Policy.* Hearings before the Subcommittee on National Security Policy and Scientific Developments of the Committee on Foreign Affairs, House of Representatives, 93rd Congress, 2nd Session, May 1, 2, 7, 9, and 14, 1974 (Washington: U.S. Government Printing Office, 1974). *Congressional Record,* Senate, S21605–21607, 16 December 1974.

21. United Nations General Assembly, First Committee, A/C.1/PV.1950, 7 November 1973.

22. *Ibid.*

23. The characterization of high-velocity projectiles as having dum-dum effects is authoritatively made in a report by the International Committee of the Red Cross (ICRC), *Weapons That May Cause Unnecessary Suffering or Have Indiscriminate Effects* (Geneva, ICRC, 1973), p. 35. Compare the more recent reasoning in the Lucerne report, *Conference of Government Experts on the Use of Certain Conventional Weapons* (Geneva, ICRC, 1975).

24. UN Report, *Respect for Human Rights in Armed Conflicts,* 5 September 1975, p. 59, and Working Paper CDDH/IV/201, which was submitted to the Diplomatic Conference on the Reaffirmation and Development of International Humanitarian Law Applicable in Armed Conflicts, 7 February 1975.

25. *Weapons That May Cause Unnecessary Suffering or Have Indiscriminate Effects* (ICRC), p. 15. (See note 23.)

26. In 1946, the Nuremburg Court confirmed that the Hague Conventions were to be considered customary law applicable to all. This pronouncement has later been reaffirmed by the United Nations International Law Commission (Chapter VIII, Section 1).

27. Lawrence C. Petrowski, "Law and the Conduct of the Vietnam War" *The Vietnam War and International Law,* ed. Richard A. Falk (Princeton: Princeton University Press, 1969, American Society of International Law), vol. 2, pp. 503, 506–507.

28. *Weapons That May Cause Unnecessary Suffering or Have Indiscriminate Effects* (ICRC), p. 13.

29. *Napalm and Incendiary Weapons,* SIPRI Interim Report (Offset, 1972, Stockholm International Peace Research Institute), p. 43.

30. *Incendiary Weapons,* A SIPRI Monograph (Stockholm: Almqvist & Wiksell, 1975, Stockholm International Peace Research Institute), p. 15. This book is conveniently collated and annotated.

31. *Ibid.,* p. 156.

32. *Ibid.,* p. 40.

33. United Nations, *Napalm and Other Incendiary Weapons and All Aspects of Their Possible Use* (New York: United Nations Publications, 1973), p. 30.

34. SIPRI, *Incendiary Weapons,* p. 153.

35. *Ibid.,* p. 154.

36. *Napalm and Other Incendiary Weapons,* pp. 5 ff.

37. SIPRI, *Incendiary Weapons,* p. 95.

38. *Napalm and Other Incendiary Weapons,* p. 55.

39. UN Report, *Respect for Human Rights,* 5 September 1975.

40. *Ibid.,* p. 55.

41. Working Paper CDDH/IV/201, 7 February 1975, pp. 6–7.

42. SIPRI, *Incendiary Weapons,* p. 23.

43. Philip Noel-Baker, *The Arms Race* (London: John Calder, 1958), p. 56. Noel-Baker holds that the prohibitive rule had been widely accepted. I am tempted to add: between wars.

44. SIPRI, *Napalm and Incendiary Weapons,* p. 15.

45. SIPRI, *Incendiary Weapons,* p. 24, quoting from League of Nations, Series of Publications: 1933.1X,2; Conf.D157(1).

46. *Documents on Swedish Foreign Policy 1972* (Stockholm: P. A. Norstedt & Söner, 1973, Royal Ministry for Foreign Affairs New Series I:C:22), p. 202, statement by Swedish Prime Minister Olof Palme, 23 December 1972. The text seems not to have been rendered in its full form abroad and has often been misrepresented as "equating Hitler and Nixon." A personal note in the margin: I was Acting Foreign Minister at the time and

concurred in the message which he read me over the telephone that Christmas night.

47. SIPRI, *Incendiary Weapons,* p. 21.

48. UN, *Napalm and Other Incendiary Weapons,* p. 56, quoting Hague Draft Air War Rules, 1923. See Chapter III, Section 2, regarding the 1932 Disarmament Conference.

49. J. M. Spaight, *Air Power and War Rights* (London: Longmans, Green & Co., 1947, 3rd ed.), pp. 259–260, and E. L. M. Burns, *Megamurder* (New York: Pantheon, 1967), pp. 40–41.

50. Burns, *Megamurder,* p. 51.

51. Winston S. Churchill, *Memoirs of the Second World War* (Boston: Houghton Mifflin, 1959), pp. 361–366. The interpretation that the British attack so angered Hitler that he was carried emotionally away and turned the attacks away from the proper strategic objectives is borne out by Burns, *Megamurder,* p. 45.

52. Burns, *Megamurder,* p. 50. This book details the dialogue between the pros who were proud of this new ruthless strategy—Churchill, his adviser Lindemann, and the chief of the new air armada, General Harris ("Bomber Harris")—and those against—scientific advisers like Professors Blackett, Zuckerman, and Tizard.

53. Burns, *Megamurder,* p. 54. Italics added. Cf. SIPRI, *Incendiary Weapons,* p. 32. Lindemann (later Lord Chernwell) is reported as having calculated "that if the bombing offensive were concentrated on the working-class areas of the fifty-eight largest German towns and cities with a population of more than 100,000 inhabitants each, it should be possible to make homeless one-third of the whole German population by the middle of 1943." Burns, *Megamurder,* p. 51.

These words have a familiar ring, as presently the same kind of calculations are basic to what is considered to constitute deterrence between the super-powers—utter devastation of their cities above 100,000 population (Chapter II).

54. Noel-Baker, *The Arms Race,* p. 411.

55. Burns, *Megamurder,* p. 54.

56. *SIPRI Yearbook 1973,* summary, pp. 143 ff.

57. Noel-Baker, *The Arms Race,* p. 410.

58. David Irving, *The Destruction of Dresden* (London: William Kimber, 1964, 3rd ed.), p. 229, quoting Churchill.

59. Taylor, *Nuremberg and Vietnam, An American Tragedy,* p. 89.

60. Experts on international law differentiate four categories: bombing nonmilitary and civilian targets, indiscriminate bombing, area bombing, and terror bombing. Other terms are zonal bombardment, saturation bombing, carpet bombing—the terror method has many names. However, international law calls for the utmost restraint in all combat tactics to limit attacks to military targets.

61. [Hamburg and Dresden] "involved huge tonnages of incendiary weapons, and both succeeded in creating fire-storms. . . . The town [of Dresden] was swollen with refugees, the presence of a great many of whom was unrecorded, and in several areas all that remained of the inhabitants were heaps

of corpses charred beyond all recognition and often in a state of complete disintegration." UN, *Napalm and Other Incendiary Weapons*, p. 45.

62. Chapter II, Section 8, makes a proposal that the United Nations conduct a special cost-benefit study of the Korean War's political, economic, and humanitarian factors.

63. Westing, "Indochina: Prototype of Ecocide," pp. 16–17. See also by the same author, "Proscription of Ecocide," *Bulletin of the Atomic Scientists*, vol. XXX, no. 1, January 1974, pp. 24–27, for information on the land-grazing tractors.

64. Henri Meyrowitz, "The Law of War in the Vietnamese Conflict," *The Vietnam War and International Law*, ed., Richard Falk, p. 555.

65. Kissinger Memorandum, 1969, *Congressional Record*, Senate, October 2, 1972, pp. S 16522–3.

66. Blix, *Area Bombardment: Rules and Reasons*, p. 41.

67. *Ibid.*, p. 3.

68. Taylor, *Nuremberg and Vietnam, An American Tragedy*, p. 207.

69. UN, *Napalm and Other Incendiary Weapons*, p. 30. Italics added.

70. *Ibid.*, pp. 39–40.

71. André Beaufre, "Battlefields of the 1980's," *Unless Peace Comes*, ed., Nigel Calder (London: Allen Lane The Penguin Press, 1968), pp. 22–24.

72. *Weapons That May Cause Unnecessary Suffering or Have Indiscriminate Effects*, ICRC, for chronology and bibliography, and *SIPRI Yearbook 1973*. United Nations, *Report on Human Rights in Armed Conflicts*, Survey prepared by the Secretariat, vol. I–II, 7 November 1973, "Existing Rules of International Law Concerning the Prohibition or Restriction of Use of Specific Weapons," for comprehensive information on the international laws on armed conflicts and several examples of national legislation.

73. UN General Assembly, First Committee, 2 November 1973. Experts were sent from Czechoslovakia, Mexico, Nigeria, Peru, Rumania, Sweden, and the Soviet Union.

74. UN General Assembly, First Committee, 30 October 1973. The legal adviser to the Swedish Foreign Office, Dr. Hans Blix, has been a brilliant crusader on all relevant issues in the UN Legal Committee as well as in the Red Cross Expert Group on Cruel Weapons and all subsequent conferences. I want to pay special tribute to him for his share in making steady progress possible.

75. *Lucerne Report* (ICRC), Geneva 1975, and *Lugano report* (forthcoming).

76. International Committee of the Red Cross, *Draft Additional Protocols to the Geneva Conventions of August 12, 1949* (Geneva, ICRC, June 1973), p. 15.

77. Left aside here are Committee I, dealing with general provisions, and Committee II on Wounded, Sick, and Shipwrecked Persons. I also pass over Protocol II, which has taken up to extraordinary new treatment the important subject of Non-International Conflicts, which per se would be worthy of a detailed comparison with the (to a large extent parallel) Protocol I, dealing with international conflicts. See the original Conference documentation in various series under the symbol CDDH, or UN, *Respect for Human Rights in*

Armed Conflicts, 5 September 1975. Annex I sets out the text of the articles so far adopted at the Committee level and Annex II, the provisions not yet adopted together with a list of proposals and amendments.

78. UN, *Respect for Human Rights in Armed Conflicts,* p. 44.

79. *United Nations General Assembly Resolution 3479 (XXX),* 11 December 1975.

80. Inga Thorsson, "Disarmament Negotiations: What Are They Doing for the Environment?," *Ambio,* vol. IV, nos. 5–6, 1975. This article is a recent summary of the broad issue as are two others in the same special number of *Ambio,* which probe the legal and scientific aspects, by Jozef Goldblat and Bhupendra M. Jasani, respectively.

81. *Ambio, ibid.,* pp. 235–236, for full text of the proposed convention. (Italics added.)

82. Working Paper CDDH IV/201, 7 February 1975, slightly modified by a paper of 15 May 1975, but not the text here quoted (RO 610/ 4 b).

83. *United Nations General Assembly Resolution 3464 (XXX),* 11 December 1975.

84. In Sweden, an ethical screening committee was set up by the government on 28 June 1954: Delegation en för folkrättslig granskning av vapenprojekt för det militära försvaret.

85. *United Nations Publication A/8052,* 1970, p. 80.

86. References to such manuals are made under specified headings for some countries in the United Nations. *Respect for Human Rights in Armed Conflicts: Survey on Existing Rules of International Law Concerning the Prohibition or Restriction of Use of Specific Weapons,* vols. I–II, 7 November 1973.

87. Geneva Conventions of August 12, 1949, in Article 44, Convention IV.

CHAPTER IX
Eliminating Biological and Chemical Means of Warfare

1. An attempt to define mass destruction weapons was made in the United Nations as early as 1948: ". . . weapons of mass destruction should be defined to include atomic explosive weapons, radioactive material weapons, lethal chemical and biological weapons, and any weapons developed in the future which have characteristics comparable in destructive effect to those of the atomic bomb or other weapons mentioned." United Nations, *The United Nations and Disarmament 1945–1970* (New York, 1970), p. 28.

2. United Nations, *Chemical and Bacteriological (Biological) Weapons and the Effects of their Possible Use: Report of the Secretary General* (New York, 1969).

World Health Organization, *Health Aspects of Chemical and Biological Weapons: Report of WHO Group of Consultants.* (Geneva, 1970).

The Problem of Chemical and Biological Warfare, vol. I, *The Rise of CB Weapons,* and vol. V, *Technical Aspects of Early Warning and Verification* (Stockholm: Almqvist & Wiksell, 6 vols., 1971–1975, Stockholm International Peace Research Institute).

3. *The Problem of Chemical and Biological Warfare*, vol. II, *CB Weapons Today*, 1973, p. 250.

4. The incitement for action came from the Hungarian delegation at the General Assembly in 1966, when they introduced a draft resolution clearly aimed at stricturing U.S. warfare in Vietnam. It demanded absolute compliance with the norms and principles of the Geneva Protocol, condemned any use of chemical and bacteriological weapons, and declared that the use of those weapons "for the purpose of destroying human beings and the means of their existence constitutes an international crime." *The Problem of Chemical and Biological Warfare*, vol. IV, *CB Disarmament Negotiations, 1920–1970*, 1971, pp. 238–242, 247–250. UN, *United Nations and Disarmament 1945–1970*, p. 335. The text was considerably watered down before becoming UN document A/RES/2162B (XXI). At the following session of the Geneva Disarmament Committee, Sweden demanded that the issue of cessation of the development and production of CB-weapons be given priority on the agenda. *Disarmament Conference Document. CCD/PV. 288.* 23 February 1967.

5. *Disarmament Conference Document CCD/231*, 6 August 1968.

6. *The Problem of Chemical and Biological Warfare*, vol. IV, *CB Disarmament Negotiations, 1920–1971*, pp. 257–260, about the opening act where the typical roles of the various groups of nations are clearly revealed.

7. UN, *Chemical and Bacteriological (Biological) Weapons*.

8. Through UN document A/RES/2603B (XXIV), it was referred to CCD for urgent consideration of prohibiting CB-weapons production.

9. Joint Memorandum by the twelve nonaligned delegations. *Disarmament Conference Document CCD/310*, 25 August 1970, and my statement introducing it in the General Assembly, First Committee, 4 November 1970.

10. *Disarmament Conference Document CCD/322*, 16 March 1971. The idea, meant to serve as a device to rescue the negotiating operations, was that commitment be made to an over-all, comprehensive agreement but with an article permitting one or several later deadlines for the entry into force of certain more detailed proscriptions.

11. *Disarmament Conference Document CCD/PV.507*, 6 April 1971.

12. *UN Document A/RES/2825 (XXVI).* See also *Arms Control and Disarmament Agreements 1959–1972* (Washington: U.S. Government Printing Office, 1972, U.S. Arms Control and Disarmament Agency publ. 62), p. 98.

13. Karin Hjertonsson, "A Study on the Prospects of Compliance with the Convention on Biological Weapons," *Instant Research on Peace and Violence* (Tampere Peace Research Institute), vol. 3, no. 4 (1973), pp. 211–224.

14. *UN Document A/C.1/PV.1834*, 23 November 1971; *UN Document AC.1/PV.1846* for a Swedish explanation of the vote on 8 December 1971. Similar arguments were heard from Brazil, France, Austria, Ghana, Pakistan. Sweden hesitated until early 1976 before ratifying the Convention.

15. Several suggestions were made to this effect during the CCD negotiations. See my statement, *Disarmament Conference Document CCD/PV.522*, 20 July 1971. Article V of the BW Convention refers only to Parties "to consult one another and to cooperate in solving any problems which may arise,"

possibly "through appropriate international procedures within the framework of the United Nations and in accordance with its Charter." (The corresponding Article III in the Sea-Bed Treaty provides for a more stepwise, less abrupt procedure for verification.)

16. Article XI in the BW Convention mentions the right for any Party to propose amendments, and Article XII stipulates that a Review Conference shall be held five years after the entry into force of the Convention, "or earlier if it is requested by a majority of Parties." ACDA, *Arms Control and Disarmament Agreements 1959–1972* (Washington: U.S. Government Printing Office, 1972. United States Arms Control and Disarmament Agency), p. 102.

17. *The Problem of Chemical and Biological Warfare,* vol. II, *CB Weapons Today,* contains a full survey and analysis of CB capabilities then existing in individual countries. *Chemical Disarmament: New Weapons for Old* (Stockholm: Almqvist & Wiksell, 1975, Stockholm International Peace Research Institute), pp. 75–93, for United States up-to-date information.

18. *Disarmament Conference Document CCD/477. Report to the United Nations General Assembly and to the United Nations Disarmament Commission,* 28 August 1975, p. 6.

19. *The Problem of Chemical and Biological Warfare,* vol. II, *CB Weapons Today,* pp. 166 ff., reports considerable evidence from writings on military strategy, field manuals, research reports, notes and maneuvers, etc. that the Soviet army is well equipped for tactical use of chemical weapons.

20. *The Problem of Chemical and Biological Warfare,* vol. II, *CB Weapons Today,* p. 165.

21. *UN Document A/C.1/PV.1716.*

22. *The Problem of Chemical and Biological Warfare,* vol. II, *CB Weapons Today,* pp. 190–191.

23. *Ibid.,* pp. 191–192, for *The White Paper 1970 on the Security of the Federal Republic of Germany and on the State of the German Federal Armed Forces,* published by the Federal Minister of Defense on behalf of the FRG Government, [643] states: "The Federal Republic neither possesses or does she store any biological and chemical weapons; she does not seek possession of, or control over, weapons of that kind, she has made no preparation for using them, does not train military personnel for that purpose, and will abstain from doing so in the future."

24. *The Effects of Developments in the Biological and Chemical Sciences on CW Disarmament Negotiations* (Stockholm: Stockholm International Peace Research Institute, 1974), for categories of most lethal gases and others.

25. *Disarmament Conference Document CCD/PV.457,* 12 March 1970.

26. The use of separate Protocols, suggested in the above quoted speech, has a long tradition; this technique was also applied to the Tlatelolco Treaty (Chapter VI, Section 10).

27. *New Times,* no. 28 (1974), p. 22.

28. *UN Document A/RES/2827B(XXVI).*

29. *Disarmament Conference Document CCD/PV.613,* 17 July 1973.

30. *Disarmament Conference Document CCD/PV.569,* 18 July 1972.

31. *Disarmament Conference Document CCD/PV.569,* 18 July 1972.

32. *Disarmament Conference Document CCD/473*, 26 August 1975.

33. *Disarmament Conference Document CCD/427*, 2 July 1974.

34. *Disarmament Conference Document CCD/420*, 30 April 1974.

35. After many years' work and several tentative working papers, it was first presented in *Disarmament Conference Document CCD/427*, 2 July 1974; and with more sophisticated elaboration in *Disarmament Conference Document CCD/461*, 29 July 1975. Both papers have in the main been authored by Johan Lundin and Lars-Erik Tammelin, who also have published individual research papers in this field.

36. *Disarmament Conference Document CCD/461*, 29 July 1975.

37. *Chemical Disarmament: New Weapons for Old*, p. 6.

38. The subject of verification, starting from national means, has been one in which the Swedish delegation has specialized. See a statement in the Geneva Committee, where I surveyed extensively the needs and opportunities for verification, beginning with the fundamental requirement of open information, further the transmission of publications on significant scientific research as well as government notifications concerning the flow of substances from production facilities to different types of users, applying possible indicators, such as number of personnel engaged in certain activities, figures for sales, and other measurable factors, ending with a firm request that it be made obligatory through the treaty text for governments to report, continuously or periodically, to an international control agency. *Disarmament Conference Document CCD/PV.463*, 9 April 1970.

39. *The Problem of Chemical and Biological Warfare*, vol. V, *The Prevention of CBW*, for a comprehensive list of suggestions; vol. VI, *Technical Aspects of Early Warning and Verification; Chemical Disarmament: Some Problems of Verification*, SIPRI Monograph (Stockholm: Almqvist & Wiksell, Stockholm International Peace Research Institute, 1973), for an examination of the types of data to be reported internationally from economic, statistical, and other methods by a national verification organization controlling potential chemical warfare materials; *SIPRI Yearbook 1975*, pp. 430–432.

40. Johan Lundin, "Considerations on a Chemical Arms Control Treaty and the Concept of Applied Verification," *FOA Reports* (Försvarets Forskningsanstalt, Stockholm), vol. 7, no. 1, February 1973, pp. 3–4.

41. *Disarmament Conference Document CCD/384*, 8 August 1972, Working Paper on domestic legislation in Sweden regarding chemical substances, intended to elicit similar reports from other countries in order to lay the basis for compilation of internationally comparable rules.

42. Alva Myrdal, "The International Control of Disarmament," *Scientific American*, October 1974, pp. 21–33.

43. *Disarmament Conference Document CCD/400*, 26 April 1973.

44. *UN Document A/RES/3465 (XXX)*.

45. *Disarmament Conference Document CCD/PV.457*, 12 March 1970.

46. Third Pugwash Chemical Warfare Workshop, London, England, *Pugwash Newsletter*, vol. 13, no. 4 (April 1976).

47. *Disarmament Conference Document CCD/PV.622*, 16 August 1973.

48. *UN Document A/C.1/PV.1950*, 7 November 1973. See also Johan Lundin, "The Scope and Control of Chemical Disarmament Treaties particu-

larly with regard to Binary Chemical Weapons," *Cooperation and Conflict,* 1973, pp. 145–154.

49. J. Perry Robinson, *Binary Nerve Gas Weapons: Their Economic, Environmental, and Security Implications for the United States, Including Their Likely Effects on the International Chemical Disarmament Negotiations.* A paper prepared for the Symposium on Chemical Weapons and U.S. Policy by the American Chemical Society, Los Angeles, 1 April 1974: and for the Pugwash Chemical Warfare Workshop, Helsinki, 16–18 April 1974. Revised version quoted in *Chemical Disarmament: New Weapons for Old,* p. 25.

50. *Chemical Disarmament: New Weapons for Old,* p. 46.

51. *Ibid.,* p. 46.

52. *Ibid.,* p. 62.

53. Johan Lundin, "Considerations on a Chemical Arms Control Treaty and the Concept of Applified Verification," *FOA Reports,* p. 152.

54. Statement by the Swedish delegate, Inga Thorsson, *Disarmament Conference Document CCD/PV.652,* 15 August 1974, with comprehensive treatment of verification possibilities in relation to the Japanese treaty draft.

55. *Chemical Disarmament: New Weapons for Old,* p. 7.

56. *U.S. Chemical Warfare Policy, Hearings Before the Subcommittee on National Security Policy and Scientific Developments of the Committee on Foreign Affairs, House of Representatives, Ninety-third Congress, Second Session* (Washington: U.S. Government Printing Office, May 1974), statement by Leon Sloss, p. 201.

57. J. K. Miettinen, "The Chemical Arsenal," *Bulletin of the Atomic Scientists,* September 1974, p. 43.

58. *Chemical Disarmament: New Weapons for Old,* p. 24.

59. *UN Document A/C.1/PV.2072,* 30 October 1975.

60. Such a stepladder scheme was *grosso modo* conceived and presented more than five years ago by the Swedish delegation to the disarmament negotiations, *Disarmament Conference Document CCD/PV.457,* 12 March 1970; it gave special attention to the varying verification possibilities. Canada in 1975 introduced a different, more permissive scheme for phasing out activities, *Disarmament Conference Document CCD/643,* 16 July 1974.

61. Verification of Transports is treated in *Chemical Disarmament: Some Problems of Verification,* and in a U.S. Working Paper, *Disarmament Conference Document CCD/437,* 16 July 1974.

62. Swedish Working Paper, Disarmament Conference Document. CCD/461, 29 July 1975.

63. *The Problem of Chemical and Biological Warfare,* vol. V, *The Prevention of CBW* and vol. VI, *Technical Aspects of Early Warning and Verification.*

CHAPTER X
Verifying Disarmament and Internationalizing Knowledge

1. From the early days of disarmament discussions in the League of Nations, particularly in the Conference of 1932, the Soviet Union has never shirked from accepting inspections as a general feature of complete disarma-

ment. Also occasionally during later negotiations on partial measures of disarmament, inspections have seemed acceptable, as was indicated in regard to the bilateral agreement on a threshold test ban (Chapter VII, Section 1). Nevertheless, the description of their stance as being in general anti-inspection remains correct.

2. Alva Myrdal, "The Game of Disarmament," UNESCO, *Impact of Science on Society,* vol. 22, no. 3 (July–September 1972), pp. 217–233. "The High Price of Nuclear Arms Monopoly," *Foreign Policy,* no. 18 (spring 1975), pp. 30–43. "Peaceful Nuclear Explosions," *Bulletin of Atomic Scientists,* May 1975, pp. 29–33, *Den Största Felräkningen*—Kapprustningen i Världen, Göteborg 1975, Göteborgs Universitet (commencement address).

3. Richard J. Barnet and Richard A. Falk, eds., *Security in Disarmament* (Princeton, N.J.: Princeton University Press, 1965), p. 21.

4. *Ibid.,* pp. 20–21.

5. Michael Howard, *Studies in War and Peace* (New York: Viking Press, 1971), p. 217.

6. *Hearing Before the Committee on Foreign Relations, U.S. Senate, 91st Congress, 1st Session; 6 February 1969* (Washington: U.S. Government Printing Office, 1969).

7. United Nations, *The United Nations and Disarmament 1945–1970* (New York, 1970), p. 88. Italics added.

8. *Ibid.,* p. 91. The titles of the draft treaties on General and Complete Disarmament launched in 1962, and not later superseded are "Draft Treaty on General and Complete Disarmament Under Strict International Control," submitted by the Soviet Union, and "Outline of Basic Provisions of a Treaty on General and Complete Disarmament in a Peaceful World," submitted by the United States.

9. Richard J. Barnet, "Inspection: Shadow and Substance," in Barnet and Falk, eds., *Security in Disarmament,* pp. 15–36; Richard A. Falk, "Inspection, Trust, and Security During Disarmament," *Ibid.,* pp. 37–49.

10. Hans A. Linde, "Organization of a 'Mixed' National and International Inspectorate," in Barnet and Falk, eds., *Security in Disarmament,* pp. 80–106; Roger Fisher, "International Police: A Sequential Approach to Effectiveness and Control," *ibid.,* pp. 240–285; Walter Millis, "The Role of Police Forces in Response to Violations," *ibid.,* pp. 286–319; Hans J. Morgenthau, "The Impartiality of the International Police," *ibid.,* pp. 320–340.

11. For both these cases see ample evidence in SIPRI studies, quoted in the chapters indicated.

12. *Disarmament Conference Document CCD/398,* 24 April 1973.

13. For strengthening certainty by relying on a decision theory model, see author's statement in *Disarmament Conference Document CCD/PV.524,* 27 July 1971, and Chapter VII, Section 5, where some important papers by Ericson are quoted which were prepared for the Swedish delegation in the Geneva Disarmament Committee. Discussions on deterrence levels must be conducted according to the specific activities to be banned. SIPRI, in relation to a ban on production of C-weapons, mentioned the possibility that a 50 percent probability of detection might constitute a sufficiently high barrier against cheating. But evidently the levels must vary according to (a) the

material opportunities to hide clandestine production and (b) the efficacy of organized monitoring.

14. ENDC, 10 March 1966.

15. United Nations, *The United Nations and Disarmament 1945–1970*, p. 239. See Chapter VII, Section 5.

16. Edward Teller, "The Feasibility of Arms Control and the Principle of Openness," in Donald G. Brennan, ed., *Arms Control, Disarmament, and National Security* (New York: George Braziller, 1961), pp. 134, 136.

17. *Ibid.*, p. 136.

18. This idea of a "feedback with the population of national communities" has recently been reaching the peace research circles through Dieter Senghaas of the Hessische Stiftung für Friedens und Konfliktsforschung, Frankfurt am Main. He advocates it as part of a new strategy for curtailing armaments: "The current arms control strategy considers control, inspection, and verification to be the business of specialists commissioned on a national level or in an international team by state administrations; in the arms control strategy described here, however, control is essentially also a matter of *self-control*. Of course, on a national level such self-control can be effective only if the policy of self-imposed arms control curtailment is supported by interest groups." Dieter Senghaas, "Arms Race by Arms Control?" *Bulletin of Peace Proposals*, 1973, pp. 373–374.

19. See *United Nations and Disarmament 1945–1970*, for comprehensive presentations of the drafts, pp. 392 ff. and 421 ff.

20. UN General Assembly, First Committee, *AC.1/PV.1260*, 31 October 1962.

21. *Disarmament Conference Document CCD/PV.560*, 28 April 1972 (the Netherlands) and *CCD/PV. 569*, 18 July 1972 (Sweden and Yugoslavia).

22. *Disarmament Conference Document CCD/400*, 26 April 1973.

23. The author's statements are contained in *Documents CCD/PV.601*, 17 April 1973 and *CCD/PV.610*, 5 July 1973. See also Alva Myrdal, "The International Control of Disarmament," *Scientific American*, October 1974, pp. 21–33.

24. *Disarmament Conference Document CCD/410*, 31 July 1973.

25. The full presentation of the Japanese proposal was made in a working paper with a Draft Convention on the Prohibition of the Development, Production, and Stockpiling of Chemical Weapons and on their Destruction, *Disarmament Conference Document CCD/420*, 30 April 1974. The U.S. in *Document CCD/360*, 20 March 1972, had made certain suggestions for negotiation.

26. *Disarmament Conference Document CCD/410*, 31 July 1973.

27. Alva Myrdal, "The International Control of Disarmament," *Scientific American*, October 1974, pp. 21–33.

28. *General Assembly Resolution 3484 B (XXX)*, 12 December 1975, was approved by 108 votes but without the concurrence of the two superpowers and most of their allies. Rumania on the one hand and Belgium, France, Italy, and the Netherlands on the other voted for the proposal, however.

29. *Disarmament Conference Documents CCD/PV.569*, 18 July 1972, and *CCD/400*, 26 April 1973.

30. Quoted from author's statement, *Disarmament Conference Document CCD/PV.610*, 5 July 1973.

31. United Nations, *Report of the Committee on the Peaceful Uses of Outer Space 1975*, Official Records of the General Assembly, Thirtieth session, supplement no. 20 (A/10020), UN General Assembly Resolution A/RES/3388 (XXX), 18 November 1975.

32. Alva Myrdal, "The International Control of Disarmament," p. 29.

33. *Disarmament Conference Document CCD/420*, 30 April 1974.

34. *Disarmament Conference Document CCD/348*, 2 September 1971.

35. *Disarmament Conference Document*, "Working paper on ways of implementing control over compliance with the convention on the prohibition of the development, production and stockpiling of chemical weapons and on their destruction," *CCD/403*, 28 June 1973.

36. *Chemical Disarmament: Some Problems of Verification*, SIPRI Monograph (Stockholm: Almqvist & Wiksell, 1973, Stockholm International Peace Research Institute), pp. 36–50. Appendix 2, "An Examination of the types of data to be reported internationally from economic, statistical, and other methods by a national verification organization controlling potential chemical warfare materials." Papers submitted for discussion at the working group meeting on 16–18 December 1972. Part A: Paper prepared by O. A. Reutov, N. N. Melnikov, and J. Moravec. The views have been restated by the Soviet delegation in *Disarmament Conference Document*, 18 July 1974.

37. *Disarmament Conference Document CCD/348*, 2 September 1971.

38. *Disarmament Conference Document CCD/PV.627*, 16 April 1974.

39. Philip Noel-Baker, "Science and Disarmament," UNESCO, *Impact of Science on Society*, vol. 15, no. 4 (1965), p. 214.

40. Reports from UN Law of the Sea Conference, final agreements still unconsummated.

41. For information, see the consecutive reports from the United Nations, or, more summarily, in *SIPRI Yearbooks*. For an early treatment of the political problems involved, see Alva Myrdal, "The Game of Disarmament," UNESCO, *Impact of Science on Society*, vol. 22, no. 3 (July–September), pp. 230 ff.

42. *Pugwash Newsletter*, vol. 13, no. 2 (October 1975), p. 108.

CHAPTER XI
In Conclusion

1. SIPRI, *Press Release: World Armaments and Disarmament, SIPRI Yearbook 1976* (Stockholm: Stockholm International Peace Research Institute, 17 June 1976).

2. *New York Times*, 13 February 1976.

3. SIPRI, *Disarmament or Destruction? Armaments and Disarmament* (Stockholm: Stockholm International Peace Research Institute, 1975), p. 5.

4. A memorable occasion was the challenge raised in 1967 by academician L. A. Artsimovitch of the Soviet Union, when he spoke about the necessity

to "nip in the bud" the potential to invent and perfect new means of mass destruction: "For instance, we might put forward a proposal to conclude a treaty banning any research and investigations for the purpose of creating new weapons of mass destruction. An international scientific-technical committee consisting of eminent trustworthy scientists, each of whom could be responsible for carrying out the treaty in his field in his own country, could become a guarantor of the fulfillment of such a treaty." L. A. Artsimovitch, "New Ideas in Disarmament," Paper delivered at the 17th Pugwash Conference on Science and World Affairs, Ronneby, Sweden, 3–8 September 1967 p. 4.

5. From a document submitted to the United Nations General Assembly, 12 December 1975, quoted in *Le Monde*, 19 June 1976 (A. Myrdal's translation). In addition, the Pope points out that "the arms race has become a cumulative process with its own inherent dynamic, independent from any attitudes of aggression and outside the contest of States" (*ibid*).

6. From the Declaration of the General Assembly of the World Council of Churches, Nairobi, 10 December 1975, quoted in *Der Quäker: Monatsschrift der deutschen Freunde*, vol. 50, no. 6 (June 1976), p. 95 (A. Myrdal's translation).

7. Although in vain, I have made certain efforts at compromise over the years, such as inviting the Chinese to concur in a joint preliminary decision to place the two crucial demands as priority items on the conference agenda. See, for example, my statement in Disarmament Conference Document CCD/PV.610, 5 July 1973, pp. 6–13.

8. From the Preamble to the United Nations Charter. United Nations Security Council Resolution 255 (XXIII), 19 June 1968, considers that "any aggression accompanied by the use of nuclear weapons would endanger the peace and security of all states," and United Nations General Assembly Resolution 1378 (XIV), 20 November 1959, is one of many which confirm that General and Complete Disarmament is a basic goal of the United Nations.

9. SIPRI, *World Armaments and Disarmament, SIPRI Yearbook 1976* (Stockholm: Almqvist & Wiksell, 1976, Stockholm International Peace Research Institute), p. 15.

10. Alva Myrdal, "The High Price of Nuclear Arms Monopoly," *Foreign Policy*, no. 18 (Spring 1975), p. 38.

11. United Nations Document A/RES/3484 B (XXX). The report is due in the summer of 1976.

12. United Nations, Department of Political and Security Council Affairs, *The United Nations and Disarmament 1945–1970* (New York: United Nations Publication, no. 70.IX.1, 1970), p. 168 et passim.

13. At the time of the Soviet-inspired so-called Stockholm appeal in 1950, Averell Harriman, who as ambassador to Moscow and in other capacities had come to know conditions in Russia better than most experts, explained that he did not share the common perception in the West that the appeal was propaganda beamed towards countries abroad. "It was directed homewards. No Russian government could keep itself in power if the people did not trust it as the champion of peace" (private communication).

14. In an interview Jimmy Carter, the Democratic candidate for the U.S.

Presidency, explained that, contrary to earlier American strategic policy, he did not believe in a "limited nuclear war." Though he lent a kind of vague support to preserving a "rough equivalence," he rejected "the basic Nixon-Ford-Kissinger strategy on the nuclear balance of power" and pointed out that the "overwhelming capability" of the two superpowers to "wreak havoc" on each other removed as a major consideration whether "one nation has a slight advantage." He declared himself against "the current practice of building new nuclear weapons to bring about agreements on arms control," the "bargaining chips" approach. *International Herald Tribune*, 9 July 1976.

index

Index

ABM Treaty (1972), 104–5, 107
Acheson, Dean, 74, 76
Acheson-Lilienthal Report (1946), 74
aerial photography, 82, 83. *See also* satellites
Africa: and China, 54; denuclearization of, 202–3; and superpowers, 61–5
African Commission of Arms and Disarmament (proposed), 203
Afro-Asian Conference (1954), 85
Afro-Asian Conference (1955), 85
air sampling, 90
air warfare, 248–55
aircraft carriers, 68; nuclear, 13
airplanes, 68. *See also specific names*
Albania, 222
Aldermaston Easter march (1960), 86, 162
Alexander II, Czar of Russia, 229
Algeria, 182
alliances: and arms race, 24; bilateral, 62; multistate, 62; postwar, 31; scissions in, 50–3. *See also specific names*

American Academy of Arts and Sciences, 210
American Association for the Advancement of Science, 237
Angola, 14, 63
Antarctic Treaty (1959), 108, 196, 314
antipersonnel weapons, 117, 239–42; banning of, 263–4
antiplant agents, 236–7. *See also* herbicides
ANZUS (Australia, New Zealand, United States Tripartite Security Pact), 55–6
area bombing, 16, 237, 251, 261; in Vietnam, 252–5
area denial, 253–5, 262
Argentina, 59, 142; and Ayacucho agreement, 201; and NPT, 168, 172, 174, 202; and nuclear material, 180, 191; and Tlatelolco Treaty, 200, 202
arms control, definition of, xvi. *See also* control issue
Arms Control and Disarmament Agency (ACDA), 46, 118

381

Arms Control Association, 173 *n*
arms industry, proposed conversion
  of, 150–5
arms limitation, definition of, xvi
arms regulation, definition of, xvi
arms race: apathy toward, 318–21;
  within arms race, 25, 113–14;
  in conventional arms, 137–58;
  economics of, 4–6, 8–10; ethical
  considerations of, 21–2, 114,
  118; expansion of, 3–22; institutionalization of, 103–8; as national policy, 10–12, 25, 321; and
  national security, 7–8, 28–9; and
  NPT, 184–5; nuclear testing and,
  208; psycho-socio-political effects
  of, 14–21; as resource drain, 7,
  12–14; reversal of, 121–2, 126–7,
  184–5; and social alienation, 19–
  20; between superpowers, 7, 8,
  24, 26, 317–18, 331–4; underwater, 96–103; vested interests
  in, 10–12, 25, 318. *See also* proliferation
Arms Race, The (Noel-Baker), 81
ASEAN (Association of South East
  Asian Nations), 63
Asia, and superpowers, 61–5
atomic bomb, 159–61. *See also*
  nuclear . . .
Atomic Energy Commission (UN),
  46, 72, 73–8
Atoms-for-Peace plan (1953), 162 *n*
Attlee, Clement, 162
Augustine, Saint, 228
Australia, 63, 165; and NPT, 171,
  172, 175; and nuclear-free zones,
  205–6; and superpowers, 55–6,
  57
Austria, 30 *n*, 85, 246
Ayacucho agreement (1974), 201–2

B–1 bomber, 12, 105, 128
Backfire bombers, 51, 128, 129
Baghdad pact, 63
Baldwin, Stanley, 68
Balkans, 204

ballistic missile submarines, 100, 105,
  106, 116, 126, 128
ban-the-bomb movements, 167, 319
Bangladesh, 205
Barnaby, Frank, 132, 319–20
Barnet, Richard, 298
Baruch, Bernard M., 74
Baruch Plan (1946), 73, 74–6, 161
Battle of Britain, 249
Beaufre, André, 257
Belgium, 31, 172
Benelux countries, 31
Bentham, Jeremy, 229
binary chemical weapons, 286–90
biological weapons, 66, 148–9, 235,
  268–77; disarmament negotiations on, 270–5; elimination of,
  264, 268–86, 290–2; protection
  against, 269–70. *See also* Geneva
  Protocol
Biological Weapons Convention
  (1971), xxv–xxvi, 272–5, 283,
  307, 314, 327
bipolar model, xii. *See also* superpowers
Blackett, P. M. S., 163
Blix, Hans, 254
Bohr, Niels, 302
Bolivia, 201
bombers, 125; strategic, 106, 126
bombing, 247–55; area, 16, 237,
  251–5, 261; in Korean War, 252–
  253; in Vietnam War, 247–8,
  252–5; in World War I, 248–9;
  in World War II, 249–52
Brandt, Willy, 35, 48, 289
Brazil, 59, 77, 88, 142, 182, 219;
  and Ayacucho agreement, 201;
  and BW Convention, 276; and
  NPT, 168, 172, 174, 202; nuclear material in, 180, 190–1;
  and Tlatelolco Treaty, 200, 202
Brezhnev, Leonid, 104–5, 106, 121,
  333
Brookings Institution, 49
Brown, George S., 16
Brussels Declaration (1874), 230
Bulganin, Nikolai, 198

Bulgaria, 109
bullets, antipersonnel, 239–42
Bundy, McGeorge, 117
Burma, 88
Burns, E. L. M., 17, 250, 251
Bush, Vannevar, 73
BW. *See* biological weapons
Byrnes, James, 74

Cambodia, 14, 63
Canada, xiii, 56, 58, 77, 109, 160–161, 208; and CB weapons, 271, 276, 281; and NPT, 165, 171–2
Carnegie Endowment for International Peace, 173 *n*
Carte Blanche (NATO military exercise), 43, 319
Casablanca Conference (1943), 251
CB weapons. *See* biological weapons; chemical weapons
CCD (Committee of the Conference on Disarmament). *See* Geneva Disarmament Committee
Cecil, Lord, 68
Center for the Study of Democratic Institutions, 27
CENTO (Central Treaty Organization), 63
Ceylon. *See* Sri Lanka
"Changing Nuclear Myths" (Barnaby), 132
chemical weapons, 21, 66, 234–9, 252, 268–9, 276, 278–86; binary, 286–90; and control, 299; disarmament negotiations on, 270–275; elimination of, 148–9, 264, 268–86, 290–2; in Indochina, 236–7; protection against, 269–70; and verification, 305–10, 312–13. *See also* Geneva Protocol
Chemical Weapons Convention (proposed), 278–86, 290, 328–9; Japanese draft of, 306–9, 312, 314
Chiang Kai-shek, 53
Chile, 58–9, 200, 201
China, xiii, 4, 5, 60, 69, 201, 222,

322; and BW Convention, 276, 277; and Hague Convention of 1899, 232; and proliferation, 164, 166, 171, 173; superpowers and, 53–5, 57, 184
Chou En-lai, 55
Churchill, Winston, 160, 164, 250, 251
Civil War, American, 229
civil wars, cruelty of, 256–7
civilian defense plans, 140
Cleveland, Harlan, 49
climate modification, 262
cluster bomb unit (CBU), 240–1, 263
Codex Alimentarius, 285
cold war, 23, 159–60
collateral damage, 47, 131
Colombia, 201
command and control system, 33
Commission for Conventional Armaments (UN), 72, 79–80, 343 *n*.7
Committee of the Conference on Disarmament (CCD). *See* Geneva Disarmament Committee
Common Market, and Africa, 63
comprehensive test ban (proposed), 208, 213, 214, 218, 221–5
Conant, James, 73
condign punishment, 74–5
Conference of Government Experts in the Use of Certain Conventional Weapons (ICRC), 244
Conference of Non-Nuclear Powers (1968), 218
Conference on Harmful Chemicals (proposed), 285
Conference on the Law of the Sea (1958), 97
Conference of Government Experts on Arms (1974, 1976), 259
containment policy, 31, 161
control issue, 293 *n*; in BW Convention, 273–5; in disarmament negotiations, 79–80; purpose of, 294–7; and requirements according to scope, 297–9; in Sea-Bed Treaty, 299; and test-ban nego-

control issue (*continued*)
  tiations, 298–9, 300–1. *See also*
  verification
Convention of the Continental Shelf
  (1958), 97
Convention on Psychotropic Substances (1971), 273
Convention on the High Seas (1958),
  97
conventional arms race, 6, 141–4,
  156–8; cost of, 137–8; limits on,
  137–8; and production disclosures, 146–8; and production,
  141–2; proposed reversals of,
  144–56, 201–2; and trade disclosures, 146–8; and trade, 141–4
conventional war. *See* limited war
countercity force (second-strike),
  116, 119, 129–30
counterguerilla warfare, 256–7
craterization, 253–4
Crimean War, 229
cruel weapons, 54, 66, 233–4;
  banning of, 148–50, 259–67.
  See also specific types
cruise missiles, 51, 128–9, 132, 134
cruisers, 67
CTB (comprehensive test ban), 208,
  213, 214, 218, 221–5
Cuba, 200; missile crisis in, 34, 58,
  88, 92, 201
CW. *See* chemical weapons
Cyprus, 30
Czechoslovakia, 31, 32, 198, 238–9

Daedalus, 163
decision theory, 211
defense industries, proposed conversion of, 152–5
Defense or Retaliation (Schmidt),
  41
defoliation, 236–7
delayed-action weapons, 240
Delta submarines, 128
Denmark, 109, 160; and NATO, 50,
  199
denuclearization: in Africa, 202–3;

in Europe, 196–9; in Latin
  America, 200–2; in South Asia,
  205–7
Depositary Powers, 170–1, 174, 307,
  327–8; in BW Convention, 273–
  275
Destin de la Paix (Moch), 27
destroyers, 67
détente, 23–4, 104
deterrence: and first-strike capability,
  115, 119–21, 129–30; minimum,
  127, 133, 134–6; and terror
  balance calculations, 118–24,
  127; and verification, 300–1;
  weaponry for, 115–17
development aid, 9–10, 24, 59, 63–4,
  153–4. *See also* military aid
Diego Garcia Island, 206
Diplomatic Conference on the Reaffirmation and Development of
  International Humanitarian Law
  Applicable in Armed Conflicts
  (CDDH), 227, 245–6, 256, 259–
  264
disarmament: agenda for, 324–6;
  apathy toward, 318–21; and CB
  weapons, 268–86; and control
  issue, 293–302; definition of, xv–
  xvi; and development, 153–4;
  General and Complete, 78–84,
  108–9, 136, 226, 297–8, 304–5,
  322; exploratory studies for, 329–
  330; history of, 343 n.7; international verification of, 304–13;
  and League of Nations, 66–9;
  and minimum nuclear deterrent,
  127, 133, 134–6; and nonaligned
  states, 326–31; and nuclear-test
  bans, 133–4; of the oceans, 98–
  103; and openness, 80, 302–4;
  pre–World War II, 66–9; proposed strategies for, 114–15,
  126–7, 133–6, 324–6; regional
  initiatives for, 149–50, 194–6;
  and superpowers, 331–4; UN
  and, 69–78, 78–84, 108–10,
  127–9; and verification, 299–302,
  304–13; and weapons gap reduc-

tion, 255–7. *See also* proliferation; *specific agreements and weapons*
Disarmament and Development (UN), 150, 152, 155, 315
Disarmament and Nuclear War: The Next Step (British Labour Party), 167
Disarmament Commission (UN), 80–3, 85, 328
disarmament dividend, 150
Dominican Republic, 58
Doty, Paul, 119–20, 126
DOW Chemical Company, 245
Draft Disarmament Convention (1933), 68
dreadnoughts, 96
Dresden, 248, 251, 252
drones, remote-piloted, 128–9
Dulles, John Foster, 32
dum-dum bullets, 232, 235, 239–42, 264
Dunant, Henri, 229, 256

Earth-Watch systems, 310
East Germany, 31–2, 34–5, 198; and NPT, 171, 172
ecocide, 237, 262
Economic and Social Consequences of Disarmament (UN), 150
Ecuador, 201
Eden, Anthony, 197–8
Eden plan, 197–8
Egypt, 14, 60, 64, 88, 208, 228, 246; and NPT, 172, 174, 189–90; and nuclear-free zones, 195, 204
Eighteen-Nation Disarmament Committee (ENDC), 72. *See also* Geneva Disarmament Committee
Einstein, Albert, 84
Eisenhower, Dwight D., 10, 33, 81–83, 114, 157, 162 *n*, 296
El Salvador, 77
Emelyanov, V. S., 214–15
Enthoven, Alain, 44
ethics: of arms race, 21–2, 114, 118, 163; of arms trade, 144; military,

266–7; of scientists, 316; of warfare, 241, 255–7
Ethiopia, 61, 88, 235
Europe: definition of, 30 *n*; demilitarized zones in, 197–9; limited-war scenarios for, 30, 33–34, 36–50, 139–40; nuclear-free zones and, 196–9; postwar, 31, 34–5; and superpowers, 31–53
Europe, Eastern, 30 *n*, 41
Europe, Western: defense strategies of, 31–5, 38–50; definition of, 30 *n*; and NATO, 50–3; and U.S., 38–41, 42–50, 51–3; U.S.S.R. and, 34–5, 36–8
Europe and Nuclear Weapons (Yefremov), 36
European Security Conference (1975), 24, 35, 49, 108, 145, 199, 303
European Space Agency, 311
excavating, with PNEs, 215–16
expanding bullets. *See* dum-dum bullets

Falk, Richard, 298
fallout, radioactive, 27, 38, 47, 84–6, 95; local, 29; long-range (worldwide), 29; preparations for, 140; underground test leaks, 178, 215–216
field manuals, examination of, 266
Finland, 195, 199
Finnish-Soviet Friendship and Assistance Agreement (1948), 199
first-strike capability: definition of, 139; and deterrence, 115, 119–121, 129–30
first use, 139, 323; of chemical weapons, 238
fissionable materials. *See* nuclear materials
flame-throwers, 246, 247, 263
flechettes, 17, 240, 252, 263
flexible-response doctrine, 33, 34, 36, 40, 41, 44

Food and Agriculture Organization (FAO), 285
food crisis, 62, 64–5
Ford, Gerald, 52, 57, 130; and SALT, 106, 121–2
forward defense strategy, 47
fragmentation bombs, 17, 148, 240, 252, 263
France, xiii, 63–4, 69, 77, 160–1, 184, 196; arms trade in, 60, 143, 144; and CB weapons, 238, 271, 273, 277; and Disarmament Commission, 80–3; and Hague Convention of 1907, 232; military spending in, 4; nuclear material in, 180, 191; and nuclear testing, 84–8, 222; postwar, 31; and proliferation, 162–6, 168, 173; and Tlatelolco Treaty, 200, 201
Franco, Francisco, 248
Fulbright, J. William, 237

Gaitskell, Hugh, 164–5
Gandhi, Mohandas, 21
García Robles, Alfonso, 59, 200
gas warfare, 232. See also chemical weapons; specific types
General and Complete Disarmament, 108, 109, 136, 297–8, 304–5; goals of, 226, 322; UN and, 78–84
Geneva Convention (1864), 229, 256
Geneva Convention (1949), 227 n, 233
Geneva Disarmament Committee (CCD), xii–xiii, 72, 95, 110; and binary weapons, 288–90; Canada and, 56, 172; and CB weapons, 269–72, 276–7, 279–86; and climate modification, 262; and control issue, 297–9; and conventional arms, 144, 145, 155; and international verification agency, 305–6, 312–13; and mini-nukes, 45–6; and nonaligned states, 327–31; and nonprolifera-

tion, 168; nuclear-free zones and, 195–6, 204; and nuclear test-ban treaties, 88–93, 209, 212, 223–5; and ocean treaties, 98–101; and PNEs, 218, 220–1; and SALT, 104, 107
Geneva Experts Conference on Nuclear Tests (1958), 87
Geneva Protocol (1925), xxv, 66, 227, 232, 234–9, 252, 258, 268–273, 277–8
Geneva Summit Conference (1955), 82, 197–8
genocide, nuclear war as, 29
Germany: and atomic bomb, 160; rearming of, 295; and World War II bombing, 248–52. See also East Germany; West Germany
Giscard d'Estaing, Valéry, 184
GNOME test (1961), 92
Goldschmidt, Bertrand, 162
Great Britain, 4, 31, 56, 63, 64, 69, 77, 109, 319; and Antarctic Treaty, 196; arms trade of, 60, 144; and atomic bomb, 160–1; and CB weapons, 238, 273, 277; and Disarmament Commission, 80–3; and Hague Convention of 1907, 232; IRBMs in, 33–4; and NPT, 170, 171, 173–7; and nuclear testing, 84–93, 103–4; and proliferation, 162–7, 169, 173; and Tlatelolco Treaty, 200, 201; and World War II bombing, 249–52
Greece, 31, 109
Grecko, Marshal, 36
Gromyko, Andrei, 75, 134
Grotius, Hugo, 67, 96, 228–9
Grünewald, Dr. Armin, 52
Guantánamo Bay, 200, 201
Guatemala, 58
guerilla warfare, 256–7
Guernica, 248
Guinea-Bissau, 14
Gulf sheikdoms, 143
gunboat diplomacy, 58–9

Hague Conference (1899), 17, 66–67, 145, 226–7, 230–1, 232, 240
Hague Conference (1907), 17, 66–67, 145, 147, 226–7, 230–2, 247, 263
Hague Law of War, 227
Helsinki Conference. *See* European Security Conference (1975)
herbicides, 234, 236–7, 270
high-velocity weapons, 148
Hiroshima, 72, 73, 84
Hitler, Adolf, 67, 68, 160, 248, 250, 314
Hoover Plan (1932), 68
Humphrey, Hubert, xxv, 93, 237
Hungary, 32, 109
hydrophones, 101

Iceland, 199
Iklé, Dr. Fred, 46, 118, 126, 216
incendiary weapons, 21, 240, 242–7, 263; and terror bombing, 252; in World War II, 242–3
India, xiii, 77, 88, 182, 228, 276; arms production in, 142; and nonproliferation, 167–8, 172–3; and NPT, 168, 169, 172–3, 191, 294; and nuclear-free zones, 205–206; nuclear material in, 179–80; and nuclear tests, 209, 213, 223, 294; and test bans, 85–6, 88, 218
Indian Ocean, as Zone of Peace, 205–7
Indonesia, 56, 63, 64
Innocent II, Pope, 228
inspections, and disarmament negotiations, 76, 80–1, 90–3, 212
intercontinental ballistic missiles (ICBMs), 103, 104–6, 125
Interim Agreement (on offensive strategic arms) (1972), 104, 105, 106
intermediate range ballistic missiles (IRBMs), 33–4, 43
International Affairs, 201
International Armed Conflicts, 266
International Atomic Energy Agency (IAEA), 76, 162 *n*, 169–70, 176–177; as nuclear banker, 192–3; and nuclear-free zones, 195; and PNEs, 220; role of, 305, 309, 310; safeguards of, and NPT, 185–93; and Tlatelolco Treaty, 200
International Authority (1946), 73, 75
International Committee of the Red Cross (ICRC), 227, 229, 244; and rules of war update, 257–65
International Conference on Human Rights (1968), 244, 257–8
"International Control of Disarmament, The" (Myrdal), 299
International Disarmament Organization (IDO), 304–5
International Geophysical Year, 90
International Law Commission Draft Code of Offenses, 233
International Verification Agency (proposed), 133, 145, 155, 284, 329; organization of, 306–13
internationalization of knowledge, 313–16
Iran, 63, 191; arms trade in, 142; and nuclear-free zones, 195, 204, 206; nuclear material in, 180, 191
Iraq, 64
Israel, 14, 51, 60–1, 238, 276; military spending of, 5; and NPT, 172, 174; and nuclear-free zones, 204–5; and proliferation, 189–90
Italy, 109, 160, 172, 235; IRBMs in, 33–4

Jackson, Henry M., 125
Japan, xiii, 4–5, 8, 56–8, 160, 295; and CB-weapons, 271, 281, 282–284, 290, 306–9, 312, 314; and Geneva Protocol, 232; and International Verification Agency, 306–9, 312, 314; nonproliferation policy of, 180–1; and NPT, 172, 174; and nuclear-free zones,

Japan (*continued*)
  206; and test bans, 85, 208, 209,
  215
Johnson, Lyndon B., 103

Kahn, Herman, 163
Kant, Immanuel, 229
Kekkonen, Urho, 199
Kennedy, Edward, 210, 215
Kennedy, John F., 33, 88, 92, 94,
  117, 235, 333
Khrushchev, Nikita, 58, 76, 81, 82,
  88, 92, 333
kill-effectiveness, 6, 7, 16
Kissinger, Henry, 29, 33, 37–9, 45,
  51–3, 163, 181, 254
knowledge, internationalization of,
  302, 313–16
Koran and rules of war, 228
Korean War, 17, 60–1, 139; bombing
  in, 252–3; treaty violations in,
  294–5
Kosygin, Aleksei, 103
Kuwait, 143

La Roque, Gene, 126
land mines, 240, 264; nuclear, 46
Laos, 63
lasers, 6, 16, 129
Lateran Council (1139), 228
Latin America: aid to, 9, 59; and
  BW Convention, 276; conventional disarmament in, 201–2;
  nuclear-free zones in, 200–2, 324;
  superpowers and, 58–9
Laws of the Sea Conference (1974–
  1976), 98, 291, 315
Lazy Dog (weapon), 240–1
League of Nations, 144–5, 235, 249;
  disarmament and, 66–9; Disarmament Conference, 149, 246–
  247; Preparatory Disarmament
  Commission, 67–8, 145
Liddell Hart, B. H., 163
limited war: European scenarios, 30,

32–4, 36–8, 40–50, 139–40; non-
  European scenarios, 60–1
Lincoln, Abraham, 229–30
Litvinov, Maksim, 68
Lucky Dragon (fishing boat), 319

M–16 rifle, 239–40
MAD (Mutual Assured Destruc-
  tion), 39, 118
McCarthy, Joseph, 82, 163
McCloy-Zorin Agreed Principles
  (1961), 297–8, 304
McGovern, George, 151
McNamara, Robert, 181
Malaysia, 63
Manifesto of 1955, 84
Manu Law of India (500 B.C.), 228
mass destruction weapons, 148–50,
  244, 268–92. *See also* biological
  weapons; chemical weapons; nu-
  clear weapons
massive retaliation doctrine, 32, 33,
  38–9, 161
Marshall Plan, 34, 35
Martens clause, 231
MARV (Maneuverable Reentry Vehicles), 128
"*maux superflus*," 260
"Means of Injuring the Enemy,
  Sieges, and Bombardments," 231–
  232
megamurder, 17, 250
Mendès-France, Pierre, 162
Mexico, xiii, 59, 175, 220, 246; and
  CCD, 88, 110
Middle Ages, war during, 228
Middle East: in European war
  scenarios, 41, 51–2, 59–60; and
  nuclear-free zones, 204–5
militarization: of nations, 18–19,
  24, 62, 138; of oceans, 96, 98–
  103
military aid, 24; to Latin America,
  59; to underdeveloped countries,
  63–4, 143; to Western Europe,
  32, 34–5. *See also* development
  aid

military bases, 64
military budgets, 146, 302
military dictatorships, 59, 138
military-industrial complex, 114, 155–6, 157–8
military policies, changes in, 129–32, 161
military research and development (R & D), 11, 313–16
Military Research and Development (SIPRI), 155
military spending: and development aid, 6, 8–10, 13–14, 138; growth of, 4–5; proposed disclosure of, 144–6
military training, examination of, 266
Military Strategy (Sokolovski), 36
mini-nukes, 45–8
mining, with PNEs, 215
Minutemen III conversions, 12
MIRV (multiple independently-targetable reentry vehicle), 105, 106, 126, 128, 132
missiles, 117, 176; ballistic, 33–4; cruise, 51, 128–9, 132, 134; Soviet, 95; strategic, 303 (*see also* strategic nuclear weapons); submarine-based, 103, 105, 106, 116, 126, 128; test ban proposed for, 133–4; warning time for, 8. *See also specific types*
Moch, Jules, 27
Molotov, Vyacheslav, 198
Molotov cocktails, 21
Monroe Doctrine, 58
Montebello Island test, 162
morality. *See* ethics
Mozambique, 14
MRV (Multiple Reentry Vehicle), 105, 106
Multilateral Force (MLF), 181
Mussolini, Benito, 235
mustard gas, 235, 281
mutual collective suicide, 40
Mutual Reduction of Forces and Armaments and Associated Measures in Central Europe (MBFR), 45, 48, 109, 199

Nagasaki, 72, 73, 84
napalm, 17, 148, 240, 242–7, 252, 263; discriminatory effects of, 255–6
Napalm and Other Incendiary Weapons and All Aspects of Their Use (UN), 244–5
Napoleon, 229
National Economic Conversion Commission, 151
national security, and arms race, 7–8, 28–9, 140
NATO (North Atlantic Treaty Organization), 24, 30 n; defense allegiances to, 49–50; and European defense, 31–4, 40–9; and "flexible response" agreement (1967), 34, 40, 41, 44; formation of, 31; military spending, 4; and nuclear-free zones, 199; Nuclear Planning Group, 42, 44; scissions in, 50–3; summit meeting (1975), 52; and Yom Kippur War, 51–2
naval armaments, 67–8, 96–103
Nehru, Jawaharlal, 85, 168
Nelson, Gaylord, 237
nerve gas, 234, 281
Netherlands, xiii, 31, 172, 200, 232, 281; and International Verification Agency, 305–9
neutrality. *See* nonalignment
New Zealand, 63, 175; and nuclear-free zones, 205–6; superpowers and, 55–6, 57
Nicholas II, Czar of Russia, 230
Nigeria, 88, 175
Nightingale, Florence, 229
Nixon, Richard, 104–5, 237, 279
"no-first-use" principle, 322, 323
Noel-Baker, Philip, 67, 68, 81, 163, 314
Non-Proliferation Treaty (NPT), xxvi, 45, 163, 168; criticisms of, 168–71; Depositary Powers of,

Non-Proliferation Treaty (*continued*)
307; Draft Protocols of, 175–6;
failure of, 171–7; Final Declaration of, 174–5, 176, 184, 186,
190; and IAEA controls, 185–93;
and information-sharing, 314;
and Latin America, 202; and
Nordic countries, 199; and PNEs,
209, 213–14, 217, 218–21; preferential treatment eliminated from,
189–92; Preview Conference of,
173 and *n*, 180, 183 and *n*, 190;
price of, 182–5; Review Conference for, 127, 171–2, 173–7,
182–4, 186, 196, 219–20, 222;
and Security Assurances, 182–4;
and verification, 305
nonalignment: disarmament strength
and, 326–31; in Europe, 30 *n*,
32, 49; and national defense, 140
nondissemination issue, 183
nonmodernization,   as   reduction
method, 126
nonreplacement, as reduction method,
126
North Atlantic Treaty Organization.
See NATO
Norway, 109, 246; and NATO, 50,
199
Norwegian   Academy   of   Sciences,
316
NPT: Paradoxes and Problems, 173 *n*
NPT. *See* Non-Proliferation Treaty
nuclear disarmament, 26; proposals
for, 126–7; UN and, 72–8, 79–
80
nuclear energy: and   IAEA   safeguards, 187–8, 190–2; and NPT,
176; and nuclear-free zones, 194;
and proliferation, 176, 177–82,
186–7
nuclear fission, 160
nuclear-free zones, 166–7, 194–6; in
Africa, 202–3; in Balkan states,
204; in Europe, 196–9; in Latin
America, 200–2; in Middle East,
204–5;   and   military   alliances,
198–9; in Oceania, 205–7

nuclear fuel cycles, 177, 179–80;
centers for, 176–7; and IAEA
safeguards, 188–9, 190–1; international control proposed for,
192–3; internationalization of,
188–9
nuclear land mines, 46
nuclear materials: black markets in,
180; IAEA safeguards on, 187–9;
international   management   for,
192–3; and NPT, 169–70, 176,
186–7; processing of, 179–80,
188–9; safeguards against theft
of, 176–7, 178, 180; transfer of,
186
nuclear shield, 134–6
nuclear test bans, 133–4; comprehensive, 208, 213, 214, 218, 221–5;
and control issue, 298–9, 300–1;
and NPT, 175–6, 185. *See also*
Partial Test-Ban Treaty; Threshold Ban Treaty
nuclear testing: atmospheric, 87, 89,
94–5, 208; over Bikini Atoll, 75,
84, 319; ceilings for, 209–10,
221; crisis in (1962–63), 88–95;
false alibis for, 208–12; moratorium on, 87; before 1962, 84–
88; in outer space, 208; peaceful,
209, 210, 212–21; thresholds for,
209–10; underground, 87, 89,
92–5, 208, 210, 221–2; underwater, 208; verification of, 209–
212
nuclear umbrella, 134
nuclear warfare, 27–9, 57
nuclear warheads, 132; multiple, 105,
106, 126–7
nuclear waste, 178–9
nuclear weapons: accuracy of, 130–
131; cost of, 138; deterrence and,
115–22, 123–4, 127, 129–30;
elimination of, 26, 72–8, 79–80,
126–7; in Europe, 33, 36, 38–40,
42–51; European targets for, 43;
explosive capacity of, 6, 26–9,
115, 117, 122; and non-use assurances, 182–4; on ocean floor,

98–103; regional systems of, 181; and rules of war update, 259; spread of, 113, 117 (*see also* proliferation); strategic, 38–40, 51, 103–7, 115, 126–7; tactical, 33, 36, 38–40, 42–51, 107, 115; and terrorism, 21. *See also* weapons
Nuremberg Principles (1946), 233, 252, 255

OAS (Organization of American States), 58
obsolescence, as reduction method, 125–6
Oceania. *See* Australia; New Zealand
oceans: disarmament of, 98–103; encroachment in, 101–2; exploitation of, 96–7, 103; militarization of, 96, 98–103; missile testing in, 133–4; treaties regarding, 96–103
oil politics, 52, 54–5, 62, 64–5
Open Skies proposal (1955), 82, 83, 296
Oppenheimer, Robert, 74, 163
Oppenheimer-Lilienthal plan, 192
Organization of African Unity, 202–203
Outer Space Treaty (1962), 108, 314
overkill capacity, 26–9, 115, 117, 122
ozone layer, and nuclear explosions, 216

Pacem in Terris III Conference (1973), 27
pacifism, ethics of, 22
Packard, David, 37
Pakistan, 9, 63, 172, 182, 276; and nuclear-free zones, 195, 205; and nuclear material, 180, 191
Palme, Olaf, 248
Panama, 59, 200, 201
Panama Canal, 59, 216
Pardo, Dr. Arvid, 97
parity principle, 72, 123–4

Parliamentary Defense Commission (Sweden, 1955), 87
Partial Test-Ban Treaty (1963), 55, 93–5, 133, 208, 271; and PNEs, 213–14, 215–16
Pauling, Linus, 86
peace research institutes, 320
Pell, Claiborne, 100
Peredelski, Marshal, 36
Peru, 175, 201
Petrowski, Lawrence C., 240–1
Philippines, 62, 63
Plowshare program, 214
plutonium, 177, 178–80, 188–9
PNEs (peaceful nuclear explosive devices), 212–17, 222–3; economic benefits of, 214–16
Poland, 35, 77, 198, 239
Polaris system, 100
Portugal, 14, 31, 51, 63
Poseidon submarines, 126
Potsdam Agreement (1945), 30
precision bombing, 251
precision-guided munitions (PGM), 129
precision targeting, 130–1
Preparatory Disarmament Commission (League of Nations), 67–68, 145
Principal Security Guarantees, 322–324
projectiles, antipersonnel, 239–42; prohibition of, 228, 229–30, 231–232, 263
proliferation: attempts at banning, 166–8; of binary weapons, 287–90; chain-reaction pattern of, 181; by lesser powers, 164–6; limits of, 177–82; and NPT, 168–177; and nuclear energy production, 176, 177–80, 186–7; and nuclear-free zones, 194–6; and PNEs, 214; prevention of, 159–207; reversal of, 182–5; and secrecy, 159–63; by superpowers, 159–63, 167–71, 182–5. *See also* arms race
Puerto Rico, 200

Pugwash movement, 26, 84, 320–1; "Pledge for Scientists," 316; Symposium (1975), 126
Pyongyang, 253

radioactivity. See fallout, radioactive
Rapacki plan, 198
Rathjens, G. W., 126
ratios, in naval armaments, 67
reactors, nuclear, 177
realistic deterrence doctrine, 34
religion, 228, 321
resource drain, arms race as, 12–14, 152–3, 155–6
"Respect for Human Rights in Armed Conflict," 266
"Respecting the Laws and Customs of Wars on Land," 231
retaliation, with chemical weapons, 238
Reuther, Walter, 151
review conferences, 307
Role of Nuclear Forces in Current Soviet Strategy, The, 36
roll-back doctrine, 32
Roosevelt, Franklin D., 73, 249
Rousseau, Jean-Jacques, 229
rules of war, 16, 66–7, 114, 139, 147–8, 226–7; history of, 227–234; updating of, 257–65. See also specific conventions
Rumania, xiii, 109, 175; and nuclear-free zones, 199, 204
Russell, Bertrand, 84, 113, 163

St. Petersburg Declaration (1868), 229–30, 242, 246
SALT (Strategic Arms Limitation Talks), xxvi, 26, 29, 51, 103–109, 121–2, 327; and control issue, 296; criticisms of, 127; and lesser powers, 164; and secrecy, 303; value of, 124–5
sanctuary doctrine, 30, 34, 36–7, 47, 51, 129, 165
Saracens, 228

Sarin, 281
satellites, 6, 54, 82–3, 91, 211–12, 295, 300, 302, 310–11, 315
Schelling, Thomas, 163
Schlesinger, James R., 39–40, 46–7, 52, 56, 130, 323
Schmidt, Helmut, 41–2, 44, 52
Schweitzer, Albert, 84
Scientific Committee on the Effects of Atomic Radiation (1955), 85
scientists: codes of ethics for, 316; protests of, 320
Scoville, Herbert, Jr., 126
Sea-Bed Treaty (1972), 99–103, 272, 299, 314
seas and sea-bed. See oceans
SEATO (South East Asia Treaty Organization), 63
second-strike capabilities, 116, 119, 129–30
secrecy: about atomic bomb, 159–161; and disarmament negotiations, xvi, 75, 80; and proliferation, 159–63; and verification, 302–4
Security Assurances Resolution (1968), 182–3
security guarantees, 196, 323–4
Security in Disarmament (Barnet and Falk), 298
seismology, and nuclear testing verification, 90–1, 209–11, 305
Shulman, Marshall, 122
Singapore, 63
Sino-Japanese War (1937–45), 235
SIPRI (Stockholm International Peace Research Institute), xix; on CB-weapons, 235, 269–70, 277, 283, 292; on conventional arms trade, 141; on cruel weapons, 241–2; on international verification, 308, 312; on multiple warheads, 106; on ocean treaties, 100–1; on plutonium production, 178–80; on R & D spending, 155–6; on strategic policies, 130
Smith, Gerald, 296

Sokolovski, Marshal, 36
Soman, 281
sonars, 101, 295
South Africa, 63, 77; and NPT, 172, 174, 203
South Korea, 9, 180, 191
Spain, 31, 172, 248
Speer, Albert, 251
Sputnik, 83, 103
spying, 295, 304
Sri Lanka (Ceylon), 205–6
SS–19 missile, 128
SSX missile, 128
Stalin, Joseph, 35, 73, 76
starvation, prohibition against, 262
Stassen, Harold, 82–3
State Treaty (1955), 30 n
Stimson, Henry, 73
Stockholm International Peace Research Institute. See SIPRI
strategic bombers, 106, 126
strategic nuclear weapons, 38–40, 51, 103–7, 115, 126–7
strategic policies, changes in, 129–132, 161
"strategy intellectuals," 163
submarine-launched ballistic missiles (SLBMs), 100, 105, 106, 116, 126, 128, 132
submarine warfare, 131–2
submarines, 68, 96, 125
Suez War (1956), 60
suitcase bombs, 21
Sukarno, 64
superdreadnoughts, 96
superpowers: and arms race, 7, 8, 24–30, 317–18, 331–4; and biological weapons, 271–2, 273, 276–7; and chemical weapons, 279–82, 290; and control issue, 293–4, 295–7, 298; détente between, 23–4; and disarmament, 24, 331–4; European war scenarios and, 30, 33, 36–50; and International Verification Agency, 310; non-European confrontations of, 53–61; and nonaligned negotiations, 326–31; and NPT,
170, 171, 173–7; and nuclear-free zones, 198–9, 205–7; and nuclear testing, 209–12; overkill capacity of, 26–9; and parity principle, 72, 123–4; and PNEs, 214–21; and proliferation, 159–163, 167–71, 182–5; and sanctuary doctrine, 30, 34, 36–7, 47, 51, 129, 165; and security guarantees, 323–4; and underdeveloped countries, 61–5. See also Union of Soviet Socialist Republics; United States
supersonic military aircraft, 7
surface vessels, 68
Sweden, xiii, 20, 54, 56, 65, 70, 246; and CB-weapons, 270, 276, 281, 282; and CCD, 88, 110; civil defense plans in, 140; conventional arms in, 142, 147, 152; and development aid, 154; nonalignment of, 30 n, 32, 199; and nondissemination issue, 183–4; nonproliferation policy of, 165, 168, 171, 172; and NPT, 171, 172; nuclear protest movement in, 86–7, 319; and rules of war undate, 258–9; and test bans, 85, 86–7, 208, 215, 218, 220, 223–225; and verification issue, 301, 305–9, 312
Swedish Parliamentary Commission, 149
Switzerland, 140, 149, 246; non-alignment of, 30 n, 32; and NPT, 172, 174
Symington, Stuart, 178
Syria, 14, 175

Tabun, 281
tactical nuclear weapons, 33, 36, 38–40, 42–51, 107, 115
Taiwan, 9
Taylor, Maxwell, 117
tear gas, 234, 236, 270
technological imperative, 11, 114, 141

technology, 113, 185; and arms race, 127–32, 141; brain power and, 155–6; and control issue, 295–6, 304; and cruel weapons, 241–2; and egalitarian warfare, 256–7, 315; and NPT, 176; and nuclear-testing verification, 211–12
Teller, Edward, 214, 302
territorial waters, rights to, 96
terror balance, 8, 116, 117; and deterrence concept, 118–22, 123–124, 127, 129
terror bombing, 245, 247–55. *See also* napalm
terrorism, weapons for, 21, 178–9, 180
test bans. *See* nuclear test bans
Thailand, 61, 63
Third World. *See* underdeveloped countries
Thirty Years' War, 228
Thomas Aquinas, Saint, 228
Thorsson, Inga, 86, 175, 192, 220
Threshold Ban Treaty (1974), 209–210, 217
Tito, Josip Broz, 81
Tlatelolco Treaty (1967), 200–2
Tokyo, 248, 252
toxins, 273 *n*
trade, in conventional arms, 141–4, 146–8
Treaty of Mutual Cooperation and Security (1960), 57
Treaty on Banning the Production of Biological Means of Warfare. *See* Biological Weapons Convention
Trettner, H. H., 42
Trident submarines, 12, 105, 128
Troubled Partnership, The (Kissinger), 39
Truman, Harry, 74, 96
Turkey, 31, 63, 109; IRBMs in, 33–4

U–2 incident, 82
Undén, Östen, xxii–xxiii, 86, 145

Undén plan, 166–7, 194, 197, 202
underdeveloped countries: and arms trade, 141–4, 148; and internationalization of knowledge, 313–316; militarization of, 5, 24, 138; military aid to, 9–10, 63–4, 143; and superpowers, 61–5
Union of Soviet Socialist Republics (U.S.S.R.), 28–9, 69, 160–1, 322; and Antarctic Treaty, 196; and Australia, 56; Baruch Plan and, 73, 74–6; and CB-weapons, 238, 271–3, 276, 279; and China, 53–55; and control issue, 293–4, 295–7, 298, 300, 303; and disarmament, 109, 331–4; and Disarmament Commission, 80–3, 85; and European war strategies, 36–8; and Latin America, 58–9; and NPT, 170, 171, 173–7; and nuclear-free zones, 197–9; and nuclear testing, 84–95, 209; and ocean treaties, 98–103; and proliferation, 160–3, 167–71; and security guarantees, 323–4; and test bans, 221–2; and Tlatelolco Treaty, 200, 201; and UN A.E.C., 73–8; and underdeveloped countries, 61–5; and Western Europe, 34–5, 36–8. *See also* superpowers
United Nations (UN): and arms trade disclosures, 147–8; and CB-weapons, 235–9, 268, 280; China and, 54–5; Committee on the Peaceful Uses of Outer Space, 311; and Development Decade, 64; and disarmament, 69–84, 108–10; Disarmament Commission, 80–3, 85, 328; and Disarmament Decade, 109; and incendiary weapons, 243–7; and information-sharing, 314; and Korean War, 60–1; and Middle East, 59–61; and nuclear-free zones, 194–5, 202–3, 204; as nuclear storehouse, 136; and proliferation, 162 and *n*; and Ra-

packi plan, 198; Resolution 41, 78–80; Resolution 242, 61; Resolution 338, 61; and rules of war, 227, 232–3; Satellite System, 311; Sea-Bed Committee, 97–8; and test-ban movement, 85–95; and Undén plan, 166–7, 194, 197, 202; and verification issue, 308–11; Working Group on Remote Sensing of the Earth by Satellites, 310; and Yom Kippur War, 51

United Nations Charter, 323; and disarmament, 69, 70, 72–3, 79

United Nations Environment Program (UNEP), 285, 309, 310

United Nations General Assembly: and CB-weapons, 268, 271, 272, 284; and disarmament, 69, 71, 76, 78–80, 127–9, 297–8, 304–305; and Geneva Protocol, 232; and International Verification Agency, 309–13; McCloy–Zorin Agreed Principles, 297–8, 304; and military spending disclosures, 145–6; nonaligned states in, 326, 327–31; and nonproliferation, 166–8; and nuclear-free zones, 194, 197, 204, 205–7; and ocean treaties, 97–103; and PNEs, 221; and rules of war, 257–8, 262, 264; and SALT, 104; and test bans, 209, 221–2

United Nations Security Council: and BW Convention, 274–5; and disarmament, 69–71, 78–80; and military spending disclosures, 145–6; and NPT, 170–1; Security Assurances Resolution (1968), 182–3; veto in, 69–71, 74, 296, 327–8

United States (U.S.), 9, 13, 14, 20, 28–9, 69, 160–1, 322; and Antarctic Treaty, 196; and Australia, 55–6; Baruch Plan and, 73, 74–76; and CB-weapons, 235–8, 271–3, 276–7, 279, 281; and China, 53–5, 60; and control issue, 293–4, 295–7, 298, 300, 303; and defense industry conversion, 151–3; and disarmament, 109, 331–4; and Disarmament Commission, 80–3; and European defense strategies, 32–5, 42–51; and European war strategies, 38–41; and Geneva Protocol, 232, 237, 273; and Hague Convention (1899), 240; and Japan, 56–8; and Latin America, 58–9; military spending in, 5–6; and NATO, 31–4; and NPT, 170, 171, 173–7; and nuclear-free zones, 197–9; nuclear policies of, 122–4; and nuclear testing, 84–95, 209; and ocean treaties, 98–103; postwar, 33–5; and proliferation, 159–63, 167–71, 189–190; and security guarantees, 323–4; and terror bombing, 247–248, 252–5; and test bans, 222; and Tlatelolco Treaty, 200, 201; and UN A.E.C., 73–8; and underdeveloped countries, 61–5; and Western Europe, 38–53; and World War II bombing, 251, 252. *See also* superpowers

United States Coast and Geodetic Survey, 90

United States National Academy of Science, 236

United States Senate Resolution 20, 121–2

uranium, 177, 178–80, 188–9

V2 rocket, 314

Venezuela, 201

venting, 215–16

verification, xvi, 80, 90–1, 298; in BW Convention, 273–5; of binary weapons, 228–9, 290–2; by challenge, 301–2, 312; and chemical weapons, 282–6, 290–2, 305–10, 312–13; definition of, 293 *n*; and

verification (*continued*)
  deterrence, 300–1; *ex ante* approach, 300–1, 302; *ex post* approach, 300–1, 302; function of, 299–300; international, 304–13; and NPT, 169; of nuclear testing, 209–12; and openness, 302–304; of PNEs, 214; of Sea-Bed Treaty, 102–3. *See also* control issue; International Verification Agency
Versailles Peace Treaty (1920), 66, 68, 232
Vienna talks (MBFR), 45, 48, 109, 199
Vietnam War, 6, 9, 14–17, 40, 60–1, 63; antipersonnel weapons in, 240–1; ANZUS and, 55–6; bombing in, 247–8, 252–5; chemical warfare in, 234, 235–237, 270; weapons of, 139, 240–241
Vladivostok meeting (1974), 106, 118, 121–2
Von Clausewitz, Karl, 229
Von Weizsäcker, Carl Friedrich, 42, 43

Wallace, Mike, 38–9
war and warfare: biological, 235; chemical, 234–9; human costs of, 14–16, 17; inegalitarian nature of, 255–7; international laws for: *see* rules of war; and militarism, 18–19; nuclear, 8, 27–9, 57; "unnecessarily cruel," 233–4; as war-breeder, 17–18. *See also* limited war; rules of war
war crimes, 233
warning times, decrease in, 8, 113
Warsaw Treaty Organization. *See* WTO
Washington Naval Arms Limitation Treaty (1922), 67, 295
weapons: cruel, 16–17, 54, 66, 148–150, 233–4, 259–67; inegalitar-
ian gap in, 255–7; incendiary, 21, 240, 242–7, 252, 263; nuclear/conventional distinction, 47–8; strategic, 103–6; technology of, 11–12, 127–32, 230; use restrictions on, 226–7. *See also* biological weapons; chemical weapons; nuclear weapons; *specific names*
Weapons that may Cause Unnecessary Suffering or have Indiscriminate Effects (ICRC), 244
West Germany, 4, 8, 34, 42, 60, 64, 319; and arms trade, 144; and CB-weapons, 277, 281; and NATO, 31, 33, 52, 81–2; nonproliferation policy of, 172, 180–181; nuclear material in, 180, 190–1; and Rapacki plan, 198
Western European Union (1948), 31
white phosphorous, 242, 243, 244–5
Wiesner, Jerome B., 28–9
Wigforss, Mr., 86
Winter War (1939–40), 249
World Conference for the Reduction and Limitation of Armaments (1932), 68
World Council of Churches, 321
World Disarmament Conference (proposed), 55, 184, 322–6; agenda for, 324–6; Principal Security Guarantees as preconditions for, 322–4; for nonaligned states, 330
World Health Organization (WHO), 269, 285, 308, 310
World Plan of Action for the Application of Science and Technology to Development, 156
World War I, 17; bombing in, 248–249; chemical warfare in, 232, 235
World War II, 17; bombing in, 249–252; incendiary weapons in, 242–243; weapons of, 314
WTO (Warsaw Treaty Organization), 4, 24, 30 *n*, 40, 53, 82

"Year of Europe" (1973), 52
Yefremov, A. Ye., 36
Yom Kippur War (1973), 51–2
York, Herbert F., 27–9, 42–3, 45,
    117, 120, 126

Ypres, 235
Yugoslavia, xiii, 77, 85, 199, 246,
    305; and CB-weapons, 276; and
    CCD, 110; nonalignment of,
    30 n, 32; and NPT, 175

About the Author

No woman in the twentieth century has played such an important role in her nation's history in so many capacities as Alva Myrdal. She has held numerous ministerial appointments, was a leader of the neutralist bloc in the Geneva Negotiations, and is the author of some of this century's pioneering works in social philosophy, population control, and equality.